DEFENDING SHAME

DEFENDING SHAME

Its Formative Power in Paul's Letters

TE-LI LAU

Foreword by
LUKE TIMOTHY JOHNSON

Baker Academic
a division of Baker Publishing Group
Grand Rapids, Michigan

© 2020 by Te-Li Lau

Published by Baker Academic
a division of Baker Publishing Group
PO Box 6287, Grand Rapids, MI 49516-6287
www.bakeracademic.com

Printed in the United States of America

Library of Congress Cataloging-in-Publication Data
Names: Lau, Te-Li, author.
Title: Defending shame : its formative power in Paul's letters / Te-Li Lau.
Description: Grand Rapids, Michigan : Baker Academic, a division of Baker Publishing Group,
    2020. | Includes bibliographical references and index.
Identifiers: LCCN 2019031876 | ISBN 9781540960146 (paperback) | ISBN 9781540962775
    (casebound)
Subjects: LCSH: Shame—Religious aspects—Christianity. | Shame—Biblical teaching. | Bible.
    Epistles of Paul—Theology.
Classification: LCC BT714 .L38 2020 | DDC 227/.06—dc23
LC record available at https://lccn.loc.gov/2019031876

20   21   22   23   24   25   26   7   6   5   4   3   2   1

In keeping with biblical principles of creation stewardship, Baker Publishing Group advocates the responsible use of our natural resources. As a member of the Green Press Initiative, our company uses recycled paper when possible. The text paper of this book is composed in part of post consumer waste.

For 'Genie

Contents

Foreword

One of the things that the historical study of Scripture can do best is make the ancient texts by which we purport to live strange and new. Because historical analysis makes the text truly other than us, it also makes it capable of challenging us. We are able to engage texts gone so suddenly strange with fresh eyes. We are able to see both them and our own lives in new ways, precisely because the differences between them appear to be both clear and sharp. When it is done well, historical analysis shakes us out of our bored habituation—our assumption that we already know what the texts say—and startles us into new insight.

Such historical analysis is not easy. It demands the closest attention to the grammar and syntax of ancient languages, as well as the larger symbolic worlds within which those languages first made sense. Such close attention to ancient language and meaning is far from easy, even among those claiming the title of scholar. When any scriptural study—such as Professor Te-Li Lau's on shame—bases itself not only on the original Hebrew and Greek of the Scripture but also on the original languages across a broad range of Greco-Roman philosophy, and then adds, as lagniappe, the contribution of Confucian thought, based on the knowledge of Chinese, a serious level of engagement, indeed, is on offer.

Readers will find here that a thoroughly contemporary and contentious issue is thrown into new light by the careful consideration of ancient wisdom from several little-known cultures, and in that light will find themselves capable of appreciating a dimension of life that up to now they have little appreciated, or even deprecated. The question pursued through all these ancient sources is the meaning and the function of shame.

As Professor Lau notes, the contemporary world is one that is particularly in need of help when it comes to the topic of shame. His description of our present discourse as "fractured" is apt. In a time and place dominated by mass and social media, we show ourselves to be at once most sensitive to being shamed and most willing to shame others. But what is most obviously lacking in our confused feelings and actions is an understanding of shame as a positive factor in building character, a positive element in pedagogy rather than a negative weapon for mutual destruction. And it is precisely this dimension that Professor Lau excavates and elevates from his knowledge of Greco-Roman, biblical, and Chinese discourse.

His specific focus is on four letters of Paul in which the language of shaming forms part of the apostle's rhetoric. His careful analysis of such language within the overall occasion and rhetorical goals of the respective letters goes a long way toward helping readers see Paul not as an abusive or oppressive leader but as a teacher whose language was always directed not to the tearing down but rather to the building up of communities and the individuals within them. He draws support for this portrayal from the analogously positive ways in which the Jewish and Greco-Roman cultures employ the language of shame. Where Paul is distinctive within his world—and this is by no means an insignificant observation—is the way shame has a "theonomous" dimension: of ultimate importance for Paul is the truth that humans stand within the "court of opinion" that is the divine gaze. Not human opinion, but divine judgment, is decisive.

The real effectiveness of this book, however, is in the way Professor Lau positions Paul as a dialogue partner, not only with ancient biblical and Greco-Roman texts on shame but equally with the powerful voice enunciated by the classical Confucian tradition and with the best in contemporary moral psychology. There is much to be learned by listening to each of these voices. Professor Lau has provided the scholarly service of accurately and empathically assessing Paul's pedagogical use of shame discourse, and he has suggested some of the ways that the several voices converge and conflict. By so doing, he has opened the possibility for us to do more than simply and reflexively either reject or submit to the voices from the past—he invites us to converse with Plutarch and Paul and Confucius. It remains for his readers to advance the conversation by following the leads he has provided.

Luke Timothy Johnson
Robert W. Woodruff Professor of New Testament
and Christian Origins, Emeritus
Emory University

Abbreviations

Old Testament

Gen.	Genesis	2 Chron.	2 Chronicles	Dan.	Daniel
Exod.	Exodus	Ezra	Ezra	Hosea	Hosea
Lev.	Leviticus	Neh.	Nehemiah	Joel	Joel
Num.	Numbers	Esther	Esther	Amos	Amos
Deut.	Deuteronomy	Job	Job	Obad.	Obadiah
Josh.	Joshua	Ps(s).	Psalm(s)	Jon.	Jonah
Judg.	Judges	Prov.	Proverbs	Mic.	Micah
Ruth	Ruth	Eccles.	Ecclesiastes	Nah.	Nahum
1 Sam.	1 Samuel	Song	Song of Songs	Hab.	Habakkuk
2 Sam.	2 Samuel	Isa.	Isaiah	Zeph.	Zephaniah
1 Kings	1 Kings	Jer.	Jeremiah	Hag.	Haggai
2 Kings	2 Kings	Lam.	Lamentations	Zech.	Zechariah
1 Chron.	1 Chronicles	Ezek.	Ezekiel	Mal.	Malachi

New Testament

Matt.	Matthew	Eph.	Ephesians	Heb.	Hebrews
Mark	Mark	Phil.	Philippians	James	James
Luke	Luke	Col.	Colossians	1 Pet.	1 Peter
John	John	1 Thess.	1 Thessalonians	2 Pet.	2 Peter
Acts	Acts	2 Thess.	2 Thessalonians	1 John	1 John
Rom.	Romans	1 Tim.	1 Timothy	2 John	2 John
1 Cor.	1 Corinthians	2 Tim.	2 Timothy	3 John	3 John
2 Cor.	2 Corinthians	Titus	Titus	Jude	Jude
Gal.	Galatians	Philem.	Philemon	Rev.	Revelation

Old Testament Apocrypha

1–4 Macc. 1–4 Maccabees   Wis. Wisdom of Solomon
Sir.   Sirach (Ecclesiasticus)

Old Testament Pseudepigrapha

Apoc. Mos. Apocalypse of Moses   Ps.-Phoc. Pseudo-Phocylides
2 Bar.   2 Baruch (Syriac Apocalypse)
4 Ezra   4 Ezra   T. Jud.   Testament of Judah

Qumran / Dead Sea Scrolls

1QH[a] Thanksgiving Hymns   4Q436   Barkhi Nafshi[c]
        (Hodayot[a])   11QPs[a] Psalms Scroll[a]

Philo

Her. *Quis rerum divinarum heres sit*   Post. *De posteritate Caini* (*On the Pos-*
      (*Who Is the Heir?*)   *terity of Cain*)
Ios. *De Iosepho* (*On the Life of*   Sacr. *De sacrificiis Abelis et Caini* (*On*
      Joseph)   *the Sacrifices of Cain and Abel*)
Mos. *De vita Mosis* (*On the Life of*   Somn. *De somniis* (*On Dreams*)
      Moses)
Mut. *De mutatione nominum* (*On the*   Spec. *De specialibus legibus* (*On the*
      Change of Names)   *Special Laws*)

Josephus

J.W. *Jewish War*

Apostolic Fathers

1 Clem. 1 Clement   Ign. *Magn.* Ignatius, *To the Magnesians*

Classical Authors

Achilles Tatius

Leuc. Clit. Leucippe et Clitophon (*The*
      Adventures of Leucippe and
      Cleitophon)

Aristotle

Eth. nic. Ethica nicomachea (*Nicoma-*
      chean Ethics)
Rhet.   Rhetorica (*Rhetoric*)

Athenaeus

Deipn. Deipnosophistae

Aulus Gellius

Noct. att. Noctes atticae (*Attic Nights*)

Cicero

Amic.   De amicitia
Att.   Epistulae ad Atticum
Clu.   Pro Cluentio
Or. Brut. Orator ad M. Brutum

Planc.   Pro Plancio
Rep.   De republica

Demosthenes

Cor.   De corona (On the Crown)
Or.   Orations

Dio Chrysostom

Or.   Orations

Diogenes Laertius

Vit. phil.   Vitae philosophorum (Lives of
Eminent Philosophers)

Epictetus

Diatr.   Diatribai/Dissertationes

Euripides

Herc. fur.   Hercules furens (Madness of
Hercules)
Hipp.   Hippolytus
Iph. aul.   Iphigenia aulidensis (Iphige-
neia at Aulis)
Med.   Medea
Orest.   Orestes
Suppl.   Supplices (Suppliants)

Herodotus

Hist.   Historiae (Histories)

Hesiod

Op.   Opera et dies (Works and Days)

Iamblichus

Vit. Pyth.   De vita pythagorica (On the
Life of Pythagoras)

Menander

Sam.   Samia

Ovid

Metam.   Metamorphoses

Plato

[*Alc. maj.*]   Alcibiades major (Greater
Alcibiades)
Apol.   Apologia (Apology of
Socrates)
Charm.   Charmides
Crit.   Crito
Gorg.   Gorgias
Leg.   Leges (Laws)
Phaedr.   Phaedrus
Prot.   Protagoras
Resp.   Respublica (Republic)
Soph.   Sophista (Sophist)
Symp.   Symposium
Tim.   Timaeus

Plutarch

Adul. amic.   Quomodo adulator ab
amico internoscatur (How
to Tell a Flatterer from a
Friend)
Crass.   Crassus
Frat. amor.   De fraterno amore
[*Lib. ed.*]   De liberis educandis (On
the Education of Children)
Rect. rat.   De recta ratione audiendi
aud.
Tranq. an.   De tranquillitate animi
Virt. mor.   De virtute morali
Vit. pud.   De vitioso pudore

Quintilian

Inst.   Institutio oratoria (The Orator's
Education)

Seneca

Ben.   De beneficiis
Ep.   Epistulae morales

Sophocles

Phil.   Philoctetes

Tacitus

Hist.   Historiae

Thucydides		**Xenophon**	
Pel. War	*History of the Peloponnesian War*	*Cyr.*	*Cyropaedia*
		Mem.	*Memorabilia*

Patristic Writings

Augustine

Exp. Gal.	*Expositio in epistulam ad Galatas*

Clement of Alexandria

Strom.	*Stromateis*

Jerome

Comm. Gal.	*Commentariorum in Epistulam ad Galatas libri III*

John Chrysostom

Hom. Gal.	*Homiliae in epistulam ad Galatas commentarius*
Hom. Phil.	*Homiliae in epistulam ad Philippenses*
Hom. Phlm.	*Homiliae in epistulam ad Philemonem*
Paenit.	*De paenitentia*

Origen

Hom. Jer.	*Homiliae in Jeremiam*

Bible Versions

LXX	Septuagint	NLT	New Living Translation
NET	New English Translation	NRSV	New Revised Standard Version
NIV	New International Version		

General and Bibliographic

BDAG	Bauer, Walter. *A Greek-English Lexicon of the New Testament and Other Early Christian Literature.* Edited by Frederick W. Danker. Translated by William F. Arndt, and F. Wilbur Gingrich. 3rd ed. Chicago: University of Chicago Press, 2000.
BDF	Blass, Friedrich, Albert Debrunner, and Robert W. Funk. *A Greek Grammar of the New Testament and Other Early Christian Literature.* Chicago: University of Chicago Press, 1961.
DPL	*Dictionary of Paul and His Letters.* Edited by Gerald F. Hawthorne and Ralph P. Martin. Downers Grove, IL: InterVarsity, 1993.
ET	English translation
FC	Fathers of the Church
frag.	fragment
JBL	*Journal of Biblical Literature*
JSNTSup	Journal for the Study of the New Testament Supplement Series
JSOT	*Journal for the Study of the Old Testament*
LCL	Loeb Classical Library
L&N	Louw, J. P., and Eugene A. Nida, eds. *Greek-English Lexicon of the New Testament: Based on Semantic Domains.* 2nd ed. 2 vols. New York: United Bible Societies, 1989.

LSJ	Liddell, Henry George, Robert Scott, and Henry Stuart Jones, eds. *A Greek-English Lexicon*. 9th ed. Oxford: Clarendon, 1996.
NIDNTTE	*New International Dictionary of New Testament Theology and Exegesis*. Edited by Moisés Silva. 5 vols. Grand Rapids: Zondervan, 2014.
NIDOTTE	*New International Dictionary of Old Testament Theology and Exegesis*. Edited by Willem A. VanGemeren. 5 vols. Grand Rapids: Zondervan, 1997.
NovTSup	Supplements to Novum Testamentum
NPNF[1]	*Nicene and Post-Nicene Fathers*, Series 1
NTS	*New Testament Studies*
OED	*Oxford English Dictionary*
OTP	*Old Testament Pseudepigrapha*. Edited by James H. Charlesworth. 2 vols. Peabody, MA: Hendrickson, 2009.
SBLDS	Society of Biblical Literature Dissertation Series
s.v.	*sub verbo*, under the word
SVF	*Stoicorum Veterum Fragmenta*. Hans Friedrich August von Arnim. 4 vols. Leipzig: Teubne, 1903–24.
TDOT	*Theological Dictionary of the Old Testament*. Edited by G. Johannes Botterweck, Helmer Ringgren, Heinz-Josef Fabry, and Holger Gzella. Translated by John T. Willis, Douglas W. Stott, David E. Green, and Mark E. Biddle. 16 vols. Grand Rapids: Eerdmans, 1974–2018.
TDNT	*Theological Dictionary of the New Testament*. Edited by Gerhard Kittel and Gerhard Friedrich. Translated by Geoffrey W. Bromiley. 10 vols. Grand Rapids: Eerdmans, 1964–76.
TLOT	*Theological Lexicon of the Old Testament*. Edited by Ernst Jenni, with assistance from Claus Westermann. Translated by Mark E. Biddle. 3 vols. Peabody, MA: Hendrickson, 1997.
WUNT	Wissenschaftliche Untersuchungen zum Neuen Testament

Introduction

A Fractured Understanding of Shame

We live in a world with a fractured understanding of shame. Unlike other negative emotions, such as sorrow or anger, which may be cathartic when experienced and processed, we generally wish to avoid shame as much as possible. The psychotherapist Joseph Burgo wrote in the *Atlantic* that we live in an "anti-shame zeitgeist."[1] Actors, psychologists, and social critics all consider shame to be the enemy that must be resisted and extirpated. Pop superstar Lady Gaga urges her fans toward self-love and confidence, never allowing themselves to be bullied or shamed. Her song "Born This Way" reminds her followers, "There's nothin' wrong with lovin' who you are. . . . Don't hide yourself in regret, Just love yourself and you're set." You should freely express your own individuality without fear of embarrassment or shame. In common parlance, you do you. American model Tyra Banks and actress Selena Gomez speak out vehemently against body shaming. Research professor Brené Brown appeared on *Super Soul Sunday* with Oprah Winfrey and declared, "I think shame is lethal, I think shame is destructive. And I think we are swimming in it deep."[2] For Brown, shame is a pernicious emotion that serves no constructive purpose whatsoever.

This sentiment concerning shame is also extant in academic circles. Shame is perceived as the primitive precursor to guilt, and its value as a moral emotion has been severely discredited.[3] Shame is heteronomous and responds to

---

1. Burgo, "Challenging the Anti-Shame Zeitgeist."
2. "Dr. Brené Brown."
3. Gilbert ("Evolution," 1225) writes, "Guilt but not shame is regarded as a moral emotion because shame is ultimately about punishment, is self-focused and 'wired into' the defense system. Shaming people can lead to various unhelpful defensive emotions, such as anger or debilitating anxiety, concealment or destructive conformity. Guilt, however, is outward focused

the opinions and judgments of others, making it unfit for a Kantian system of morality. Guilt, however, responds to the inner judgments and sensibilities of the autonomous self. Beginning at a later stage in human development than shame, guilt is perceived to be more advanced and better than shame.[4]

University campuses are also not exempt. In the name of emotional well-being and individual self-fulfillment, fragile undergraduates demand trigger warnings on reading assignments that might be provocative or upsetting. They also push campus administrators to create "safe spaces" that will shield them from frank speech and uncomfortable ideas. These spaces allow full self-expression without fear of shame and discomfort. Eric Cartman, one of the main characters in the animated sitcom *South Park*, expresses this idea succinctly in a particular episode when he sings, "There is no shame in my safe space."[5]

The anti-shame zeitgeist is nourished in part by the current ethos of therapeutic individualism. In this ethos, the individual self is the sole arbiter of authentic moral knowledge, and personal growth is the central purpose of human existence. External forms of authority are no longer structures to which the self must conform; rather, they are something from which the self must be liberated. Moral obligations are no longer disciplines that must be maintained; rather, they are chains that must be shaken off so as to attain maximal happiness and positive self-esteem. The individual self or psyche is the preoccupying focus of attention in this ethos. Individual emotional fulfillment or self-actualization is not just a personal good but a social obligation. Needless to say, shaming criticism of one's failings is taboo.[6]

The aversion toward shame also arises because we all recognize its potential to be destructive. Toxic shame plays a prominent role in the dynamics that lead to suicidal thoughts and behavior.[7] The shame of sexual assault can break a person's sense of self-worth and may even push some to kill themselves, especially if photos of the attack are circulated on social media. Honor or shame killings are also endemic in parts of the world. The killing of the

---

and is about responsibility and caring feelings for others. Moreover, in a shame system people can behave very immorally in order to court favor with their superiors and avoid being rejected for not complying with requests or orders. Prestige seeking and shame avoidance can lead to some very destructive behaviors indeed."

4. See Tangney and Dearing, *Shame and Guilt*.

5. "Safe Space," episode 5 of season 19 of *South Park*, directed by Trey Parker, aired October 21, 2015.

6. For more information on the therapeutic culture, see Rieff, *Triumph of the Therapeutic*; Polsky, *Rise of the Therapeutic State*; Nolan, *Therapeutic State*; Moskowitz, *In Therapy We Trust*; Sommers and Satel, *One Nation under Therapy*; Aubry and Travis, *Rethinking Therapeutic Culture*.

7. Martínez de Pisón, *Death by Despair*.

Pakistani social media star Qandeel Baloch in 2016 is one such example. In a defiant press conference, her brother claimed that he was proud to kill her because she brought shame on their family with her provocative Facebook posts. Shame *has the capacity* to push us toward unhealthy, self-destructive, and violent patterns of behavior. Whether shame is *necessarily* destructive is a question that needs to be probed.

Despite the aversion to shame, we nonetheless witness how segments of our society have a primal urge to shame others. We see how people are pilloried savagely for posting an ill-conceived comment on social media.[8] The pronouncement of collective judgment is swift and furious, and the online shaming quickly devolves into a voyeuristic spectator sport as each accuser calls for a pound of flesh. The intent of the shaming is generally punitive rather than redemptive, and the gleeful brutality of the punishment in no way matches the severity of the crime. The virtual targets of such shaming often lose their jobs. They are also permanently traumatized as their poorly conceived tweets and respective backlashes live on forever in the blogosphere.

Despite the aversion to shame, we also see government entities using shame to encourage tax scofflaws to pay their taxes. The tax boards of states such as California, Vermont, and Delaware publish the names, addresses, and amount owed by tax delinquents on their respective websites. Removal of this humiliating information is pursuant to the full payment of taxes owed. Just the threat of being listed is sufficient in most cases to get reluctant taxpayers to pay. More creative ways to shame delinquents are adopted by government entities in other countries. In one of the suburbs of the Indian commercial capital of Mumbai, officials found that posting the names of delinquent taxpayers was not sufficiently effective since their websites were not heavily trafficked. They then decided on a more unorthodox approach. They employed drummers to accompany tax collectors to the homes of delinquent taxpayers. When the musicians arrived banging on their instruments, neighbors peered outside and gawked at the racket. Since the introduction of these percussionists, collection of property tax revenues has jumped 20 percent.[9]

The fractured and conflicting understanding of shame also percolates in the church. Many churches follow the anti-shame zeitgeist of mainstream society and adopt the therapeutic ethos of the larger culture. Therapy informs the calling and identity of ministers to the extent that Christian ministers and secular therapists perform many similar roles.[10] Churches prefer to "stay

8. See Ronson, "One Stupid Tweet."
9. Parussini, "If You Don't Pay."
10. For a defense of the psychotherapeutic ethos within the church, see Muravchik, *American Protestantism.*

positive" in their teaching, pastors proclaim the gospel in therapeutic idioms, and few churches practice formal discipline. According to the sociologist Christian Smith, the dominant religion among Christian American teenagers is a Christianized version of moralistic therapeutic deism—a system in which "God wants people to be good, nice, and fair to each other" and in which "the central goal of life is to be happy and to feel good about oneself."[11] This is not a religion of sin, righteousness, justice, holiness, and repentance but a religion of feeling good and inner peace. The language of remorse, rebuke, shame, discipleship, and the cross is replaced by the feckless language of happiness and niceness.

The movement away from shame is also fueled by the recognition that some within the church suffer from chronic shame. Many people experience shame only for a short span of time, but those who suffer from chronic shame develop ingrained patterns of seeing themselves as shameful and unworthy. The sociologist Julius Rubin provocatively argues that certain forms of Protestant pietism gave rise to "religious melancholy," a distinctive psychopathology that induced a neurotic personality haunted by shame, guilt, and anxiety.[12] While the causal relationship of Rubin's thesis is not convincing, we are nonetheless aware of individuals who are weighed down by chronic shame and are unable to accept the gracious forgiveness that God provides. Women who have had abortions fall dangerously within this group. They regret their actions and experience emotional trauma. Given the church's stance on the sanctity of human life, such women are plagued by shame. They are afraid to tell others what they consider to be a shameful secret, and some are hesitant to join recovery groups lest their identities be known. Consequently, they do not receive the healing they desperately need. Their shame continues to fester.

On the other extreme, we see some segments of the church embracing shaming techniques that stigmatize and destroy. Most infamous in this regard is Westboro Baptist Church in Topeka, Kansas. The church is well known for its picketing and hateful vitriol, and the church's URL (www.godhatesfags .com) unabashedly parades their contempt for LGBTQ people. The use of shame is also clearly seen in historical sources. John Demos notes that public humiliation was the primary instrument of moral and social control among the early Puritans. Some of the favorite punishments, with occasional refinements, were "sitting in the stocks; standing on a pillory; wearing a so-called 'badge of infamy' (in the manner of Hawthorne's scarlet letter) or a simple 'paper' describing the offense in question; branding (in effect, a way of making

11. Smith, *Soul Searching*, 162–63.
12. Rubin, *Religious Melancholy*.

the 'badge' permanent); being dragged through the streets, tied to a 'cart's tail'; standing in the gallows with a rope tied around one's neck."[13] The common element that connects all the above is public exposure.

While some segments of Christianity may not actively shame others, they nevertheless find themselves shamed by the larger society. This arises because they affirm values that run counter to the liberal conventional ethos. The reigning political and social authority therefore shames these Christian segments so as to destroy their resolve to hold these values. For example, LGBTQ activist groups urge the government to publish a "shame list" of faith-based institutions that request Title IX exemption from transgender rules.[14] The Department of Education agreed to publish such a list in 2016. These activist groups also urge the NCAA to divest from all faith-based colleges that sought such waivers; the NCAA has, however, declined to take any action, for now.

In a world with a fractured understanding of shame, we possess a deep antagonism to shame. It shrivels our self-esteem and pushes us to hide from humanity. Yet we intuitively recognize that shame is fundamental to moral character, for none of us wish to be absolutely shameless. And if the nature of shame has a certain positive valence, what about the appropriateness of using shame as a means to reform behavior or punish misdemeanors? And if shaming is apt, how should such acts be conducted and by whom? These are difficult questions. Shame presents us with a hornet's nest of issues.

A Way Forward

The extirpation of shame is ill-advised, if not impossible. As a human emotion, shame is part of who we are. It is an inevitable aspect of the human experience, just as fear, sadness, and joy are. "To extirpate shame is to cripple our humanity."[15] As a moral emotion, shame functions as a critical component of our moral apparatus. It helps us discern what is noble and base and provides the motivational energy that impels us to do good and to avoid doing bad. As a social emotion, shame is the glue that holds relationships and communities together. It has the potential to construct a decorous and harmonious society—a society in which individuals are sensitive to the social norms of the community and who respect the honor of others. What we need is not the extirpation of shame but a nuanced understanding of the

13. Demos, "Shame and Guilt," 71.
14. This shaming and ostracizing strategy follows the propaganda campaign advocated by Kirk and Madsen, *After the Ball*.
15. Schneider, *Shame, Exposure, and Privacy*, xv.

complexity of shame that leads to human flourishing. The apostle Paul can help us point the way.

Paul sets before us a model in which shame can be meaningfully employed to bring one to ethical and spiritual maturity. He considers shame as a necessary element in moral formation, and he clearly understands certain behavior to be shameful. In line with Jewish sentiments of his day, Paul considers homosexual acts as shameless acts that arise from degrading passions (Rom. 1:26–27). He also castigates those who are shameless and who indulge in every sordid debauchery and impurity (Eph. 4:19).[16] Their behavior is so deplorable that Paul considers it shameful even to mention what they do in secret (Eph. 5:12). In contrast to those whose god is their belly and whose glory is their shame, Paul exhort his readers to live carefully since their true citizenship is in heaven (Phil. 3:19–20). By cultivating a proper sense of shame, they will live lives that are prudent and self-controlled (1 Tim. 2:9; 2 Tim. 1:7; Titus 2:2, 5, 6, 12).

The classification of certain behavior as "shameful" is understandable, but Paul's views on *acts of shaming* need further clarification. On the one hand, Paul criticizes the use of shaming rhetoric as practiced by some of his readers. He berates them for using civil litigation to accrue honor on themselves and to shame their opponents (1 Cor. 6:1–11). He rebukes the wealthy Corinthians for humiliating, in the Lord's Supper, those who have nothing (1 Cor. 11:22). He also warns the church not to show disdain or contempt to those who are young (1 Tim. 4:12; Titus 2:15).

On the other hand, Paul himself engages in shaming rhetoric. He rebukes and shames believers when they do not walk in line with the gospel. When the morals of the Corinthians deteriorated to such an extent that there were litigations among themselves and hedonistic overindulgence, Paul explicitly rebukes them, saying, "I say this to your shame" (1 Cor. 6:5; 15:34). When the Galatian church abandoned the gospel for the law, Paul rebukes and shames them with pointed rhetorical questions: "You foolish Galatians! Who has bewitched you? . . . Are you so foolish? . . . Did you experience so much for nothing?" (Gal. 3:1–4). Paul does not only shame his converts; he also has no qualms about shaming other apostles when their actions compromise the

---

16. In contrast to the major scholarly opinion that the disputed Pauline letters are pseudonymous, I assume Paul either authored or supervised the writing of these letters. Even if these letters are inauthentic, they are nevertheless Pauline in character. They therefore cannot be ignored in any attempt to reconstruct the theological ethics of the apostle in whose name they are written. For a brief defense of the authorship of the various Pauline letters, see Johnson, *Writings of the New Testament*. Arguments for each specific letter can be found in various monographs and articles, such as Roon, *Authenticity of Ephesians*; van Nes, *Pauline Language*.

gospel. When Peter came to Antioch and stopped eating with the gentiles because he was afraid of the circumcision group, Paul confronts Peter "to his face" (Gal. 2:11). He points out Peter's hypocrisy "in front of everyone" (Gal. 2:14). The public nature of Paul's confrontation would be perceived as a shaming experience by all who were present.

Paul's shaming rhetoric and action is not an apostolic prerogative. Paul intends it to be part of the disciplinary measures that the church is to enact against its errant members. Thus, in 2 Thessalonians 3:14, Paul tells the Thessalonian church to take special note of those who do not heed the moral teaching presented in his letter. Having identified them, the church is not to associate with them in order that they may be shamed. Such shaming action is not meant to be punitive but redemptive. For Paul quickly reminds the church not to regard the errant as enemies; rather, the church is to admonish them as they would a brother or sister (2 Thess. 3:15). In 1 Timothy 5:20, the church is to confront elders who persist in sin, rebuking them before everyone so that the rest of the elders will be afraid and not follow their sinful behavior.

Apart from actively shaming others, Paul also encourages his readers to live exemplary lives, full of integrity and gracious loving so that their enemies might be ashamed of their animosity toward believers. In Romans 12:20, Paul tells the church to respond practically to the needs of their enemies, giving them food and water when they are hungry and thirsty. Such actions will heap "burning coals" on the heads of their enemies; that is, their enemies will experience the burning pangs of shame. In Titus 2:7–8, Paul instructs his protégé Titus to show himself to be a model of good works and to demonstrate integrity, gravity, and sound speech in his teaching so that his opponents might be ashamed.

The above examples show that certain acts of shaming are prohibited, but others are necessary. In the latter case, Paul and the church not only actively shame by word or action but also passively shame others through their good conduct. The rationale for such actions must be that Paul considers the shame experience to be salutary for shaping one's identity and behavior. He appeals to shame and recognizes its value as a moral emotion. But certain questions are not so easily resolved. How does Paul envision his shaming rhetoric to function? What is the relationship between shame and moral formation? What is the relationship between shame, as an emotion, and moral beliefs? Are there limits to the use of shame? How do Paul's religious convictions affect his use of shame? Does the Holy Spirit play any role in this process? What is the relationship between shame and moral conscience? These questions have not been vigorously pursued in the history of interpretation of Pauline ethics.

Lacunae in Pauline Studies

Despite the presence of shame in the Pauline Letters, surprisingly little has been written regarding Paul's use of shame for transforming one's identity and behavior. There are books that deal with Pauline ethics and books that emphasize Paul's use of shame; I am, however, unaware of any monograph-length work that constructs a Pauline ethic of shame. Books on Pauline ethics scarcely discuss Paul's moral psychology. They do not examine his use of emotions, let alone shame, for moral formation. For example, the word "shame" only appears once or twice in the main texts of Victor Furnish, *Theology and Ethics in Paul* (1968); Brian Rosner, *Understanding Paul's Ethics* (1995); or James Thompson, *Moral Formation according to Paul* (2011). The situation is only marginally better in Daniel Harrington and James Keenan, *Paul and Virtue Ethics: Building Bridges between New Testament Studies and Moral Theology* (2010), and David Horrell, *Solidarity and Difference: A Contemporary Reading of Paul's Ethics* (2016). Nevertheless, the word still appears less than ten times. These authors do not index shame as a category, nor do they examine it extensively.

Studies that recognize the theme of shame in Paul, on the other hand, do not *adequately* emphasize its use for moral formation. Such studies employ cultural and anthropological models of honor and shame, defining shame vis-à-vis honor and understanding both as social values. Bruce Malina defines honor as "the value of a person in his or her own eyes (that is, one's claim to worth) *plus* that person's value in the eyes of his or her social group. Honor is a claim to worth along with the social acknowledgment of worth."[17] Shame is divided into two categories. On the one hand, to "have shame" (positive shame) or a sense of shame means "sensitivity about one's own reputation, sensitivity to the opinion of others."[18] Honor and shame are synonymous in this context (honor and shame-as-honor). On the other hand, to "be shamed" (negative shame) or dishonored refers to "the state of publicly known loss of honor."[19] Honor and shame are opposites in this context (honor vis-à-vis shame-as-dishonor).

There are recognized hazards in the application of cultural and anthropological models to New Testament texts.[20] Nevertheless, when the necessary correctives are put in place, the application of honor and shame categories can yield fruitful results by helping us understand the social world of the

---

17. Malina, *New Testament World*, 30.
18. Malina, *New Testament World*, 47.
19. Malina and Pilch, *Social-Science Commentary*, 370.
20. See deSilva, *Despising Shame*, 11–23.

texts. The relevance to moral formation is also readily apparent. Since concern for honor permeates every aspect of life, the pivotal social value of honor leads one to adopt certain mannerisms, postures, and actions, while the pivotal social sanction of shame for noncompliance directs one to avoid others. Honor and shame are used strategically as instruments of moral persuasion, and the vocabulary of praise and blame are viewed as social sanctions for moral behavior. At the same time, the recognition that honor and shame are social constructs reminds us that what is disgraceful within one group may be considered honorable in another. For example, while crucifixion is seen as a horrifying and humiliating death within the larger Greco-Roman world, Paul construes a crucified Messiah as God's power and wisdom for the church (1 Cor. 1:22–25).[21] Counter-definitions of what constitutes the honorable and shameful show how subgroups within a dominant culture construct an alternative court of reputation to prevent its members from conforming to values of the wider society.[22]

There are nevertheless limitations to this line of study. An honor-shame approach defines shame vis-à-vis honor and understands both of them primarily as social values. It does not focus on the shame experience, nor does it understand shame as a moral emotion. It may explain how a community maintains social control, but it does not focus on how an individual such as Paul brings about moral reformation in his converts via the practice of psychagogy.[23] It may discuss the strategic use of honor and shame as external instruments of persuasion, but, in doing so, it does not explain *how* shame can internally reform the individual mind and conscience. Honor and shame studies thus negatively predispose us to consider shame to be heteronomous rather than autonomous or theonomous. An honor-shame approach also does not locate Paul's use of shame within the moral psychology of his day. Finally, given their focus on the social dimension, honor and shame studies do not address the role of the Spirit in moral formation. In summary, an honor-shame approach has benefits, but it is not sufficiently refined to examine the

---

21. See also Neyrey, "Despising the Shame of the Cross," 114, who notes that the Fourth Gospel portrays Jesus's crucifixion as a "status elevation ritual" rather than a "status degradation ritual." He remarks, "The gospel inculcates an ironic point of view that death and shame mean glory and honor. The mock coronation of Jesus, which in the eyes of outsiders means shame, truly betokens honor from the viewpoint of insiders" (126).

22. For the construction of an alternative court of reputation in Hebrews, see deSilva, *Despising Shame*, 276–313.

23. Psychagogy, or "guidance of the soul," centers on "care for the young" (Epictetus, *Diatr.* 3.21.18). It describes the practice whereby a mature guide brings about moral transformation in a novice by shaping the novice's view of himself and the world. For studies on Pauline psychagogy, see Glad, *Paul and Philodemus*; Vegge, *2 Corinthians*.

role of shame for moral formation. My study builds on the contributions of the honor-shame approach but seeks to rectify its deficiencies. I understand shame primarily as a moral emotion and focus on the ethical significance of the shame experience in Pauline texts.

My Project

This study examines Paul's use of shame for Christic formation within his Jewish and Greco-Roman context and compares it with various contemporary perspectives. Specifically, I argue that Paul uses shame as a pedagogical tool to admonish and transform the minds of his readers into the mind of Christ and that his rationale can best be grasped through comparison with analogous perspectives, both within and without his cultural context. Unlike Aristotle or the Stoics, Paul does not present us with a systematic analysis of the relationship between shame and moral beliefs. Nevertheless, one can discern from his various writings a pattern that effectively functions as the basis for constructing a Pauline ethic of shame. My interest lies in the ethical significance of shame, not so much in the phenomenology, sociology, or psychology of shame. These other approaches will be examined only insofar as it helps to elucidate the rationale underlying Paul's use of shame for Christic formation. I examine not only how Paul uses the category of shame to inculcate a Christian identity and ethos but also how and why he shames others when they fail to conduct their lives in a manner worthy of the gospel.

This study on Paul's use of shame for moral formation proceeds in three parts: framework, exegesis, and engagement. Part 1 provides the framework and background that informs our reading of Paul. Chapter 1 defines key terms and lays out the presuppositions of this project. Chapter 2 examines the role of shame in various theories of moral progress promoted by various Greco-Roman authors. Chapter 3 examines the same topic in several Jewish writings.

Part 2 is the exegetical task. Chapter 4 examines how Paul explicitly and implicitly shames others in 1 Corinthians and Galatians. Chapter 5 examines how Paul uses honor and shame categories to instill in his readers a proper sense of shame so that they might live worthy of the gospel. The texts in focus are Philippians and Philemon. Chapter 6 synthesizes the exegetical data and constructs a coherent understanding of Paul's use of shame for moral formation.

Part 3 engages Paul's vision with contemporary perspectives. Chapter 7 brings Paul into conversation with minority voices in our world that advocate a positive role for shame. Chapter 8 does the same with contemporary challenges to a positive use of shame.

PART 1

FRAMEWORK

Part 1 provides the framework for my project and the conceptual background for our reading of Paul. Chapter 1 defines key terms and clarifies potential confusions surrounding the issue of shame. Chapter 2 examines how Greco-Roman authors understand shame and its role in moral progress. Chapter 3 does the same from the perspective of Jewish authors.

1

Definitional Background

The literature on shame is vast, and the study of shame has been approached from different disciplines: political science, education, philosophy, literature, ethics, history, neuroscience, psychology, psychoanalysis, cultural anthropology, social anthropology, sociology, law, and criminology. In this chapter, I present my understanding of the nature and character of shame. Shame can broadly denote the objective reality of disgrace or the subjective experience of pain that arises from falling short of some standard. Studies on honor and shame have adequately covered the former; I focus on the latter here. I examine how shame is an emotion and refine my understanding of shame by differentiating it from humiliation, embarrassment, and guilt. I then highlight certain conceptual confusions that surround the study of shame and define various terms so as to clear away this fog. I give some necessary precautions in a cross-cultural examination of shame. I then conclude with a succinct definition of shame.

Shame and Emotion

I take it to be uncontroversial that shame is an emotion. There is no definite consensus on how to define emotions, and this is not the place to give a detailed account of the nature of emotions. Nevertheless, some general observations that will orient us to the task ahead are in order.

Emotions are hard to define. On the one hand, William James defines emotions as the bodily feeling that arises from physiological changes that follow the perception of some exciting fact.[1] They are the raw sensations of visceral disturbances due to the stimulation of the nervous system. On the other hand, Robert Solomon defines emotions as judgments about ourselves.[2] Anger is the judgment that someone has wronged me; shame is the judgment that I am responsible for an inappropriate or offensive situation.

Such simplistic binaries fail to capture the complex nature of emotions. A much more promising definition of emotion is suggested by the philosopher Aaron Ben-Ze'ev. He writes, "An emotion is something that is generated by perceived changes; its focus of concern is personal and comparative; its major characteristics are instability, great intensity, partiality, and brief duration; and its basic components are cognition, evaluation, motivation, and feelings."[3] We can examine the basic components of emotion: *cognition* consists of information concerning the event or situation; *evaluation* appraises the personal significance of the event or situation; *motivation* addresses the action tendencies, desires, or readiness to act in these circumstances; and *feelings* are the consciousness of our bodily state.[4]

Ben Ze'ev's definition that emotions are generated by perceived changes and that they are personal reminds us that the emotion cannot be abstracted from the conditions that elicit it, from the evaluation of those conditions, and from the feelings and desires that stir within us. An emotion cannot be relegated to one of its components; it is the whole story, the entire script, the unfolding experience of its basic components. Theorists disagree about which specific components should be included.[5] Ben Ze'ev lists four, but "five appear in most theories in one form or another: (1) objects, causes, precipitating events, (2) appraisal, (3) physiological changes, (4) action tendencies/action/ expression, and (5) regulation."[6]

1. James ("What Is an Emotion?," 189–90) writes, "My thesis . . . is that *the bodily changes follow directly the* PERCEPTION *of the exciting fact, and that our feeling of the same changes as they occur* IS *the emotion*."

2. Solomon (*Passions*, 183) writes, "What is an emotion? An emotion is a *judgment* (or a set of judgments), something we *do*. An emotion is a (set of) judgment(s) which constitute our world, our surreality, and its 'intentional objects.' An emotion is a basic judgment about our Selves and our place in our world, the projection of the values and ideals, structures and mythologies, according to which we live and through which we experience our lives."

3. Ben-Ze'ev, "Thing Called Emotion," 56.

4. It is debated whether emotions necessarily involve noncognitive *feelings*. For arguments that they do not, see Nussbaum, *Upheavals of Thought*, 56–64; Roberts, *Emotions*, 65–69.

5. For some samples, see Kleinginna and Kleinginna, "Emotion Definitions"; Mesquita and Frijda, "Cultural Variations in Emotions"; Scherer, "What Are Emotions?"

6. Planalp, *Communicating Emotion*, 11 (italics removed). The first four components in the list are self-explanatory. Regulation is the inhibitory control or voluntary enhancement of the emotion. It can affect all four other components of the emotional process. Planalp gives the following example on p. 31. We regulate emotion (e.g., fear) by dealing with the object

Of the above five components, those that are most culturally sensitive and dependent would be the precipitating event, the action tendencies, and the regulation of that emotion. But what is essential and constitutive of the emotional experience is the appraisal or evaluative component.[7] The evaluative element makes the emotional experience what it is, differentiating it (e.g., anger) from other states (e.g., jealousy or pride). Moreover, the evaluative element is also causally responsible for the emotion and gives the reason for a person to be in that particular state. To be afraid is to evaluate or appraise a situation, object, or event to be dangerous with a significant degree of probability; to be overcome by grief is to realize that someone to whom I am deeply attached and who is irreplaceable has been permanently taken from me. Emotion words are not just labels for bodily sensations. An experience of fear, grief, or anger relates to the external world, and emotions are ways of perceiving and responding to changes in that world. To experience an emotion thus is to construe a personally significant event or situation in a particular way. In essence, emotions or emotion lexemes are the interpretive schemes of various script-like or narrative forms that give meaning and shape to the human experience of some self-relevant condition.[8]

When we apply the five components of an emotional experience to shame, we discover the following. The *precipitating event* can vary widely. It includes being seen doing bad things, being associated with people of ill repute, being rejected in an electoral venue, or failing an academic exam. It is important to note that shame is not produced by any specific event, for the same event can happen to two different people with two different emotional responses. As

---

(avoiding the car in my path), managing the appraisal (telling myself I have plenty of room to spare), regulating the physiological change (deep breathing), and managing the action tendency (screaming will not help).

7. See Taylor, *Pride, Shame, and Guilt*, 1–5; Cairns, *Aidōs*, 5–14; Kaster, *Emotion, Restraint, and Community*, 8–9. The importance of appraisals is also seen in Roberts, *Emotions*, 60–179, who defines emotions as concern-based construals. In his view, construals are akin to perceptions, and they can have the same immediacy as sense perceptions. Although they are interpretations, the interpretation is built into the experience. Experientially, "a construal is not an interpretation laid over a neutrally perceived object, but a characterization of the object, a way the *object* presents itself" (80). Roberts's analysis is helpful in showing that the evaluation can be deliberate or immediate. In some instances, the evaluation (e.g., my evaluation that a snake right beside my feet is dangerous) need not enter consciousness. It can happen so fast (perhaps accelerated by past evaluations that lead me to believe that snakes are dangerous) that it can be seen as an instinctual reflex.

8. Shweder, "'You're Not Sick,'" 32–33. Kaster (*Emotion, Restraint, and Community*, 8) similarly writes, "Any emotion-term is just the lexicalized residue of what happens when the data of life are processed in a particular way—through a sequence of perception (sensing, imagining), evaluation (believing, judging, desiring), and response (bodily, affective, pragmatic, expressive)—to produce a particular kind of emotionalized consciousness, a particular set of thoughts and feelings."

discussed above, what is central is the individual's *interpretation and appraisal* of that event. In shame, the constitutive element is negative self-evaluation, the awareness of being seen to fall short of some perceived standard or ideal. The presence of an other may be the catalyst, but the evaluation constitutive of shame still depends on the self. As Douglas Cairns remarks, "In every case shame is a matter of the self's judging the self in terms of some ideal that is one's own."[9] The discomforting and perplexing experience of shame may have physiological, behavioral, and evaluative elements, but what distinguishes shame from other emotions is the evaluative component. The *physiological changes* may include an increased heart rate or the sensation of feeling hot. The *action tendency* may be to avert one's gaze and hang one's head. The *regulation* of the shame emotion may be denial, laughing about one's transgressions, or embracing the criticism and seeking to do better the next time.

Shame, Humiliation, and Embarrassment

In the above section, I noted that the fundamental and constitutive element of shame is the negative self-evaluation brought about by the awareness of being seen to fall short of some standard, ideal, or goal. This can be sharpened by comparing shame with two closely related emotions, embarrassment and humiliation.

Andrew Morrison argues that embarrassment, shame, and humiliation are almost interchangeable and that they differ primarily in intensity.[10] Humiliation is the most intense and embarrassment the least intense version of interpersonal shame. Embarrassment, shame, and humiliation can be accompanied by the same physiological symptoms (blushing, feeling hot, perspiration, trembling, or increased heart rate) and behavioral signs (pursed lips, squirming, a desire to hide or be alone, averting one's gaze, bowing or lowering of the head). But I think what differentiates them definitively is the appropriate evaluative criteria, even if it is the case that the relevant evaluative criteria for humiliation make it the most intense and for embarrassment the least intense of the three emotions.[11]

Humiliation is elicited when the self perceives that an other displays an attitude of disgust and contempt for the self. Both shame and humiliation see the self as falling short of some ideal or standard. Central to humiliation, however, is not this self-reflection but the unjust experience of being put into that state by a contemptuous other. It does not consider the self as blameworthy.

9. Cairns, *Aidōs*, 16.
10. Morrison, *Culture of Shame*, 40–41.
11. So also Tarnopolsky, *Prudes, Perverts, and Tyrants*, 156.

Rather, it focuses on the external attribution of this negative evaluation so that there are tendencies toward revenge.[12] Shame may be brought on by an external other, but it focuses more on the internal attribution of the negative evaluation, involving primarily the self reflecting on the self.

In contrast to humiliation, shame and embarrassment are not prompted by a contemptuous assessment of the self, and one can feel shame or embarrassment before an other who displays a significantly less negative attitude. Both shame and embarrassment are related to exposure. Some assert that shame involves a violation of a moral norm and embarrassment a social norm or etiquette. It is, however, misleading to limit shame to a breach of a moral norm. For one can experience shame as a result of one's dyslexia or stutter, but we would never assert that one is morally culpable for one's dyslexia. A more fruitful criterion for distinguishing shame and embarrassment is the evaluation whether, in the moment of exposure, a significant character flaw has been revealed (shame) or merely an apparent flaw (embarrassment).[13] Moreover, one may experience embarrassment simply for being the center of attention even when no apparent flaw is revealed. I provide two examples. First, imagine a situation where I am introduced before giving an after-dinner speech at a conference. The person introducing me extols my credentials and expertise. The emotion I might experience in this moment of exposure is probably embarrassment rather than shame since no character flaw, real or apparent, has been revealed. Now, imagine that as I give my speech, I suddenly notice that there is a piece of spinach stuck between my teeth. I enter a state of fluster and feel exposed. If I believe that a discrediting fact of my character has been truly revealed (I am a careless sloven), I would describe myself as ashamed. However, if I believe that the situation does not truly reflect a flaw of my character, although everyone's attention is on the piece of spinach and I can imagine how the audience might think it to be a flaw, I would describe myself as embarrassed rather than ashamed.

Shame and Guilt

Many consider shame and guilt to be different emotions, but the specific factors that differentiate them are strongly debated. Attempts to distinguish

---

12. Gilbert, "What Is Shame?," 9–11.

13. Sabini, Garvey, and Hall ("Shame and Embarrassment Revisited," 104) write, "People refer to themselves as experiencing shame when they believe that a real flaw of their self has been revealed, they refer to themselves as experiencing embarrassment when they believe that others have reason to think a flaw has been revealed."

shame and guilt generally fall into three categories: (1) distinction based on the degree the person focuses either on the self or the behavior, (2) distinction based on the public and private nature of the transgression, and (3) distinction based on the nature of the eliciting event.[14] These approaches are not mutually exclusive, and some adopt a mix of them. I assess these approaches and conclude with some remarks about their relevance to my project.

Distinction 1: Self or Behavior

The dominant approach for distinguishing shame and guilt centers on the degree to which the person construes the emotion-eliciting event as a failure either of self or of behavior. In her landmark work *Shame and Guilt in Neurosis*, the psychoanalyst Helen Lewis argues that the key difference between shame and guilt centers on the role of the self in these experiences. Both shame and guilt are self-conscious emotions, emotions that have as components "consciousness of the self . . . and evaluation of the self against some standard."[15] Nevertheless, the specific evaluation is what differentiates shame from guilt. Specifically, the focus of evaluation in shame is the *self*, while the focus in guilt is the *thing* done.[16] This differential emphasis on self ("*I* did that horrible thing") vis-à-vis behavior ("I *did* that horrible *thing*") leads to different phenomenological experiences. Shame is a painful experience that is accompanied by the desire to shrink, to withdraw, and to hide. With its acute awareness of one's flawed self, shame is accompanied by a sense of worthlessness and powerlessness. Guilt, although painful, is nevertheless a less devastating experience as it does not affect one's core identity. Rather, people who experience guilt focus on the transgression, wishing they could undo or seeking to make amends for their actions.[17]

It is, however, doubtful whether these distinctions between shame and guilt can be so clearly discerned. Cairns writes, "It may be tidy to claim that shame involves thoughts like 'What a terrible person I am!' and guilt thoughts like

---

14. Tangney, Stuewig, and Mashek, "Moral Emotions," 348.

15. Fischer and Tangney, "Self-Conscious Emotions," 14.

16. H. Lewis (*Shame and Guilt in Neurosis*, 30) writes, "Shame . . . involves more self-consciousness and more self-imaging than guilt. The experience of shame is directly about the *self*, which is the focus of evaluation. In guilt, the self is not the central object of negative evaluation, but rather the thing done or undone is the focus. In guilt, the self is negatively evaluated in connection with something but is not itself the focus of the experience." Similarly, Nathanson (*Shame and Pride*, 19) writes, "Whereas shame is about the *quality* of our person or self, guilt is the painful emotion triggered when we become aware that we have acted in a way to bring harm to another person or to violate some important code. Guilt is about *action* and laws. Whenever we feel guilty, we can pay for the damage inflicted." See also M. Lewis, "Self-Conscious Emotions."

17. See Tangney and Dearing, *Shame and Guilt*, 10–25.

'What a terrible thing to do!' and to argue that 'What a terrible person I am to do such a terrible thing!' indicates a concurrence of shame and guilt, but it is unlikely that the real world can admit such a sharp conceptual distinction. . . . Quite simply, self-image will constantly be called into question by specific acts, and in such situations the sharp distinction between shame and guilt will begin to disappear."[18]

This does not necessarily mean that shame and guilt are identical. Bernard Williams suggests that shame and guilt can be evoked by the same action.[19] Nonetheless, shame and guilt focus primarily on different directions of an emotional response to an action. Williams writes, "The action stands between the inner world of disposition, feeling, and decision and an outer world of harm and wrong. *What I have done* points in one direction toward what has happened to others, in another direction to what I am. Guilt looks primarily in the first direction. . . . Shame looks to what I am."[20] Shame is not a general negative evaluation of the self but a negative evaluation in light of some specific shortcoming. When the shortcoming is dependent on some action that is contrary to one's moral standards, shame invariably references both conduct and self-image. Similarly, guilt that is caused by a specific act is nevertheless caused by a specific act that runs counter to an ideal self. Guilt must therefore also reference both an ideal self and conduct. The distinction between self and conduct may be possible to draw in the abstract, but it is difficult to maintain in practice. Shame and guilt reflect the reciprocal relation between self and action, and shame and guilt interweave as we construct and assess our identity in relation to others.

Distinction 2: Public or Private

The second approach distinguishes shame and guilt on the basis of the public or private locus of the negative evaluation. Shame arises from public exposure of one's shortcoming, but guilt stems from private self-reproach that arises from one's conscience. David Ausubel clarifies, "Shame may be defined as an unpleasant emotion by an individual to an actual or presumed negative judgment of himself by others resulting in self-depreciation vis-à-vis the group," and "guilt may be conceptualized as a special kind of negative

18. Cairns, *Aidōs*, 24. Kaufman (*Psychology of Shame*, 6) likewise writes, "The assumption that we feel guilty about deeds but feel shame about self is equally in error. The target of shame can be either the self or the self's actions, just as one can feel guilty about deeds or else feel essentially guilt-ridden as a person. From the perspective of affect theory, one can feel shameful about deeds as well as guilty about self."

19. So also Rawls, *Theory of Justice*, 445.

20. Williams, *Shame and Necessity*, 92–93.

self-evaluation which occurs when an individual acknowledges that his behavior is at variance with a given moral value to which he feels obligated to
conform."[21]

This distinction between shame and guilt was not only applied to individual emotional experiences; it was also applied to cultures. According to
these theorists, the distinction between shame and guilt cultures relies on a
distinction between internal and external sanctions. Shame is caused by fear
of external sanctions, especially the disapproval of others; guilt relies on internal sanctions that stem from one's individual conscience, especially one's
own disapproval of oneself. Ruth Benedict writes,

> A society that inculcates absolute standards of morality and relies on men's
> developing a conscience is a guilt culture by definition. . . . True shame cultures
> rely on external sanctions for good behavior, not, as true guilt cultures do, on an
> internalized conviction of sin. Shame is a reaction to other people's criticism. A
> man is shamed either by being openly ridiculed and rejected or by fantasying to
> himself that he has been made ridiculous. In either case it is a potent sanction.
> But it requires an audience or at least a man's fantasy of an audience. Guilt does
> not. In a nation where honor means living up to one's own picture of oneself, a
> man may suffer from guilt though no man knows of his misdeed and a man's
> feeling of guilt may actually be relieved by confessing his sin.[22]

With these criteria, Benedict considers Japan to have primarily a shame
culture and America a guilt culture.[23] E. R. Dodds uses Benedict's terminology and suggests that the transition from Homeric Greece to Archaic Greece
represents a shift from a shame culture to a guilt culture.[24] Although Dodds
uses the terms only as descriptions without assuming any theory of cultural

21. Ausubel, "Relationships between Shame and Guilt," 382, 379. Gehm and Scherer ("Situation Evaluation," 74) argue that "shame is usually dependent on the public exposure of one's
frailty or failing, whereas guilt may be something that remains secret with us, no one else
knowing of our breach of social norms or of our responsibility for an immoral act." See also
Smith et al. ("Role of Public Exposure," 145), who write, "The results . . . provide evidence that
public exposure is more associated with shame than with guilt. The manipulation of public
exposure had a strong effect on the explicit measure of shame, whereas it had no effect on the
corresponding measure of guilt."
22. Benedict, *Chrysanthemum and the Sword*, 222–23.
23. Lebra ("Shame and Guilt," 193) considers both shame and guilt to be "allocentric in that
they are based upon the actor's ability in empathy to 'take the role of other' . . . or to be aware
of his self as an object of sanction. . . . In the case of shame, others are visualized as audience
or spectators, whereas in the case of guilt they appear as victims of or sufferers from one's
action." Using these definitions, she reverses Benedict's position regarding Japanese emotions.
She argues that "guilt is anchored more firmly than shame in the Japanese moral system, and
that shame emotions, therefore, are often translated into guilt terms" (207).
24. Dodds, *Greeks and the Irrational*, 28–63.

change, those influenced by social Darwinism will assume that the shift from a shame culture to a guilt culture marks a sign of progress.

It appears valid that shame should reference the concept of an external audience. There are nevertheless difficulties with this approach since one can feel shame even when alone. If we resort to the weaker claim that shame only requires an imaginary audience to bring it about, we must then affirm that this kind of shame depends less on the expected judgments of the audience than on the discrepancy one sees between the self and some ideal standard. The fear of shame has then in effect been internalized, and the public-private distinction between shame and guilt falls apart. Gabriele Taylor considers the role of an audience as a catalyst for self-evaluation, but it is self-evaluation that is constitutive of shame, not the presence of a real or imagined audience.[25] Shame still requires the presence of an audience or an *other*, but the *other* may be internalized such that one can be an *other* to oneself. Consequently, the distinction that shame is heteronomous while guilt is autonomous falls apart.

If the public-private criterion cannot be used to distinguish shame from guilt, then Benedict's assessment that external-internal sanctions form the differentiating factor between shame and guilt cultures is also open to criticism. Millie Creighton defends Benedict against others who wrongly critique her for assuming that guilt was absent in Japan. She, however, writes that "the one area in which it is valid to severely criticize Benedict involves her designation of shame cultures as relying on external sanctions of control while guilt cultures rely on internal sanctions of control."[26] If both shame and guilt share a certain degree of internalization, then the sharp antithesis between shame and guilt disappears, and with it the antithesis between shame and guilt cultures. This is not to say that there is no such thing as a shame culture or a guilt culture. Rather, the difference between a shame culture and a guilt culture must be one of degree and emphasis rather than of kind.[27] Similarly, this is not to say that there are no differences between Japanese and American societies, nor between ancient Greek societies and ours. Rather, it is a caricature to label Japan a shame culture and the United States a guilt culture. A caricature may capture the prominent features of its subject and present it in an easily understandable form to others, but it is inappropriate to suggest that a caricature delivers all the subtle variations and complex distinctions that are present in reality.

25. Taylor, *Pride, Shame, and Guilt*, 57–68.
26. Creighton, "Revisiting Shame and Guilt Cultures," 282.
27. See Cairns, *Aidōs*, 27–47; Gill, *Greek Thought*, 20–27.

Distinction 3: Nonmoral or Moral

The third approach distinguishes shame and guilt on the nature of the eliciting event.[28] Shame is invoked by moral and nonmoral failures, while guilt arises from moral transgressions. There are at least two implications of this approach. First, since shame is invoked by moral and nonmoral failures, there is a tendency to differentiate between two kinds of shame on the basis of the moral and amoral nature of the failure.[29] On the one hand, moral shame stems from a failure that reveals a character flaw (e.g., someone who is caught shoplifting). On the other hand, amoral shame stems from a failure that does not reveal a character flaw (e.g., someone who is dyslexic and stumbles through a public reading of Scripture in a church service). In the case of the dyslexic, amoral shame is clearly distinguished from guilt as we would not want to imply that the person is responsible for his dyslexia. Second, since both moral shame and guilt can be invoked by moral failures, psychologists who adopt this approach also use one or two of the other approaches to distinguish shame and guilt. For example, some distinguish shame and guilt not only on the nature of the situational antecedent but also on the private-public locus of the negative evaluation.

Assessment

The multiplicity of approaches to distinguish shame and guilt suggests the difficulty of differentiating these two moral emotions despite our intuitive sense that they are different. The words "shame" and "guilt" are sometimes used interchangeably, and research subjects in psychological experiments are at times not able to distinguish them.[30] Moreover, the psychometric scales that are used to measure shame and guilt at times fail to distinguish them adequately.[31] Stephen Pattison remarks, "It is probably futile to try and make any absolute distinction between these two concepts or states in terms of common parlance."[32] Part of this confusion may arise because shame and guilt experiences overlap or co-occur at the same time, and people use both shame and guilt to cover the full range of their experience without

28. Psychologists who adopt this approach include Ferguson, Stegge, and Damhuis, "Children's Understanding"; Olthof et al., "Shame and Guilt in Children"; Smith et al., "Role of Public Exposure."

29. Ausubel, "Relationships between Shame and Guilt," 382.

30. N. Harris, "Dimensionality of the Moral Emotions."

31. See Kugler and Jones, "Conceptualizing and Assessing Guilt," 324, Blum, "Shame and Guilt," 91.

32. Pattison, *Shame*, 43.

being able to articulate the different facets that give rise to each emotion separately.[33]

The overlap between shame and guilt may be explained by the argument that guilt is not an emotion in itself. Contrary to most researchers, Andrew Ortony argues that guilt is not an emotion; it is a socio-legal condition, an external objective description.[34] The reason why many wrongly think that guilt is an emotion is because they do not pay careful attention to the distinction between *feeling* X and *being* X. The failure to note this difference "can result in inadvertently attributing to non-affective conditions properties that belong, not to the conditions themselves, but only to the associate (affective) *feeling* conditions."[35] For true emotions, both of the statements "I feel X" and "I am X" will refer to emotional states and will be roughly equivalent (e.g., "I feel angry" and "I am angry"). For non-emotions, both statements will not refer to emotional states and both will not be equivalent. Thus, "I feel guilty" refers to an emotional state, but not "I am guilty." The latter is the external description of the socio-legal condition of a person. The former is a matter of feeling what a guilty person feels, and that might include shame, sadness, fear, regret, and remorse.[36] Thus, while shame is a unitary affect, guilt is a socio-legal state that elicits multiple affects.

The assertion that guilt is not an emotion is also borne out in the second edition of the *Oxford English Dictionary* (*OED*). The *OED* defines guilt primarily as "a failure of duty, delinquency; offence, crime, sin."[37] The definitions *OED* gives focus on acts, responsibility, and state of culpability. There is no mention of emotion or feeling in any of the dictionary definitions except for entry 5d, which notes that guilt is "misused for 'sense of guilt.'" The *OED* also recognizes an implicit connection between shame and guilt in defining *sense of shame* as "the consciousness of this emotion, guilty feeling."[38] Since one source of shame is the consciousness of having done something wrong, the socio-legal condition of being guilty would elicit shame.

It is beyond the scope of this project to adjudicate whether guilt is an emotion, but the above discussion concerning the difficulty of distinguishing shame and guilt has several implications. First, since both guilt and shame share a certain degree of internalization, our study and analysis of shame should not commit us to focus only on external sanctions without any appreciation of

33. Smith et al., "Role of Public Exposure," 140.
34. Ortony, "Is Guilt an Emotion?" See also Elison, "Shame and Guilt."
35. Ortony, "Is Guilt an Emotion?," 285.
36. Sabini and Silver, "Emotion Names and Experiences," 6–7.
37. *OED*, s.v. "guilt," *sb.* 1.
38. *OED*, s.v. "shame," *sb.* I.1.c.

some internalized standard. Second, even though emotion lexemes in other cultures and languages may be quickly glossed in English as "shame," a careful study of these lexemes should not preclude their characterization in terms of guilt. Third, many psychologists have a decidedly negative view toward shame vis-à-vis guilt; they consider shame to be maladaptive. June Tangney and Ronda Dearing write, "The literature strongly suggests that shame is the more problematic emotion, linked to a range of psychological symptoms. In contrast, 'pure' guilt, uncomplicated by shame, does not lead to psychological symptoms and can, in fact, be quite adaptive."[39] The difficulty of absolutely distinguishing shame and guilt should lead us to question the validity of such statements. Moreover, it should caution us not to allow simplistic distinctions to cloud our understanding of the material that follows and should prompt us to consider the possibility that shame can play a positive role in moral formation.

Conceptual Clarifications

Much conceptual confusion surrounds the issue of shame. This arises out of the different ways in which shame lexemes work not only in the English language but also in other languages. When someone says, "Don't you have any shame?" and another retorts, "I don't need any more shame!" they may be referring to different types of shame. In order to clarify this confusion, we need to distinguish between the occurrent experience of shame, dispositional shame, retrospective shame, prospective shame, and acts of shaming.

The *occurrent experience of shame* is the discomforting and painful emotion that arises when one is aware of certain inadequacies of the self under the gaze of an other. As an occurrent emotion, it is an emotion experienced as actually occurring at the present moment and is typically accompanied by the affective behavior of blushing, pursed lips, constricted posture, gaze aversion, and hanging the head.[40]

Dispositional shame (sense of shame or shamefastness) is the disposition, inclination, and inhibition that restrains one from pursuing certain actions that are shameful without implication that shame is actually being experienced by the person. For example, the statement "I am ashamed of being seen as a coward" informs you not about an occurrence of shame in me but about a disposition of mine to experience shame in that particular situation. I take it as obvious that the occurrent experience of shame must be

---

39. Tangney and Dearing, *Shame and Guilt*, 127.
40. See Keltner and Harker, "Nonverbal Signal of Shame."

prior to the dispositional sense, for the statement "I will not do X lest I be shamed" implies a previous occurrence of shame and an inhibition toward future occurrences.[41]

Some consider the understanding of shame as sense of shame or shame-fastness to be quite distinct from the understanding of shame as an emotion: one is a disposition to experience shame, and the other is the occurrent experience of shame; one is considered an ethical trait, the other an emotion; one has a positive connection, the other negative.[42] It should, however, be noted that the distinction between the dispositional and the occurrent senses of the emotion is not sharp.[43] For the disposition must quickly lead to the occurrence of the emotion, given the right stimuli. Since the disposition so readily leads to the embodied experience of the emotion, the dispositional shamefast person habitually lives with a foretaste of shame at the back of the throat.[44] It is this habituation with the prospect of the occurrent experience of shame that gives dispositional shame the power to restrain. Without the proleptic emotive component inherent in its structure, dispositional shame lacks the inner strength to circumscribe inappropriate behavior and ceases to be an ethical trait.

The tight relationship between the dispositional and the occurrent senses of shame is mitigated in English, for we typically differentiate between the two using different words: "sense of shame/modesty/shamefastness" and "shame." The ancient Greeks and Romans, however, used the same lexeme (αἰσχύνη, αἰδώς, *pudor*) for the dispositional and the occurrent understandings of shame. Thus, the relationship between them appears seamless and uniform.

Retrospective shame and *prospective shame* refer respectively to situations where the evil that makes one feel shame is either in the past/present or in

---

41. This understanding of occurrent and dispositional shame corresponds to the first two definitions of *shame* in the second edition of the *OED*: "1.a. The painful emotion arising from the consciousness of something dishonouring, ridiculous, or indecorous in one's own conduct or circumstances (or in those of others whose honour or disgrace one regards as one's own), or of being in a situation which offends one's sense of modesty or decency. . . . 2. Fear of offence against propriety or decency, operating as a restraint on behaviour; modesty, shamefastness." The distinction between occurrent and dispositional senses of an emotion is found also in the Greco-Roman world. Cairns (*Aidōs*, 398) notes that Aristotle "has a developed terminology which makes similar distinctions: a *pathos* is an affect, and is always occurrent, but behind *pathē* lies capacities (*dunameis*), and settled states (*hexeis*), both of which may involve some kind of non-occurrent disposition towards the various emotions."

42. Miller (*Anatomy of Disgust*, 34) writes, "The shame doing the inhibiting is not the emotion shame, but the sense of shame, the sense of modesty and propriety that keeps us from being shamed."

43. Cairns, *Aidōs*, 158.

44. Kaster, *Emotion, Restraint, and Community*, 16–17.

the future. The former is a kind of shame that is consequent upon having done bad acts (either in the past or present); the latter looks to the future and restrains one from performing bad acts. Note that there is some ambiguity in prospective shame. It can refer either to (1) the prospect of shame (or sense of shame) that restricts one's behavior or (2) the occurrent experience of shame at a prospective blow to one's honor.[45] Given this ambiguity, the distinction between retrospective and prospective shame does not exactly map onto the difference between the occurrent experience of shame and the dispositional sense of shame.[46]

Acts of shaming are what an individual or collective agent does to bring about the occurrent experience of shame in an individual or collective group. This can be mediated through words, actions, or a combination of both. How a self responds to the occurrent experience of shame brought about by an other's act of shaming depends on a variety of factors. They include the intensity of the affective experience; the social relationship between the self and the other; how the self views the attitude and intent of the other; the social context in which the act of shaming occurs; the self's experience of previous shaming incidents; the intrapsychic shame scripts that run in that individual's mind; and the ways in which other parties or social scripts tell the self how it should respond to such acts of shaming. The multiplicity of factors suggests that any attempt to shame a person for some supposed good may lead to an indeterminate response. This does not necessarily mean that shaming should not be used as a pedagogical tool for moral formation. Rather, any use of it must be framed in a way that minimizes misunderstanding and be accompanied with full awareness of the potential harm that it can inflict.

Cross-Cultural Examination of Shame

This study is focused not on shame per se but on the use of shame for moral formation. Nevertheless, we need to examine briefly how the different authors we engage understand shame. As we are interacting with texts in multiple languages, we cannot take it for granted that the emotional lexemes in Greek, Latin, Hebrew, and Chinese correspond exactly to contemporary English terminology.[47] This assertion immediately raises several questions. How can

---

45. Nieuwenburg, "Learning to Deliberate," 466n16.
46. Tarnopolsky, *Prudes, Perverts, and Tyrants*, 58n8.
47. W. Harris (*Restraining Rage*, 36) remarks, "The study of classical emotions has been seriously impeded by our failure to realize . . . that the relevant Greek and Latin terminology is very unlikely to correspond neatly to modern English usage."

we meaningfully examine the emotion-talk of another culture, especially one that is removed from us in time?[48] Are the emotions of the Greeks, Romans, Jews, and Chinese the same as ours? Is there a universal set of emotions that is experienced by every culture?

In *The Expression of Emotions*, Darwin extended his idea of evolution to the emotional life of humans, suggesting that certain expressive features are innate and universal. Neo-Darwinists such as Paul Ekman build on Darwin's work and devise experiments to prove that there is a basic set of emotions that are universally shared and that can be universally recognized from facial expressions regardless of language and culture.[49] This principle can be articulated as follows: "There is considerable evidence indicating distinct, prototypical facial signals that across a variety of cultures can be reliably recognized as corresponding to at least six different emotions (happiness, sadness, surprise, disgust, anger, and fear), and possibly others, including interest, shame, and contempt."[50] The work of Ekman has not gone unchallenged. Anthropologists argue that human behavior and emotions are decisively determined by one's respective culture. Drawing on her work among the Ifaluk people, Catherine Lutz claims that "emotional experience is not precultural but pre*eminently* cultural. . . . The complex meaning of each emotion word is the result of the important role those words play in articulating the full range of a people's cultural values, social relations, and economic circumstances."[51] The linguist Anna Wierzbicka also challenges Ekman's categorization of basic emotions in English lexical categories. She notes that "the speakers of other languages in fact think about human experience in terms of other, non-matching, conceptual categories . . . ; they do not 'read' any human faces as 'angry,' 'sad,' or 'fearful,' but rather interpret them in terms of their own language-specific categories."[52]

The views adopted by universalists and social constructivists should not be construed as mutually exclusive and exhaustive.[53] Robert Solomon remarks, "There is nothing in the nature of emotion . . . that assures universality, but

48. For discussions of methodological issues, see C. Barton, *Roman Honor*, 1–17; Cairns, "Ethics, Ethology, Terminology"; Kaster, *Emotion, Restraint, and Community*, 6–12; Konstan, *Emotions of the Ancient Greeks*, 3–40.
49. See Ekman, *Emotion in the Human Face*.
50. Smith and Scott, "Componential Approach," 229 (references removed).
51. Lutz, *Unnatural Emotions*, 5–6.
52. Wierzbicka, *Emotions across Languages and Cultures*, 169.
53. Mallon and Stich ("Odd Couple") reconcile the two views by noting the confusion in the meaning and reference of emotion terms. Social constructivists employ a "thick" description of the emotion term, paying attention to the antecedent conditions as well as the socially learned response that varies from culture to culture. Universalists, on the other hand, employ a narrow view of the meaning and reference of the emotion term, focusing on a core element or an innate emotion prototype.

neither is it so obvious that emotions differ so much from place to place either."[54] Emotions have universal and culture-specific aspects, making dialogue between other cultures and our own possible. Although the nuances of emotional lexemes may be socially constructed, we are still able to make some sense of them. If it were not so, contemporary readers would not be able to make sense of the emotions found in an English translation of the *Iliad* or the "Rasādhyāya" (the sixth chapter of *Nāṭyaśāstra*, a Sanskrit text written between the third and fifth centuries CE).[55] Cultural psychologists recognize this phenomenon, noting that "contemporary non-Hindu researchers in the United States and Europe are likely to find the account of the 'basic emotions' in the 'Rasādhyāya' both familiar and strange." A comparison of the Sanskrit list of nine basic emotions with those that Ekman derived from facial expressions shows that "the two lists do not seem . . . to be closely coordinated, although they are not totally disjoint either."[56]

Given this similarity and dissimilarity between emotional lexemes in different languages and cultures, what is the minimal mandatory meaning that shame must have? What is the abstract idea or underlying concept that sets a mandatory limit on all instances of shame lexemes? Cultural psychologist and anthropologist Richard Shweder proposes this definition: "Shame is the deeply felt and highly motivating experience of the fear of being judged defective."[57] Such a definition is fundamentally in line with our earlier statement that the constitutive element of shame is negative self-evaluation, the awareness of being seen to fall short of some ideal or goal. Having articulated the abstract idea that undergirds every cultural-specific definition of shame, we should not lull ourselves into thinking that the shame that another culture experiences is the same as ours, for we do not experience the abstract idea of shame in itself. Every mental state that we experience is never the abstract concept but the more substantive, full-bodied, and cultural-specific manifestation of that abstract idea, colored with its local meaning.

As we examine the shame lexemes of different sets of texts, we must be mindful of how a particular culture concretizes the abstract concept with its

---

54. Solomon, "Philosophy of Emotions," 14.

55. Williams (*Shame and Necessity*, 88) also recognizes this: "In [my] discussion, I have been using the English word 'shame' in two ways. It has translated certain Greek words, in particular *aidōs*. It has also had its usual modern meaning. I have been able to use it in both these ways without its falling apart, and this shows something significant. What we have discovered about the Greeks' understanding of these reactions . . . applies equally well to what we recognize in our own world as shame. If it were not so, the translation could not have delivered so much that is familiar to us from our acquaintance with what we call 'shame.'"

56. Shweder et al., "Cultural Psychology of the Emotions," 411.

57. Shweder, "Deep Cultural Psychology of Shame," 1115 (italics removed).

distinctive character and meaning. This can be done by noting how members of various cultural groups are alike or different with respect to the components of the shame experience. This approach minimizes the danger of simplification (where we simply assume that Greek or Hebrew emotional lexemes map directly onto their English equivalents) and helps us appreciate how shame may be understood differently in the Jewish, Greco-Roman, and Chinese worlds.

Conclusion: What Is Shame?

I first defined emotion as a script comprising five components: (1) precipitating event, (2) appraisal, (3) physiological change, (4) action tendency, and (5) regulation. Of these five components, the appraisal element differentiates one emotional experience from another.

Applying the above five components to the emotional experience of shame, I noted that precipitating events, action tendencies, or even physiological changes in the shame experience may differ for different individuals and even different episodes in the same individual. Nonetheless, the central constitutive element of the shame experience is the negative appraisal or self-evaluation by the individual. I thus define shame as *the painful emotion that arises from an awareness that one has fallen short of some standard, ideal, or goal.*

2

Greco-Roman Backgrounds

This chapter examines how various Greek and Roman authors understand shame and its role in moral progress. The primary literature on this topic is vast. Major writers include Homer, Sophocles, Euripides, Protagoras, Plato, Aristotle, Philodemus, Cicero, Dio Chrysostom, Seneca, and Epictetus. It is impossible to investigate adequately each person in the space of a chapter. I only survey the writings of representative thinkers so as to understand the conceptual background that will inform our reading of Paul. Specifically, I examine the moral education of pre-Socratic philosophers, the shaming elenchus of Socrates, the moral psychology of Aristotle, and the moral philosophy of various thinkers in the Hellenistic period. A concluding section summarizes the key findings of this chapter and draws out the implications for my overall project.

The Vocabulary of Shame

Before I begin my survey of the various thinkers, it is necessary to make some preliminary lexical remarks. Several Greek words fall within the concept of shame. They are αἰδώς (shame, sense of honor), αἰσχρότης (shamefulness), αἰσχύνη (shame, modesty), ἀσχημοσύνη (shameless deed), ἀτιμία (dishonor), ἐντροπή (shame), δειγματισμός (putting to shame), ὄνειδος (disgrace), and ταπεινός (lowly). Within the primary literature that I examine, two occur repeatedly—αἰδώς and αἰσχύνη. The frequency of these two lexemes shows their importance and requires some comment on their meaning and significance.

LSJ defines αἰδώς as "a moral feeling, *reverence, awe, respect* for the feeling or opinion of others or for one's own conscience, and so *shame, self-respect* . . . , *sense of honour.*"[1] Douglas Cairns, who has written the definitive work on αἰδώς, defines it as "an inhibitory emotion based on sensitivity to and protectiveness of one's self-image."[2] It is always prospective and inhibitory in the earliest authors such as Homer, and the notions of shame ("I feel shame before [someone]") and respect ("I respect [someone]") are fused together. From the sixth century BCE onward, the word αἰδώς also acquired the retrospective sense—one experienced shame for past events. The link between αἰδώς and τιμή (honor, reverence) is fundamental throughout the history of its usage, but the crucial point is that αἰδώς includes a concern for both one's honor and that of others.[3] Αἰδώς is thus not so fixated on the pursuit of one's own prestige that it impinges on the prestige of others. Moreover, the pursuit of one's honor never implies concern for one's outward reputation to the exclusion of one's internal self-image. The code of honor that αἰδώς subscribes to is concerned with the internal possession of true excellence, rather than only being seen by others to have attained it.

As for αἰσχύνη, LSJ defines it primarily as "*shame, dishonor*" and secondarily "like αἰδώς, *sense of shame, honour.*"[4] The term αἰσχύνη thus encompasses both prospective and retrospective aspects of shame. In this regard, the semantic meaning of αἰδώς and αἰσχύνη overlap, and it is not clear whether they are synonymous. Aristotle frequently uses the two terms interchangeably, and Plutarch considers the terms to be synonymous.[5] But classical Stoic theory, as reported by Diogenes Laertius, makes a distinction between them: αἰδώς is a *good emotion* (εὐπάθεια) under the genus of *caution*, while αἰσχύνη is an *ordinary emotion* (πάθη) under the genus of *fear.*[6] The net effect of this framework is that αἰδώς is restricted to the Stoic sage, in whom it guards against the pursuit of any unworthy action. The rest of humanity, however, succumbs to αἰσχύνη, the fear of ill repute. The fourth-century bishop Nemesius also distinguishes between these two terms, noting that the one who feels αἰσχύνη is shamed for what he has done, but the one who feels αἰδώς fears

---

1. LSJ, s.v. "αἰδώς."
2. Cairns, *Aidōs*, 2.
3. Cairns, *Aidōs*, 432.
4. LSJ, s.v. "αἰσχύνη."
5. Plutarch, *Vit. pud.* 2 (529d). If there is a distinction between αἰδώς and αἰσχύνη, it may parallel the distinction between *verecundia* and *pudor*. For a sensitive analysis of the similarities and differences between these two Latin words, see Kaster, *Emotion, Restraint, and Community*, 61–65.
6. Diogenes Laertius, *Vit. phil.* 7.116. See the discussion in Graver, *Stoicism and Emotion*, 208.

that he will fall into some disgrace.[7] He adds that the ancients often call αἰδώς αἰσχύνη, but remarks that in doing so they misuse the terms. David Konstan notes that Nemesius is the first to differentiate between αἰδώς and αἰσχύνη on the distinction of prospective and retrospective shame.[8] He nevertheless asserts that Nemesius is certainly wrong about this distinction in classical Greek because both prospective and retrospective senses of shame coexist in the term αἰσχύνη.

The data suggests that certain Greek authors use αἰδώς and αἰσχύνη synonymously, while others make a slight distinction between them. In either case, αἰδώς is the more archaic term and has a loftier connotation than αἰσχύνη. Cairns crisply summarizes his findings: "In ordinary Greek *aidōs* and *aischunē* are synonyms . . . , but *aidōs* is the older and more poetic term, and it draws its claim to be considered as a virtue from its use in highly poetic contexts where something of the importance originally accorded the concept is preserved."[9]

Cairns's remarks are primarily directed to the time of Aristotle. Nevertheless, they are still pertinent to the Hellenistic period, for Dio Chrysostom, writing in the first century CE, also affirms that αἰδώς is the more poetic form of αἰσχύνη.[10] Given the significant semantic overlap between these two terms, our analysis of the role of shame in moral progress should at the very least include texts that focus on both of these terms.

Pre-Socratic Philosophers

The pre-Socratic philosophers were early Greek thinkers not influenced by the thought of Socrates. Although most of them were engaged in cosmological speculation, some explored questions about ethics, not least the role of shame for moral formation. Two such thinkers are Protagoras and Democritus.

Protagoras

We have little material that comes directly from Protagoras's hand, but the Great Speech in Plato's *Protagoras* (320C–328C) is one of the main sources that may give us access to his moral thought. What concerns us primarily in the speech is the social nature of αἰδώς and its role in maintaining civic order.

---

7. *SVF* 3.416.19–20 = Nemesius, *On the Nature of Man*, chap. 20.
8. Konstan, *Emotions of the Ancient Greeks*, 97.
9. Cairns, *Aidōs*, 415.
10. Dio Chrysostom, *Or.* 13.7: "The poet uses 'awe' [αἰδώς] instead of 'shame' [αἰσχύνη] as is the custom the poets have." Unless otherwise stated, translations of nonbiblical Greek and Latin texts are from the LCL.

In the Great Speech, Protagoras presents a myth that relates a two-stage account of human development. The first stage is brutish and uncivilized. Although humans have the wisdom and skill to meet the physical needs of food and shelter, they are not able to live communally through their lack of civic art. The second stage is civilization as Zeus intervenes in human history with his two gifts: *justice* (δίκη) and *shame* (αἰδώς).[11] These two gifts allow humanity to live together peacefully under the bonds of friendship. Unlike the previous skills or crafts that were already given, these two gifts are given not to select individuals but to all. Zeus further lays down the law that these two gifts should be taught to all men such that "he who cannot partake of [αἰδώς] and [δίκη] shall die the death as a public pest" (322D). In the discursive section following the telling of the myth, Protagoras replaces αἰδώς with *temperance* (σωφροσύνη, 323A), reflecting a tradition that sees the importance of prospective shame (αἰδώς) as a cardinal social virtue or excellence.[12]

In the myth, αἰδώς is presented as a divine gift; in the subsequent discussion, Protagoras notes that σωφροσύνη must be acquired through education. Given the equivalence of αἰδώς and σωφροσύνη, one must also assume that αἰδώς should be inculcated in the population through education.[13] Thus, good men "teach and admonish [their sons] from earliest childhood till the last day of their lives" (325C). Insofar as what is considered honorable and shameful is not instinctively understood, "the nurse, the mother, the tutor, and the father himself strive hard . . . [to] teach and impress upon [the child] that this is just, and that unjust, one thing noble, another base [αἰσχρόν], one holy, another unholy, and that he is to do this, and not do that" (325D). This elementary education is then supplemented by formal schooling under a master who pays more attention to the "children's good behavior than over their letters and harp-playing" (325D–E). After the years of formal schooling, the laws of the city continue the process of education. Protagoras compares the laws to letters drawn in a writing tablet for the "less advanced pupils" (326D), suggesting that the laws and its corresponding punishment function as external corrections for those who have not yet internalized the social virtues.

Protagoras sees αἰδώς as a major element of virtue (ἀρετή). He stresses the importance of acquiring αἰδώς during a child's formative years and of the necessity to pursue the *noble* and avoid the *base* (αἰσχρόν). The intended

11. "Δίκη and αἰδώς" is a traditional formula. It is found, for instance, in Hesiod, *Op.* 192.

12. The link between σωφροσύνη and αἰδώς is clearly seen in Plato, *Charm.* 160E; *Phaedr.* 253D. According to Stobaeus, the Stoics consider αἰδημοσύνη (a cognate of αἰδώς) a virtue, a species of σωφροσύνη. See *SVF* 3.264.9–10.

13. For the link of αἰδώς with education, see also Theognis, *Elegiac Poems* 409–10; Euripides, *Iph. aul.* 561–67; Thucydides, *Pel. War* 1.84.3.

result of this education is that αἰδώς, with its cognitive ability to differentiate between right and wrong, becomes so ingrained that it automatically constrains the adult citizen from pursuing every action that is expedient.[14] As a dispositional trait that manifests the emotion in its occurrent sense, αἰδώς causes one to experience shame at the prospect of failing one's social and moral responsibility. It makes one sensitive to the social norms of the community and enables humanity to live together harmoniously. As such, αἰδώς is more than an inhibiting emotion such as the fear of touching a hot stove; it is primarily a social emotion that enables us to connect with those around us. Moreover, as a gift given only to humanity, αἰδώς is a human emotion that is not shared with other species.

Democritus

Democritus recognizes the importance of shame for moral development. He notes that in order for change to occur, "the man who does shameful deeds must first feel shame [αἰσχύνω] in his own eyes" (B 84).[15] Once shame has done its work in awakening the individual to his error, repentance for these shameful deeds will result in the salvation of his life (B 43).

Given the importance of shame in moral progress, Democritus follows Protagoras in advocating for the moral education of the young so as to produce αἰδώς (B 179). He nevertheless recognizes a major issue with Protagoras's program—the social nature of αἰδώς, coupled with the use of laws to carry on the process of education, may only foster mere conformity. Democritus perceives the inability of external punishments to deter in every case, for the one who is prevented by social customs or law from wrongdoing will probably do it in secret (B 181). Democritus addresses this issue by linking αἰδώς with conscience. Instead of external sanctions, the force that drives an individual not to do bad must arise from duty or the sense of what must be done (B 41). One's duty is driven not by the external opinions of others but by an internalized standard of right and wrong that is bound up with a proper sense of shame. Thus Democritus says, "One must not respect [i.e., feel shame before, αἰδέομαι] the opinion of other men more than one's own; nor must one be more ready to do wrong if no one will know than if all will know. One must respect [i.e., feel shame before, αἰδέομαι] one's own opinion most, and this must stand as the law of one's soul, preventing one from doing anything

---

14. Protagoras's sentiment is shared by his contemporaries. For example, see Euripides, *Suppl.* 911–17.

15. English translations of Democritus are from Freeman, *Ancilla to the Pre-Socratic Philosophers.*

improper" (B 264). He expresses the same idea in fragment 244 using αἰσχύνω instead: "Do not say or do what is base, even when you are alone. Learn to feel shame [αἰσχύνω] in your own eyes much more than before others." For Democritus, shame functions as a prospective check that inhibits evil deeds, not because it is liable to censure from other members within the community but because it fails to meet the internalized standards of right and wrong.[16]

Socrates

Socrates did not leave any written works, but scholars generally assume that the early dialogues of his student Plato present us with a reasonable portrayal of the historical Socrates. The early dialogues, in alphabetical order, are the *Apology, Charmides, Crito, Euthyphro, Gorgias, Hippias Minor, Ion, Laches,* and *Protagoras.* The *Meno* is a transitional dialogue between the early and middle dialogues. In this section I will focus on Socrates's shaming elenchus (ἔλεγχος) as seen primarily in the *Gorgias.*[17]

Certain interpretations of Socrates's ethics argue for an intellectualist perspective. This view stems from statements that Socrates makes in the *Meno,* which argue that the difference between good and evil people is not in the nature of the things they desire (i.e., that good men desire good things and evil men desire evil things). Rather, all people desire good things, but good and evil people have different beliefs about what is good and evil. Thus, "when people act badly or viciously or even just out of moral weakness, that will be merely a result of intellectual mistake."[18] The way to change one's ethical behavior, then, is to change one's belief. Thus, "*only philosophical dialogue can improve one's fellow citizen.*"[19]

Other scholars, however, note that Socrates does not just engage his interlocutors in ratiocination; he also employs shame to persuade his interlocutors toward virtue.[20] Socrates plays on his interlocutor's sense of shame, and he actively shames them in his elenchus. For example, Socrates, in the *Gorgias,* refutes each of his interlocutors not so much by appeals to logic but by appeals to shame. Gorgias initially declares that the rhetoric he teaches is morally

16. Cairns, *Aidōs,* 363–70.
17. The verb (ἐλέγχω) that Socrates uses for his shaming elenchus carries the archaic sense of "*disgrace, put to shame*" (LSJ, s.v. "ἐλέγχω"). For an example, see Plato, *Soph.* 230C–D.
18. Penner, "Socrates," 165.
19. Penner, "Socrates," 164. See also Rowe, "Socrates in Plato's Dialogues," 166.
20. See Kahn, "Drama and Dialectic"; McKim, "Shame and Truth"; Woodruff, "Socrates and the Irrational"; Moss, "Shame, Pleasure, and the Divided Soul"; Gish, "Rivals in Persuasion"; Futter, "Shame as a Tool"; Brickhouse and Smith, *Socratic Moral Psychology.*

neutral and that he cannot be responsible for how his students employ such tools of persuasion, yet Socrates shames him into conceding that he could and should teach his students justice. Polus initially declares that suffering injustice is worse than doing it, yet Socrates shames him into conceding that justice is better than injustice. Finally, Callicles advocates the life of maximum desire and maximum fulfillment, yet Socrates finally shames him into conceding that hedonism is false—some pleasures need to be restrained.

In the above refutations, Socrates shames his interlocutors by proving that their position is incoherent—they have betrayed values that are entirely their own. Harmony with oneself is important; it is therefore appropriate to feel shame when there is conflict among one's beliefs. Even Socrates himself would be shamed if he was refuted and shown to have inconsistent beliefs.[21]

In the following sections, we will examine three questions: Why does Socrates use shame as a tool of moral persuasion in his refutation? When is shaming refutation necessary? And is Socratic shaming refutation effective?

The Reason for Shaming Refutation

At the outset, we must recognize that Socrates does not employ shame to attack or retaliate against an interlocutor. He considers it wrong ever to harm anyone, even in return for the harm that one receives.[22] A more fruitful approach to understanding Socrates's use of shame would be to observe the medical imagery that he uses. Socrates frequently compares vice to disease, himself to a doctor, and his refutations to medical practice. The pleasures of vice and injustice damage the soul, hindering its ability to manage, rule, and deliberate. The more these pleasures are indulged and satisfied, the more the soul is lulled into thinking that the pleasures afforded by the vices are indeed good. To cure their damaged souls, wrongdoers must submit themselves to shaming refutations as the sick would to the painful regimen of a doctor.[23]

Socrates finds shame to be a particularly useful instrument for curing souls because shame powerfully counters the lure of pleasure. As a painful medicine, shame provides the necessary jolt that rouses one from the moral stupor induced by the saccharine and opioid pull of pleasure. The searing pain cuts through the fog of muddled thinking, enabling the patient to realize finally that the pleasures desired are truly destructive to the moral soul. Thus, shame effectively dislodges and clears away the false beliefs in Socrates's interlocutors.[24]

21. Plato, *Gorg.* 522D.
22. Plato, *Apol.* 25C–26A, 29B, 37A–B; *Crit.* 49A–C; *Gorg.* 479C–E.
23. Plato, *Gorg.* 478C–D, 480C–D.
24. Sanderman, "Why Socrates Mocks His Interlocutors."

It "force[s] them to confront the incoherence of their own position, and thus to make a first step towards that recognition of their ignorance which is the beginning of wisdom."[25]

The painful occurrent experience of shame brought about by acts of shaming has the potential to alter our dispositional sense of shame because it introduces a new perspective into our psyche. It forces us see that we have been trapped in the court of public opinion, and encourages us to see ourselves from the gaze of an other and from a different court of opinion.[26] When Socrates seeks to transform Alcibiades's ambition, he first unsettles the young man's deep self-confidence through shame. He remarks to Alcibiades, "But surely that is disgraceful [αἰσχρόν]; . . . are you not ashamed [αἰσχύνω] to be unable . . . to answer a question upon it? Does it not seem disgraceful [αἰσχρόν]?"[27] In one short paragraph, Socrates uses variations of the word "shame" three times to bring Alcibiades to examine himself. Before Socrates came along, Alcibiades was not aware of his own limitations. It is only after Socrates's shaming refutation and the accompanying occurrent experience of shame that he admits, "I fear that for some time past I have lived unawares in a very disgraceful [αἴσχιστα] condition."[28] The awareness of our own limitations and ignorance before the gaze of an other makes possible the receipt of new ideas, and it is the prerequisite for true knowledge and wisdom.[29]

At the same time, the rebuke given by the other can also direct our attention to a divine court of opinion. At the end of the dialogues in the *Gorgias*, Socrates presents a myth. The myth recounts the trial that humans must face at the end of their life and that determines whether they are sent to the Isles of the Blest or to Tartarus. The men on trial stand naked and alone before the divine judge so that the judgment may be just. In this way, those who committed injustice will have the ugly scars of false oaths, license, luxury, insolence, and incontinence whipped on their souls, visible to all.[30] The naked-

25. Kahn, *Plato and the Socratic Dialogue*, 141.

26. Tarnopolsky, *Prudes, Perverts, and Tyrants*, 99–100.

27. Plato, [*Alc. maj.*] 108E–109A.

28. Plato, [*Alc. maj.*] 127D. The occurrent experience of shame is critical to Alcibiades's description of the effect that Socrates had on him in Plato's *Symposium*. Alcibiades states, "And there is one experience I have in presence of this man [Socrates] alone, such as nobody would expect in me,—to be made to feel ashamed [αἰσχύνω] by anyone; he alone can make me feel it" (Plato, *Symp.* 216B).

29. This sentiment is shown when Socrates gives Meno the moral lesson from the shame felt by the slave boy who realizes that he is not able to answer Socrates's question: the boy is now ready to learn. See Plato, *Meno* 84A–C.

30. Plato, *Gorg.* 523E–525A.

ness and judgment tropes in this myth are tropes commonly connected to shame, strongly suggesting that this myth serves as an illustration of Socrates's shaming elenchus. In his shaming rhetoric, Socrates presents the painful medicine of having our wrongdoings exposed before one whose court of opinion supremely matters. In contrast to the verdict of a human court, Socrates sets before Callicles the portrait of a court whose opinion is far more important— the court of the divine judge.

In summary, Socrates uses shame as a tool in moral persuasion. In his refutations, he uses shame to target an interlocutor's appetites, pleasures, and false beliefs about what is good. He brings about the occurrent experience of shame to dislodge his interlocutor's vested interest in the court of public opinion, replacing it with a different court of opinion. One must be afraid not of the shame imposed by the many but of the shame brought about by a trusted moral philosopher (as between Alcibiades and Socrates) or a divine judge (as seen in the myth told to Callicles at the end of the *Gorgias*).[31] Instead of the public court of opinion, the philosopher's or the divine court of opinion must dominate and eventually form the fundamental court of opinion within the individual. The interlocutor's conscience is then fashioned according to the true belief that virtue is necessary and important.

The Necessity of Shaming Refutation

I have earlier noted that certain interpretations of Socrates's moral psychology argue for an intellectualist perspective. This is apparent as Socrates does not always resort to shaming refutation in his attempts to persuade others; he may at times use rational arguments. For example, when Crito urges him to flee Athens, Socrates remarks that reason and rational argumentation must inform their decision-making.[32] On the other side, we have already noted that Socrates mocks and shames Gorgias, Polus, and Callicles. This raises the question: When does Socrates consider shaming refutation to be a necessary tool in moral persuasion?

One may reasonably suppose that Socrates engages in shaming refutation when rational arguments will not work. This is borne out in the exchange between Socrates and Callicles. From the beginning of the discussion, Callicles

31. See Plato, *Crit.* 46C–48A, where Socrates attempts to dissuade Crito from his concerns about the opinions of many by advocating αἰσχύνη only from the one who truly knows about right and wrong.

32. Plato, *Crit.* 46B.

refuses to listen to reason. He attacks Socrates and his methods. He disparages Socrates's lifelong pursuit of philosophy and claims that such a person is "in need of a whipping."[33] In response to these attacks, Socrates increases the intensity of his refutation and finally succeeds in shaming Callicles to concede that not all hedonistic pleasures are good. This exchange shows that rational argumentation is ineffective against those who will not listen. Shaming refutation is the appropriate remedy.

There may be another factor for the necessity of shaming refutation: when the logical consequences of an interlocutor's belief structure are particularly disastrous. For example, Callicles believes that the superior man should "let his desires be as strong as possible . . . and satisfy each appetite in turn with what it desires."[34] He also considers insatiate hedonism to be a virtue.[35] Such a belief structure would lead to a life that is centered on maximal pleasure and maximal fulfillment. The consequences of such a life would be disastrous. One would be a slave to one's appetites, and these appetites would destroy one's soul, one's most precious possession.[36] Given these severe consequences, Socrates feels compelled to shame Callicles in order to reform his belief structure. Now, it is worthwhile to compare Callicles's particular beliefs with Crito's. Crito's objective is for Socrates to escape his death sentence. While such a proposition is still unacceptable to Socrates, it does not appear to be nearly as reprehensible as Callicles's undisciplined life. Single acts of wrongdoing damage the soul, but persistent wrongdoings allow these injuries to fester, leading the soul to become incurable and ruined. Socrates will shame his interlocutors if the consequences of their false beliefs are sufficiently disastrous—if they have the potential to damage the soul beyond all possibility of repair.

When does Socrates consider shaming refutation to be necessary? We cannot answer this question definitively. For to answer it presupposes that Socrates had a particular method, and some have argued that Socrates had no single method of refutation. He employed different arguments and strategies depending on the situation at hand.[37] Socrates does not always resort to shaming refutation. Nevertheless, the above discussion suggests that there are some occasions when such painful treatment is necessary.

33. Plato, *Gorg.* 485D.
34. Plato, *Gorg.* 491D–492A.
35. Plato, *Gorg.* 492D.
36. In his conversations with Gorgias and Polus, Socrates claims that the purpose of his elenchus is to rid his interlocutors of the "greatest evil" of the soul. See Plato, *Gorg.* 458A, 477A.
37. See Carpenter and Polansky, "Variety of Socratic Elenchi"; and Brickhouse and Smith, "The Socratic *Elenchos*?"

The Effectiveness of Shaming Refutation

Socrates's shaming elenchus may at times be effective, as it was when it shook Alcibiades's confidence. Nevertheless, the *Gorgias* notes that Socrates very often fails to persuade his interlocutors. Gorgias agrees with Socrates only out of shame for conventional morality; Polus regards Socrates's claims as incredulous even though he is refuted; and Callicles becomes so annoyed with Socrates that he withdraws from the conversation, leaving Socrates to go on alone and answer his own questions. Socrates may have refuted all of them, but this does little to shake them from their commitment to their original views.

Toward the end of the *Gorgias*, Socrates addresses his own failure to persuade. He admits that his speeches usually fail to persuade because they are "not aimed at gratification, but at what is best instead of what is most pleasant."[38] He considers himself a doctor and likens his philosophy to painful surgery or cautery that is essential to the well-being of his patients' souls. His interlocutors, however, are like children who prefer sweet treats rather than bitter pills. Socrates's shaming elenchus "*could* free people of the greatest of evils if they would submit to it, but . . . they often refuse. Many people are not persuaded by Socrates—do not relinquish the beliefs he refutes, do not leave off valuing less important things in favor of justice and philosophy—and therefore get no real discipline and no real benefit from his 'cures.'"[39]

The *Gorgias* paints a worrying picture for moral education. It shows the danger posed by the appetitive parts of the soul. These appetites lead people to vice and undermine rational attempts to lead people to virtue. Moreover, they may be so ingrained in some that they are too powerful for shame's prompting to overcome. The occasional failure of Socrates's shaming elenchus should not lead us to think that we should dispense of shame in moral formation. Rather, it suggests that a proper sense of shame needs to be inculcated much earlier in the formative years of a person before one's appetites become too entrenched. Such a perspective is not found in Plato's early dialogues, and we cannot attribute it to the historical Socrates. Nevertheless, such a view is included in Plato's account of the soul in his later work, the *Republic*.

In the *Republic*, Plato presents a tripartite schema of the soul: reason, spirit, and appetite. Reason, the part of the soul that differentiates between good and bad, is undeveloped in children. Spirit, the part of the soul that feels shame, is, however, present from the beginning.[40] Spirit, moreover, can be

---

38. Plato, *Gorg.* 521D.
39. Moss, "The Doctor and the Pastry Chef," 235.
40. Plato, *Resp.* 441A–B. The association of shame with spirit is readily seen in the allegorical psychology of the *Phaedrus*. There, the soul is again composed of three parts: the

shaped from the earliest years to dispel the lure of appetites. If uncorrupted, spirit can then support reason in its conflict against appetite. In Plato's view, spirit is indispensable for moral formation because it is the link between the rational (reason) and the nonrational (appetites). Unlike reason, spirit is a powerful motivational force in those who are not virtuous, especially in those whose reason is not sufficiently developed. Unlike appetite, spirit is malleable and can be shaped so as to lead those who are not virtuous toward virtue. Thus, nurses and mothers use prescribed stories, music, and poetry not to target reason but to mold the spirit of their children. They teach their children to discern between the ugly and the beautiful, the shameful and the good.[41] They cultivate their children's sense of shame so that they will instinctively avoid the shameful and lean toward the admirable. In so doing, they strengthen a child's spirit so that it can be an ally of reason against the appetites.

The *Republic* develops the idea of shame in the *Gorgias* and presents a new vision for its role in moral education. It shows "that shame can be a more effective tool of persuasion than reason, that shame is more effective against pleasure in a person who has a strong sense of honor, ambition, and pride in manliness, and that shame is connected to how an agent sees himself. It does all this by assigning feelings of shame and admiration to a part of the soul distinct from both appetite and reason, which has a crucial role in mediating between the two—in helping reason to overcome appetite and keep it under control."[42] The *Republic* affirms that shame is an indispensable tool for moral cultivation. Shame guides the soul to choose the good, revealing the value of virtue and quenching the appeal of pleasure. It does this not because it intrinsically knows the good and the noble but because it can acquire that skill through education.

Aristotle

I noted briefly in the previous section that Socratic ethics can be interpreted from an intellectualist perspective. Aristotle definitively overturns this Socratic

charioteer and his two horses. When presented with an object of erotic desire (a boy), the charioteer (corresponding to reason) wishes to refrain. One horse (corresponding to appetite) always tends toward base pleasures and desires sexual gratification. The other (corresponding to spirit), however, sides with the charioteer and is "constrained then as always by [shame, αἰδώς]" (254A) so as not to leap upon the boy. In the ensuing struggle, the base horse "pulls shamelessly [ἀναίδεια]" (254D) toward the boy. But the noble horse "in his shame [αἰσχύνη] and wonder wets all the soul with his sweat" (254C), struggling with the charioteer until they are able to subdue the unruliness of the base horse.

41. See Plato, *Resp.* 378C, 388D, 401E, 403C.
42. Moss, "Shame, Pleasure, and the Divided Soul," 167.

intellectualistic model, for he gives nonrational factors a prominent role in moral development. He considers cognitive and emotive dimensions to be necessary for acquiring virtue, giving emotions an important role in moral persuasion.[43] The prominence of emotions in Aristotle's moral psychology presents us with an excellent opportunity to study the role of shame in moral formation as he explicitly considers shame to be an emotion. Our study will proceed in three parts. I first present Aristotle's definitions of emotion and shame. I then explore his understanding of the role of shame in rhetoric and moral persuasion. Lastly, I explore the role of shame in learning to be good.

Definitions of Emotion and Shame

The fullest and clearest treatment of emotions (including shame) bequeathed to us by the ancient Greeks is found in Aristotle's *Art of Rhetoric*. This placement tells us that Aristotle analyzes emotions for their role in the art of persuasion. His definition of emotions is telling: "The emotions [πάθη] are all those affections which cause men to change their opinion in regard to their judgments, and are accompanied by pleasure and pain; such are anger, pity, fear, and all similar emotions and their contraries."[44] Aristotle characterizes emotions with two main points: (1) emotions cause men to change their evaluation and judgment on various matters, and (2) every emotion is accompanied by pain and pleasure. The first point shows that judgment and belief are essential to the working of emotions. From chapter 1, we know that feelings are a function or result of our interpretation and judgment of an event.[45] Aristotle, however, notes that the reverse is also true: emotions affect our beliefs and judgments, "for the judgments we deliver are not the same when we are influenced by joy or sorrow, love or hate."[46] Thus, evaluation or judgment is not only constitutive of the emotion but also dynamic; judgments and beliefs give rise to the formation of emotions, which in turn affect other beliefs or the emotions themselves.[47]

---

43. Price ("Emotions in Plato and Aristotle," 138) writes, "Ethical education in Aristotle is emotional education."

44. Aristotle, *Rhet.* 2.1.8, 1378A20–23.

45. Aristotle anticipated this modern view, for he considers cognition and appraisal essential to emotional response. For example, he defines anger as a desire for revenge accompanied by pain "for [διά] a real or apparent slight" (*Rhet.* 2.2.1, 1378A30–32). Similarly, he defines fear as a painful feeling "caused by [ἐκ] the impression of an imminent evil" (2.5.1, 1382A21–22). In both cases, the perceived slight or evil are not merely characteristics that accompany anger and fear respectively; they are the efficient causes and the necessary elements for an essential definition of anger and fear. See Fortenbaugh, *Aristotle on Emotion*, 12.

46. Aristotle, *Rhet.* 1.2.5, 1356A15–16.

47. Konstan, *Emotions of the Ancient Greeks*, 37.

Aristotle's major treatment of shame in *Rhetoric* occurs in section 2.6. He begins with this definition: "Let shame [αἰσχύνη] then be defined as a kind of pain or uneasiness in respect of misdeeds, past, present, or future, which seem to tend to bring dishonor [ἀδοξία]; and shamelessness [ἀναισχυντία] as contempt and indifference in regard to these same things."[48] Two observations are worth noting.

1. Aristotle considers shame to be a painful or uneasy response to *misdeeds*, which appear to bring dishonor. He continues with the implication: "If this definition of shame is correct, it follows that we are ashamed of all such misdeeds as seem to be disgraceful. . . . Such are all those that are due to vice."[49] Note that in both statements Aristotle says that shame is a negative response not to dishonor but to *evil deeds* (ἀπὸ κακίας ἔργα), which lead to such a state. He then provides examples of these vices: "such as throwing away one's shield or taking to flight, for this is due to cowardice; or withholding a deposit, for this is due to injustice. And illicit relations with any persons, at forbidden places or times, for this is due to licentiousness."[50] Aristotle provides other examples, and each example includes "three elements that together prompt the emotion of shame: a particular act (throwing away one's shield in battle); the fault of character that is revealed by the act (cowardice); and the disgrace or loss of esteem before the community at large."[51]

Aristotle's definition shows that the shame he focuses on is the response not to any kind of dishonor but to a particular kind of dishonor—that which is the consequence of evil deeds, which stem from a vicious character (vicious character → evil deeds → dishonor). Thus, when Aristotle later says that "shame is an impression about dishonor,"[52] or when he says in the *Nicomachean Ethics* that shame is a certain fear of dishonor (φόβος τις ἀδοξίας),[53] these shortened definitions should be understood by the fuller definition. The dishonor (and its opposite, honor) that Aristotle has in mind is intimately connected with our actions and our character. We must therefore make a distinction between the good fear of dishonor and the mere desire to avoid dishonor even when one is at fault; we must make a distinction between the good love of honor and the mere desire to be honored even when one does not deserve it. In both cases, the former is Aristotle's primary understanding. For Aristotle, shame

48. Aristotle, *Rhet.* 2.6.2, 1383B13–17.
49. Aristotle, *Rhet.* 2.6.3, 1383B17–20.
50. Aristotle, *Rhet.* 2.6.3–4, 1383B20–23.
51. Konstan, *Emotions of the Ancient Greeks*, 101.
52. Aristotle, *Rhet.* 2.6.14, 1384A23–24.
53. Aristotle, *Eth. nic.* 4.9.2, 1128B11–12; 3.6.3, 1115A13–14.

does not solely depend on the opinions of others. It is primarily grounded on one's moral character and responsibility.

2. Aristotle's definition of shame notes that the misdeed we commit can be *past*, *present*, or *future*. Thus, the key element in his definition is "seem to tend to bring": the perception and appraisal of a particular event. We can remember past events, interpret present events, and anticipate future events. But if we construe or appraise these events (past, present, or future) as bringing about dishonor, the pain or discomfort that follows is shame. Some modern writers distinguish prospective from retrospective shame, considering the former an ethical trait and the latter an emotion or experience. Aristotle, however, understands both uniformly as an emotion under the category of shame.

The Role of Shame in Rhetoric and Moral Persuasion

Aristotle does not explicitly indicate the role of shame in rhetoric, but he does provide some tantalizingly brief statements about the role of emotions in rhetoric. In this section, I explore the role that emotions may play in Aristotle's rhetoric and moral persuasion.[54] Since Aristotle defines shame as an emotion, the following discussion is applicable to shame, mutatis mutandis.

As we noted above, Aristotle defines emotions to be feelings that change human beings so as to affect their judgment. Emotions alter our judgment so that the same things are viewed quite differently under different emotional circumstances. "For opinions vary, according as men love or hate, are wrathful or mild, and things appear either altogether different, or different in degree; for when a man is favorably disposed towards one on whom he is passing judgment, he either thinks that the accused has committed no wrong at all or that his offense is trifling; but if he hates him, the reverse is the case."[55] Aristotle does not explicitly explain how emotions affect judgment,[56] but these statements make clear that emotions affect the severity of judgments and may change them altogether.

The appeal to emotions may be abused so as to be manipulative, but manipulation does not appear to be Aristotle's intent for three reasons. First, Aristotle criticizes the authors of earlier handbooks as fundamentally manipulative since they advocate techniques to sway the emotions of their listeners without considering issues that are pertinent to the specific case at hand. Such irrelevant emotional appeals include describing events that do

---

54. On the legitimacy of "appeal to emotions" as part of an orator's task, see Brinton, "Pathos and the 'Appeal to Emotion.'"

55. Aristotle, *Rhet.* 2.1.4, 1377B31–1378A4.

56. For some suggestions, see Leighton, "Aristotle and the Emotions."

not impinge on the matter in dispute. On the contrary, Aristotle argues that emotional arousal and the overall purpose of rhetoric is to provide *proper* grounds for conviction—grounds that depend on the underlying strength of the speaker's position.[57] Second, Aristotle bases his understanding of emotions on cognitive thought.[58] The pairing of reason with emotion removes the irrationalism that is commonly found in emotional manipulation. Third, Aristotle's rhetorical program is directed at discovering and establishing truth.[59] When we couple this goal with Aristotle's understanding of shame (a kind of pain in regard to deeds that arise from a vicious character), we find that the evocation of shame helps the listener discern the true state of his or her character. This ethical dimension aimed at the good of the listener obviates the falsehood and insincerity that is present in emotional manipulation.

Aristotle considers the evocation of emotions in a learner of virtue to be appropriate because the moral life is not just about right doing but also about right feeling.[60] It is not only acting in a certain way but also responding in a certain way when acted on; it is both action and passion.[61] What this means is that if the correct action is chosen without the appropriate motivating or reactive emotion, Aristotle would not consider it a truly virtuous act. An action is virtuous only if it is done in the way that a virtuous person would do it. Consequently, the management and habituation of emotions are important aspects of moral formation. The moral teacher will evoke in the learner the requisite emotions, not just because the person who feels rightly will act rightly but because feeling rightly is itself part of a noble character.[62] For Aristotle, feeling rightly is a matter of observing the mean in relation to the emotions, not being in excess or in deficit of it. When the doctrine of the mean is applied to shame, the one who is praised is not the bashful or the shameless. The bashful is ashamed of everything, while the shameless is deficient in shame or abashed at nothing. The one

57. Dow, *Passions and Persuasion*, 58–63, 107–27.
58. Nussbaum, *Therapy of Desire*, 78–101.
59. Engberg-Pedersen, "Ethical Dimension."
60. Aristotle, *Eth. nic.* 2.6.10, 1106B16–17: "Moral virtue . . . is concerned with emotions *and* actions" (emphasis mine).
61. Kosman, "Being Properly Affected"; Sherman, *Making a Necessity of Virtue*, 24–98.
62. Striker ("Emotions in Context," 297) writes, "If emotional dispositions are what underlies virtue of character, the influence of emotion on judgment cannot be regarded as merely distorting, a distraction, as it were, from rational thought. An orator's attempt to arouse or dispel emotions should also not be seen as mere manipulation, or as an attempt to produce conviction by illegitimate means. If morally good people can be expected to have certain characteristic emotional responses, then the influence of emotion may sometimes be what is needed to see things in the right way."

who is praised is the modest man (ὁ αἰδήμων); he has an intermediate and proper sense of shame.[63]

The evocation of emotions is also appropriate because it can focus attention on a particular issue, deepen conviction, and provide rhetorical amplification.[64] Aristotle recognizes that proofs for a particular judgment come in three forms: ethos (ethical proofs that establish the speaker's credibility), pathos (psychological proofs that bring the audience into a state favorable to the speaker's arguments), and logos (logical and reasoned arguments in support of the speaker's position).[65] Of these technical means of persuasion, Aristotle considers logos to be primary. It is *the* argument, and demonstration by logos argument addresses the issues being discussed most directly. Appeals to pathos (and ethos) are legitimate only insofar as they are an integral part of the orderly exposition of the logos argument.[66] While appeals to logos are persuasive, it may be insufficient in some situations where the listener suffers a weakness of judgment and is not able to judge according to the premises of which he is convinced.[67] In these situations, ethos and pathos proofs complement the logos proof, stabilizing the process of judgment formation.[68] These additional appeals provide further proof or confer more epistemic good standing on the earlier conclusion. In particular, emotions can focus attention on prior cognitions or thoughts such that they are taken more seriously.[69] For example, I may provide you with logical arguments for why throwing your shield and running away during battle is a bad thing—it stems from cowardice. But if I am also able to evoke the feeling of shame and connect it with both the act and the character flaw, it makes sense to say that I have provided you with a deeper knowledge of courage.

The Role of Shame in Learning to Be Good

Shame is the linchpin in Aristotle's moral psychology that enables a learner of virtue to become virtuous. The arguments to validate this assertion are involved; nevertheless, a rehearsal of these arguments will demonstrate the critical role that shame plays in moral development.

63. Aristotle, *Eth. nic.* 2.7.14, 1108A30–35.
64. Amplification (αὔξησις) exalts or amplifies a theme. See Aristotle, *Rhet.* 2.26.1, 1403A20–21; Cicero, *Or. Brut.* 36.125.
65. Aristotle, *Rhet.* 1.2.3, 1356A1–4.
66. Cooper, *Reason and Emotion*, 393.
67. Rapp, "Moral Psychology of Persuasion."
68. Aristotle, *Rhet.* 2.1.2, 1377B21–24.
69. Stocker, "Emotional Thoughts," highlights the importance of emotions in drawing focus and attention.

Aristotle declares in the *Nicomachean Ethics* that just as learners of an art or craft acquire expertise via practice, so also learners of virtue. Beginning students of virtue become just, temperate, or courageous by performing the same kinds of actions that are characteristic of virtuous people. Aristotle remarks, "We become just by doing just acts, temperate by doing temperate acts, brave by doing brave acts."[70] But this learning-by-doing thesis presents a challenge, for the suggestion that learners are able to perform virtuous actions *assumes* that these students are *already* virtuous. Aristotle recognizes this problem and solves it by distinguishing between (a) doing virtuous actions and (b) doing virtuous actions virtuously. In order for someone to do virtuous actions *virtuously* rather than in accordance with virtue, three conditions must be present: knowledge, motivation, and stability. The act must be done with knowledge, the agent must intentionally choose the act and choose it for its own sake, and the act must arise from a stable disposition of the agent's character.[71] This strict definition for "doing virtuous actions *virtuously*" suggests a more relaxed definition for "doing virtuous actions"—namely, that the triple requirements of knowledge, motivation, and stability are *not* necessary conditions. In other words, learners of virtue can do virtuous actions even when these three conditions are not *completely* met.

The general outline of Aristotle's program is clear; the specific details are not. While learners of virtue can perform virtuous actions without completely fulfilling all three requirements, these actions cannot be performed in any random way. They must still be performed "well" ($εὖ$).[72] Practice by itself does not lead one to acquire virtue; it must be the right kind of practice. But what constitutes the right kind of practice? Aristotle conceives that the learner can perform virtuous actions by not *completely* fulfilling the triple requirements. It is, however, not clear which of the requirements should be weakened or to what degree they should.

Modern commentators agree that of the three requirements, some knowledge is essential.[73] The practice or habituation of virtuous actions cannot be a mindless mechanical reproduction of the external behavior performed by virtuous agents. The learners' minds must be involved, and their cognitive processes need to be engaged in order to determine what is just, temperate, or courageous under different circumstances. Modern commentators also agree that of the three requirements, the actions of learners cannot proceed from a

---

70. Aristotle, *Eth. nic.* 2.1.4, 1103A34–B2.
71. Aristotle, *Eth. nic.* 2.4.3, 1105A31–33.
72. Aristotle, *Eth. nic.* 2.1.6, 1103B11.
73. Sorabji, "Role of Intellect in Virtue," 216; Sherman, *Fabric of Character*, 7; Broadie, *Ethics with Aristotle*, 103.

firm and unchangeable character. For learners do not yet possess virtue—the stable disposition of the soul.[74] The only debatable element among the three requirements is thus motivation.

Some commentators argue that the actions of learners do not proceed from virtuous motivation.[75] Since virtuous motives are the purview *only* of virtuous agents, the actions of learners cannot proceed from virtuous motives. These actions are virtuous in that they are the right actions under the circumstances, externally indistinguishable from those performed by virtuous people. But they differ from the activities of virtuous people in two aspects: they are not performed from a stable disposition of character, and they lack virtuous motivation. There is, however, a problem in this formulation. If the actions of learners do not proceed from virtuous motives, how does practice or habituation eventually lead learners to achieve virtue so that they desire virtuous acts for their own sake? In other words, there is a gap between the motivationally neutral actions of the learners and the virtuous disposition that these actions are supposed to produce. It is here that shame enters our discussion.

Howard Curzer attempts to bridge the "moral upbringing gap" by suggesting that practice alone is insufficient. A catalyst is needed, and the catalyst is the pain of αἰδώς (shame).[76] Αἰδώς serves as a catalyst in four ways: (1) it negatively reinforces bad behavior; (2) it functions as a salience projector, impressing the viciousness of wicked acts on the learner's mind; (3) it prompts the learner to think about what should have been done; and (4) it develops the learner's ability to evaluate different acts in new situations.[77] Led by αἰδώς, the learner comes to choose not acts that they think are virtuous but acts that are truly virtuous.

Curzer's proposal is intriguing, but it is not fully satisfying. His view assumes that the practice of virtuous acts prompted by external pain accomplishes the transformation of a learner to a virtuous person. But the motivation provided by external pain is not a motivation to perform a virtuous act "well." It motivates the learner to do whatever it takes to avoid the pain; but as soon as the rod of shame is absent, the learner has no reason to choose a virtuous act for its own sake. In other words, the "moral upbringing gap" still persists.

74. Aristotle, *Eth. nic.* 6.2.2, 1139A22.

75. Broadie, *Ethics with Aristotle*, 88; Irwin, *Aristotle*, 195; Vasiliou, "Virtue and Argument," 52n22.

76. Curzer, *Aristotle and the Virtues*, 318–66. For a contrasting proposal affirming that the catalyst is pleasure rather than pain, see Burnyeat, "Aristotle on Learning to Be Good."

77. Curzer, *Aristotle and the Virtues*, 336–40.

Marta Jimenez presents a more satisfying proposal to close the gap.[78] She still affirms the important role of shame in moral formation, but she abandons the argument that the actions of learners *do not proceed* from virtuous motivation. Instead, the actions of learners *do proceed* from virtuous motivation *some of the time*. Learners can sometimes perform actions for the sake of the noble because of their sense of shame. As they progress in virtue, learners increasingly perform their actions from virtuous motivation until they have developed the stable disposition to do so.

According to Jimenez, Aristotle considers shame to be particularly relevant for true progress toward virtue because it provides three important factors: the motivating, the cognitive, and the hedonic.[79] Learners with a sense of shame have a genuine love for the noble and an aversion toward the base (the motivating); they have some conception of what is noble and base, despite not possessing the understanding (φρόνησις) of the virtuous (the cognitive); and they have the ability to take pleasure in the noble and to be pained by the base (the hedonic). Through these three factors, shame provides learners with the requisite grasp and love of the noble. The actions of learners are not done with the full knowledge, motivation, and stability of virtuous agents; nevertheless, the partial knowledge and motivation by which these actions are carried out are conducive to the development of virtue.

Aristotle also considers shame to be important for moral development in the young because it is a proto-virtuous emotion. On the one hand, shame is not like a virtue because it lacks the stability that virtuous dispositions have.[80] Shame is also not like a virtue in that it is not present in the virtuous man. If shame is the feeling caused by base actions, the virtuous man can never feel shame, for he never does any base action. On the other hand, shame is like a virtue in that it is praiseworthy and essential in the young. Aristotle envisages the learner as a young person who is led by his emotions because his cognitive faculties are not developed.[81] As an emotion, "shame is the semi-virtue of the learner"[82] that is able to guide him to walk the middle path, between blindly following his appetites on one side and acting from a stable virtuous disposition on the other.

Jimenez's proposal is subject to a critique that shame cannot provide the right motivation for the development of virtue; for some claim that the goal of shame is not the noble but the pursuit of honor and the avoidance of re-

---

78. Jimenez, "Virtue of Shame."
79. Jimenez, "Virtue of Shame," 161–73.
80. Aristotle, *Eth. nic.* 4.9.1, 1128B10–11.
81. Aristotle, *Eth. nic.* 4.9.3, 1128B16–19.
82. Burnyeat, "Aristotle on Learning to Be Good," 78.

proach. Learners who are motivated by shame are therefore concerned only with external recognition and the opinions of others, rather than with a sincere desire to do what is good. This objection does not stand, because Aristotle's understanding of shame is much more nuanced. It is true that Aristotle considers shame to be the fear of disrepute and to depend on the opinions of others. But we have earlier noted that this shortened definition of shame needs to be understood within the framework of the fuller definition that relates shame to evil deeds and vicious character. Aristotle thus shows that there is a way of loving honor whereby those who seek honor do so on the basis of virtue.[83] In other words, they only do things that truly deserve honor, not anything that will bring external recognition; they affirm a noble love of honor, not just the mere desire to be honored. Cairns remarks, "The code of honor to which *aidōs* [shame] relates demands individual determination actually to possess an excellence, not merely that one should seem to others to possess it."[84] Learners of virtue who are motivated by a sense of shame thus truly desire virtue.[85]

The Hellenistic Period

The importance of shame for moral education continued into the Hellenistic period. Many philosophical schools affirmed the importance of cultivating a proper sense of shame in the moral development of children. They also believed that retrospective shame was salutary. Thus, they shamed others with the intent of producing the occurrent experience of shame within the individual or collective body, causing them to see themselves as others see them. In this section, I sample the views of Philodemus, Musonius Rufus, Seneca, Epictetus, Plutarch, and Dio Chrysostom. We shall see that their views echo the sentiments of their predecessors. Thus, my treatment of each writer will be brief.

Philodemus

The Epicurean Philodemus affirms the deliberate use of mental pain in moral formation. In order to change his students' ethical thinking, he advocates the use of frank criticism (παρρησία) that stings or, literally, "bites"

---

83. Aristotle, *Eth. nic.* 1.5.5, 1095B26–30.
84. Cairns, *Aidōs*, 432.
85. Williams (*Shame and Necessity*, 81) notes that the role of shame in moral development is not "immaturely heteronomous, in the sense that it supposedly pins the individual's sense of what should be done merely on to expectations of what others will think of him or her."

their hearts. The discomfort from such criticism leads them to give up their pride and obey admonitions.[86]

Frank criticism is the mark of true friendship. It is inspired by an unfeigned goodwill that uses plain language to spur one another on to maturity, and it is close in meaning to ἐλέγχω (reprove) and νουθετέω (admonish). Philodemus does not explicitly draw out the emotional implications of frank criticism, but the emotion of shame appears to be the predominant one that he has in mind.[87]

Philodemus recognizes that different students will respond differently to frank criticism. The response of the "weak," obedient ones will differ from the "strong," disobedient ones. The teacher therefore needs to adapt his methods to different students, delivering different intensities of criticism. Toward the "weak" who err, he will reproach "in moderation" (frag. 6) and mix his censure with praise. But toward the "strong who will scarcely change {even} if they are shouted at" (frag. 7), he will adopt a harsh form of frank criticism, criticize with "all passion and <[blame] . . . >" (frag. 10), and say "again <and again, 'You are doing [wrong]' . . . >" (frag. 11).

The Stoics—Musonius Rufus, Seneca, and Epictetus

The prominent Stoics within the Hellenistic period include Musonius Rufus, Seneca, and Epictetus. Musonius Rufus stresses the importance of virtue for living the good life. He never defines virtue, but he vigorously propounds the four cardinal virtues: prudence (φρόνησις), justice (δικαιοσύνη), temperance (σωφροσύνη), and courage (ἀνδρεία). In line with other philosophers such as Protagoras, Musonius links temperance (σωφροσύνη) with a proper sense of shame (αἰδώς). He stresses the necessity of cultivating this sense of shame in kings, women, men, students, and children. This moral education must begin from an early age. Thus, both male and female children, straight from infancy, should be taught "that this is right and that is wrong, . . . that this is helpful, that is harmful. . . . Then they must be inspired with a feeling of shame [αἰδώς] toward all that is base [αἰσχρός]. When these two qualities have been created with them, man and woman are of necessity self-controlled [σώφρων]."[88]

Seneca considers the capacity to feel shame to be a necessary condition for moral progress,[89] and he recognizes its role in reforming the moral perspec-

---

86. Philodemus, *On Frank Criticism*, frags. 64, 66.

87. See Armstrong, "'Be Angry and Sin Not,'" 98–100.

88. Musonius Rufus, *Lect. 4: Should Daughters Receive the Same Education as Sons* (Stobaeus 2.31.123; ET *Musonius Rufus*, 47–49).

89. Seneca, *Ep.* 25.2.

tive of a person. He employs shaming and biting rhetoric to expose brutally, but honestly, the folly of humanity. For example, Seneca remarks in a letter to Lucilius that one should humor, for a while, a person who is grieving. Those who continue to indulge in grief, however, should be rebuked so as to recognize that there are even follies in grief. Thus, Seneca berates his diatribe interlocutor, "Are you not . . . ashamed [*pudeō*] to cure sorrow by pleasure [that comes from constantly recalling the past]?"[90]

Epictetus is no different in the use of harsh rhetoric. He employs a purgative elenchus. He harangues his students with these words: "Men, the lecture-room of a philosopher is a hospital; you ought not to walk out of it in pleasure, but in pain."[91] The pain inflicted by a teacher should cause students to evaluate their own lives and prod them toward the virtuous ideal. For Epictetus, this is a life that possesses αἰδώς. People who are motivated by αἰδώς may be inhibited by fear of social disapproval or by concern to maintain their own social standing. But αἰδώς can also function as a form of self-evaluation that is manifested in attitudes of shame and self-respect. This latter understanding is Epictetus's view. For him, "αἰδώς plays the role of the conscience: a self-evaluation that restricts conduct, 'from within.'"[92]

Plutarch

The Platonist Plutarch also draws the connection between moral progress and the occurrent experience of retrospective shame. He notes that repentance (μετάνοια) is brought about by reason when the psyche experiences biting pain along with shame (αἰσχύνη).[93] If students do not experience remorse on their own accord, the teacher must exercise frank criticism. The rebukes and admonitions that seek to reform the hearers must penetrate like a biting drug, cause sweating and dizziness, and "burn with shame [αἰσχύνη] in the soul."[94] Plutarch points to Socrates as an exemplar. He notes that the elenchus of Socrates kept Alcibiades in check and "drew an honest tear from his eyes by exposing his faults, and so turned his heart."[95]

Like Philodemus and other philosophers, Plutarch notes that harsh criticism needs to be balanced with praise. In the education of children, "rebukes and praise should be used alternately and in a variety of ways; it is well to

---

90. Seneca, *Ep.* 99.29.
91. Epictetus, *Diatr.* 3.23.30.
92. Kamtekar, "ΑΙΔΩΣ in Epictetus," 159–60.
93. Plutarch, *Tranq. an.* 19 (476f). See also *Adul. amic.* 12 (56a).
94. Plutarch, *Rect. rat. aud.* 16 (46d).
95. Plutarch, *Adul. amic.* 29 (69f).

choose some time when the children are full of confidence to put them to shame [αἰσχύνη] by rebuke, and then in turn to cheer them up by praises, and to imitate the nurses, who, when they have made their babies cry, in turn offer them the breast for comfort."[96] Plutarch advocates the use of frank speech among friends, but it, like any other medicine, needs to be applied at the appropriate time.[97] Thus, he cautions that it should preferably be done in private. He recounts how Pythagoras once shamed a student in the presence of several other people.[98] The student was so distraught that he subsequently hanged himself. From that time forth, Pythagoras never admonished anybody when someone else was present.

The use of pain in moral formation is not strange to Plutarch, as he considers it the direct application of Platonic moral psychology. Yet he critiques the Stoics at this point, given the school's commitment to the extirpation of emotions (ἀπάθεια).[99] One may claim that the Stoics were inconsistent, or that their ideas were so paradoxical that they needed to resort to non-Stoic ideas in their explanation to students. But Margaret Graver is probably right in saying that the Stoic understanding of ἀπάθεια is *not* the extirpation of *all* affect-laden responses, but only those that are directed toward externals.[100] There is a set of emotional experiences that are appropriate within the Stoic framework, and these are directed to integral matters of good and evil.

Dio Chrysostom

Dio Chrysostom is a moral philosopher who eclectically combines Stoic, Cynic, and Platonic ideas. He uses the rhetoric of shame masterfully when he addresses the Rhodian assembly in *Oration* 31.[101] The Rhodian assembly was in the habit of recognizing its benefactors by erecting statues in their honor. After the city was flooded with statues, the assembly introduced cost-saving and space-saving measures by simply having the name of any new benefactor engraved on an already existing statue, after first chiseling out the name of the previous benefactor. Dio's strategy here is to shame the Rhodians for dishonoring the memory of their benefactors for the sake of money. He compares the statues to actors who assume different roles at different times—at one time a Greek, later a Roman or Macedonian or Persian. He thinks that even the

---

96. Plutarch, [*Lib. ed.*] 12 (9a).
97. Plutarch, *Adul. amic.* 25 (66b).
98. Plutarch, *Adul. amic.* 32 (70f–71a).
99. Plutarch, *Virt. mor.* 12 (452c).
100. Graver, *Stoicism and Emotion*, 210–11.
101. See also *Or.* 48.15–16, where he shames the Bithynians for their disunity.

masons will blush for shame when they are instructed to carry out this task. He further shames the Rhodians by reminding them of their recent past when they did not choose a dishonorable course of action (declaring bankruptcy) for the sake of monetary gain even though they were in an economic crisis. Instead, they incurred civic debt in order that there might be no blemish on their honor. Their past nobility stands in stark contrast to their present disgrace, a disgrace made all the more shameful given their present economic prosperity. Throughout the speech, Dio refers to that which is αἰσχρόν in order to exhort the Rhodians to change their practices. He incredulously remarks, "Can it be that you are unaware of the shame which attaches to this practice, and how ridiculous you make yourselves by this deception practiced by your state, and that too so openly?"[102]

In line with many other moral philosophers before him, Dio compares the task of moral correction to medicine. To reform the moral soul of a person, the moral philosopher, like any good physician, must not be afraid to employ harsh medicine. And this bitter medicine includes the rhetoric of shame. Nevertheless, harsh words need to be balanced with gentle ones, and blame must be balanced with praise. Dio describes the ideal Cynic as one who leads all men to virtue and sobriety, "partly by persuading and exhorting, partly by abusing and reproaching, . . . 'With gentle words at time, at others harsh.'"[103]

Synthesis and Overview

This chapter surveys various thinkers concerning their understanding of shame and its role in moral progress. In this concluding section, I synthesize the above data under two categories: (1) the Greco-Roman construal of shame and (2) elements in the Greco-Roman role of shame for moral formation.

The Greco-Roman Construal of Shame

My survey suggests that two lexemes are critical to understanding the Greco-Roman construal of shame: αἰδώς and αἰσχύνη. Although certain authors maintain a distinction between them, the two terms came to be fundamentally synonymous in ordinary Greek. Both embody prospective and retrospective aspects of shame, and both can denote a sense of shame or the occurrent experience of shame itself. Despite these similarities, αἰδώς bears a

---

102. Dio Chrysostom, *Or.* 31.153.
103. Dio Chrysostom, *Or.* 77/78.38.

richer heritage and carries a loftier connotation. It occurs frequently in poetic and religious contexts, while αἰσχύνη is found more in ordinary parlance.

As the myth of Protagoras relates, a sense of shame and the ability to feel shame is considered a gift from Zeus. It is a major element of virtue as it is linked to prudence, self-knowledge, and self-control (σωφροσύνη). As a dispositional trait, it gives us the cognitive ability to differentiate between the noble and the base. As an inhibitory emotion, it leads us to respect the honor of others and restrains us from acting on our every whim and fancy. As a social emotion, it sensitizes us to the social expectations of the community and enables us to live communally.

The social dynamics of shame easily lead to the familiar criticism that an ethical life girded by shame is fundamentally heteronomous, subject to public opinion and regulated by external sanctions. The Greco-Roman understanding of shame is sufficiently strong and complex to dispose of this criticism. Democritus, for example, recognizes the inability of external sanctions to deter wrongdoing in every case and resolves the problem by linking shame with the individual conscience. He effectively moves the court of opinion from the external to the internal, from an other-directed shame to a self-directed shame. The individual thus has his own standard of right and wrong. His sense of shame must touch his inner core, and he must feel shame before his own eyes rather than the eyes of others. Thus, he will reject any base action not only because it is liable to attract the censure of others but also because it fails to meet his own set of ideals.

The Greco-Roman understanding of shame finds its fullest treatment in Aristotle. He explicitly considers shame to be an emotion. It is the pain that comes from the imagination of dishonor. But the dishonor that Aristotle has in mind is that which arises from evil deeds and stems from a wicked character. By relating shame to dishonor, evil deeds, and vicious character, Aristotle highlights the moral and ethical dimension of shame. He is aware that shame and causal responsibility may not necessarily go hand in hand; nevertheless, his discussion centers on those scripts of shame that arise from one's moral failure. Thus, in Aristotle's ethical framework, the avoidance of dishonor prompted by a sense of shame must not imply a concern for my external reputation to the neglect of my internal character. The learner of virtue who is motivated by a sense of shame truly desires virtue, not just the adulation from the crowds. Such a person is concerned with the actual possession of true excellence, rather than only being perceived by others as possessing it.

The above brief survey highlights several elements that disrupt the binary categories of guilt and shame that some modern psychologists construct, according to which guilt focuses on deeds while shame focuses on the self. In Aristotle's framework, shame results from particular acts, and it is possible to make amends for these offenses by apologizing or some form of compensation. These are limited acts and do not entail the annihilation of one's sense of self. This Aristotelian emphasis on deeds and moral responsibility, coupled with Democritus's linkage of shame and conscience, suggests that the Greco-Roman understanding of shame may at times encompass our modern understanding of the emotion of guilt. This observation is a reminder that psychological ideas may not correspond exactly across linguistic and cultural boundaries. Despite sharing common elements in their phenomenology and associations, the Greco-Roman understanding of shame and the modern Western notion of shame are not exactly coextensive.

Elements in the Greco-Roman Role of Shame for Moral Formation

Shame plays a major role in the Greco-Roman system of moral formation. I examine this role in three ways.

The Inculcation of Prospective Shame in Moral Education

The Protagorean myth sees prospective shame, dispositional shame, or sense of shame as a virtue that is absolutely essential for communal living. It promotes sensitivity to the customs and values of a particular community, and it creates harmony and unity as all citizens conform to a common set of values and expectations. As the myth reminds us, those who do not partake of it are consigned to death as a public pest. Given its importance, prospective shame must be taught to all humankind. The ability to feel prospective shame may be innate, but the content that leads us to construe something as shameful is not. We acquire it by education and habituation, and we develop it through instruction and socialization.

The importance of inculcating prospective shame in the moral education of children is echoed by many subsequent thinkers such as Democritus, Plato, Aristotle, Musonius Rufus, and Plutarch. They encourage parents, tutors, and nurses to instruct the child to pursue the honorable rather than the shameful, the just rather than the unjust, and the noble rather than the base. Moral education must begin in the earliest years while the soul is still malleable so that the values imparted in the process of education may become internalized. Consequently, the prospect of acting appropriately becomes an automatic response in adulthood. The presence of a proper sense of shame in an adult is the product of a good upbringing, and its absence is the sign of a defective education.

The Application of Retrospective Shame in Shaming Refutation

The purpose of inculcating prospective shame in children is to develop their sensitivity toward bad things so that they will be ashamed with regard to disgraceful acts. Not all, however, develop this necessary sensitivity. Instead of feeling pain with regard to bad things, some are contemptuous and indifferent toward them. They exhibit shamelessness instead of shame. How then can these individuals be encouraged to exchange their shamelessness for a sense of shame?

Protagoras suggests that laws and punishment could function as external corrections for those who have not internalized the requisite social values. Many others, such as Socrates, Philodemus, Epictetus, Plutarch, and Dio Chrysostom, advocate the use of shaming refutation. Democritus is helpful in understanding the thinking behind this strategy. He says that the one who does shameful things must first feel shame. When shame has done its work of conviction, remorse for these shameful deeds will bring about moral salvation. Moral philosophers therefore see the first task of moral correction to be the evocation of shame in the shameless.

Using medical analogies, these moral philosophers see their role as physicians and their shaming refutation as the painful medicine that will cure the souls of their patients. The sting of shame rouses individuals from their moral stupor. It reveals their ignorance and inconsistencies, allowing them to see things from a different perspective. It leads them to remorse and causes them to exchange their self-will for deference.

Shaming refutation is a double-edged sword, and it is not always effective. In some cases it leads the interlocutor to experience remorse and repentance (e.g., Alcibiades); in others it leads to anger (e.g., Callicles) or even suicide (e.g., Pythagoras's student). Thus, shaming refutation should not be the immediate instrument of choice. Persuasion and dialogue should be employed first. However, when rational arguments fail, when the individual is particularly arrogant and dismissive, or when the consequences of a faulty belief structure are particularly disastrous, shaming refutation may be necessary to awaken the individual from folly. Nevertheless, shaming refutation must be mixed with praise and gentle admonition so that the individual is not overwhelmed with grief or anger.

The Efficacy of Shame within Aristotelian and Stoic Moral Psychology

The above survey demonstrates that shame plays an important role in moral formation. The primary reason why shame is able to do so is that it is a self-conscious moral emotion, providing the ability for self-evaluation according to some moral standard. I delineate the significance of this statement in four moves.

First, according to Aristotle, shame is remarkably suited to guide the young, who are primarily led by their emotions. The reasoning abilities of the young are not robustly developed. The young are impulsive and do not have stability in judgment formation. They follow their feelings rather than their minds. As an emotion, shame has the potential to function as a moral compass, steering them away from bad appetites and guiding them to choose the noble and the good.

Second, Aristotle's rhetorical theory informs us that emotions have the ability to change our judgments. Not only does our interpretation or judgment of an event give rise to specific emotions, but the introduction of a subsequent emotion can also change that initial judgment. For example, I may feel pride in being financially savvy so as to hide my wealth in offshore accounts. However, if someone is able to evoke shame in me, my perception of those same actions will change; I will view them as dishonest and reprehensible. The dynamic interplay between emotion and beliefs gives shame the ability to influence one's belief structure.

Third, the moral life is not only about right doing but also about right feeling. Within the matrix of right feelings, the affective experience of shame at the prospect of doing bad or becoming bad is clearly one of them. Aristotle considers shame to be a praiseworthy possession among those who are learning to be virtuous. The Stoics consider αἰδώς (sense of shame or caution against good censure) to be a good emotion or proper feeling (εὐπάθεια) that is present in sages.[104] The affective experience of shame is bound up with a virtuous life.

Fourth, shame provides learners with three factors—the motivating, the cognitive, and the hedonic—that help them make progress in the path toward virtue. Learners with a sense of shame are motivated to pursue the noble and avoid the base, they have a conception of the noble that enables them to differentiate between the good and the bad, and they enjoy pleasure from noble activities and suffer distress from base ones. All of these factors provide learners with a receptivity toward ethical arguments and equip them with the conditions that allow them to perform virtuous deeds in a manner that is conducive to attaining virtue.

---

104. Graver (*Stoicism and Emotion*, 254n27) considers αἰδώς to be "at all times an affective response. It is not *merely* an inclination to judge certain actions appropriate or inappropriate in relation to one's self-conceived role in life, but also, and fundamentally, a disposition to experience a certain feeling which is manifested in blushing as well as aversion."

3

Jewish Backgrounds

This chapter examines how Jewish authors understand shame and its role in moral progress. Given the space constraints of a chapter, I will necessarily be selective. I survey only representative writings so as to understand the conceptual background that will inform our reading of Paul. I first provide an overview of shame vocabulary and investigate the foundational event of Genesis 2–3. I then examine the role of shame in the covenant community of Israel, the Deuteronomic covenant, the book of Ezekiel, and Sirach. A concluding section summarizes the key findings of this chapter.

The Vocabulary of Shame

The main vocabulary for shame in the Hebrew Bible comprises the substantival and verbal roots of בּוֹשׁ (be ashamed, put to shame), כלם (be shamed, humiliated), and חפר (be dismayed, feel ashamed).[1] These words often appear in parallel, and the differences in meaning between them are slight. Nevertheless, there are perceptible differences. For example, in comparison to כלם, בּוֹשׁ has a more passive connotation; even in its causative form, the emphasis is on how "a person endures it."[2]

The above shame words have two senses.[3] The first is a *subjective sense*. These shame words can depict the subjective experience of shame (to be

---

1. Avrahami ("בּוֹשׁ in the Psalms") argues that the primary meaning of בּוֹשׁ is not "shame" but "disappointment, failure, frustration." Wu (*Honor, Shame, and Guilt*, 100–104) concurs, although he notes that בּוֹשׁ can be used in contexts where "shame" is a suitable translation.
2. H. Seebass, "בּוֹשׁ," *TDOT* 2:52.
3. Klopfenstein, *Scham und Schande*, 207.

ashamed, to feel humiliated). Retrospectively, the occurrent emotional experience results from the failure to perform one's duty, as when farmers are not able to produce a harvest (Jer. 14:4; Ezek. 36:30; Joel 1:11) or when seers are not able to obtain an answer from God (Mic. 3:7). It can also come about as a result of misplaced trust (Isa. 1:29; 23:4) or disappointing news (Jer. 49:23). Prospectively, this emotional experience occurs when one imagines a scenario that runs counter to one's ideal or boast. This prospective shame then curtails potentially shameful conduct. For example, Ezra was ashamed to ask the king for military protection against enemies (Ezra 8:22). He had earlier stressed the power of God to deliver him, and any request now for soldiers would diminish the power of God in the eyes of the king. The second is an *objective sense*. Shame words can also depict the objective reality of disgrace (to be humiliated or put to shame). This state of humiliation can stem from the failure of political alliances (Isa. 20:5) and idols (Ps. 97:7; Isa. 42:17; Jer. 2:26–27; Hos. 10:6) upon which one puts trust and hope. It denotes the disgrace of a defeated enemy (2 Kings 19:26; Isa. 19:9; 37:27; Ezek. 32:30; Zech. 10:5). The division between objective and subjective senses may be helpful, but the two cannot be maintained as hermetically sealed categories. In many cases, the subjective sense is embedded with the objective sense, and vice versa.[4]

The above shame vocabulary is most prevalent in the Major Prophets. Martin Klopfenstein notes that of the 167 occurrences of the root בושׁ in the Hebrew Bible, 99 occur in the Prophets, and of the 69 occurrences of the root כלם, 39 occur in the Prophets.[5] This distribution arises not because there was a major cultural transformation in later Israelite history, where "this dimension of being human was discovered on the broader plain . . . for the first time in the period of great prophets."[6] Rather, the increasing covenantal faithlessness of Israel led Yahweh to raise up prophets that communicated his word of judgment and hope. Through the shame discourses of the prophets, Yahweh appeals to his people to repent so as to stave off the impending judgment.

If the semantic range of shame is widened to include words that focus not on the subjective experience of shame but only on the objective state of disgrace or the act of shaming, we can include words such as בזה (to despise), זלל (to despise or treat lightly), קלה (to treat contemptuously), קלל (to diminish, dishonor, or treat with contempt), חרף (to reproach, revile, or taunt), מכך (to lower), and שׁפל (to humiliate or abase). These words have conceptual

---

4. P. J. Nel, "בושׁ," *NIDOTTE* 1:662.
5. Klopfenstein, *Scham und Schande*, 29, 118.
6. Seebass, "בושׁ," *TDOT* 2:52.

opposites that denote social significance.[7] For example, קלל (to be light or insignificant) is opposed to כבד (to be heavy or significant), and שפל (to be low) is opposed to רום (to be high). The concept of honor and shame lies behind these words. Honor increases status and causes one to be heavy or significant. Shame decreases status and causes one to be light or insignificant.

The absence of the above lexica in any particular context does not imply the absence of shame, since the concept of shame underlying the lexica may be inferred by contextual clues. For example, acts of shame and shaming can be denoted in passages that speak of spitting in the face (Num. 12:14; Deut. 25:9; Job 17:6; 30:10), striking the cheek (Job 16:10; Lam. 3:30), pulling or shaving the beard (2 Sam. 10:4; Isa. 7:20; 15:2; 50:6), uncovering the nakedness of another (2 Sam. 10:4–5), feeding captive kings with scraps from the table (Judg. 1:7), licking the dust of another's feet (Ps. 72:9; Isa. 49:22–23), treating captives as animals (2 Kings 19:28; Ezek. 19:4), and mutilating enemies (Judg. 1:6–7; 1 Sam. 10:27–11:11).[8]

Genesis 2:25 and 3:7

The earliest occurrence of "shame" in the Old Testament is Genesis 2:25: "And the two of them, the man and his wife, were naked; yet they were not ashamed." In the garden of paradise, Adam and Eve existed in a state of innocence, unity, and unimpeded freedom. In a sinless world, the primary characteristic that the author depicts is the absence of shame.

The absence of shame, in general, need not be a good thing. It can indicate the total lack of moral sensitivity, such as a shameless man who feels no compunction for the evil he does; it can denote the lack of moral or social maturity, such as a child who is blissfully unaware that nudity is shameful; or it can represent a perfect state in which there is no sin or guilt, a state in which the person is perfectly at peace. In this context, the last option is preferable given the function of Genesis 2:25.

Genesis 2:25 functions as a transition between chapters 2 and 3. It summarizes the earlier material and points forward to the new. The biblical story unfolds in chapter 3 with the disobedience of humanity to God's command. When they ate of the fruit, their eyes were opened and they knew that they were naked; so they sowed fig leaves and made loincloths for themselves (3:7). When God asked where they were, Adam responded, "I heard the sound of

---

7. While these words have conceptual opposites, Jumper ("Honor and Shame," 119) notes that the primary shame lexica (בוש, כלם, and חפר) have no antonyms.
8. See Lemos, "Shame and Mutilation of Enemies."

you in the garden, and I was afraid because I was naked; so I hid" (3:10). We can make several observations concerning shame in this narrative.

1. Shame is prevalent throughout the narrative. It is only explicitly mentioned in 2:25, but its reach extends into chapter 3. Shame is first connected to nakedness in 2:25, and subsequent mention of the word "naked" in 3:7, 10, 11, recalls the earlier connection. Nakedness, which formerly signified innocence, is now an objective marker of shame. Subsequent biblical records highlight this fact. Appearing naked before God is an abomination (Exod. 28:42–43), and nakedness is forced on prisoners of war (Isa. 20:3–4; 47:2–3) or on adulterous nations (Jer. 13:26; Lam. 4:21; Ezek. 16:37, 39; Hos. 2:3, 10; Nah. 3:5) as a sign of disgrace and humiliation. Nakedness, which formerly signified healthy relationships, now becomes a source of mental and emotional trauma. It is a source of subjective shame. The text does not explicitly say that the man and woman were ashamed, but the thought is indirectly expressed through their "hiding" actions. The sociologist Thomas Scheff notes that the behavioral response to shame is hiding, both verbal and nonverbal.[9] This includes physical hiding, looking down to escape the gaze of another, or speaking in an inaudible voice to hide the content of one's speech. Adam and Eve hid their shameful parts,[10] and they hid from God. Their external actions manifest their internal and subjective shame.

2. Shame is a relational concept, and it is a social emotion. It is generated by a fractured relationship or a threat to the social bond. The covering of fig leaves demonstrates Adam and Eve's alienation and concealment from each other,[11] and their hiding from God reflects their separation from him. The disordered relationships with fellow humans and with God result in shame: shame before one another and shame before God. But shame not only arises from a disunion with others but also speaks of a disunion within ourselves. Dietrich Bonhoeffer remarks, "Shame arises only out of the knowledge of humankind's dividedness . . . , of the world's dividedness in general, and thus also of one's own dividedness."[12]

3. Moral shame in Genesis 2–3 is the subjective expression of objective guilt. The experience of shame need not arise from a moral failure, but the Genesis account unmistakably highlights the theological character of shame.[13] One of the consequences of sin is moral shame. The text states that when the man and woman ate of the fruit, "then the eyes of both of them

---

9. Scheff, *Microsociology*, 86.
10. The male genitals are referred to as "shameful parts" (מְבֻשִׁים; Deut. 25:11).
11. Blocher, *In the Beginning*, 174.
12. Bonhoeffer, *Creation and Fall*, 101.
13. Klopfenstein, *Scham und Schande*, 33.

were opened, and they knew that they were naked" (3:7). Eating from the tree of the knowledge of good and evil is not an innocuous act; it constitutes a deliberate repudiation of God's explicit command in 2:17. When they ate of the fruit, they disobeyed God. In setting the self as *autonomous* from the Creator, they reject and resent the self as *given* by the Creator.[14] They repudiate the glory that God had originally intended for them and assumed instead the mantle of shame.[15] In this act of defiance, their eyes were opened; they discovered that their soul was threadbare, and they recognized their beggarly moral condition. In wanting to "be like God" (3:5), they discover the chasm between their intent and reality. This negative self-evaluation is the constitutive element of their shame (recall the definition of shame given in chapter 1 as the painful emotion that arises from an awareness that one has fallen short of some standard, ideal, or goal). The divine interrogation in 3:8–13 heightens the tension of this negative self-evaluation. God asks the man, "Where are you? . . . Who told you that you were naked? Have you eaten from the tree of which I commanded you not to eat?" (3:9, 11). He questions the woman, "What is this you have done?" (3:13). These questions are not meant to elicit information; they are rhetorical. The judge of the universe is calling the humans to demand an account for their conduct.[16] It is a call for self-examination, and the self-examination here inevitably leads to shame.

4. Genesis 2–3 suggests that nonmoral shame is also a function of sin. Shame can be invoked by nonmoral failures. For example, one can experience shame because of rape, childlessness, or widowhood. Although one does not deserve this humiliation because of any specific transgression that one has done, one nonetheless experiences shame because of the sin that others commit or because of the dysfunction that comes from living in a fallen world. If Adam's sin in Genesis 2–3 is understood as the cataclysmic event that brought about the entrance of sin into the world and the state of fallenness for all humanity and creation (3:14–19; cf. Rom. 5:12), then we can say that nonmoral shame is a reflection of sin. It is a symptom of the sin of Adam. We may then follow Johanna Stiebert in describing the relationship of moral and nonmoral shame to sin in this manner: moral shame denotes transgression; nonmoral shame connotes transgression in that it is a symptom of transgression.[17]

14. Blocher, *In the Beginning*, 174.
15. Apoc. Mos. 20.2–4 (OTP 2:281) reads, "Why have you [Satan] done this to me [Eve], that I have been estranged from my glory with which I was clothed? . . . I looked for leaves in my region so that I might cover my shame [αἰσχύνη]."
16. Cassuto, *Book of Genesis*, 1:155.
17. Stiebert, *Construction of Shame*, 46–47.

5. Shame is the necessary experience of sinful humanity. Given the foundational role of Adam as the progenitor of all humanity, Genesis suggests that sin and shame are part of the human experience. Later Jewish texts develop this thought in three ways. First, various texts affirm that all humanity is sinful. Psalms 51:5, 58:3, and 143:2 state that sin is inevitable. Philo notes that, even without faulty instructors, "the soul is its own pupil in the school of guilt."[18] It is impossible for humans to exist without a tendency toward evil.[19] Prayers in the Second Temple period also declare that sinful tendencies are unavoidable and are part of the human condition.[20] Second, certain Jewish texts note the pivotal role of Adam in the plight of humanity. Both 4 Ezra and 2 Baruch lament Adam's sin and blame him for the subsequent sins of humanity.[21] Moreover, 4 Ezra explicitly states that humanity's desire to sin is inherited from Adam such that it is "innate and inevitable."[22] There has never been a time when humanity has not sinned (3:35). All humans are sinful (4:38), and there is no human that has not sinned (7:46). Third, if sin is part of the human condition, so is shame. The Hodayot, a collection of hymns found in Qumran, is striking. In 1QH^a the speaker affirms his identification with the sin and shame of humanity. He writes, "Yet I am a vessel of clay and a thing kneaded with water, a foundation of shame and a well of impurity, a furnace of iniquity, and a structure of sin, a spirit of error, and a perverted being, without understanding, and terrified by righteous judgments."[23] These texts do not explicitly state that shame is the result of sin, but they suggest that shame cannot be extirpated as long as sin abounds.[24]

6. Only God is able to deal adequately with humanity's shame. Despite the coverings that Adam and Eve constructed for themselves (Gen. 3:7), God intervenes and provides clothes for them (3:21). God's provision suggests that Adam and Eve's earlier effort is inadequate. The inadequacy is further seen in the specific coverings that each construct. Adam and Eve sewed skimpy loincloths (חֲגֹרָה) out of fig leaves, but God provides long tunics (כְּתֹנֶת) from animal skins.[25]

---

18. Philo, *Her.* 295.

19. Philo, *Mut.* 183–85.

20. 11QPs^a XXIV, 11–13a; 4Q436 1 I, 10–II, 4.

21. 4 Ezra 3:20–22, 25–26; 4:30; 7:118–20; 2 Bar. 48:42–43.

22. Brand, *Evil Within and Without*, 282.

23. 1QH^a IX, 23–25. See also 1QH^a V, 31–32. ET Schuller and Newsom, *Hodayot*.

24. In the New Testament, the apostle Paul also traces the sin of humanity to Adam. Paraphrasing Paul, we might say: Just as sin entered the world through one man (Rom. 5:12), so also shame entered the world through one man. Just as all sinned and fall short of the glory of God (Rom. 3:23), so also all bear the shame of Adam.

25. The only other occurrences of כְּתֹנֶת in Genesis are to denote the tunic that Jacob made for Joseph (37:3, 23, 31–33).

In providing these garments, "God does (3:21) for the couple what they cannot do for themselves (3:7). They cannot deal with their shame. But God can, will, and does."[26] If Adam and Eve are representatives of humanity, then this story tells us that only God can adequately deal with humanity's shame; humanity's efforts are inadequate.

Shame and the Covenant Community

We noted in the previous section that shame is a relational concept and that shame is a social emotion. Shame is not only symptomatic of and arises from a fractured relationship but is also a tool that can be applied by one party over against another to indicate that their relationship is frayed. Given this dynamic, shame is used as a sanction of social behavior, especially in communities that are closely knit or group oriented.

In this section, I examine how shame regulates human relationships within the covenantal community of Israel and functions as a sanction of social control.[27] I pay attention to the ways in which shame guards boundaries, delimiting that which is acceptable or unacceptable. I also note how shame is employed when these boundaries are transgressed. I end with the reminder that though the use of shame within the covenantal community can be understood from a purely sociological perspective, it is also theological.

Shame as a Guard to Boundaries

Shame serves to maintain and guard boundaries; it demarcates that which is forbidden, despised, insignificant, and taboo. The boundaries vary; they can be ethnic, linguistic, cultic, cultural, or moral. In this brief section, we examine how shame delimits and guards both the moral and cultic boundaries within the covenantal community of Israel.

Moral Boundaries

A society can circumscribe appropriate moral behavior by publishing a list of commands and prohibitions. But it can strengthen the prohibitions by labeling those acts as odious and shameful. Such shaming labels attach a negative valence or stigma to forbidden practices. They warn the community that those who transgress the moral boundaries of the community and practice

26. Brueggemann, *Genesis*, 50.
27. See Bechtel, "Shame as a Sanction."

deviance will be shamed accordingly. Seen in this light, shame is a powerful instrument that can be used to control behavior.[28]

Regulations governing the Israelite covenantal community provide us with several examples where shame labels are explicitly used. For example, Leviticus 18:17 forbids sexual relations with both a woman and her daughter or granddaughter. This prohibition is then strengthened by affixing the incestuous act with the label "It is depravity [זִמָּה]." In a similar fashion, Leviticus 18:22 prohibits a homosexual act and stigmatizes it with the label "It is an abomination [תּוֹעֵבָה]"; and Leviticus 18:23 prohibits bestiality with the label "It is a perversion [תֶּבֶל]." The use of the formula "It is X" labels and attaches a social value to a particular behavioral pattern. It subsumes those acts under the categories of abomination, depravity, or perversion.

There are variations to the shaming label, for the label can be attached not to the act but to the person itself. Deuteronomy 22:5 forbids women from wearing men's clothing and men from wearing women's clothing, because "*whoever* does these things is an abomination to the LORD your God." Similarly, Deuteronomy 25:13–16 prohibits the use of inaccurate weights and measures. The reason is that "*everyone* who does these things, *everyone* who acts dishonestly is an abomination to the LORD your God." The application of the shame label to the person rather than the act intensifies the experience of shame, for the self can no longer be dissociated from the act. The act so overwhelms the identity of the person that the self becomes an abomination.

Cultic Boundaries

Within the Israelite covenantal community, honor and shame are associated with the language of purity and defilement. That which is pure is honored and desired; that which is defiled is shamed and avoided. Anything that threatens the purity of the community is considered unclean. "Uncleanness" or "dirt" is "matter out of place."[29] It must therefore be shunned and expelled from the community, relegated to the category of the shameful. For example, lepers or those having skin discharges are considered diseased and unclean. They must wear torn clothes, let their hair be disheveled, cover their lips, and cry out "Unclean! Unclean!" (Lev. 13:45). The leper is not described as "shameful," nor does he cry out "Disgraced! Disgraced!" Nevertheless, the depiction of the leper with their torn clothes, unkempt hair, and covered lips describes a

---

28. Aristotle, *Rhet.* 2.6.26, 1385A: "People do and do not do many things out of a sense of shame." See also Scheff, "Shame and Conformity."
29. Douglas, *Purity and Danger*, 35, 40.

person who is disgraced.[30] Since lepers have the potential to defile others, they must also be put out of the camp (Num. 5:2–3)—in the place of impurity,[31] the place that is farthest away from God and the tabernacle, the place where lawbreakers are executed (Lev. 24:14, 23; Num. 15:35–36), and the place where the toilet with shameful things (lit. "nakedness of a thing," Deut. 23:15 [ET 23:14]) are found. Banishment from a community is shameful. In Numbers 12:14, Miriam is shut out of the camp for seven days. Her punishment is described as "being humiliated [כלם]." The ostracism and marginalization of the leper thus reveals a diminished status within society and marks the leper out as persona non grata.

The distinction between the moral and cultic is blurry.[32] Moral sin defiles a person and the land (Lev. 18:23, 27), and defilement is sometimes equated explicitly with sin and transgression (Lev. 16:16, 19; 18:25). Ezekiel associates idolatry with defilement (Ezek. 14:11; 20:7, 18, 31; 23:7, 13–17, 30, 38; 36:18, 25; 37:23); and a priest who is ceremonially unclean sins when he eats of the sacred offering (Lev. 22:2–9). Given the overlap between moral and cultic boundaries, it is not surprising that shame serves to guard and delimit both sets of boundaries.[33] Shame ultimately designates that which is to be avoided.

Shaming Punishment as a Sanction of Behavior

Within the covenantal community of Israel, shame is not only employed to guard boundaries; it is also used when those boundaries are crossed. Deuteronomy 25:1–12 is instructive in this regard. It lays out three cases in which shaming the offender is a major component of the punishment.

The first legislation (25:1–3) concerns a legal dispute between two persons. If a judge determines that the one in the wrong deserves to be flogged, that person is made to lie down and is beaten in his presence. The punishment is clearly meant to be shameful. To have your offense revealed publicly at the gate, to be made to lie prostrate in a position of helplessness, and to be beaten in front of the judge and anyone else who might pass through are indeed shameful. Nonetheless, the legislation sets a limit on the amount of lashes that the person can receive. The offender cannot be given more than forty; otherwise, "your brother will be degraded [קלה] before your eyes"

---

30. In Mic. 3:7, covering the lips is a sign of shame for seers and diviners who fail to receive an answer from God.

31. Weinfeld, *Deuteronomy and the Deuteronomic School*, 225.

32. See Milgrom, "Rationale for Cultic Law."

33. The collocation of shame, impurity, and sin is clearly seen in 1QHª, one of the hymns of the Hodayot used in the Qumran community. For example, see 1QHª V, 31–32; IX, 23–25.

(25:3). In essence, the legislation advocates shaming punishment but prevents excessive shaming.

The second legislation concerns levirate marriage (25:5–10). If the brother of the deceased refuses to perform the duty of a brother-in-law in marrying the widow and raising an heir to carry on the deceased's name, the widow is to lodge her complaint to the elders at the city gate. The elders will then summon the man. If the brother persists in refusing to fulfill his duty, the widow will shame him in the presence of the elders and all who might be witnessing. She will take off one of his sandals, spit in his face, and proclaim, "This is what is done to the man who does not build up his brother's house" (25:9). These actions induce shame for three reasons. First, the brother-in-law has to put up with the aggressive actions of a woman, thereby destroying his image of the "dominant" male. Second, spitting in one's face is an overt display of contempt. Spit defiles a person, for bodily fluids are generally unclean and dangerous once discharged from the confines of the body.[34] Numbers 12:14 gives evidence of the shame that is borne by one who is spat on. Speaking of Miriam, the text notes, "If her father had spit in her face, would she not be disgraced for seven days?" Finally, the brother-in-law and his family will suffer ongoing shame as it gains the disgraceful reputation as "the house of him whose sandal was pulled off" (25:10).

The third legislation concerns the intervention by the wife of one of the fighters in a brawl between two Israelites (25:11–12). If the woman reaches out to seize the private parts of her husband's opponent, she is to be punished—her hand is to be cut off. The retribution is harsh and humiliating, for it leaves her with a physical defect. The mutilation brands her with a permanent stigma that cannot be erased. The punishment thus does not induce a temporary shame-affect in the offender. Rather, the public and irreversible stigma induces a permanent shame-affect.

The last legislation is puzzling, for it is the only mutilation punishment prescribed in the Old Testament. Moreover, the harshness of the penalty, emphasized by the comment "Show her no pity" (25:12), goes against the leniency and humanitarianism of 25:3. Furthermore, we know of no example in biblical literature where the mutilation prescribed by the law is enforced. Even the principle of *lex talionis* is not literally applied in Israel,[35] and the Talmud requires appropriate monetary compensation instead. All these reasons lead P. Eddy Wilson to suggest that this particular law is written not so much to be enforced as to deter. The force of the law lies in its threat of stigmatiz-

---

34. Douglas, *Purity and Danger*, 121.
35. Rad, *Deuteronomy*, 129.

ing shame, and "the law is written in the most extreme language possible to provide the greatest deterrent."[36]

The primary function of shaming punishments is not so much retribution as deterrence. The punishments are carried out in a public place so that the maximal number of people are aware of the offense. In certain cases, the entire community are themselves invited to participate in the punishment (Deut. 13:9; 17:7; 21:21; Josh. 7:24). When the people function as the executors of justice, they internalize the standards of the community. They become keenly aware that every stone they cast has the potential to be thrown back at them if they themselves break the law. Finally, the legal code in Deuteronomy also emphasizes its deterring force. Four times after the pronouncement of capital punishment, the text says, "Then all Israel shall hear and fear, and no longer do any such evil thing in your midst" (Deut. 13:11; 17:13; 19:20; 21:21).

Shame and Appearances

The above discussion demonstrates the importance of shame in regulating the moral, cultic, and legal relationships within the community. These examples lead scholars to conclude that the culture of Deuteronomy is permeated with a "strong shame-cultural element."[37] The regulations are crafted for a community that is sensitive to one another's behavior, and they focus on the public nature of the offense. Consequently, "sanctions become less dependent on administered system of penalties and more dependent on social and religious pressures within the community."[38]

The danger of such a strong shame element is that emphasis is placed on appearances rather than on the substance of the issue. This can be noted by the various legislations that begin with the "If there be found" formulas (Deut. 17:2; 21:1; 22:22; 24:7). Taking Deuteronomy 24:7 as an example, the legislation could simply have been written as "If a man steals" rather than "If a man be found stealing." The present formula, however, focuses not on the fearfulness of the crime but on the fearfulness of the appearance of the crime. There appears to be more concern for the inadequacy that is revealed than for the crime itself. But this need not be the case, for the axis of shame in Deuteronomy is not only sociological but also theological. There is a focus on appearances in the eyes of the beholder, but the ultimate and final beholder is not the people—it is God. He is the one who "walks in the midst of the camp," observing and watching the hearts and actions of the community.

36. Wilson, "Deuteronomy XXV 11–12," 234.
37. Daube, "Culture of Deuteronomy," 27.
38. Carmichael, *Laws of Deuteronomy*, 47.

"Therefore, [the] camp must be holy" and ready for his scrutiny at all times (Deut. 23:14).[39] On his inspection tour, God must not see anything indecent among the people lest he turn away from them. The role of the community, then, is to ensure that everything is presentable for the inspection by the great king, by God himself. Within this framework, shame is not heteronomous in that it locates the individual's sense of what should be done solely on the expectation of the community. When the observer or discoverer is God himself, the motivation of shame is internalized into the conscience of the individual.

Deuteronomic Covenant

In the previous section, we examined how shame functions horizontally within the human community. Here we examine how shame operates vertically within the divine-human relationship. The Deuteronomic covenant is fundamental to regulating the divine-human relationship between God and Israel, especially in regard to Israel's tenure in the promised land. It lays out how the relationship is to be manifested and maintained. It also stipulates the kind of nation that God wants Israel to be—a holy nation that is set apart from all the other nations so that it might reveal the nature and character of God.

Traditional shame vocabulary (בוש, כלם, and חפר) is absent or rare in covenantal texts. This does not mean that the concept of shame is absent, for the concept is expressed through other lexemes (such as קלה or קלל) and contextual clues. Specifically, while emotive words that denote the subjective sense of shame are absent, value-laden words that denote the objective state of shame and disgrace are present. In this section, I will examine the presence of shame in one central covenantal text: the blessings and curses of Deuteronomy 28.

It is generally recognized that the Deuteronomic covenant is similar in form to the ancient Near Eastern vassal treaty. Within the treaty framework, Deuteronomy 28 corresponds to the "blessings and curses" component. It outlines the consequences in the maintenance and breach of the treaty, functioning as incentives and disincentives for covenantal fidelity.

The blessings and curses can be understood in honor-shame categories. The blessings are listed in 28:1–14. There will be abundant prosperity, their children and harvest will be plentiful, success will follow all the work of their hands, and they will lend to many nations but borrow from none. Although enemies may arise, they will be defeated. The blessings given

39. Daube, "Culture of Deuteronomy," 46.

to Israel consist primarily of economic and military successes, and these blessings increase Israel's prestige and honor. The emphasis on honor is highlighted by the status language that brackets this section of blessings in Deuteronomy 28. In 28:1 Yahweh proclaims that he will set Israel "high above [עֶלְיוֹן] all the nations of the earth." In 28:13 Yahweh again reiterates that he will make Israel "the head [רֹאשׁ], not the tail [זָנָב]." They will "always be at the top [מַעַל], never at the bottom [מָטָּה]." By sandwiching the economic and military blessings of 28:2–12 within the frame of honor language, the passage suggests that these blessings are meant to establish Israel's honor among the nations.[40]

The curses are listed in 28:15–68. The content of the curses, in many instances, is the mirror opposite of the blessings, and there are verbal similarities between the two. For example, every blessing in 28:2–6 finds its converse in the curses of 28:15–19.

Blessings	Curses
These blessings shall come upon you and overtake you (v. 2)	These curses shall come upon you and overtake you (v. 15)
Blessed shall you be in the city (v. 3)	Cursed shall you be in the city (v. 16)
Blessed shall you be in the field (v. 3)	Cursed shall you be in the field (v. 16)
Blessed shall be the fruit of your womb, the fruit of your ground, . . . both the increase of your cattle and the issue of your flock (v. 4)	Cursed shall be the fruit of your womb, the fruit of your ground, the increase of your cattle and the issue of your flock (v. 18)
Blessed shall be your basket and your kneading bowl (v. 5)	Cursed shall be your basket and your kneading bowl (v. 17)
Blessed shall you be when you come in (v. 6)	Cursed shall you be when you come in (v. 19)
Blessed shall you be when you go out (v. 6)	Cursed shall you be when you go out (v. 19)

The similarities between the blessings and the curses suggest that just as the blessings raise Israel's prestige and honor, the curses bring humiliation and shame on Israel. The motif of shame is amplified in the following curses: the Israelites will flee from battle in ignominious defeat; their dead will not be given a proper burial but will be food for unclean birds and wild animals; their betrothed brides will be forcibly taken and raped by other men; and they will become objects of ridicule in the land in which they are

40. The emphasis on honor is seen earlier in the covenant-renewal ceremony of Deut. 26:16–19. When Israel takes on the obligation to keep all the Lord's commandments, Yahweh will "set you high above all nations that he has made, in praise and in fame and in honor" (26:19).

exiled. More significantly, the passage uses the exact status language of the blessing in 28:13 and converts it into a curse in 28:43. Instead of being raised above the nations, Israel is now lowered. The foreigners among them will rise higher (מָעַל), but Israel will sink lower (מָטָה); the foreigners will be the head (רֹאשׁ), but Israel will be the tail (זָנָב). The section of curses ends with a sobering warning. Israel's status will be worse than that of slaves. They will be *unwanted* slaves—they will offer themselves for sale as slaves, but no one will buy them (28:68).

The ultimate source of the blessings and curses are not the nations or nature. It is Yahweh. As Yahweh is ultimately the Lord of history and of nature, he alone is the one who has the power to bless and to curse; he alone is the one who has the prerogative to honor and to shame (28:63). Consequently, whatever honor Israel possesses, it possesses it as a gift from God; whatever shame Israel suffers, it suffers it as God's judgment on his people.

The distribution of blessings and curses by Yahweh is not arbitrary. It is contingent on Israel's fidelity toward the covenantal stipulations. The criteria for covenantal fidelity is described in various ways, but the fundamental refrain that echoes throughout this chapter is to "obey [שׁמע] Yahweh" (28:1, 2, 13, 15, 45, 62) and "keep [שׁמר] his commands" (28:1, 9, 13, 15, 45). Israel is not to turn aside from the commands of the Lord so as to follow other gods and serve them (28:14). It is not to forsake Yahweh (28:20). On the contrary, Israel is to serve him joyfully and gladly (28:47). If Israel maintains covenantal fidelity, it will be blessed, and these blessings establish Israel's honor among the nations. If Israel is faithless, it will be cursed, and these curses establish Israel's disgrace among the nations. The cause-and-effect relationship is unmistakable.

If the blessings and curses can be understood in honor-shame categories, the criteria for covenantal faithfulness can also be understood similarly. In other words, covenantal faithfulness can be construed as that which honors God, and covenantal faithlessness as that which dishonors God. Deuteronomy 28:58 bears this out, for it suggests that obeying Yahweh's commands is fundamentally equivalent to honoring him. In this verse, "to observe all the words of this law" is explicated by the following infinitival clause "to fear this honored and awesome name, the LORD your God."[41]

The above suggestion shows that the covenantal relationship can be understood in honor-shame categories. If Israel honors Yahweh by obeying his commands, Yahweh will in turn honor Israel. If Israel dishonors Yahweh by

---

41. The word "name" can represent one's honor and reputation. See A. S. van der Woude, "שֵׁם," *TLOT* 1356–57.

despising his commands, Yahweh will in turn dishonor and shame Israel.[42] This reciprocal honor-for-honor and shame-for-shame relationship finds support in the concept of *talion* that undergirds the Deuteronomic understanding of justice (cf. Exod. 21:23–25; Lev. 24:18–20; Deut. 19:21). It is also succinctly affirmed in 1 Samuel 2:30, where Yahweh declares, "Those who honor me I will honor, and those who despise me shall be treated with contempt."

Ezekiel

Within the prophetic literature, the relationship between judgment, shame, and deliverance typically follows a normative pattern. Disobedience to the covenantal obligations brings forth the covenantal curses, and the covenantal curses that fall on Israel bring judgment and shame (Jer. 9:19; 14:2–4; Ezek. 7:17–18; 22:4–5). Shame is a consequence of judgment, and shame is at times equated with the impending judgment (see Mic. 2:6).[43] Internalization of this shame and acknowledgment of the shamefulness of sin lead to repentance and confession (Ezra 9:6; Jer. 3:25; 31:19; Dan. 9:7).[44] According to the covenantal formula (Deut. 30:1–5), genuine repentance leads to divine forgiveness and deliverance. Exiles who are scattered over all the nations will be regathered, and the shame they experienced will be replaced with honor as their fortunes are restored (Zeph. 3:19–20). If "judgment brings disgrace, salvation leads to the removal of shame."[45] Instead of the shame of abandonment by Yahweh, Israel will receive the honor of a double portion in God's estate; instead of the disgrace of military defeat, Israel will experience joy (Isa. 61:7). These promises of deliverance are also often accompanied with assurances that they will never again be put to shame or disgraced (Isa. 45:17; 49:23; 54:4; Joel 2:27; Zeph. 3:11).

Overall, the sequential relationship between judgment, shame, and deliverance can be diagrammed as follows: disobedience of covenantal obligations → covenantal curses and shame in front of the other nations → internalized shame concerning one's sin → repentance → restoration → objective honor. Central to this normative sequence is the prerequisite of shame for deliverance and restoration.

---

42. See Olyan, "Honor, Shame, and Covenant Relations," 204–8.

43. S. Wagner, "כלם," *TDOT* 7:195.

44. In Jer. 31:19, penitential confession is accompanied by a recognition of one's shame and disgrace ("I am ashamed [בוש] and humiliated [כלם], because I bear the disgrace [חֶרְפָּה] of my youth"). Such a contrite stance contrasts with Israel's earlier refusal to acknowledge her shame ("You have the brazenness of a prostitute; you refuse to be ashamed [כלם]," Jer. 3:3).

45. Hadjiev, "Honor and Shame," 334.

The book of Ezekiel also relates shame to deliverance. But, remarkably, Ezekiel reverses the usual sequence. Shame is not presented as the prerequisite for deliverance but is the result of divine salvation and restoration. A comparison of Ezekiel and Jeremiah is instructive. Both books share the same concern with the absence of positive shame (prospective shame) in Israel and the need for negative shame (retrospective shame) in light of its shameful deeds. Nevertheless, "in Jeremiah the people never experience shame *after* Yahweh has acted to deliver them; in what is considered the more theologically normative sequence, repentance and shame precede deliverance."[46] Ezekiel, on the other hand, is different. In six sections of the book, Israel feels shame only *after* God restores his people (16:53–63; 20:43–44; 36:31–32; 39:25–29; 43:10–11; 44:10–14).[47] This is surprising because God's deliverance and restoration should remove the typical causes of shame within the ancient world.[48] Israel should therefore not have any cause for shame before the nations. This is true. But as we shall see, restored Israel experiences a different kind of shame. It experiences shame before Yahweh; it comes to a true self-knowledge in light of remembering who Yahweh is. Space does not permit me to examine all six passages; I will only focus on Ezekiel 16 and 36.

Ezekiel 16:1–63

Ezekiel 16 contains the most extensive treatment of shame in the entire book. The chapter begins with the commission of the prophet Ezekiel to confront Israel concerning its abominations (16:2). The central problem is Israel's adultery and shamelessness. It engages in shameful acts, but it does not consider them to be shameful. Israel lacks self-awareness and has no sense of shame.

In his indictment, Ezekiel highlights the shamelessness of Jerusalem by noting how she (the passage personifies Jerusalem as a woman) is much worse than the traditional representatives of moral depravity. The Philistines were commonly perceived by Jews to be morally suspect, but even they are appalled by Jerusalem's lewd conduct (16:27). Prostitutes were roundly condemned in Israelite society, but Ezekiel notes that typical prostitutes fared "better." They at least demanded payment for their sexual favors; Jerusalem, on the other hand, paid her customers instead (16:30–34). Finally, Samaria and Sodom, paragons of immorality, will appear righteous in comparison to the depraved corruption of Jerusalem (16:47–52).

---

46. Lapsley, *Can These Bones Live?*, 130n51.
47. Ortlund, "Shame in Restoration in Ezekiel," 1.
48. Simkins, "'Return to Yahweh.'"

The punishment for Jerusalem's shamelessness is shame and more shame. If Jerusalem delights in shameful deeds, Yahweh will pour more shame on her. He will gather all her lovers and expose her nakedness before them (16:37). Her lovers will also strip her. They will summon a mob to stone and hack her to pieces (16:39–40). But despite all this shaming punishment, there is no mention of compunction or remorse on the part of Israel. She remains hardened.

Jerusalem's ability to feel shame comes about only as a result of Yahweh's restoration. This is clearly noted in the last two verses of the chapter.[49] After Yahweh reestablishes his covenant with Jerusalem, she will finally acknowledge Yahweh and recognize him as the covenantal-faithful Lord ("you will know that I am the LORD," 16:62).[50] The purpose of this acknowledgment is expressed in the following clause: "so that [לְמַעַן] you shall remember [זכר] and be ashamed [בּוֹשׁ], and never again open your mouth because of your disgrace [כְּלִמָּה], when I forgive you for all you have done" (16:63). The language of "remember" does not just denote recalling to mind what was forgotten. Rather, it means "to take into account," noting the implications or consequences that such recall entails.[51] In 16:62–63, Jerusalem's renewed knowledge of Yahweh leads to the recognition of his grace, coupled with the concomitant acknowledgment of her ungrateful response. Feelings of shame and humiliation naturally follow. This change is striking, for the "brazen prostitute" (16:30) is now able to feel shame for both her past sins and undeserved atonement. In the postrestoration life, she will be able to see herself as Yahweh sees her. She will stand in humble silence because she finally recognizes her unfaithfulness in fulfilling the covenantal obligations.[52] The entire sequence of events described above can be depicted as follows: Yahweh's unilateral restoration → knowledge of Yahweh → Jerusalem's self-knowledge → Jerusalem's experience of shame.

Ezekiel 36:16–38

In Ezekiel 36, Jerusalem's betrayal of the covenantal obligations defiles the land. Yahweh judges them according to their conduct and scatters them throughout the nations. Their exile, however, impugns the honor of Yahweh before the nations (36:20), for it was commonly believed that the fortunes

---

49. The same sequence is also found in 16:53–54. Here Yahweh remarks that he will restore the fortunes of Sodom, Samaria, and Jerusalem "so that [לְמַעַן] you [Jerusalem] may bear your disgrace and be ashamed of all that you have done in consoling them." The purpose clause indicates that Jerusalem feels shame only *after* Yahweh has restored her.

50. Zimmerli, "Knowledge of God."

51. H. Eising, "זָכַר," *TDOT* 4:67.

52. Odell, "Inversion of Shame."

of a nation reflected on the reputation of its god.[53] Yahweh himself cannot experience shame for doing something shameful or for failing to accomplish what he sets out to do. He is, after all, a holy and powerful god. Nonetheless, Yahweh allows himself to be so intimately connected with Israel through the covenant that its humiliation also becomes his.

Yahweh rehabilitates his honor by restoring all the blessings of the Mosaic covenant. He does it not for Israel's sake but for his own honor (36:22, 32). He will gather the exiles back into the promised land. He will transform their hearts so that they will be able to follow his decrees and keep his law (36:26–27), forestalling the possibility of another exile and the opportunity for the nations to impugn Yahweh's name again. He will also rejuvenate the land so that it is fruitful. Consequently, Israel will "no longer suffer disgrace before the nations because of famine" (36:30).

The consequence of Yahweh's salvific act is not the total removal of shame. Yahweh will no longer make Israel hear the insults of the nations or bear the disgrace of the peoples (36:15), but the removal of this public dimension of shame before the nations is to be substituted by another—the private experience of shame before Yahweh. When Yahweh completes his restorative work, Israel will "remember" (זכר) its wickedness and "loathe" (קוט) itself for its sins and abominations (36:31). The indicative mood of these verbs suggests that shame is a spontaneous reaction, but the switch to the imperative in the following verse ("Be ashamed [בושׁ] and disgraced [כלם]," 36:32) indicates that it is also the appropriate response. Shame is the appropriate response or result of restoration; it is not presented here as the prerequisite for restoration.

Israel's shame stems from a renewed self-knowledge that is fundamentally tied to a renewed knowledge of Yahweh. Both knowledge of self and knowledge of Yahweh result from Yahweh's restorative act (36:31, 38), but the relationship between them is not as clearly portrayed as in Ezekiel 16. We may presuppose from the earlier chapter that a proper knowledge of Yahweh leads Israel to a renewed awareness of its evil ways. But it is also apparent that a proper knowledge of Yahweh is possible only insofar as Israel comes to a true knowledge of its infirmities and sins—a knowledge that results in shame before Yahweh's unmerited favor.

Ezekiel 36 also advances the theme of shame in restoration with the promise of an inner transformation (36:26–27). It shows that judgment and unmerited restoration are effective in transforming the moral vision of Israel only insofar as the hearts of the nation are transformed from that of stone to that of flesh. Shame concerning one's sin is brought about by the convicting work of the

---

53. In Jer. 50:2 the protective deities of Babylon, both Bel and Merodach, are humiliated as Babylon is captured.

Holy Spirit. A renewed knowledge of Yahweh is possible only when Israel is indwelt by the Holy Spirit, and a renewed knowledge of self is possible only when Israel is given a heart to know Yahweh as the covenantal Lord (cf. Jer. 24:7).

Shame in Restoration

Our study in Ezekiel reveals several aspects to shame. First, shame has both objective and subjective aspects. Shame can be understood objectively as a disgrace or a loss of status, but it can also be understood subjectively as a feeling of unworthiness or self-loathing. Second, the manifestation of divine judgment on Israel in exile and famine are dishonorable states of affairs before the nations. This "shame in judgment" has a public dimension as Israel's disgrace (objective shame) is recognized "before others"—before the various nations and the peoples. Third, Israel never internalizes this "shame in judgment"; it is unable to see its depravity and experience its disgrace. Israel is objectively shamed before the nations, but it does not subjectively experience this shame. Fourth, the manifestations of divine restoration in the regathering of the exiles and the provision of an abundant harvest removes Israel's objective shame before the nations. Fifth, although restored Israel no longer has reason to be ashamed before the nations, it nevertheless experiences shame and self-loathing (subjective shame). This "shame in restoration" exists only in relation to Yahweh, not to anyone else; it has a private dimension.

In Ezekiel, Israel does not experience shame in its judgment when there are objective reasons to be ashamed. It nevertheless experiences shame in its restoration when there are no objective reasons to be ashamed. How are we to explain this inversion of shame?

Ezekiel shows that punishment does not necessarily bring penitence. Given the hardness of humanity's heart, judgment may only spur the sinner toward further sin. Contrition, remorse, and shame come about by a divine act. The cause of Israel's objective shame has always been its failure to honor Yahweh and respond appropriately to his love and faithfulness. The *efficient* cause of Israel's subjective shame, however, is Yahweh's unilateral act that exchanges Israel's heart of stone for a heart of flesh (36:26). The use of "heart" (לֵב) language is significant because the heart is the organ of knowledge that notes deviations from God's will; it functions as the conscience of the person.[54] When Yahweh replaces Israel's heart of stone with a heart of flesh, he transforms Israel's epistemic abilities so that it is able to see things from Yahweh's perspective and be stricken by its past misdeeds.

54. H.-J. Fabry, "לֵב," *TDOT* 7:426.

Ezekiel shows that remorse and shame for what one has done is intimately tied to self-knowledge and knowledge of Yahweh. Shame is a manifestation of self-knowledge, for the language of self-loathing is often preceded by זכר, "to remember" (16:61; 20:43; 36:31). Self-knowledge is a function of one's ability to "remember" and take into account one's past sins. At the same time, Israel's self-knowledge or remembering is tightly interwoven with the divine recognition formula ("Know that I am Yahweh").[55] One may then say that "Israel knows itself only *vis à vis* YHWH and through acknowledgement of the actions by which YHWH is revealed as its sole and sovereign God. For Israel, remembering the past and acknowledging YHWH are inseparable elements of a complex interaction."[56] Israel cannot truly know itself without knowledge of Yahweh. At the same time, Israel cannot truly know Yahweh without knowledge of itself, without remembering the death from which it was saved through Yahweh's mercy, and without experiencing shame for its guilt.[57]

This inversion of shame must also be understood within the rhetorical function of the book of Ezekiel. Thomas Renz suggests that the book's aim is to shape the self-understanding of a community in crisis. The "exilic community is to define itself not by the past but by the future promised by Yahweh."[58] They are to "disassociate themselves from their past and associate themselves with Ezekiel's portrayal of a new Israel."[59] They are to agree with Yahweh's judgment over Jerusalem, to give up any delusions of innocence, and to be ashamed of their guilt as they marvel at Yahweh's mercy. Authentic existence before the creator and covenant God is to dwell in continual nakedness before him. We stand before the judge as one who knows what he already knows: that any good we have comes from him alone, for by ourselves we are wretched creatures. Without this shame for our moral and spiritual bankruptcy, we will never appreciate the immeasurable grace and love that God has given to us.

Sirach

Sirach (or the Wisdom of Ben Sira) is the final Jewish text we will examine in this chapter. It is pertinent to our study because it presents us with an example

---

55. In Ezek. 16:61–63 we have the sequence "You will remember your ways. . . . You will know that I am the LORD. . . . You will remember and be ashamed." In 20:42–44 we have the sequence "You will know that I am the LORD. . . . You will remember your conduct. . . . You will know that I am the LORD."

56. E. Davis, *Swallowing the Scroll*, 115. See also Lapsley, *Can These Bones Live?*, 157.

57. Ortlund, "Shame in Restoration in Ezekiel," 15.

58. Renz, *Rhetorical Function*, 249.

59. Renz, *Rhetorical Function*, 131.

of not only how honor and shame were understood in Wisdom literature but also how they were employed in Jewish literature within the Second Temple period.

Ethic of Caution: Developing a Proper Sense of Shame

As Wisdom literature, Sirach lays out clear instructions for what pious Jews should and should not do. This ethic of caution is unmistakable, for the phrase "Do not X" occurs 240 times in the NRSV translation of this work. For example, it warns its readers not to have many confidants (8:17–19; 13:12–13) nor to criticize others without first investigating the facts (11:7). They are not to do anything on a whim (32:19), and they must guard themselves in every act (32:23). Sirach's ethic of caution is seen most vividly, however, in its instruction concerning daughters. It advises fathers to monitor them closely lest they make the fathers "a laughingstock to [their] enemies, a byword in the city and the assembly of the people, and put [them] to shame in public gatherings" (42:11).[60]

Other Wisdom literature, such as Proverbs, also displays an ethic of caution that is grounded in honor and shame. Sirach's emphasis on honor and shame, however, "goes far beyond anything that we find in the Hebrew tradition."[61] The rationale for doing X is not so much that those who do X will live, but that they will not fall into disgrace and disrepute. Jack Sanders remarks, "For Ben Sira, shame lurked everywhere, and one's approach to life needed to be cautious at every point."[62] Sirach's ethic of caution is thus propelled by a fear of shame. The text implores its readers to develop a proper sense of shame, not to deter them from pursuing honor but to help them attain it.

The responsibility for cultivating this sense of shame falls primarily on fathers and teachers. They are not to spoil and overindulge their children. Rather, they are to teach and chastise them so that they will not grow up to be unruly and stubborn (30:1–12). They are to discipline them at every turn lest the children become shameless and ultimately bring disgrace on their own fathers (30:13). Children also bear responsibility for their own development. They must be humble (3:17–29) and be receptive to disciplinary rebuke. If they are willing to listen to such instruction, they will gain knowledge and come to honor (6:18–22; cf. Prov. 13:18).

The cultivation of a proper sense of shame is bound up with the acquisition of wisdom. Sirach depicts wisdom like cords or a yoke (6:24, 25, 30; 51:26)

---

60. English translations of the Apocrypha follow the NRSV.
61. Collins, *Jewish Wisdom in the Hellenistic Age*, 76–77.
62. Sanders, "Ben Sira's Ethics of Caution," 99–100.

that constrain children to walk the path of honor rather than the path of shamelessness (30:13). Similarly, wisdom is like a glorious robe and a splendid crown (6:29–31), bestowing honor to those who wear it. Ultimately, the one who has wisdom will never be put to shame (24:22) and will inherit glory and an everlasting name (4:13; 15:6; cf. Prov. 3:16–17, 35; 8:18). One's name is important in the worldview of Sirach, for the Hebrew text has no notion of the afterlife.[63] Thus, the only reward or compensation after death is one's posthumous reputation.

Apart from wisdom, Sirach's ethic of caution is inculcated by cultivating a proper fear of the Lord. Such a move is not surprising, for Sirach not only repeats the teaching of Proverbs that "the fear of the Lord is the beginning of wisdom" (1:14) but also goes on to say that it is the fullness of wisdom (1:16), the crown of wisdom (1:18), and the root of wisdom (1:20). Fear of the Lord entails patience (1:23–24), discipline, fidelity, humility (1:27), and sincerity (1:28–29). Those who fear the Lord will not disobey his words (2:15; 23:27) but will seek to please him (2:16) and humble themselves before him (2:17). They will never sin against him in order to save face (42:1). They will gladly accept his discipline (32:14) and will genuinely repent when rebuked (21:6). In essence, they will reverence God, possess a high regard for his honor and requirements, and develop a proper sense of shame before him. As Sirach affirms, "The one who has a sense of shame will fear the Lord" (26:25).[64] Those who are shameless, however, live in self-willed autonomous defiance of the God who created both them and the universe.

Constructing a Different Court of Opinion

Sirach presents us with an example of how honor and shame were understood and used in the Second Temple period. Jews in the second century BCE faced a crisis. Politically, Israel was a pawn as it was passed back and forth between Ptolemaic and Seleucid powers. Culturally, Judaism was a minority culture within the dominant culture of Hellenism. Living in a world dominated by Greek values, ideas, and ideals, many Jews questioned the utility and viability of their Jewish heritage. For example, 1 Maccabees 1:11–15 describes renegade Jews who were ashamed of their Jewish way of life. Some went so far as to cover the marks of circumcision, so that they would not suffer ridicule when they participated naked in the Greek gymna-

---

63. There are allusions to the afterlife in the Greek translation; see 7:17b and 48:11b LXX.
64. Similarly, T. Jud. 16:2 states that shamelessness (ἀναισχυντία) is caused by the departure of the fear of God.

sium in Jerusalem. The priesthood was not immune to these challenges. Enticed by the excitement generated by Hellenistic influences, priests neglected their ministry at the temple altar. They instead rushed to participate in the activities of the gymnasium, "disdaining the honors prized by their ancestors and putting the highest value upon Greek forms of prestige" (2 Macc. 4:13–15).

Ben Sira lived just before Hellenization reached its prime during the reign of Antiochus IV Epiphanes. There were nonetheless existing tendencies pulling in that direction. Thus, he writes to combat the onslaught of Hellenistic liberalism against Jewish ideals.[65] He does not eschew the wisdom of foreign sages, but he opposes any compromise of the Jewish law.[66] He employs honor and shame language to exhort his readers to follow the Torah, arguing that true honor is obtained only by pursuing the wisdom that is to be found in the law of Moses. In doing so, he constructs a different court of opinion whose verdict about what is truly honorable and shameful differs from that which is currently in vogue. He establishes the Torah of Moses and the fear of Yahweh as the lens through which honor and shame must ultimately be determined. Any action and attitude must ultimately be evaluated and adjudicated within this divine court of opinion.

Ben Sira argues that lasting honor cannot be found in wealth, strength, power, or social status (5:1–3). Rather, true honor is found by those who fear the Lord (10:19, 20, 22), for the fear of the Lord brings glory, pride, and a crown of joy (1:11). Even though princes and rulers may be honored, "none of them is greater than the one who fears the Lord" (10:24; cf. 25:10–11). True honor is also found in wisdom that comes from the Lord, for wisdom bestows high honor on those who hold fast to her (1:19).

Ben Sira also differentiates between proper and improper shame. In 4:21 he notes that "there is a shame that leads to sin, and there is a shame that is glory and favor." Within the context of his program to counter Hellenism, the shame that leads to sin is shame toward one's Jewish heritage (cf. 4:20).[67] The shame that merits glory and favor, however, is shame for one's sin and transgression against the dictates of Torah. Ben Sira further delineates what is considered proper and improper shame in 41:16–42:5. Pious Jews should be ashamed of sexual immorality, falsehood, crime, breach of the law, theft, the breaking of an oath, lack of social manners, immoral actions, abusive language, and the betrayal of secrets. The first thing that they must never be

---

65. Hengel, *Judaism and Hellenism*, 1:138.
66. DeSilva, *Introducing the Apocrypha*, 161.
67. Skehan and Di Lella, *Wisdom of Ben Sira*, 176.

ashamed of, however, is God's law and covenant (42:2). Similarly, Ben Sira enjoins his readers never to be ashamed to praise God (51:29).

Apart from detailing the values that constitute true honor and shame, Ben Sira concretizes these concepts by valorizing individuals who exemplified them. In a lengthy section (44:1–50:21), Ben Sira recalls Israel's ancestors who performed praiseworthy acts so as to move his audience toward Torah fidelity and honor. For example, Abraham is unparalleled in honor, for he kept the law of God and proved steadfast when put to the test (44:19–20). Ben Sira balances his positive exemplars with negative counterparts. Solomon, for example, is censured. His honor is stained, for he broke the Deuteronomic stipulation prohibiting Israelite kings from acquiring many foreign wives (47:19–21; cf. Deut. 17:17). All the kings of Israel, except for David, Hezekiah, and Josiah, were great sinners, "for they abandoned the law of the Most High" (49:4). Through these examples, Ben Sira reminds his readers, on the one hand, that covenantal faithfulness results in a legacy that is praised by subsequent generations. On the other hand, covenantal unfaithfulness brings lasting disgrace. Those who forsake the Torah have no name. There is no memory of them; "they have become as though they had never been born" (44:9).

Ben Sira argues that the divine court of opinion is paramount, for only God is to be feared (1:8). He is the only one who is wise (1:8), he sits on the throne (1:8), he rules over the nations (10:4–5, 8), he appoints their rulers (10:14), he controls nature (43:13–25), and he is infinitely worthy of more praise than we can lavish on him (43:27–32). Like Socrates in Plato's *Gorgias*, Ben Sira sets before his readers the portrait of a divine judge whose opinion ultimately matters. All honor and glory rightly belong to God, and they are his to give to whomever he chooses. His decision to reward some and punish others is perfect and just, for he sees everything (17:15). Since nothing is hidden from his sight (23:18–19), Jews cannot hope that their decision to adopt Hellenistic values will be hidden from God. Rather, they must regulate the entirety of their lives in the fear of the Lord. Ben Sira underscores the importance of the divine court of opinion by ending his work with the injunction for pious Jews to carry out their duty faithfully, for God will reward them in his own time (51:30; cf. 12:6; 17:23; 35:13, 24).

Synthesis and Overview

As with the chapter on the Greco-Roman backgrounds, I synthesize the findings of the above sections under two categories: (1) the Jewish construal of shame and (2) elements in the Jewish role of shame for moral formation.

The Jewish Construal of Shame

Multiple words within the Jewish texts denote shame. The main roots בוש, כלם, and חפר denote either subjective or objective shame—the subjective experience of shame (one who is ashamed) or the objective reality of disgrace (one who is shameworthy). Other roots such as חרף, קלל, קלה, זלל, בזה, מכך, and שפל denote the objective state of humiliation or the act of shaming. The first group of words, being emotive shame words, have no antonyms; the second group find their conceptual opposites in an honor-shame system.

Honor and Shame

Honor and shame are values whose specific content needs to be determined according to the values of the appropriate court of opinion. Within the Israelite worldview, there are two main courts of opinion: the human or public court of opinion and the divine court of opinion. The divine court of opinion is significantly more important and overrides any public court of opinion. Yahweh is the ultimate source and giver of honor, and he alone determines how shame and honor are to be defined, measured, and distributed. The covenantal stipulation is one example of this standard. If Israel honors Yahweh and obeys his commands, it will be blessed and honored before the nations; if it dishonors Yahweh and disobeys his commands, it will be cursed and shamed before the nations. Within the prophetic literature, honor and shame are closely linked to judgment and salvation. Judgment entails the curses of the covenant—destruction, death, famine, military defeat, nakedness, and exile, all of which bring disgrace. If Israel takes these curses to heart and repents of its sin, Yahweh will restore its fortunes. Thus, if judgment brings shame, salvation is the removal of shame and the restoration of honor.

Emphasis on the divine court of opinion gains renewed emphasis in Sirach. Facing the corrosive influence of Hellenism in the second century BCE, Ben Sira forcefully argues that the entirety of one's life must be lived before the court of Yahweh. Lasting honor is to be found only by those who fear the Lord and embrace the wisdom of Torah. Jews must not be ashamed of Yahweh and his laws, even as the entire world is pulled into the vortex of Hellenism, for the opinions of those who do not fear the Lord are unreliable guides to true honor and shame.

If honor and shame are determined by Yahweh and are a function of obedience to Yahweh, then honor is not ultimately determined by the accumulation of worldly possessions (be it wealth or power). If honor is not determined by the accumulation of possessions, then honor is not a limited good. If honor is not a limited good, then the quest for honor need not be a zero-sum exchange transacted in a series of agonistic challenge-ripostes. Honor need not be gained at the expense of shaming another. All nations and all peoples can be honored if they faithfully serve Yahweh. Similarly, all nations and all peoples can be shamed if they are faithless and chase after other gods.

Shame and Conscience

If shame is to be fundamentally understood in relation to Yahweh, then shame cannot be merely understood on the horizontal level. It is more than failing to meet the ideals of one's community and losing face before one's social group. On the contrary, it is fundamentally related to what one perceives to be right and wrong as determined from Yahweh's perspective. If we internalize Yahweh's perspective, then our sense of shame effectively functions as our conscience. It should restrain us from any behavior that dishonors God, and it should shame us when we transgress God's command. Far too often, however, the prophets castigate Israel for not having a proper sense of shame or conscience. Israel acts shamefully and commits abomination, but it does not feel shame nor does it know how to blush (Jer. 3:3; 6:15; 8:12; Zeph. 3:5). What is needed is a reconfiguration of the "heart" or conscience so that Israel is able to perceive and evaluate things from Yahweh's perspective.

Shame and Guilt

The biblical evidence does not put shame and guilt as binary opposites, as psychologists are wont to do. In the Scriptures, "guilt does not refer, in the first instance, to the *feeling* of having transgressed an internalized moral code, so much as the *fact* of having transgressed YHWH's moral code."[68] If guilt refers primarily to the fact of having transgressed Yahweh's stipulations and if Scripture frequently use "shame" words to denote the subjective experience of objective guilt, then "subjective shame includes subjective remorse."[69] Shame does not necessarily denote transgressions; it can be invoked by both moral and nonmoral failures. Nevertheless, when shame stems from the recognition that one has done wrong, this subjective experience of moral shame, such as that displayed by Israel because of God's salvation (Ezek. 36), should be understood as remorse. It expresses deep regret, sorrow, and compunction for past moral failings.

---

68. Wu, *Honor, Shame, and Guilt*, 174. Milgrom (*Cult and Conscience*, 9–12) argues for a consequential אשׁם, noting that the word must mean "feel guilty." His work, however, has been criticized. Instead of "feel guilty," I understand אשׁם to mean "become guilty or culpable."

69. Klopfenstein, *Scham und Schande*, 209. He further remarks that Hebrew knows no distinct verb for "to feel remorse" and that נחם only occasionally conveys the sense of feeling remorse for an offense.

Elements in the Jewish Role of Shame for Moral Formation

The role of shame for moral formation can be seen in two spheres: the divine-human relationship and the human community.

The Role of Shame and Shaming in the Divine-Human Relationship

The role of shame in the divine-human relationship is fundamentally seen in the Deuteronomic covenant. It lays out the stipulations that Israel is to obey and enumerates the blessings and curses that would ensue. Obedience to Yahweh results in continual enjoyment of the blessings, but disobedience brings curses. The blessings of the covenant increase Israel's honor over the nations, but the curses bring humiliation and shame. Together, the blessings and curses function as incentives and deterrents for Israel toward covenantal faithfulness.

When Israel disobeys Yahweh and is judged accordingly, it is objectively shamed and called to repent. If this objective shame is internalized and subjectively experienced, it can cause Israel to realize its sin and prompt it toward repentance. In this scenario, subjective shame comes *before* restoration, and genuine repentance leads to divine forgiveness. The curses that Israel previously suffered will be replaced with blessings (Deut. 30:1–10). Instead of divine abandonment, exile, loss of land, military defeat, famine, and infertility, there will be divine presence, regathering of exiles, repossession of land, military victory, prosperity, and fertility. Instead of the objective shame that Israel previously suffered, there will be greater honor. Instead of the subjective experience of humiliation, there will be the subjective experience of joy.

The objective shame that is brought on by divine judgment and punishment does not always effect repentance. In Ezekiel, Israel engages in shameful deeds but is unable to perceive that what it is doing is shameful. When Yahweh judges and shames Israel before the nations, it remains hardened. Israel does not acknowledge its guilt, nor does it subjectively experience its objective shame. Consequently, it remains unrepentant. Israel experiences shame for its guilt only *after* Yahweh transforms its heart and places his Spirit in the community. This transformation results in a new moral vision of Yahweh and of Israel's self-identity, and it manifests itself in the subjective experience of shame and remorse for past guilt in light of Yahweh's mercy.

The above two responses to shaming punishment show different sequences between shame and restoration. In the former, subjective shame comes *before* restoration; in the latter, subjective shame comes *after* restoration. In the former, subjective shame is the prerequisite for restoration; in the latter, subjective shame is the result. These two different relationships show the tension between human responsibility and divine initiative. The former, with its call to repentance and shame, underscores Israel's responsibility. The latter, with its unilateral divine transformation that brings about a new perspective, underscores divine initiative and grace. The relationship between human responsibility and divine initiative is intricately balanced, although different texts may emphasize one or the other for rhetorical reasons. Deuteronomy emphasizes the former, Ezekiel the latter.[70]

The Role of Shame and Shaming within the Human Community

According to the Jewish texts, the earthly analogue to the divine court of opinion is the Israelite community. Israel is not to adopt the values and customs of the surrounding nations; on the contrary, Israel is to manifest visibly the values of Yahweh. It is within the community that one commends and receives commendation for acting according to the statutes and ideals stipulated by Yahweh. It is also within the community that one discourages and receives shame for acting contrary to the dictates of Yahweh. Shame plays an important role in this mechanism of commendation and censure.

Within the Israelite community, shame serves as a sanction of social control. It accomplishes this in two primary ways: prospectively and retrospectively. Prospectively, shame delimits and guards boundaries. It clarifies that which is morally suspect and cultically unclean or taboo; in essence, it denotes that which is undesirable and which should be avoided. By classifying certain actions as "an abomination" or "a depravity," the Israelite community employs shame labels that function in the same way that the "shame" (αἰσχρόν) label functions in the Greco-Roman world—they stigmatize and deter unacceptable behaviors.

Retrospectively, shame is employed when social deviance occurs. Guilty persons are publicly shamed in the eyes of the community because they have transgressed its social norms. Nevertheless, the textual evidence suggests that shaming punishment is ultimately meant to be restorative. Apart from the case of the woman who seizes the private parts of her husband's opponent (which I previously argued is not meant to be applied literally), shaming punishment is not meant to stigmatize a person permanently. On the contrary, excessive shaming is forbidden (Deut. 25:3) so that the guilty party has the opportunity to reintegrate into the community.

Reintegration of offenders is possible because the primary function of shaming punishment is not the destruction of the core identity of individuals, nor is it retribution. It is deterrence. It seeks to reform future behavior

70. See Joyce, *Divine Initiative and Human Response in Ezekiel*.

by invoking remorse in those being shamed and by moralizing with them concerning the evil of their actions. Since the offenders have a defective sense of shame that did not stop them from committing deviance, they are publicly shamed with the hope that they might be able to perceive their actions from the perspective of the community. If they are able to experience subjectively the shame of their punishment, the remorse that they feel for their past actions should prompt them to develop a much more robust sense of shame for the future.

Shaming punishment deters future deviance not only in the guilty party but also in the spectators to the punishment. As spectators witness or even participate in the punishment, they internalize the standards of the community. Their sense of shame or conscience is resensitized in conformity with the ideals of the community, for they know that they will suffer the same fate if they violate the spoken or unspoken rules of the community.

PART 2

EXEGESIS

Part 2 constructs Paul's ethic of shame. I first begin with an exegetical analysis of his use of shame through two axes: retrospective and prospective, both of which were introduced in chapter 1. Retrospective shame refers to situations where the event that causes one to feel shame is in the past or present; prospective shame refers to situations where the event is in the future. Paul uses both of these moments in his rhetoric of shame as he seeks to transform the perspective of his readers. Chapter 4 focuses on the former, chapter 5 on the latter.

After this exegetical analysis, I synthesize the findings in chapter 6.

4

Paul's Use of
Retrospective Shame

This chapter examines Paul's use of retrospective shame in two letters: Galatians and 1 Corinthians. Both letters are written to churches that are experiencing severe problems. The Galatian churches are on the verge of apostasy, and the Corinthian church is marked by moral failures and schisms. Faced with these issues and their arrogant attitude toward him, Paul explicitly and implicitly shames them for the wrong they are doing or have done. He does this so as to bring about the occurrent experience of shame in his readers, with the hope that they would reform their thinking. Given the constraints of space, I only investigate select passages from each letter. The analysis of each letter concludes with a summary of the findings.

Galatians

Paul's Letter to the Galatians describes churches that are in confusion. After Paul left the churches that he planted in the Roman province of Galatia during his first missionary journey, certain Jewish-Christian missionaries from Judea arrived. Paul refers to these outsiders as "troublemakers" (1:7; 5:10) or "agitators" (5:12). They persuaded the Galatians to turn away from the truth of the gospel to a different gospel, which was really not a gospel at all (1:6–7). They imposed on the gentile Galatian believers some requirements of the Jewish law, particularly circumcision (6:12–13) and the observance of special days within the Jewish sacred calendar (4:9–10). The arguments of these agitators were so persuasive (3:1; 5:7–8) that even though the Galatians started their journey of faith according to the teachings of Paul (5:7), they quickly began to implement the policies advocated by the agitators (4:9–11). They had, however, not taken the step of circumcision. When Paul heard of this development, he feared that his efforts in planting these churches would be wasted (4:11). He sent them a passionate letter, urging them to stand firm in their Christian freedom (5:1).

There are no explicit shame lexemes in this letter, nor does Paul baldly state that he writes to shame them. Nonetheless, the overall tenor of the letter points in this direction. The Galatians are in fact not the only ones that Paul shames in this letter. Paul reports an earlier incident in Antioch where he publicly shamed Peter in front of everyone. In this section, I examine Paul's rebuke of Peter followed by his rebuke of the Galatians. A summary concludes this section.

Paul's Shaming Rebuke of Peter

The account of Paul's shaming rebuke of Peter is given in Galatians 2:11–14. When Peter visited the church in Syrian Antioch, he initially made it a practice of eating with the gentile believers. The comment that Peter lived like a gentile (2:14) suggests that he ate unclean food, probably on the basis of the vision that he received in Acts 10. When certain men from James arrived, however, Peter changed his eating practice. He "withdrew and separated himself" from the gentiles because he feared "those of the circumcision" (2:12). Since Peter was one of the acknowledged pillars of the Jerusalem church (2:9), other Jews followed suit. So influential was Peter that "even Barnabas" (2:13) was led astray and followed Peter's separatist behavior. Paul's pathos is palpable in the expression "even Barnabas," for Barnabas was his advocate (Acts 9:27), mentor (11:25–26), companion (11:27–30), and colleague (Acts 13). This Barnabas previously stood with Paul and resisted the false brothers in order that the truth of the gospel might be preserved (Gal. 2:5); this Barnabas was Paul's ministry colleague *to the gentiles* (2:9). But alas, this Barnabas was finally led astray by Peter, the supposed pillar of the church.

From Paul's perspective, Peter stood condemned before God. His actions were hypocritical (2:13), motivated by fear of human beings rather than of God (2:12). He played the role of an observant Jew, even though his earlier willingness to eat with gentiles revealed his true convictions. More importantly, Peter was not acting rightly with regard to the truth of the gospel (2:14). Paul therefore confronted Peter and publicly exposed his sin (2:11).

A Shaming Rebuke

Although Paul does not explicitly say that he shamed Peter, the language of "opposed him to his face," "condemned," "I saw," and "before everyone" evokes the concept of shame. The use of these terms in Galatians 2:11–14 suggests that Paul intends his readers to understand his confrontation of Peter as shaming rebuke. I explain this in three moves.

1. Paul presents Peter as a hypocrite, worthy of condemnation. The verbal root behind the word typically rendered "hypocrisy" in 2:13 is ὑποκρίνομαι. Although this verb has a neutral valence in classical Greek ("to act" or "to play the part in a drama"), it almost always occurs in a negative sense in Hellenistic Jewish literature.[1] Philo considers hypocrisy to be an evil worse than death (*Ios.* 68), the work of a base and servile soul (*Spec.* 4.183). The Psalms of Solomon metes out stern justice on hypocrites (4:6–8, 20). The Gospel of Matthew is also decidedly harsh, for it assigns hypocrites to Gehenna, the place where "there will be weeping and gnashing of teeth" (24:51). As a result of Peter's hypocrisy, he "stands condemned" (Gal. 2:11)—condemned not by the verdict of mere humans but by God himself. Judgment brings disgrace, and condemnation brings shame.[2] As the condemned stands shamed before their judge, so also Peter stands shamed before God.

2. Paul's description of Peter's action in 2:12 connotes shameful cowardice. Most translations render the Greek phrase ὑπέστελλεν καὶ ἀφώριζεν ἑαυτόν as "he drew back and separated himself." However, the Greek verb for "draw back" (ὑποστέλλω) can also mean "shrink back" in a cowardly manner so as to hide from observation.[3] The use of "separate himself" (ἀφώριζεν ἑαυτόν) is also significant. Paul earlier used this verb to describe God's action in setting him apart and appointing him for God's ministry toward the gentiles (1:15). Peter, however, separates or excludes himself from God's redemptive work among the gentiles.

Peter shrank back because he feared "those of the circumcision" (2:12). This phrase is highly cryptic. Who were they? Why was Peter afraid of them? Paul does not clarify, and scholars offer diverse interpretations.

A sympathetic reading might take "those of the circumcision" to refer to unbelieving Jews in Jerusalem. Given the increasingly radical Zealot movement,[4] Peter then feared that news of his fraternization with gentiles would either

---

1. See U. Wilckens, "ὑποκρίνομαι, συνυποκρίνομαι κτλ.," *TDNT* 8:563–66.
2. See the parallelism between shame and condemnation in Sir. 5:14.
3. See BDAG, s.v. "ὑποστέλλω," 2a; Heb. 10:38. Hengel (*Saint Peter*, 59) suggests the possibility of such a reading but dismisses it without giving a reason.
4. See Jewett, "Agitators." For an expansion of Jewett's thesis, see Gibson, *Peter between Jerusalem and Antioch*.

incite militant Jews to cause trouble for the Jerusalem church or jeopardize his own reputation and ministry toward the Jews (2:7–8). Moreover, Peter, the apostle to the circumcision, might not have *fully* understood the implications of the gospel with regard to Jew-gentile relationships.[5] His concern for the work in Jerusalem conflicted with his growing theological understanding. Caught between a rock and a hard place, Peter chose the path of pragmatic expediency rather than theological convictions.

A polemical reading might take "those of the circumcision" to refer to "certain men from James" (2:12) and other Jewish Christians who stressed the necessity of circumcision.[6] Peter feared the opinion of these men; perhaps he did not want to be shamed by them for being a less-than-observant Jew, or he did not want to forfeit his prominent position as missionary to the Jews.[7] He originally received gentile believers "into true fellowship. But now apparently he regarded such liberal conduct as a thing to be ashamed of and to be concealed."[8] Peter then playacted the role of an observant Jew in order to gain the approval of these Jewish Christians. If this reading is right, the language of "hiding and shrinking away" coupled with "fearing the opinion of others" portrays Peter as a moral hypocrite and a disgraceful coward. In seeking to impress people through hypocrisy, Peter was more concerned about his status with men than with the truth of the gospel. Consequently, he stood condemned before God.

Between the above sympathetic and polemical readings, the first reading is stronger in light of Peter's defense of his conduct with Cornelius in Acts 10–11.[9] Nevertheless, Paul does not paint a flattering portrait of Peter. The lack of specific details, coupled with the suggestive language of hypocrisy and fear, presents Peter as a people pleaser—a posture diametrically opposite to Paul's (Gal. 1:10).

3. The public rather than private nature of Paul's rebuke accentuates the sting of shame. Aristotle quotes the proverb "The eyes are the abode of shame" and notes that one feels shame more intensely when the acts that elicit it are in the eyes of others and in public.[10] It is thus significant that Paul uses "I saw" in 2:14. Paul didn't say that he *heard* about Peter's actions or he *knew* about Peter's actions. He *saw* it, but no one else saw it for what it was. Thus, Paul

---

5. Silva, *Interpreting Galatians*, 156.
6. So Burton, *Epistle to the Galatians*, 107. See also the NLT and the NET.
7. Wechsler, *Geschichtsbild und Apostelstreit*, 334.
8. Machen, *Origin of Paul's Religion*, 101.
9. See also Carson, "Mirror-Reading."
10. Aristotle, *Rhet.* 2.6.18, 1384A36. See also Achilles Tatius, *Leuc. Clit.* 2.29: "Shame enters through the eyes."

had to confront Peter "to his face" (2:11), and he had to rebuke him "before the entire church" (2:14). Both Peter and the entire church needed to *see* the sin for what it was. The intensity of Paul's rebuke is multiplied because of Peter's position among the church. Aristotle remarks that people feel shame more intensely before those who admire them.[11] Peter's influence within the Antiochene church was considerable—the other Jewish believers and even Barnabas were misled by him (2:13). Since Peter was highly esteemed within the church, the sting of Paul's rebuke would have been sharply felt.

The Reason for the Rebuke

The textual evidence demonstrates that Galatians 2:11–14 should be read as a shaming rebuke of Peter. But why did Paul shame Peter?

The motive behind Paul's shaming rebuke of Peter has garnered much discussion within the history of the church. Jerome, following Origen and John Chrysostom, argues that the supposed dispute between Paul and Peter was a staged pretense for their respective audiences. Peter knew that the Mosaic law was abrogated, but he was afraid that Jewish Christians would be offended by his actions and consequently leave the faith of Christ. Thus, he withdrew from the gentiles in order to give the pretense that he was an observant Jew. Paul was not flustered by Peter's action, because he understood his good motive and agreed with him. He only pretended to rebuke Peter so that the gentile Christians would not be led astray by Peter's action. This "temporary deception" or noble lie by both apostles served to maintain the faith of both Jewish and gentile Christians.[12]

Augustine had serious misgivings about Jerome's interpretation. He was concerned that Jerome's hermeneutical moves would undermine the authority of Scripture because it allowed deception for noble motives, a case of the ends justifying the means. He therefore rejects Jerome's interpretation, noting that Peter did err and Paul did truly rebuke Peter for his hypocrisy. Calvin and Luther follow Augustine's assessment, and so has the majority of biblical interpreters since then.

What is problematic about Peter's action in Antioch is his about-face, his theological hypocrisy. Peter's initial table fellowship and *subsequent* withdrawal signified that gentile believers were second-class members within the church. Jewish believers were the favored sons; gentile believers were at best on the fringe of the Christian community. By treating gentile believers as secondary participants within the church, Peter implied that he would not

---

11. Aristotle, *Rhet.* 2.6.14–15, 1384A26.
12. Jerome, *Comm. Gal.* 2:11–13 (FC 121:106).

fully recognize them as God's people unless they "became Jews" (ἰουδαΐζω; 2:14).[13] Thus, Paul faults Peter not for observing the Jewish customs but for imposing (ἀναγκάζω) it on the gentiles.[14] In so doing, Peter was not acting according to the truth of the gospel (2:14); his conduct subverted the doctrine of justification by faith. Even though these gentile believers had come to faith in Jesus Christ, they now also had to take up the law to reestablish fellowship with Jewish believers.

Paul is justified in rebuking Peter, for his sin was not trivial. It concerned, as Luther opined, "the most important doctrine of Christianity"—the doctrine of justification by faith.[15] It did not matter if Peter was the chief of the apostles, for a herald's authority was ultimately derived from the true gospel, not vice versa. Thus, anybody, including Paul himself or even "an angel from heaven," who promotes a defective gospel will face God's wrath (1:8). No one, regardless of status, is exempt from discipline.

Paul's Shaming Rebuke of the Galatians

Paul's shaming rebuke of the Galatians is not localized to a singular passage nor limited to a particular rhetorical device. In this section, I examine Paul's shaming rhetoric in three key areas: the epistolary structure of Galatians, his portrayal of the addresses, and his portrayal of the agitators.

Epistolary Structure

The basic Pauline letter form comprises four parts: opening, thanksgiving, body, and closing. While the body is central to determine the rhetorical thrust of the letter, the other three parts are not merely formulaic and superfluous. Paul adapts these conventional elements to suit his rhetorical agenda, so that he shames his audience in the very form of the letter.

The Letter to the Galatians begins with Paul identifying himself as an apostle (1:1). When Paul claims apostolic status in his letters, he often traces that status to the will of God. Galatians is no different in this regard. It is, however, the only Pauline letter that negates the possibility of any human

---

13. Although BDAG, s.v. "ἰουδαΐζω," renders the verb as "live in Judean or Jewish fashion," the context suggests the stronger nuance of "to become a Jew." Josephus uses the verb in this sense when he records how the Roman Metilius, in order not to be killed, promised to "turn Jew [ἰουδαΐζω], and even to be circumcised" (*J.W.* 2.454).

14. The verb ἀναγκάζω (compel) occurs three times in Galatians. In 2:3 the leaders of the Jerusalem church *did not compel* Titus to be circumcised. In 2:14 and 6:12 Peter and the false teachers *compel* the Galatians to adopt Jewish traditions and be circumcised. Through the use of ἀναγκάζω, Paul hints that Peter's actions are similar to the false teachers.

15. *Luther's Works*, 26:114.

source for this calling ("sent not from people nor by a human person," 1:1). This clarification has an apologetic and polemic function. Paul defends his apostolic status against insinuations by the agitators, insisting that he received his commission directly from God without human mediation. At the same time, Paul implicitly rebukes and accuses his readers for forgetting that he is an apostle with divine authorization.

The thanksgiving section typically follows the letter opening. Peter O'Brien notes that this section fulfills several functions: epistolary (introducing the main theme of the letter), pastoral (demonstrating Paul's care for the church), didactic (emphasizing various truths), and paraenetic (exhorting the church toward different ethical imperatives).[16] Thus, the thanksgiving section is not a perfunctory or meaningless device; it sets the overall tone and theme of the letter.

Galatians is striking as there is no thanksgiving section. There is no benediction or thanksgiving for what God has done in the lives of the readers; there is also no prayer of intercession for the readers. Instead, the first Greek word that Paul begins with after the salutation is an exclamation of astonishment ("I am astonished [θαυμάζω]," 1:6). Such an opening projects the stern and dour mood of the letter.[17] There is no thanksgiving section because Paul cannot give thanks for their precarious spiritual state.[18] Instead, the opening section signals "an indignant spirit."[19] The verb θαυμάζω conveys not only astonishment but also hurt and disappointment.

The conclusion of Galatians mirrors the opening, exemplifying the strained relationship between Paul and the readers. Paul does not close with his customary personal greetings. The peace benediction of 6:16 also deviates from Paul's customary practice, for "nowhere else does the apostle give to the peace benediction or any of his other benedictions such a conditional aspect."[20] This conditional element implicitly threatens his readers. They are in danger of receiving a curse (1:8–9), rather than a blessing, if they do not conform to his rule. Paul continues with a rebuke in the next verse ("Finally, let no one cause me trouble," 6:17). They are to stop causing Paul further trouble, the implication being that they have caused him sufficient trouble.[21]

16. O'Brien, *Introductory Thanksgivings*, 261–63.
17. Weima, *Paul the Ancient Letter Writer*, 80–89.
18. Arzt-Grabner, "Paul's Letter Thanksgiving," 156; Lambrecht, "Paul and Epistolary Thanksgiving."
19. John Chrysostom, *Hom. Gal.* on 1:1 (*NPNF¹* 13:1).
20. Weima, "Sincerely, Paul," 317.
21. R. Fung, *Epistle to the Galatians*, 313.

Portrayal of the Galatians

Paul does not paint a positive portrait of the Galatians. In the opening "I am astonished" statement, Paul accuses them of ingratitude toward and betrayal of God. They are fickle, "quickly deserting" (1:6) God without a moment's hesitation. Paul emphasizes their treachery by highlighting what God and Christ have done for the Galatians. God is the one who called them to live in grace (1:6), who gave them the Spirit and worked miracles among them (3:5), who adopted them as sons even though they were formerly slaves (4:6–7), and who took the initiative to effect this transformation (4:9). Christ is the one who died for their sins (1:4), who became a curse so that he might redeem them from the curse of the law (3:13). In light of what God and Christ have done for the Galatians, their "turning back" (4:9) or defection demonstrates a profound lack of gratitude and sense of shame. As Seneca bluntly remarks, "Not to return gratitude for benefits is a disgrace, and the whole world counts it as such."[22] In repudiating the divine benefits they received, the Galatians forsake the Lord and incur shame.

The Galatians are betraying not only God but also Paul, their champion. Paul is the one who fought on their behalf. He stood firm for the gospel so that its truth might remain *for them* (2:5). He endures persecutions for the gospel (5:11), bearing its marks on his body (6:17). However, the loyalties of the Galatians toward Paul stand only insofar as he is present among them. As soon as his back is turned, they let others court them (4:18). Paul emphasizes the intensity of the betrayal he feels by comparing their past attitude toward him with the present. With a series of emotional arguments,[23] Paul rehearses their former ties of friendship (4:13–15). When Paul first preached the gospel to them, they did not treat him with contempt or scorn even though he was ill. Instead, they welcomed him as a messenger from God. They would have torn out their eyes and given them to him if they could. Given this history, Paul plaintively asks, "Where then is your former graciousness and willingness to be a blessing to me?" (4:15).

Paul's portrait of betrayal shames his readers. In the ancient world, betrayal of friendship ties is shameful.[24] But if the betrayal of friends is shameful, how much more the betrayal of one's family members?[25] Paul is more than their friend. He is their brother (1:11; 3:15; 4:12, 28, 31; 5:11, 13; 6:1)—a true

---

22. Seneca, *Ben.* 3.1.1.

23. See Martin, "Voice of Emotion."

24. Euripides, *Med.* 501; *Suppl.* 296; Sophocles, *Phil.* 906. Athenaeus (*Deipn.* 15.695C–696A) records the following Athenian drinking poem: "Anyone who refuses to betray a friend has tremendous honor among both mortals and gods, in my opinion."

25. Euripides, *Med.* 166–67, 695; *Hipp.* 1290–91; *Orest.* 499.

brother, unlike the false brothers who intend to make them slaves (2:4). He is also their mother, and they his dear children (4:19). He suffered the pains of childbirth when he first delivered them into the faith. Paul shames them now, however, for making him undergo the anguish of childbirth "again" (4:19).

Apart from betrayal, Paul also rebukes the Galatians for being foolish ("O you foolish Galatians," 3:1; "Are you so foolish?" 3:3). The emotive particle "O" and the double use of "foolish" (ἀνόητος) only imbue the rebuke with more bite. The foolish are not ignorant. They are unwilling to use their mental faculties to understand; thus they lack discernment and judgment.[26] They have no sense of shame, and they do not respect the proper boundaries of the community.[27] Thus, Paul rebukes the Galatians for blurring the boundaries between a community circumscribed by allegiance to Christ and a community circumscribed by adherence to the Mosaic law. Fools also fail to remember what they ought to know, or they fail to draw out the right implications of what they already know. Thus, Paul reminds the Galatians in exasperation, "As we have said before, so now I say *again*" (1:9); "Do you want to be enslaved to them *again*?" (4:9); "Do not be subject *again* to a yoke of slavery" (5:1); "*Again* I declare" (5:3); "I warn you, as I did *before*" (5:21). Finally, fools labor in vain. Thus, Paul laments that their defection will invalidate the Spirit's work in their lives (3:4). But not only will what they have experienced be in vain; Paul's labor on their behalf would also be "wasted" (4:11).[28] This injustice to Paul would be all the more egregious since Paul is one who does not wish to run his race "in vain" (2:2). In calling the Galatians foolish, Paul warns that their end result is not honor but shame. For "the wise inherit honor, but fools get only shame" (Prov. 3:35).

Portrayal of the Agitators

Paul portrays those who are attempting to sway the Galatians in an extremely negative light. He does not name them so as to caricature them as wicked stereotypes.[29] They are "troublemakers" (οἱ ταράσσοντες, 1:7; 5:10),

---

26. L&N, 32.50, s.v. "ἀνόητος."

27. The word "foolish" is generally contrasted with "wise" (σοφός) or "prudent" (σώφρων). From our survey of the Greco-Roman background of shame in chapter 2, we have seen that "prudence" or "temperance" (σωφροσύνη) is closely linked to a proper sense of shame. The prudent person respects the proper social boundaries and thus preserves his honor. The fool, on the other hand, is shameless. He does not show proper concern for his honor nor for the honor of the group to which he belongs.

28. John Chrysostom (*Hom. Gal.* on 4:11 [*NPNF*[1] 13:31]) notes that Paul crafted 4:11 "so as thoroughly to shame them, . . . saying, as it were, make not vain the labors which have cost me sweat and pain."

29. Marshall, *Enmity in Corinth*, 341–48.

"agitators" (οἱ ἀναστατοῦντες, 5:12), shadowy characters who pervert the gospel (1:7) and infiltrate the community so as to enslave its members (2:4). They use witchcraft, seeking "to cast an evil eye" (3:1) on the gullible readers.[30] They harbor ulterior motives and hidden agendas (4:17), concerned only about their own honor (6:12). They are children of Hagar, the bondwoman (4:29). They are morally depraved, hypocrites. They advocate circumcision but do not keep the law themselves (6:13). They prevent the Galatians from being persuaded by the truth (5:7), they act against God (5:8), they exert a corrupting and perverse influence (5:9), they are under God's curse (1:8–9), and they will finally be punished by God (5:10). Moreover, Paul crudely insults them with the sarcastic comment "I wish those who are troubling you would go so far as to castrate themselves" (5:12). Paul's opposition to these people is clear, for he vilifies them.

The vilification of one's opponents is a common polemical device.[31] The purpose of these utterances is not so much to denote as to connote, not so much to describe as to evaluate—to signify that those described are opponents and should not be trusted. The "perlocutionary aim . . . [is] primarily not to characterize the adversaries, but to put pressure on the readers/audience to dissociate themselves from them and reaffirm their allegiance to the author's position."[32] Paul's negative portrayal hammers a wedge between the Galatians and the agitators, forcing them to reconsider their opinion of the troublemakers. In essence, Paul asks his readers: Why do you believe such reprehensible people? Why are you enamored of them? Do you not know that they do not have your best interests at heart? Why would you want to be associated with such losers? Do you not know that you will be shamed if you continue to be associated with such shameful people? Do you not know that you will ultimately be cursed if you continue to identify with them and follow their teaching?

Through the negative caricature of the agitators, Paul seeks two interrelated goals: to influence the Galatians to reject the agitators and their gospel *and* to cleave to him and his gospel. Persuading the Galatians to reidentify with him cannot be separated from the task of alienating them from the agitators. But the focus of reidentifying with Paul is not so much on him as a person as on his gospel and his Lord. Thus, it must be remembered that "severing the Galatians from the Judaizers and regaining their loyalty should not be

30. Although Paul's usage here is probably metaphorical, the reference to a word associated with sorcery is intended to portray the agitators in a negative light. See Tolmie, *Persuading the Galatians*, 104.

31. See Johnson, "New Testament's Anti-Jewish Slander."

32. Du Toit, "Vilification," 412.

seen as a goal in itself, but as a means of regaining their allegiance to the one and only true gospel."[33] Allegiance to Paul is allegiance to his gospel and the Christ of the gospel.

Understanding Paul's Shaming Rhetoric in Galatians

Let me draw some conclusions regarding Paul's use of shame in Galatians.

Rationale for Public Censure

Galatians explicitly affirms that Paul shamed Peter in front of the entire church. The question naturally arises: Why did Paul not counsel Peter in private according to the Jesus tradition found in Matthew 18? Was he not familiar with it? Rudolf Bultmann famously quipped, "Jesus' teaching is— to all intents and purposes—irrelevant for Paul."[34] David Wenham, however, argues that there is cumulative evidence to indicate Paul's knowledge of the Jesus traditions. In particular, he notes the presence of common ideas and vocabulary between 1 Corinthians 5:3–5 and Matthew 18:15–20.[35] If we assume that Galatians was written before 1 Corinthians 5,[36] we can conclude that Paul was familiar with the Jesus tradition regarding church discipline, at least by the time of writing Galatians.

The text in Galatians 2 does not mention whether Paul first approached Peter in confidence. Perhaps he did; perhaps he did not. But given the gravity of the situation, a private rebuke would be insufficient. For Peter's sin was not private, known only to a few persons. No, it was committed openly, and its pernicious effects embroiled the entire church. According to Paul, "the rest of the Jewish Christians joined Peter in his hypocrisy, so that even Barnabas was led astray by their hypocrisy" (2:13). In order to arrest the leavening effects of sin (cf. 5:9) and restore the entire community to health, Paul had to confront Peter openly. A public sin that is known to the entire church *must* be publicly rebuked so that everyone, both the offender and the church, will receive instruction and be put right (cf. 1 Tim. 5:20).[37]

Appeals to Logos, Pathos, and Ethos

As I noted in chapter 2, Aristotle considers appeals to pathos to be ineffective without concomitant appeals to logos and ethos. Since shaming refutation

---

33. Du Toit, "Alienation and Re-identification," 280 (italics removed).

34. Bultmann, "Significance of the Historical Jesus," 223. More recently, Fredriksen (*From Jesus to Christ*, 174) writes, "About Jesus of Nazareth Paul evinces little interest."

35. Wenham, *Paul*, 210–13.

36. So F. Watson, *Paul, Judaism, and the Gentiles*, 59.

37. Augustine, *Exp. Gal.* 15.8–9; Calvin, *Institutes* 4.12.3.

is primarily an appeal to pathos, it also requires the other two modes of persuasion in order to strengthen its overall rhetorical force.

Paul's appeal to logos in support of his shaming refutation is clear. He provides examples (e.g., Abraham), definitions (e.g., seed in 3:16), contrasts (e.g., curse/blessing, flesh/spirit, law/Christ, slavery/freedom, bondwoman/freewoman), and logical deductions. The frequent use of the logical conjunctions "for" (γάρ) and "because" (ὅτι) also signals the use of enthymemes.

Effective shaming rebuke also requires a solid ethos or unimpeachable character on the part of the speaker. The stronger the rebuke, the greater the need for a respectable ethos.[38] The speaker must establish credibility so that the audience will give the arguments a fair hearing. In Galatians, Paul establishes his credentials masterfully, not least in the opening verse, where he emphasizes his divine call (1:1). Subsequent moves in the letter refine his ethos. For example, he asserts that he is not a people pleaser (1:10); he notes that believers praised God because of him (1:24); he claims that the pillars of the Jerusalem church gave him the right hand of fellowship (2:9); he reminds the Galatians that they once welcomed him as an angel of God, as Christ Jesus himself (4:14); he invites his readers to imitate him (4:12–20); and he maintains that he is one who boasts in the cross (6:11–17). Paul's defense of his character serves not so much to answer the accusations lobbed against him as to present a foil demonstrating the shameful character of the agitators. More importantly, Paul's defense presents him as "a paradigm of the gospel of Christian freedom which he seeks to persuade his readers to reaffirm in the face of the threat presented by the troublemakers."[39]

Harsh and Gentle

The overall rhetorical flow of Galatians affirms that Paul does not only use harsh rhetoric. Like a skillful doctor, Paul balances his shaming refutation with gentle words so that the bitter pill of correction is more easily swallowed. He "[varies] his discourse according to the need of his disciples, at one time using knife and cautery, at another, applying mild remedies."[40]

In Galatians, Paul's gentle words comprise statements that demonstrate his genuine concern for his readers. He is the one who stands resolutely against even one as prominent as Cephas so that the truth of the gospel might remain with them (2:14). He is deeply concerned about their spiritual well-being (4:11, 20). He does not flatter them; instead, he speaks the truth to them even

---

38. Sampley, "Paul's Frank Speech," 299.
39. Lyons, *Pauline Autobiography*, 171.
40. John Chrysostom, *Hom. Gal.* on 1:1–3 (*NPNF*[1] 13:1).

at the risk of being misinterpreted as an enemy (4:16).[41] He is their spiritual mother, suffering the throes of labor until Christ is formed in them (4:19). He takes no pleasure in shaming them. He is truly perplexed about their condition and wishes that the circumstances were different so that he could change the tone of his voice (4:20). John Chrysostom, who is well versed in ancient rhetoric, senses Paul's concern, pain, desperation, and tears in this last verse. He writes, "Paul admonished them sharply, and endeavored to shame them, then in turn soothed them, and lastly he wept. And this weeping is not only a reproof but a blandishment; it does not exasperate like reproof, nor relax like indulgent treatment, but is a mixed remedy, and of great efficacy in the way of exhortation."[42] By expressing genuine concern for his readers, Paul demonstrates that he does not hold them in contempt. This mitigates the likelihood that his shaming refutation can be misconstrued as a humiliating attack. Moreover, Paul declares that they have not personally wronged him (4:20). Thus, his sharp rebuke does not arise from a desire for revenge but from genuine concern for them.

Rationale for Shaming Refutation

In Galatians, Paul shames his readers not for their moral failings but for their theological folly concerning the heart of the gospel—justification by faith (2:15–21). He does not shame them because they are ignorant of the gospel. He shames them because they *deliberately* reject the true gospel, denying the spiritual progress they have made and failing to recognize the implications of their actions. He shames them because their very actions bring them to the precipice of damnation, to apostasy. Given the particularly disastrous consequences of their belief structure, Paul dare not just apply logical, dispassionate arguments.[43] He must pull out all the stops and engage them in the core of their being—he must engage them with heated emotion. Thus, he shames them, rebukes them, pleads with them, and vilifies the agitators.

Mechanism of Shaming Refutation

Paul uses shame as a salutary tool so that the Galatians are able to perceive accurately their predicament. He wants to transform their minds so that they are capable of self-testing, self-examination, and self-reflection. There is a

41. Well-intentioned rebuke can be easily misinterpreted. See Plutarch, *Adul. amic.* 12 (56a–b); Cicero, *Amic.* 24.89.
42. John Chrysostom, *Hom. Gal.* on 4:20 (NPNF[1] 13:33). His reference to "mixed remedy" echoes the "mixed method" of praise and blame in Philodemus, Plutarch, and Dio Chrysostom.
43. Paul's rationale here parallels Socrates's shaming rebuke of Callicles, for both the Galatians and Callicles held faulty belief structures that lead to disastrous consequences.

heavy cognitive component in Paul's shaming refutation. Paul describes the Galatians as "foolish" (ἀνόητος, 3:1)—those who lack a discerning mind.[44] Paul also corrects their thinking with cognitive verbs: "I want you to know" (γνωρίζω, 1:11); "you know" (γινώσκω, 3:7; 4:9; οἶδα, 2:16; 4:8, 13). Paul moreover expresses confidence that they will eventually "hold the right perspective" (φρονέω, 5:10). This overall cognitive emphasis suggests that Paul's shaming refutation seeks to transform the mind.

The purpose of such transformation is to make the mind capable of self-reflection. In Galatians, Paul's shaming rebuke challenges his readers to reconsider their preconceived notions of identity and behavior. It compels them to see themselves not from the agitator's perspective but from God's. Paul wants them to realize that their desire to be circumcised is fundamentally incompatible with their identity as children of God, as children of Abraham, and as those who belong to Christ (3:29). For any attempt to be justified through the law invalidates the grace of God and the significance of Christ's death on the cross (2:21). Within the divine court of opinion, the Galatians are shameworthy. Thus, they should reject the teachings of the agitators; they should reaffirm their commitment to Christ and the truth of the gospel.

Goal of Shaming Refutation

Paul uses shame as a tool to transform the mind so that it is capable of self-evaluation, but the ultimate goal of Paul's shaming refutation is to transform the perspective of the Galatians so that their identity and behavior are firmly rooted in the crucified Messiah. In essence, the goal of Paul's shaming refutation is Christic formation. This can be inferred as follows. The body of the Letter to the Galatians can be structurally divided into two major sections: a rebuke section (1:6–4:11) followed by a request section (4:12–6:10).[45] Within this framework, the imperative "become like me" (4:12) is critical. It sits at the turning point as the letter pivots into the request section. Moreover, it is the first imperative directed to the Galatians in the entire letter. This suggests that the goal of Paul's shaming refutation is for the Galatians to imitate him.

The imitation of Paul is not so much a call to be loyal to him as a call to be loyal to his crucified Lord, for the ethos and perspective of Paul, which the Galatians are to imitate, has already been alluded to in the autobiographical sections of the prior chapters. He is one who is loyal to the truth of the gospel (2:5, 14). He is one who is united with the crucified Messiah (2:19); his

---

44. The adjective ἀνόητος is the alpha privative or opposite of "having the mind" (τὸ νοῦν ἔχον). See Plato, *Tim.* 30B.

45. Hansen, *Abraham in Galatians*, 27–54.

identity and behavior are conformed to the cruciform image of Christ (2:20). Thus, Paul's call for the Galatians to imitate him is a call to be conformed to the image of Christ, both in their thinking and in their doing. Paul uses shame as a tool to remind the Galatians that since they have been united with Christ in baptism, they are to put on Christ (3:27)—to understand the significance of the cross and to follow the pattern of his life until Christ is formed in them (4:19).

First Corinthians

First Corinthians describes a divisive church with factions running along socioeconomic and party lines (1:10; 3:4–5; 11:18–19; 12:25). Although the majority of its members came from the lower classes, a few were wealthy, influential, and of noble birth (1:26). Since the "haves" sought to solidify their social identity by highlighting their wealth, knowledge, status, and spiritual gifts, they had no qualms about bringing lawsuits against their Christian brothers (6:1–11) and shaming the "have-nots" in the Lord's Supper (11:22).

Not only were there internal divisions within the community, but there was also tension between the church and its founding apostle. Some within the community sat in judgment of Paul (4:18; 9:3) and questioned his apostleship. They considered his rhetorical skills weak (2:1–5), doubted his reliability, and were uninspired by his physical presence. They thought his gospel and preaching to be rudimentary, like milk for babes (3:2). Finally, they questioned Paul's prophetic authority (14:37–38). These criticisms undermine not only Paul's authority as a model of imitation but also his authority to instruct.

One theme that recurs throughout the letter is the community's arrogance and complacency regarding ethical issues. This attitude probably began with several individual leaders but quickly spread throughout the community. Their reliance on worldly wisdom and their claims to a higher spiritual existence led to self-sufficiency instead of dependence on Christ. They were hubristic, believing they had the freedom to do anything without compunction (6:12).

Faced with these challenges, Paul forcefully presents a powerful theology of the cross and offers the cruciform pattern of Christ as the paradigm of the Christian life. Moreover, he employs the rhetoric of shame as a pedagogical tool to transform the mind of his readers into the mind of Christ. As 1 Corinthians is the only letter in which Paul explicitly states his intention to shame his readers (6:5; 15:34), it deserves special attention in our analysis of Paul's shaming rhetoric. I examine how and why Paul explicitly and implicitly shames his readers, paying particular attention to 4:14; 5:9; and 6:5. A summary concludes our analysis of 1 Corinthians.

"I Write These Things Not to Shame You" (4:14)

Paul in 4:14 states, "I write these things not with the intent to shame [ἐντρέπω] you." At first blush, Paul's demurral is surprising since the catalog of afflictions in 4:8–13, with its dripping irony and sarcasm, appears designed to shame his readers. Moreover, the very fact that Paul needs to make an explicit denial is evidence that he believes his response will shame them. The argument that Paul's denial indicates his reluctance to "demolish their self-respect" or "crush them with self-recrimination" is not fully satisfactory by itself.[46] After all, Paul is clearly not shy to shame them explicitly in 6:5 and 15:34. But if Paul is not afraid to shame his readers in subsequent chapters, why does it appear that he is reluctant to do so in 4:14? This question necessitates another look at 4:14.

My exegesis unfolds in three parts. First, a contextual and lexical examination of Paul's shame language in 4:14 suggests that Paul distinguishes between a rhetoric of shame that destroys and a rhetoric that builds. Second, the "not . . . but" (οὐ . . . ἀλλά) construction of 4:14 does not mean that "shame" and "admonition" are polar opposites. Rather, Paul advocates the use of shame as a pedagogical tool for admonition. Third, the goal of Paul's admonition is the transformation of the Corinthians' mind into the mind of Christ.

Two Uses of Shame

Paul's shame language in 4:14 must be understood contextually and lexically. In doing so, I propose that Paul differentiates between two uses of shame: a rhetoric of shame that tears down and a rhetoric that builds up. Specifically, there is a rhetoric of shame that the wandering sophists employ and that Paul repudiates. Nevertheless, there is also a rhetoric of shame that a loving father might employ to admonish his children; this is the rhetoric that Paul employs. This proposal will be borne out by a contextual reading of 4:14 and supported by a brief lexical analysis of Paul's shame vocabulary.

Stephen Pogoloff notes that the rhetorical situation that Paul confronts in 1 Corinthians 1–4 was a community shaped by the social norms of the visiting sophists.[47] Imitating the sophists' passion for ambition, the Corinthians prized competitive rhetoric, which focused not only on self-praise but also on

46. Contra Thiselton, *First Epistle to the Corinthians*, 369.
47. Pogoloff, *Logos and Sophia*.

the abuse and dishonor of one's competitor.[48] Moreover, the Corinthians, with their penchant for litigation (6:1–11), would surely be familiar with the use of invectives and emotional ploys to decimate the reputation and character of one's opponents.[49] Seen within this zero-sum framework where one won at the expense of others, Paul's defense of his apostleship and rebuke of the Corinthians could be perceived as an invective that attempts to ridicule and humiliate them. Paul's denial in 4:14 should then be understood as a refusal to adopt the combative rhetoric of the sophists. He does not intend to use the rhetoric of shame the same way the sophists did—that is, to destroy and humiliate. But is there something more to his understanding of the rhetoric of shame? I think there is.

Paul's attitude toward the rhetoric of shame is consonant with his attitude toward rhetoric in general. In 1 Corinthians 1–4, Paul both opposes *and* uses rhetoric. Paul's statements that his preaching was "not with eloquent wisdom" (1:17), "not in lofty words or wisdom" (2:1), and "not in plausible words of wisdom" (2:4) should not be construed to mean that Paul was a bumbling orator, that his preaching lacked persuasion, or that he did not adopt a communicative strategy. Rather, Michael Bullmore rightly argues that "it [is] against a particular strain of Greco-Roman rhetoric that Paul [sets] forth his own statement of rhetorical style."[50] Paul disowns the bombastic rhetoric and stylistic virtuosity that elevated the orator at the expense of the message. He instead adopts an unadorned style that draws no attention to itself and serves to highlight the message of the cross. In a similar manner, Paul both opposes *and* uses the rhetoric of shame. Just as he repudiates sophistic practices in 1 Corinthians 1–4, so also he rejects the sophistic rhetoric of shame. Nevertheless, just as Paul does not completely disavow rhetoric, so also he does not completely disavow a rhetoric of shame if it is used to promote the message of the cross.

Apart from this contextual evidence, there is also lexical evidence that Paul distinguishes between two rhetorics of shame: a rhetoric that exalts oneself at the expense of others and a rhetoric that challenges others to see the error of their ways in light of the message of the cross. The verb generally rendered as "to shame" in 4:14 is ἐντρέπω. This verb and its nominal form ἐντροπή are not

---

48. Schmitz ("Second Sophistic," 309) writes, "One-upmanship was a standard attribute of sophists, and exposing a rival as ignorant or putting an attacker to shame with a witty and devastating retort was part of a sophist's job."

49. The *Rhetorica ad Herennium* suggests that it is appropriate at the beginning of a speech to stir up "hatred, unpopularity, or contempt [on our adversaries] . . . by adducing some base, highhanded, treacherous, cruel, impudent, malicious, or shameful act of theirs" (1.8).

50. Bullmore, *St. Paul's Theology of Rhetorical Style*, 224.

common in Paul's extant literature (ἐντρέπω 3x; ἐντροπή 2x).⁵¹ His favorite word for shame is the αἰσχ- word group (αἰσχρός 4x; αἰσχρότης 1x; αἰσχρολογία 1x; ἀνεπαίσχυντος 1x; αἰσχύνω 2x; αἰσχύνη 2x; ἐπαισχύνομαι 5x; and καταισχύνω 10x). Richard Trench remarks that ἐντρέπω differs from the αἰσχύνω word group in that the former "conveys at least a hint of that change of conduct, that return of a man upon himself, which a wholesome shame brings with it in him who is its subject."⁵² This sense may arise from the word's etymology (τρέπω means "to turn"), but it is doubtful if this sense is inherent in the word since the ἐντρέπω and αἰσχύνω word groups are used interchangeably in the LXX.⁵³ Nevertheless, Paul's usage of ἐντρέπω/ἐντροπή suggests that he might attribute to them the positive valence that Trench commends. Whenever Paul explicitly shames an individual or calls on the church to shame an individual as part of a disciplinary measure, he uses the ἐντρέπω rather than the αἰσχύνω word group (1 Cor. 6:5; 15:34; 2 Thess. 3:14; Titus 2:8). In no instance does Paul use the αἰσχύνω word group when he shames, or calls on the church to shame, others.

When, however, Paul describes the negative actions of his readers in shaming others, he uses καταισχύνω.⁵⁴ Thus, "any man who prays or prophesies with something on his head shames [καταισχύνω] his head, but any woman who prays or prophesies with her head unveiled shames [καταισχύνω] her head" (1 Cor. 11:4–5). The classic example is 1 Corinthians 11:22, where Paul castigates the Corinthians for shaming (καταισχύνω) those who have nothing. The sample size is admittedly small; nevertheless, these examples suggest that it is Paul's idiolect that the ἐντρέπω word group connotes a constructive and positive role for shame.⁵⁵

If Paul's use of ἐντρέπω in 4:14 indicates a constructive form of shame, how then do we make sense of the negating "not"? The clause "I am writing these things *not* [οὐκ] *to shame you positively* [ἐντρέπω]" appears to contradict my understanding of Paul's rhetoric of shame, as Paul seems to repudiate even a positive use of shame. It may be possible to explain this negating clause as an example of irony and sarcasm: Paul intends to shame his readers, even though he formally denies it. Nevertheless, the following "but" (ἀλλά) clause discounts this possibility. There is a better answer, and for this we need to examine the "not . . . but" (οὐ . . . ἀλλά) construction in 4:14.

---

51. The statistics in this section are based on the entire Pauline corpus of thirteen letters.
52. Trench, *Synonyms of the New Testament*, 69.
53. See Pss. 34:4, 26; 39:15; 43:16; 68:20; 69:3; 70:24; 108:29; Isa. 41:11; 44:11; 45:16–17 (LXX).
54. Paul also describes God's shaming judgment with καταισχύνω (see 1 Cor. 1:27). In using the same verb for the Corinthians and God, Paul may suggest that the Corinthians are usurping God's prerogative to judge.
55. So also M. Silva, "αἰσχύνη, κτλ," *NIDNTTE* 1:185.

The "Not . . . But" Construction: Shame as a Pedagogical Tool

In 4:14 Paul states, "I write these things *not* [οὐ] with the intent to shame you, *but* [ἀλλά] with the intent to admonish you as my beloved children." The "not . . . but" construction here does not mean that "to shame" (ἐντρέπω) and "to admonish" (νουθετέω) are polar opposites. While the construction frequently pits the two phrases as antithetical, it can also express a comparison ("not primarily X, but Y") "in which the first element is not entirely negated, but only toned down."[56] The "but" phrase is clearly emphasized but not at the expense of the "not," especially when the first element supports the second. In 4:14 the "not . . . but" construction clearly highlights the importance of admonition vis-à-vis shaming. This, however, does not mean that shaming is completely negated; it is only made subservient to admonition. Paul does write in part to shame his readers; nevertheless, that shaming rhetoric must serve the higher goal of admonition. In other words, *Paul repudiates any shaming that does not undergird the task of admonition, but he supports any that does.*

My reading of 1 Corinthians 4:14 is confirmed in 2 Thessalonians, a letter written within a few years of 1 Corinthians and written in Corinth. In 2 Thessalonians 3:14–15, Paul uses the same two lexemes as 1 Corinthians 4:14—ἐντρέπω and νουθετέω. He directs the church to expel refractory members of the community *so that they might be ashamed* (ἐντρέπω). Note that there is no ambiguity regarding the intention to shame here. Nevertheless, in their shaming, the community is not to regard such members as enemies but to admonish (νουθετέω) them as believers. Both 2 Thessalonians 3 and 1 Corinthians 4 therefore call for a rhetoric of shame, but a rhetoric that serves as a pedagogical tool to admonish.

The line between rebuke and ridicule is thin. Those who are shamed can easily misinterpret the blunt frankness of genuine friends. Consequently, Paul needs to clarify the intent of his shaming rhetoric lest he be misconstrued as intending to humiliate his readers.[57] He needs to clarify that the rhetoric he uses is ultimately for their good, for building them up and not tearing down (cf. 2 Cor. 10:8; 13:10). If he did not do so, his rhetoric of shame would only humiliate; it would not instruct and admonish.[58]

---

56. BDF §448(1). BDF gives the following examples: Mark 9:37; Matt. 10:20; John 12:44; Acts 5:4. Other examples include 1 Cor. 1:17; 2 Cor. 2:4, 5; 7:12.

57. Frank speech may be misinterpreted as capricious fault-finding rather than admonition. See Plutarch, *Adul. amic.* 26 (66e).

58. Admonition differs from humiliation. See *Gnomologium Byzantium* 59: "Admonition [τὸ νουθετεῖν] differs greatly from insults. For the former is gentle and friendly, while the latter is harsh and insolent. The former corrects those who sin, but the latter merely censures" (Wachsmuth, *Studien zu den griechischen Florilegien*, 176).

Appropriating the Mind of Christ

If we are correct that the rhetoric of shame serves as a pedagogical tool for admonition, what is its goal? The verb νουθετέω (to admonish) derives from νοῦν τίθημι, meaning "to impart a mind or understanding" or "to put in the right mind." The reference to mind (νοῦς) is illuminating since the word has appeared before in 1 Corinthians.

The first occurrence is in 1:10, where Paul rebukes the Corinthians for their divisions and quarrels (1:10–11) and exhorts them to be in agreement, that "you might be united in the same mind [νοῦς] and in the same purpose" (1:10). The divisions within the community reflect their lack of a common mind within the body of Christ with the result that Christ is divided (1:13). The fragmented minds of the Corinthians are to be replaced by a common mind, the singular mind of Christ. This notion is already hinted at in 1:9, where Paul remarks that they were called into fellowship with Christ (1:9; cf. also 10:15–16). Paul's use of fellowship (κοινωνία) language evokes the Greco-Roman understanding of friendship,[59] a concept in which friends hold all things in common.[60] Friendship is life together, and the unity between friends is so intimate that a friend is considered another self.[61] Friends are of one soul and heart.[62] Friends share the same mind and the same frame of reference.[63] Thus, if the Corinthian believers have been called into fellowship with Christ, they must exhibit the same mind and same frame of reference as Christ. That is, they must adopt the cruciform mind of Christ.

The second explicit mention of "mind" (νοῦς) is in 2:16. Here Paul claims that those without the Spirit are not able to know the things of God. Believers, however, have the "mind of Christ" (νοῦς Χριστοῦ) so that they are able to know the plan of God as encapsulated in the gospel. This verse therefore affirms the normativity of the mind of Christ for the Christian community. It seems very likely, then, that this verse relates back to the first reference of mind in 1:10, clarifying that "the same mind" the Corinthians are to adopt in 1:10 is the mind of Christ in 2:16.[64]

The word "mind" (νοῦς) does not just denote the ability of thought; it is the "constellation of thoughts and assumptions which makes up the con-

---

59. Aristotle, *Eth. nic.* 8.12.1, 1161B: "All friendship [φιλία] . . . involves community [κοινωνία]."
60. Iamblichus, *Vit. Pyth.* 19.
61. Aristotle, *Eth. nic.* 9.4.5, 1166A.
62. Aristotle, *Eth. nic.* 9.8.2, 1168B.
63. Cicero, *Planc.* 5; *Amic.* 4,15.
64. So Jewett, *Paul's Anthropological Terms*, 377–78.

sciousness of the person and acts as the agent of rational discernment and communication."[65] It is the mode of thought, framework, belief structure, and moral consciousness that provides the criteria for judgment and actions. In remarking that believers have the "mind of Christ," Paul communicates that the mind the Spirit inculcates in the life of the community is the cruciform pattern of Christ. The mind of *Christ* does not center on special knowledge, mystical thoughts, or ecstatic experiences. It instead focuses on displaying the lifestyle of a crucified Christ or Messiah, since all major references to Christ so far in the letter have been that of a crucified Christ (1:17, 23–24, 30; 2:2). It calls for giving up one's rights, putting to death one's selfish ambitions, humbling oneself, and serving others so that the body may be built up. It is a life characterized by self-giving love in which power is mediated through weakness; it is a life transformed by the cross.

The next occurrence of a word that is related to the νοῦς (mind) lexeme is "admonish" (νουθετέω) in 4:14. The word is used here "to depict the pedagogical task of putting persons in the right mind,"[66] and there is little doubt that the right mind the Corinthians are to adopt is the mind of Christ mentioned in 2:16. After developing a robust theology of the cross centered on the cruciform mind of Christ, Paul concludes 1 Corinthians 1–4 by reminding them that he has written all these things to admonish them, to put them in the right mind of Christ. The "mind of Christ" is available to the community by the Holy Spirit; nevertheless, the Corinthians must cultivate and adopt the cruciform pattern of Christ in their communal lives, in their interactions with one another. As a loving father, Paul helps the Corinthians in this process by instructing and admonishing them.

Paul's rhetoric of shame plays a fundamental role in his admonition and transformation of their minds into the mind of Christ. The situation of the Corinthians has become so deplorable that Paul's language cannot just provide information. Rather, it must challenge them at a personal level. It is in this regard that the verb "admonish" (νουθετέω) differs from "teach" (διδάσκω). The latter's "primary effect is on the intellect"; the former "describes an effect on the will and disposition, and it presupposes an opposition which has to be overcome."[67] Instead of plain speech, Paul uses the forceful language of shame to compel his readers not to read the text as bland information. Rather, they are to sit up and take notice as his words pierce their hearts. Given their narcissistic tendencies and selfish ambitions, it is

---

65. Jewett, *Paul's Anthropological Terms*, 450.
66. Jewett, *Paul's Anthropological Terms*, 380.
67. J. Behm, "νουθετέω, νουθεσία," *TDNT* 4:1019.

not enough for them to know that they have done wrong; they need to be shaken from their complacency.[68]

"Do Not Associate with Sexually Immoral People" (5:9)

First Corinthians 5 describes a situation in which a man has an ongoing sexual relationship with his father's wife (5:1). This practice was not only strictly forbidden in the Old Testament (Lev. 18:7–8) but was also considered repulsive in the Roman world.[69] Instead of grieving over the sin, the community was "proud" and "boastful" (1 Cor. 5:2, 6). They believed that the Spirit had lifted them above the earthly things of the world. They boasted in their freedom, considering such sexual immorality to be of no consequence to their new plane of existence.

Paul castigates the church for their moral apathy and pronounces a prophetic judgment on the man who committed the immoral act. When the community is gathered together with Paul in the Spirit, they are to judge this person with the power of the Lord (5:4) and hand the individual to Satan. This cryptic judgment probably means that the individual is to be expelled from the community (5:2, 7, 13), "putting him outside the sphere of God's protection within the church and leaving him exposed to the Satanic forces of evil in hopes that the experience would cause him to repent and return to the fellowship of the church."[70] Paul explains this judgment by clarifying an earlier letter he had written to them (5:9–13). The community is not to mingle or associate indiscriminately with any so-called brothers or sisters who are sexually immoral or greedy, or who are idolaters, revilers, drunkards, or swindlers; they are not even to eat with them (5:11).[71] Such sins cannot be taken lightly since those who commit them will not inherit the kingdom of God (6:9–10).

Paul exhorts the church to expel the individual who committed the immoral act in order to protect the church from slander by outsiders (5:1) and from the corrupting influence of the sin (5:6). More importantly, the intent of this action is redemptive. The proximate purpose of the expulsion is shame, but the ultimate purpose is salvation on the day of the Lord. The intent of the expulsion is to shame primarily the individual and secondarily the com-

---

68. Cf. Quintilian, *Inst.* 6.1.8: "Emotional appeals are necessary if truth, justice, and the common good cannot be secured by other means."

69. Cicero, *Clu.* 5.12–6.15; Martial, *Epigrams* 4.16; Gaius, *Institutes* 1.63.

70. South, *Disciplinary Practices in Pauline Texts*, 43.

71. The sins mentioned in 5:11 parallel the list of vices in Deuteronomy that warrant exclusion from the covenant community. See Rosner, *Paul, Scripture, and Ethics*, 69–70.

munity. The sinning individual is explicitly shamed as he is ostracized by his social group (cf. 2 Thess. 3:14); the community is implicitly shamed as Paul rebukes them for condoning this sin. The shame that the individual and the community experiences should lead them to repent of their sins. As they are humbled, the individual and the community learn that their boasting is not good (5:6). Instead of boasting in themselves, they are to boast only in the Lord (1:30). The anticipated result of the discipline is the salvation of the *spirit* as the *flesh* is destroyed (5:5). The salvific purpose extends not only to the individual but also to the community since the community is complicit in the sin of the offender. In other words, the flesh-spirit language references both individual and community.

The flesh-spirit (σάρξ-πνεῦμα) language in 5:5 recalls the fleshly-spiritual (σάρκινος, σαρκικός-πνευματικός) language in 3:1, for this is the only other place where flesh-spirit language is used with reference to the Corinthians. The Corinthians consider themselves *spiritual*, but their thinking and behavior demonstrate that they are only *fleshly* (3:3). The sexual immorality of the individual in 1 Corinthians 5 and the community's complacency regarding it further prove that they are indeed fleshly. If the link between 5:5 and 3:1 holds, then the flesh that is to be destroyed in 5:5 is not the man's physical flesh or body but the individual's and the community's fleshly stance of self-sufficiency and self-congratulation. The spirit that is saved is the individual's and the community's spiritual stance in orientation to God. The spirit that is saved is the spirit that enables them to be spiritual rather than fleshly, the spirit that enables them to discern the things of God and grasp the cruciform mind of Christ (2:10–16). Paul highlights the cruciform pattern of Christ in 1 Corinthians 5. Christ, after all, is the Passover lamb that has been sacrificed (5:8) on the cross. Consequently, those who pattern their minds after the mind of Christ must celebrate the Passover not with the old yeast of malice and wickedness but with the new unleavened bread of sincerity and truth.

The salvation of the individual differs a little from that of the community. As his spiritual stance is saved, the man will be restored back to fellowship with the community. Such redemptive restoration is confirmed in 2 Corinthians 2:6–8. Paul writes, "The punishment inflicted by the majority against *such an individual* [ὁ τοιοῦτος] is sufficient; so now you should rather forgive and console lest *such an individual* [ὁ τοιοῦτος] be overwhelmed with excessive grief. Therefore, I urge you to reaffirm love for him." The phrase "such an individual" (ὁ τοιοῦτος) also occurs in 1 Corinthians 5:5, 11. It is not clear whether 2 Corinthians 2 and 1 Corinthians 5 refer to the same offender, but most interpreters agree that the punishment in 2 Corinthians 2 includes exclusion from communal activities. Thus, Paul teaches that there must be a limit to the shame that the community can inflict on the offending individual. If the shaming punishment leads to grief and repentance, the individual should be restored to the fellowship of the community, as the goal of the disciplinary measure has been reached. If the shaming punishment extends indefinitely such that there is no hope for restoration, the individual may adopt an attitude of shamelessness to anesthetize the pain.

"I Say This to Your Shame" (6:5)

The problem in 1 Corinthians 6:1–11 centers on Christians taking fellow Christians to local magistrates over "trivial cases" (6:1–2). The plaintiff and the defendant were probably social equals of high status and were leaders within the Christian community.[72] Paul rejects such a practice since the local courts were generally corrupt (6:1). Moreover, civil litigations were conducted with utmost acrimony.[73] Such proceedings therefore contributed to the divisions within the church (1:10–11).

Paul rebukes and shames the Corinthians with a series of rhetorical statements that show his horror and frustration: "Do you dare take it to court?" (6:1); "Do you not know?" (6:2, 3, 9); "Are you not competent?" (6:2); "Can it be that there is no one wise among you?" (6:5); "And this before unbelievers?" (6:6); "Why not rather be wronged? Why not rather be defrauded?" (6:7). He shames the plaintiff for initiating legal proceedings, and he shames the community for not doing anything about it. To ensure that they fully understand the gravity of the situation, Paul plainly states, "I say this to your shame [ἐντροπή]" (6:5). The use of ἐντροπή recalls the earlier use of ἐντρέπω in 4:14. If our reading of 4:14 is correct, we might expect that Paul's shaming rhetoric here also serves a pedagogical tool. This is accomplished in three ways.

1. *Paul's shaming rhetoric parallels and foreshadows God's shaming judgment.* In 6:4–5 Paul's shaming rhetoric alludes to God's shaming judgment in 1:27–31. The frame of reference in these two passages is different: the world in 1:27–31 and the church in 6:4–5. Nevertheless, just as God in 1:27–31 shames (καταισχύνω) the strong and wise of the world by choosing the despised of the world (τὰ ἐξουθενημένα; i.e., the Corinthians), so also Paul in 6:4–5 shames (ἐντροπή) the strong and wise within the church by telling them to appoint the despised within the church (τοὺς ἐξουθενημένους; i.e., the "have-nots" [cf. 11:22]). If the strong and wise within the church should have disputes concerning matters of this world, they should appoint (καθίζετε) for themselves

72. Chow, *Patronage and Power*, 123–30.
73. See Kelly, *Civil Judicature*, 98–99.

judges who are of no account within the church.[74] The plaintiff would consider such a proposal ludicrous, for it would be shameful for him to have his case tried before a social inferior. But that is Paul's point. The plaintiff should be ashamed of initiating legal proceedings against a brother, for such proceedings signify the total collapse of the community long before any verdict is delivered in court (6:7). In this way, Paul's shaming rhetoric parallels God's shaming judgment.

But Paul's shaming rhetoric also differs from God's shaming judgment. The shame that God pronounces on the world refers to his judgment on his enemies; the shame that Paul seeks to bring about, however, refers to the painful experience that is meant to cause the plaintiff to relinquish the desire to litigate. If the plaintiff does not heed Paul's shaming rhetoric, however, he will face God's final shaming judgment, since those who uses the local magistrates' courts to wrong and defraud their brothers are in danger of not inheriting the kingdom of God (6:8–9). In this way, Paul's shaming rhetoric foreshadows God's shaming judgment.

2. *Paul's shaming rhetoric reminds them of their present identity in the crucified Messiah.* Paul shames the Corinthians, rhetorically asking, "*Do you not know that* the saints will judge the world?" (6:2); "*Do you not know that* we will judge angels?" (6:3); and "*Do you not know that* the unrighteous will not inherit the kingdom of God" (6:9). These questions indicate Paul's intense frustration ("Surely, you must know this!") and his belief that the underlying issue at hand is fundamental for Christians to grasp. The use of "know" (οἶδα) recalls Paul's earlier discussion in 2:6–16. As those who have received the Spirit so that they might know (οἶδα) what God has freely given to them (2:12), Paul expected them to know that they will judge angels and that God's judgment will come on the unrighteous. But such eschatological knowledge cannot stay in the abstract; it must influence the worldviews, perspectives, and self-identity of those who have the "mind of Christ" (2:16).

3. *Paul's shaming rhetoric reminds them of the wisdom that is centered on the cross.* Paul's rhetorical question in 6:5 ("Can it be that there is nobody among you wise enough?") is a shaming indictment of the Corinthians. They considered themselves wise by the standards of this age (3:18), for they knew how to manipulate the legal system to their benefit. But Paul berates them for not having true wisdom. As those who are of Christ, they should have wisdom that is centered on the crucified Messiah. He is the one who became wisdom to them from God (1:30).

---

74. I take καθίζετε as an ironic imperative rather than as an indicative. See Kinman, "'Appoint the Despised as Judges!'"

Understanding Paul's Shaming Rhetoric in 1 Corinthians

At this point we are ready to draw some conclusions regarding Paul's use of shame in 1 Corinthians. I argue that 1 Corinthians 4:14 functions as the paradigm of Paul's shaming rhetoric. It is a paradigm that uses shame as a pedagogical tool for Christic formation. Paul's rhetoric is both harsh and gentle. Despite the possible severity, Paul recognizes the importance of his shaming rhetoric, for it foreshadows God's shaming judgment. If his readers do not respond to the escalating severity of his rhetoric, they will face God's condemnatory judgment. I now expand on these points.

Paradigm of Paul's Shaming Rhetoric

First Corinthians 4:14 ("I write these things not primarily to shame you but to admonish you as my beloved children") serves as the paradigm for understanding Paul's rhetoric of shame, including its use implicitly in 5:9 ("Do not associate with sexually immoral people") and explicitly in 6:5 ("I say this to your shame"). My reasons are as follows:

1. There is no substantive tension between 4:14; 5:9; and 6:5. For in all three passages, Paul advocates the use of shame, properly understood.

2. The first occurrence of the ἐντρέπω/ἐντροπή word group and the first explicit mention of Paul shaming anyone occur in 4:14. For this reason, Paul must first clarify here the function of his rhetoric of shame lest it be misunderstood by the Corinthians. Once he has explained that his shaming rhetoric is not meant to destroy but to build up and admonish, he can then use it without further clarification in 5:9 and 6:5. In this way, 4:14 functions as the paradigm for understanding Paul's subsequent uses of shame.

3. It is generally recognized that 1:10–4:21 functions as the locus classicus for Paul's theology of the cross. The purpose of 1:10–4:21, however, is not to provide an abstract theological reflection of the crucifixion but to provide the theological criterion for the rest of the letter.[75] Paul's *theologia crucis* in 1 Corinthians 1–4 thus functions as a central theme for the entire letter, for it functions as a prism with which to evaluate not only Paul's own ministry but also the life of the Corinthian church. Now, if Paul's *theologia crucis* is central, 4:14 must also be paradigmatic for the letter. For its placement at the conclusion of 1 Corinthians 1–4 and its explanation that Paul's shaming rhetoric serves to inculcate the

---

75. Hafemann, *Suffering and the Spirit*, 59.

cruciform mind indicate how this verse is one practical outworking of Paul's *theologia crucis* in the Corinthians' life.

The Mind of Christ

Our analysis of 4:14 shows that Paul uses shame as a pedagogical tool to transform the minds of his readers into the mind of Christ. Paul's shaming rhetoric suggests that he cannot change the practical decision-making ability of those who are arrogant and shameless without first engaging their sense of shame.[76] He affirms the positive role that retrospective shame can play and advocates a guarded use of shaming to cause his readers to examine their own lives from a different moral framework. This is accomplished in the following two ways:

1. *Critique to evaluate past actions.* Paul's shaming of the Corinthians forces them to evaluate themselves and their past actions from the gaze of an other. The Corinthians were puffed up, one over against another (4:6). Their notions of superiority, sense of entitlement, and arrogant behavior stemmed from "a failure in self-knowledge."[77] If the Corinthians are to improve morally, they must first see themselves for who they really are since "the knowledge of sin is the beginning of [moral] salvation."[78] Shaming rhetoric is suited for this task. When Paul shames the Corinthians, he shatters their complacency and puts before them a mirror or frame of reference with which to see themselves.[79] Through the painful emotive experience of shame, Paul calls them to examine themselves in light of the cruciform pattern of Christ.

2. *Critique to evaluate future actions.* Paul's shaming rhetoric not only forces the Corinthians to evaluate their *past* actions from the gaze of an other but also encourages them to inculcate a framework with which to evaluate all *future* actions. In several instances, Paul shames the Corinthians with "not rather" (οὐχὶ μᾶλλον) rhetorical questions: "Should you not rather have mourned?" (5:2); "Why not rather be wronged? Why not rather be defrauded?" (6:7). These rhetorical questions explicitly address what the Corinthians should have done in that present situation—that

76. See *Gnomologium Byzantium* 58.

77. Marshall, *Enmity in Corinth*, 205.

78. Seneca, *Ep.* 28.9. See also Thom, *Pythagorean Golden Verses*, 163–67, where he examines the call for self-examination found in *Golden Verses* 40–44. He notes that self-examination is the "*sine qua non* for any progress in virtue" (163).

79. In this regard, Paul's shaming rhetoric is similar to the shaming elenchus put forward by the Eleatic Stranger (in Plato's *Sophist*) to cast out the conceit of cleverness in ignorant men (Plato, *Soph.* 230C–D).

is, they should have mourned, and they should have let themselves be wronged and defrauded. Nevertheless, the questions implicitly also set the framework and perspective by which they should respond in the future.

When people who are shamed agree that the rebuke was justified and their actions were indeed shameful, they invariably adopt a mindset and disposition to avoid similar shameful actions in the future. In this way, shaming rhetoric shapes the moral disposition and conscience of people, causing them to evaluate whether future actions are shameful or good. If we are correct that Paul's rhetoric of shame functions to inculcate the mind of Christ in the Corinthians, then it is readily apparent that Paul's rhetoric shapes the moral disposition and conscience of his readers since the cruciform mind of Christ functions as the theological criterion to evaluate all communal life.

It is important to note that the purpose of Paul's shaming rhetoric, seen in the above light, is not only to curtail or modify behavioral actions. These are only the tip of the iceberg. What is more fundamental is the deep underlying value structure that gives rise to these actions. By transforming the minds of his readers into the mind of Christ, Paul moves past the superficial task of behavior modification to value transformation. He works from the inside out, realigning their mode of thought and moral conscience so that their lives eventually display the marks of a crucified Messiah.

Harsh and Gentle

As in Galatians, Paul mixes harsh rhetoric with gentle words. Shaming rhetoric is not the only tool in his toolbox such that every situation is a nail to be hammered by shame. Soothing words are also judiciously employed. In 1 Corinthians, Paul offers little praise or commendation apart from the opening thanksgiving. Nevertheless, in 11:2 he praises the Corinthians for remembering him and maintaining the traditions just as he had handed them to the community. It is possible to take this praise as ironic or as a rhetorical *captatio benevolentiae* to introduce 1 Corinthians 11–14. However, Richard Hays's reconstruction of the situation is more persuasive.[80] The Corinthians expressed their intention to follow Paul's directives concerning traditions but have genuine questions about matters of head coverings. Anthony Thiselton shrewdly remarks that "Paul always stands warmly alongside those who admit to perplexity or seek advice. It is when they claim no need of advice, or act unilaterally with complacency rather than consultation, that he becomes

---

80. Hays, *First Corinthians*, 182–83.

sharply polemical."[81] This stance is confirmed in 4:21, where Paul warns the Corinthians as a father, "What do you wish? Shall I come to you with a rod [ῥάβδος], or with love and a gentle spirit?" Paul does not seek confrontation, but if some persist in ignoring his teaching, he will have no choice but to be harsh and use the rod of shaming discipline.[82]

Sign of Prophetic Judgment

Despite challenges from some within the Corinthian church, Paul was deeply conscious of his apostolic authority. As an apostle of Christ Jesus by the will of God (1:1), as a laborer belonging to God (3:7), as a servant who has been entrusted with the mysteries of God (4:2), as one deeply aware that all his actions will be judged by the Lord (4:4), as one who communicates the Lord's command (14:37), Paul saw himself as the direct mediator of the gospel as well as its authoritative interpreter. Consequently, his shaming rebuke of the Corinthian community for failing to conduct their lives in line with the gospel carries not only his own apostolic authority but also the authority of God, foreshadowing in a limited way the shaming judgment that God brings on the so-called wise and strong (1:27).

Such an understanding is confirmed in 5:3–5, where Paul declares, "I have already passed judgment *in the name of our Lord Jesus* on the man who has done such a thing" (5:4). Paul passes a prophetic judgment on the man who was sleeping with his father's wife, but the authority of this judgment is not his own—it is that of the risen Lord Jesus. Moreover, the execution of this judgment is also done *"with the power of our Lord Jesus"* (5:4).

Putting It Together

We can now suggest how the mind of Christ, Paul's shaming rhetoric, and God's judgment can be understood together. I shall do this by way of 11:31–32. In 11:27–34 Paul notes that some of the Corinthians fell sick or died because they partook of the Lord's Supper in an unworthy manner. They would not have come under this judgment of sickness if they examined or evaluated (διακρίνω, 11:31) themselves. Nevertheless, God's disciplinary judgment (κρίνω, 11:31) of sickness and death is meant to be instructive (11:32a). The Corinthians are to learn from it so that they would not be finally condemned (κατακρίνω, 11:32b) with the world. The line of thought is that self-judgment may help us avoid God's disciplinary judgment; nevertheless,

---

81. Thiselton, *First Epistle to the Corinthians*, 810.
82. Philo, *Post.* 97: "The rod [ῥάβδος] is a symbol of discipline, for there is no way of taking to heart warning and correction, unless for some offences one is chastised and *brought to a sense of shame*" (italics mine).

that disciplinary judgment is intended to help us avoid God's stronger judgment of condemnation. There is thus an escalation of severity in each level of judgment: self-judgment (διακρίνω) → God's disciplinary judgment (κρίνω) → God's condemnatory judgment (κατακρίνω).[83]

In the sequence of judgments above, Paul's shaming rhetoric functions similarly to God's disciplinary judgment. If the Corinthians self-examine their lives according to the mind of Christ, they will not be shamed by Paul. Nevertheless, Paul's shaming rhetoric is meant to be instructive—to function as a pedagogical tool to transform their minds into the mind of Christ. It is also meant to be redemptive, with the result that the spirit is saved as the flesh is destroyed (5:5). If they disregard Paul's shaming discipline, however, they run the risk of not inheriting the kingdom of God (6:9–10) and of being condemned with the world (11:32).

Summary

This chapter examined Paul's use of retrospective shame in Galatians and 1 Corinthians. In both letters, Paul shames others because of their moral or theological failings. He evokes the painful experience of shame in them so that they can see themselves from a new frame of reference, so that they can reevaluate their identity and behavior in light of the cross. Paul uses shame as a pedagogical tool to transform their minds into the mind of Christ, enabling them to remember their true identity in Christ and to evaluate both their past and their future actions in light of the cruciform pattern of Christ. In essence, Paul uses shame for Christic formation.

Paul's shaming rhetoric is harsh. He therefore takes extra measures so that his rhetoric is not misunderstood. He supports his rhetoric with logical arguments. He balances his harsh tone with gentle words. He establishes the credentials that grant him the credibility to speak into the lives of his readers, reminding them that he is their mother, father, brother, and friend. His shaming rhetoric wounds, but the wounds from a friend can be trusted (Prov. 27:6).

---

83. Note the same κρινω root in διακρίνω, κρίνω, and κατακρίνω, suggesting that these three stages of judgment are related.

5

Paul's Use of Prospective Shame

This chapter examines Paul's use of prospective shame. Here I examine how Paul uses honor and shame categories in Philippians to cultivate a dispositional sense of shame in his readers. I also analyze how Paul uses shaming rhetoric to persuade Philemon to accept Onesimus back as a brother. Paul uses prospective shame in both of these letters, for the shameful events that he highlights have not occurred. They are possible futures that Paul wants his readers to avoid. As in the previous chapter, I only investigate select passages from each letter. The analysis of each letter concludes with a summary of the findings.

Philippians

Paul founded the church at Philippi in about 50 CE. The relationship between the church and Paul is marked by mutual affection and warmth. From its inception, the church supported his ministry (Phil. 1:5; 4:15–16; 2 Cor. 8:1–5; 11:9). Paul, likewise, expresses deep appreciation for the church. This is evident in his letter to them. He longs for them with the affection of Christ Jesus (Phil. 1:8), considers them his crown and joy (4:1), and calls them his beloved friends (2:12; 4:1). Indeed, the language of friendship permeates the entire letter.

Despite the positive assessment of the Philippian church, there are nevertheless concerns. Internally, some within the church are selfish and conceited, looking out only for their own interests (2:3–4). Others grumble and argue (2:14); while still others, such as Euodia and Syntyche, do not get along with one another (4:2). Externally, gentile opponents are intimidating the Christian community, frightening some and tempting others to abandon their struggle for the gospel (1:27–28). Jewish Christian teachers are also misleading gentile Christians to follow Jewish practices (3:2). Against these challenges, Paul urges the Philippians to conduct their lives in a manner worthy of the gospel of a crucified Messiah (1:27).

Given the warm and friendly relationship between church and apostle, Paul does not need to rebuke and shame his readers into compliance.[1] Unlike the Corinthian church, they readily accept his apostolic authority and always obey his instructions—not only in his presence but much more in his absence (2:12). Nevertheless, since honor and shame are pivotal values in the first-century Greco-Roman world, Paul invariably uses them in his exhortation. This section examines Paul's use of prospective shame in Philippians, analyzing how he cultivates in his readers a dispositional sense of shame that is consonant with the mindset of Christ. I proceed with the following moves. First, I examine Paul's exhortation to live worthy of the gospel. Second, I consider Paul's presentation of the story of Christ, whose obedience to God forms the supreme example of what it means to live worthy of the gospel. Third, I investigate Paul's exhortation to follow the story of Jesus. Finally, I synthesize the preceding exegetical data and conclude with some observations concerning Paul's rhetoric of honor and shame in Philippians.

"Live Worthy of the Gospel of Christ"

Paul exhorts the Philippians in 1:27a with the following: "Only, live your lives in a manner worthy of the gospel of Christ." The use of "only" at the beginning of the sentence highlights the comprehensive nature of this imperative. Duane Watson considers this command to be "the main proposition" of the letter; subsequent admonitions, statements, and narratives expand and elaborate what it means to live worthy of the gospel.[2] The imperatival verb "live your lives" (πολιτεύεσθε) carries the nuance of citizenship. With this verb as well as the adverb "worthy" (ἀξίως), Paul's exhortation alludes to the

---

1. Even if we consider the rebuke of Euodia and Syntyche (4:2–3) to be an example of retrospective shaming, we should take note of its mild and gentle tone. Paul does exhort them to work together in harmony, but he also commends them. They have struggled along with him in gospel ministry, and their names are in the book of life. Moreover, Paul names Euodia and Syntyche publicly not because he wants to humiliate them but because their disagreement is already well known in the church.

2. Watson, "Rhetorical Analysis," 78. See also Brucker, *"Christushymnen" oder "epideiktische Passagen"?*, 294–95; Debanné, *Enthymemes in the Letters of Paul*, 96; Witherington, *Paul's Letter to the Philippians*, 29.

civic duty of Roman citizenship. Citizens are not to say or do anything that brings shame and dishonor to their city.[3] Rather, they are to conduct themselves in a manner "worthy" of the ethos and demands of the body politic, discharging their responsibilities with honor, integrity, and sensibility.[4] But in a surprising twist, Paul exhorts his readers to live worthy, not of the gospel of Caesar, but of the gospel of the crucified Messiah—the content of which loudly proclaims that Jesus Christ, not Caesar, is Lord (2:11). Their true citizenship (πολίτευμα, 3:20) is in heaven, not in a Roman colony. Thus, they are to live according to the honor and shame values established by God, not according to the prevailing social norms of Roman Philippi. The exhortation to live worthy *of the gospel* recalls God's prior salvific action in their lives and presents the gospel as the norm by which the Philippians are to regulate their lives. Paul expands on what it means to live by this norm in the following verses. It entails standing together firmly for the gospel in the face of external threat (1:27b–30) and living together harmoniously for the gospel in the face of internal threat (2:1–4).

In 1:27b–30 Paul writes that living according to the norm of the gospel entails standing firm with one common purpose—striving together for the faith and persevering against their enemies for the gospel. Although the community faces opposition (1:30), Paul exhorts them not to be intimidated. The presence of attacks and reprisals against the Christian community shows that the norms of the gospel runs counter to the dominant cultural rhetoric.[5] Paul warns his readers that everyone looks out for their own interests rather than that of Jesus Christ (2:21). Many also live as enemies of the cross of Christ (3:18), and their enmity is evident in their behavior. Instead of fixing their minds on the cruciform pattern of Christ, these enemies set their minds on earthly things. They worship their sensual appetites and take pride in matters that should be considered shameful (3:19). In essence, Paul remarks that their quest for real honor is ill-founded. Such enemies of the cross may appear to

---

3. Just as a city could honor or shame its citizens, so a citizen could honor or dishonor a city. See Lendon, *Empire of Honour*, 78–89.

4. The adverb ἀξίως is related to ἀξίωμα ("that of which one is thought worthy, an honor" [LSJ]), a word used synonymously with "honor" (τιμή) and "glory" (δόξα). Moreover, the root word ἄξιος is a common epithet applied to benefactors of a city (Luke 7:4). For example, Demosthenes claims that he is worthy (ἄξιος) of praise because his civic service (πολίτευμα) brought glory, honor, and power to the city of Athens (*Or.* 18.108).

5. Using several descriptors, Paul presents the group of believers at Philippi as a minority subgroup against dominant forces, amounting only to a few stars amid the vast and dark expanse of a crooked and perverse generation (2:15). Paul emphasizes the numerical force of their opponents, using numeral adjectives such as "everyone" (οἱ πάντες, 2:21) and "many" (πολλοί, 3:18). Moreover, his exhortation not to be intimidated suggests that the believers were truly intimidated by the attacks of the larger Philippian populace (1:28).

have honor according to the dominant cultural rhetoric of Philippi, but their real destiny will be made manifest in the eschatological judgment—they will face eternal destruction (3:19). Those who intimidate the minority Christian population may appear to have power and status. But Paul remarks that this persecution and the Philippians' courage in the midst of such opposition is a divine sign to the persecutors (1:28). Regardless of whether the persecutors perceive its significance, it is a sign not only of their coming destruction but also of the Philippians' salvation. The certainty of these affairs is guaranteed by none other than God himself (1:28).

Living worthy of the gospel requires not only perseverance in the face of external threat but also steadfast resistance against internal dissension and strife (2:1–4). The community is to have a common mind by loving one another reciprocally, being one in spirit, and orienting their minds on the one central thing of significance—the gospel (2:2). At the same time, the community is to reject the one-upmanship that comes with selfish ambition (2:3). This quest for social honor is ill-founded.[6] It is empty and vain (2:3), as they are looking for honor where it cannot be found. True honor and glory belongs to God (1:11; 2:11; 4:20), and it is his to give. Those who seek it must therefore live according to his mandate. Thus, instead of elevating their own status, they should humbly consider others better than themselves (2:3). Instead of seeking their own advantage, they should seek the interests of others (2:4).

Paul calls believers to conduct their lives as honorable citizens of heaven. They must stand firm as they contend for the gospel (1:27–28). They will face suffering and opposition (1:29–30), and they will be able to stand only if they remain united (2:1–4).

The Story of Christ: Humiliation and Exaltation

The Christ hymn (2:6–11) portrays Christ as the supreme example of humility and ultimately of what it means to conduct oneself worthy of the gospel. The logical flow of 1:27–2:11 can be outlined as follows:

- The command to live as honorable citizens of heaven entails standing firm in the midst of opposition (1:27–30).

6. Inscriptions found in Roman Philippi testify that the elite and non-elite of that city were preoccupied with honor, rank, and social status. Hellerman (*Reconstructing Honor*, 109) remarks, "What is indisputable is that persons in first-century Philippi felt strongly compelled to proclaim publicly the honors they had received and their social location in the pecking order of this highly stratified Roman colony. Christians in the colony would hardly have been immune to these social pressures."

- Such steadfastness is impossible without Christian unity (2:1–2).
- Christian unity comes about only when believers adopt an attitude of humility (2:3–4), and the ultimate example of such humility is Christ (2:5–11).

The Christ hymn of 2:6–11, however, does not relate only to 2:1–4; it reaches all the way back to 1:27, presenting Jesus as the ultimate example of what it means to conduct oneself worthy of the gospel.[7] Moreover, the story of Christ's humiliation and exaltation offers the promise of vindication for those who stand firm for the gospel against external opposition and for those who use their status and power for the benefit of others within the community.

In presenting Christ as the ultimate example of the ethical demands of 1:27–2:4, the Christ hymn reconstructs a counterculture of honor and shame for the community of faith. Following Ernest Lohmeyer, I divide the hymn into two strophes with three stanzas each.[8] The first strophe (2:6–8) details Christ's repudiation of the quest for honor through self-assertion; the second (2:9–11) describes how honor within the community of faith should be truly understood.

The first strophe presents Christ's humiliation in three progressively degrading positions of status that function as a *cursus pudorum* (a succession of ignominies), a parody of the *cursus honorum* (a sequence of offices that an aspiring politician would pursue).[9] These progressive steps are as follows: equality with God (stage 1) → assuming the form of a slave (stage 2) → public humiliation in the crucifixion (stage 3).

Stage 1 depicts Christ's divine nature and preeminent status as one who is clothed in the garments of divine glory (2:6). But in contrast to Roman rulers who claimed divine status to enhance their own honor, Christ did not count equality with God as something to be exploited for his own advantage. Rather, he willingly sacrificed his own status for the benefit of others.

Stage 2 shows Christ making himself nothing (2:7), taking the shameful status of a slave. It is well acknowledged that slaves in the Roman world occupied the most dishonorable position. Dio Chrysostom writes, "Men desire above all things to be free and say that freedom is the greatest of blessings, while slavery is the most shameful and wretched of states."[10] But Christ's self-humiliation does not stop there; the hymn goes one step further.

7. Fowl, *Story of Christ*, 77–101.
8. C. Brown, "Ernst Lohmeyer's *Kyrios Jesus*."
9. Hellerman, *Reconstructing Honor*, 129.
10. Dio Chrysostom, *Or.* 14.1.

Stage 3 portrays Christ's complete degradation. As he humbles himself and becomes obedient to God, Christ suffers the most loathsome and debasing public humiliation possible in the Roman world—death by crucifixion (2:8).[11] Tacitus remarks that crucifixion is a "slave's punishment,"[12] meaning that it is the worst form of punishment. It is fit only for the dregs of society. Christ's death on the cross, then, forms the nadir of his downward spiral of self-abasement.

The use of "slave" and "cross" in the Christ hymn connects Jesus with "the most dishonorable public *status* and the most dishonorable public *humiliation* imaginable in the world of Roman antiquity."[13] Paul's purpose in doing so is to redefine a new structure of honor and shame for the Philippian community. "Slave" and "cross" may signify opprobrium. "Humility" is the shameful attitude adopted by slaves;[14] it is an obstacle to the quest for honor (φιλοτιμία) in the Greco-Roman world. Nevertheless, these social markers of shame are nullified and transformed in God's economy. What is more important is one's humility and obedience toward God (2:8), obedience to the point where previously constructed symbols of shame are no longer relevant.

The second strophe of the hymn validates and approves the necessity of obedience. As a consequence of Christ's obedience in condescension and humiliation, God now acts on his Son's behalf. While Christ was the subject of the main verbs in 2:6–8, God is now the subject. He highly exalts Christ and gives him a name that is above all other names. The word "name" (ὄνομα) does not just identify a person but also signifies "something real, a piece of the very nature of the personality whom it designates, expressing the person's qualities and powers."[15] Here the name given to Jesus is "Lord," the name of God himself. It is a high honor, given the jealous nature of God to guard his glorious name (Isa. 42:8). The purpose of this exaltation is that all might worship Christ and that all might acknowledge him as Lord. The exaltation of Christ does not diminish God, for the hymn makes clear that Christ's glory is derivative—God exalted him and conferred him with a superlative

11. See Hengel, *Crucifixion in the Ancient World*; Chapman, *Perceptions of Crucifixion*; Cook, *Crucifixion in the Mediterranean World*, 418–23.

12. Tacitus, *Hist*. 4.11.

13. Hellerman, *Reconstructing Honor*, 131. Similarly, John Chrysostom, *Hom. Phil.* 7 (*NPNF*[1] 13:215), writes, "All deaths are not alike; His death seemed to be the most ignominious of all, to be full of shame."

14. The "humility, humble" (ταπεινός) word group generally has a negative meaning in classical and Hellenistic usage, denoting the lowly, servile, weak, ignoble, or shameful conditions of slaves. For the link between humility and shame, see Demosthenes, *Cor.* 178; Plutarch, *Crass.* 17.3; *Adul. amic.* 23 (64e).

15. BDAG, s.v. "ὄνομα," 1.d.

title. Consequently, the exaltation of Christ further results in glory to God the Father (2:11).

As a moral exemplar, Christ demonstrates an orientation toward God and his glory that relativizes all other socially constructed norms for honor and shame. God is the one to whom all honor and glory is due. Consequently, those whom he honors are truly honored.[16] He alone has the ultimate authority to confer honor that is of lasting significance. The divine court of opinion, of whom God is the presiding judge, must therefore outweigh any other courts of opinion. The symbols of "slave" and "cross" may signify shame in the Roman world, but such symbols instead signify honor in the divine economy when they are juxtaposed with "self-humbling obedience" toward God.

Imitating the Story of Christ

Paul exhorts his readers to imitate the story of Christ as presented in the Christ hymn. He urges them to conform their minds (φρονέω) to that of Christ, adopting the same mindset and perspective that Christ himself held (2:5). The verb φρονέω "expresses not merely an activity of the intellect, but also a movement of the will; it is both interest and decision at the same time."[17] It encompasses one's mindset, affection, and attitude. The heavy occurrence of φρονέω in Philippians (ten of the total twenty-three Pauline occurrences are found here) is supplemented by other comparable "knowing" language. For example, Paul prays that their love would abound more and more in *knowledge* and *insight* (ἐν ἐπιγνώσει καὶ πάσῃ αἰσθήσει, 1:9); he *considers* (ἡγέομαι) everything as loss because of the surpassing value of *knowing* (γνῶσις) Christ (3:8); and he exhorts the Philippians to *set their mind* (λογίζομαι) on things that are true, noble, right, pure, lovely, admirable, excellent, and praiseworthy (4:8). These other verbs are similar to φρονέω in that they extend beyond intellectual thought and refer to attitudes and mental patterns that motivate action. Together with φρονέω, Paul uses these verbs to shape a cruciform worldview or mindset.[18] He inculcates in his readers a Christian moral reasoning so that they are able to live lives worthy of the gospel. Enemies of the cross set their

16. The honor that one gains from the praise of a prestigious individual *corresponds in proportion* to the prestige of that individual. See Lendon, *Empire of Honour*, 48–50, for examples in the Roman world where letters of recommendation from exceedingly prestigious men were collected and hoarded.

17. M. Silva, "φρονέω," *NIDNTTE* 4:620.

18. Meeks ("Man from Heaven," 333) writes, "This letter's most comprehensive purpose is the shaping of a Christian *phrōnesis*, a practical moral reasoning that is 'conformed to [Christ's] death' in hope of his resurrection."

minds on earthly things (3:19); believers, however, are to embrace the same mindset of Christ (2:5), imitating his pattern of behavior.

Christ is the supreme exemplar that believers are to imitate. Paul, however, also provides other exemplars whom the Philippians personally know. One such exemplar is Paul himself (3:17). Using antithetical parallelism, Paul's autobiographical account in Philippians 3 shows how conforming one's mind to the cruciform pattern of Christ should cause one to reevaluate the prevailing honor and shame values of society. Paul notes that the Judaizers stake their confidence on the flesh (i.e., on oneself or one's accomplishments); he, how-ever, boasts in Christ Jesus (3:3). If the Judaizers have reasons to be confident in the flesh, Paul has more (3:4). He is not their equal but their superior, pos-sessing more credentials than any Judaizer. He was circumcised on the eighth day, a member of the people of Israel, of the tribe of Benjamin, a Hebrew of Hebrews, and a Pharisee. He was zealous for the law, evidenced in his perse-cution of the church. Moreover, he observed the law so scrupulously that he considered himself faultless, when evaluated by the standard of righteousness determined according to a Pharisaic interpretation of the law (3:5–6). Paul used to consider his genealogical pedigree, education, and conduct profitable assets (3:7) in the honor and shame ledger of first-century Judaism. Never-theless, he now emphatically regards them as liabilities (3:7–8), even as abhor-rent and offensive as dung (3:8). The righteousness that is gained by obeying the law is now rejected in favor of a righteousness that is based on faith in Christ (3:9). The righteousness that was based on one's own achievement is now repudiated for a righteousness that is based on one's faith in God (3:9).

Although not explicitly stated, the event that brought about this recon-figuration of honor and shame values in Paul's life is his conversion. When God was pleased to reveal his Son to Paul on the Damascus Road, the Mes-siah Jesus so mightily apprehended Paul (4:12) that Christ is now the basis, motive, and purpose of Paul's entire life. The compass that reorients Paul is fundamentally Christ. The reason that Paul rejects his past achievements is the incomparable value of knowing Christ personally and intimately as "*my* Lord" (3:7–8). But Christ is not only the reason for Paul's rejection of his past; Christ is also the purpose, motivation, and goal of Paul's new orienta-tion in life. Paul's supreme goal now is to gain Christ (3:8). This entails being completely united with him (3:9), knowing the power of his resurrection, participating in his suffering, and being conformed to the cruciform pattern of his death (3:10). All these various statements describe Paul's ultimate goal and ambition. The singular focus of Paul's life is to forget the past, both his failures and achievements, and to strive toward the prize of God's upward calling (3:14)—the complete gaining of Christ. Paul lives with an eye toward the day of Christ (1:6, 10; 2:16; 4:5), when his imitation of Christ's story is complete. On that day, Christ's humiliation and exaltation will truly become Paul's own story, for his Savior and Lord, Jesus Christ, will return and transform his "body of humiliation" to be like Christ's "body of glory" (3:20–21). On that day, he will receive his ultimate vindication in the heavenly court (1:19). He may experience the shame of imprisonment and execution in this life, but Paul is confident that on that day he will not be shamed in any way as he stands before God (1:20).

Other exemplars that Paul provides include Timothy (2:19–24) and Epaphroditus (2:25–30). Paul commends Timothy as someone of kindred spirit (2:20) who seeks the things of Christ (2:21) and serves as a son alongside Paul in the work of the gospel (2:22). He lauds Epaphroditus as his brother, fellow worker, and fellow soldier who almost died for the work of Christ (2:30). Paul praises Timothy and Epaphroditus because both exemplify lives that are committed to the gospel. The community therefore does well not only in imitating the lifestyle of such men (3:17) but also in receiving and honoring them (2:29).

In summary, the story of Christ's humiliation and exaltation functions as an important paradigm for the Philippian community. Paul exhorts his reader to have the same mindset (φρονέω) as Christ. He accomplishes this lexically through the use of other "knowing" terms. At the same time, he provides other exemplars that illustrate concretely what it means to imitate the story of Christ.

Synthesis: Understanding Paul's Honor and Shame Rhetoric in Philippians

The above three exegetical sections show Paul using honor-shame categories to address the challenges facing the Philippians. I summarize his honor-shame rhetoric in two moves. First, I analyze how Paul constructs an alternative court of opinion that seeks to subvert the dominant culture's understanding of what is honorable and shameful. Second, I examine how Paul inculcates the values of this alternative court of opinion in his readers through the development of a dispositional sense of shame that is consonant with the mindset of Christ.

Constructing an Alternative Court of Opinion

Honor and shame are powerful motivators for certain actions and behaviors. Honor inspires conduct that is considered honorable, and shame discourages conduct that is shameful. Thus, it is not surprising that Paul uses such categories in his exhortation. What should be noted, however, is that Paul advocates an honor-shame system that relativizes and undermines the dominant cultural rhetoric of his day. The reigning political and social authority "displays the pretention to incarnate the moral values of the society which it governs, to 'command what is right and prohibit what is wrong.'"[19] A minority subgroup may, however, subvert the reliability of public opinion regarding that which is honorable and shameful by constructing a different "court of opinion" that sets forth the counter-definitions of the group. Consequently, in a complex society, things that are considered shameful in one subgroup may be deemed honorable in another.

In Philippians, Paul constructs an alternative court of opinion, with its counter-definitions of honor-shame values, in the following manner.[20]

1. Paul argues that God is the ultimate judge whose opinion and evaluation matters. He is the one to whom all glory and praise is due (1:11; 2:11; 4:20). He is the one who has the final authority to exalt and to honor someone with a title that is above every other title (2:9). More importantly, he is one who awards the prize at the end of one's life (3:14). Paul's use of "prize" and "calling" alludes to the Panhellenic games. After each event, the presiding judge would summon the victorious athlete to come forward. F. F. Bruce notes, "On a special occasion in Rome this call might come from the emperor himself; how proudly the successful athlete would obey the summons and step up to the imperial box to accept the award."[21] As the ultimate judge of human life on the final day of judgment, God has the power to overturn society's standard and institute his own criteria of honor and shame. Paul's readers would do well therefore to conduct their lives according to God's mandate. It is this divine court of opinion, not society's, that ultimately matters.[22]

2. The earthly analogue to the divine court of opinion is the community of faith, for it is here that the particular values of the community are instilled and reinforced. Paul accomplishes this task within the Philippian community in several ways:

a. He elevates individuals who exemplify values that are dear to the community. This list invariably includes Christ, but Paul also commends individuals whom the community personally know—Timothy and Epaphro-

---

19. Pitt-Rivers, "Honour and Social Status," 22.
20. For similar work done on the book of Hebrews, see deSilva, *Despising Shame*, 276–313.
21. Bruce, *Philippians*, 121.
22. Epictetus also exhorts his students to please God rather than humans: "When you come into the presence of some prominent man, remember that Another looks from above on what is taking place, and that you must please Him rather than this man" (*Diatr.* 1.30.1–2).

ditus. Such individuals should be honored and imitated *because* of their work for Christ (3:17). For example, the community is to welcome and honor Epaphroditus *because* he almost died for the work of Christ (2:29–30). The foil to such heroes of the community are the villains—enemies of the cross of Christ (3:18). The community is to beware of such dogs, evildoers, and mutilators of the flesh (3:2).

b. Paul encourages members of the community to be united around the core fundamental values of the gospel. The presence of "knowing/thinking" language (such as φρονέω, ἡγέομαι, λογίζομαι, σκοπέω, and γινώσκω) shows Paul's intent to shape the minds of his readers into that of Christ. In essence, Paul wants them to embrace the perspective and worldview that Christ himself held. They are to reconfigure their value system so that it is ultimately congruent to that of the gospel, not of the world.

c. Paul exhorts the community to strengthen the social cohesion of the community, solidifying the "plausibility structure" that supports the gospel worldview with its honor-shame categories.[23] "The firmer the plausibility structure is, the firmer will be the world that is 'based' upon it."[24] Thus, believers are not to do anything out of selfish ambition, valuing others above themselves (2:3); they are to look out not only for their own interests but also for the interests of others (2:4); they are not to grumble and argue (2:14); and they must make special effort to reconcile members whose discord threatens the unity of the church (4:2–3).

3. Paul reminds his readers that the basis of their honor is Christ. Within the community's court of opinion, the standards of honor and shame differ from that of the larger society. Believers cannot be driven by selfish ambition or vain conceit (2:3). They should instead despise achievements that cater to society's passion for ambition, considering them as dung or liabilities (3:7–8). Believers are also not to worship their sensual appetites and brag about their shameful indulgences (3:19). In contrast to these values, believers are to find honor in their relationship to Christ. Christ is the one who is exalted to the highest place and who is given the name that is above every name. He is the one before whom every knee in heaven and on earth and under the earth will bow (2:9–10). He alone possesses true lasting honor. Consequently, any

---

23. According to Berger (*Sacred Canopy*, 45), a plausibility structure is the social "base" that is required for the continuing existence of a socially constructed and socially maintained world.

24. Berger, *Sacred Canopy*, 47.

honor that believers hope for can only be attained via their association with Christ—through knowing him, gaining him, uniting with him through faith, participating in his sufferings, and becoming like him not only in his death but also in his resurrection (3:7–11).

4. Paul reinterprets the discouraging and shameful experiences of the suffering community. It is not clear what specific suffering the community faces. But if the Philippians are undergoing the same struggle that Paul himself experienced when he was in Philippi and that he is now still having (1:30), the suffering would include being stripped, flogged, and imprisoned (cf. Acts 16:22–24). Such afflictions are clearly shameful according to the standards of the world.[25] Nevertheless, Paul reinterprets them in three ways:

a. Paul draws out the positive implications of such shameful experiences. His imprisonment has resulted in the progress of the gospel both within and without the Christian community (1:12); the whole imperial guard is aware that his imprisonment is for Christ (1:13); believers are encouraged to do the work of evangelism (1:14); and even some of Caesar's household have converted to the Christian faith (4:22).

b. Paul uses several metaphors to reframe how believers are to envision their life. Using athletic metaphors, he says that believers should consider their affliction within the context of a contest.[26] They must forget what lies behind and fix their eyes on the prize. Using cultic metaphors, Paul says that believers must consider their entire life as a sacrificial service.[27] Martyrdom is a drink offering acceptable to God.

c. Paul recasts their afflictions from God's perspective. These intimidations do not portend their doom. Rather, these persecutions are a sign from God that confirms their salvation and their opponents' destruction (1:28). Suffering is not a misfortune or calamity that unexpectedly arises. Rather, God has *given* (χαρίζομαι) them the privilege not only to suffer on behalf of Christ but also to believe in Christ (1:29). Their suffering is a gracious gift from God, just as their faith is a gracious gift. As a gift, suffering should be accepted rather than refused. For the rejection of a gracious gift signals discontent and insults the giver.

25. Paul writes that he was shamefully mistreated (ὑβρίζω) at Philippi (1 Thess. 2:2). Fisher (*Hybris*, 493) notes that the core essence of ὕβρις in ancient Greece is "the deliberate infliction of shame and dishonor."

26. The athletic terms include συναθλέω (1:27), ἀγών (1:30), τρέχω (2:16), κοπιάω (2:16), διώκω (3:12, 14), βραβεῖον (3:14), σκοπός (3:14), and κλῆσις (3:14).

27. Note the cultic terms in 2:17 (σπένδω, θυσία, and λειτουργία), 3:3 (λατρεύω), 4:4 (ἀγνός), and 4:12 (μυέω).

5. Paul encourages his readers to persevere by holding out the certainty of greater glory in the future (prospective honor). The eschatological framework that undergirds Paul's construction of an alternative court of opinion is his understanding of the present experience as both "already" and "not yet." The resurrection of Christ and the gift of the Holy Spirit indicate that the eschatological age of salvation has already begun. Nevertheless, the consummation of that salvation awaits the return of their Savior on the "day of Christ" (1:6, 10; 2:16). On the basis of their present experience of salvation and their anticipation of a future culmination of that salvation, Paul exhorts his readers to express the reality of their future eschatological salvation in the here and now (2:12). Their present life must be constrained not by the exigencies of the present but by the values and perspectives of a future eschatological reality. Their present life may be marked by suffering; nevertheless, Paul encourages them to press on by making repeated references to the promise of vindication in the day of Christ (1:6, 9–11, 27–28; 2:14–16; 3:10–14, 17–21; 4:5). Their vindication consists of a future resurrection that is guaranteed by the power of Christ's resurrection (3:10–11). Their vindication consists of a future glorification (3:21) that is guaranteed by the work of God in their lives: God has begun a good work in them, God is working in them, and God will bring it to completion in the day of Christ (1:6; 2:13). The certainty of this future vindication then enables them to participate in the cruciform pattern of Christ and to be content in any and every situation, whether in plenty or in want (4:11–12).

Cultivating a Dispositional Sense of Shame

The above section shows how Paul primarily uses honor discourse to motivate his readers to adopt the values of his alternative court of opinion. He honors Timothy and Epaphroditus for the work they have accomplished on behalf of the gospel (retrospective honor), holding them out as models of imitation. He also holds out the promise of greater honor (prospective honor) if they persevere in the race of life. Paul's honor rhetoric in Philippians is further buttressed by the strong presence of *joy* (χαρά, χαίρω, συγχαίρω; 16x), an emotion that one experiences when one is honored.[28]

---

28. The relationship between joy and honor is clearly seen in Philippians. For example, Paul tells the Philippians to welcome Epaphroditus with great *joy* and to *honor* him (2:28); Paul considers the Philippians to be his *joy* and *crown* (4:1); and Paul *rejoices* because the Philippians honored him by renewing their concern for him (4:10). Similarly, Plutarch writes that it is "an uncle's duty to *rejoice* [χαίρω] and take pride in the fair deeds and *honors* [τιμή] and offices of a brother's son and to help to give them an incentive to honorable achievement" (*Frat. amor.* 21 [492c]; italics mine).

The preponderance of honor discourse should not lead us to suppose that Paul refrains from utilizing a rhetoric of shame, for the development of a sense of honor *is* the development of a sense of shame. In the honor-shame culture of the Roman world, one's goal was understandably to obtain the largest possible share of creditable attention (honor) while avoiding the least possible experience of discreditable attention (shame). Consequently, it was necessary to clothe oneself with a sense of shame (cf. 1 Tim. 2:9), for the absence of shame signifies license and the lack of discipline.[29] Sensitivity toward shame is essential for obtaining honor. Robert Kaster writes, "Honor and shame were . . . experienced as complementary, rather than opposed. Those who did not have what we would call . . . a 'sense of shame' could not expect to gain much honor; those who valued honor most highly could expect to experience shame most intensely."[30] Carlin Barton puts it more starkly: "To have a sense of honor in ancient Rome was to have a sense of shame. . . . The ancient Romans did not distinguish a passive, defensive shame from an active, aggressive honor. . . . For us, honor and shame, like autonomy and dependence, internality and externality, are abstract dichotomies. For the ancient Roman, honor *was* shame."[31]

In Philippians, the exhortation to act honorably (sense of honor) as children of God who shine like stars in the sky is at the same time a warning (sense of shame) not to dishonor their heavenly Father by behaving in a manner that is no different from the crooked and perverse generation (2:14–15).[32] The community's desire for Christ to return and honor them, transforming their lowly bodies into glorious bodies (3:21), is at the same time a desire that they would not be put to shame and consigned to destruction (3:19). In all cases, the sense of honor that drives them to press on toward the prize is at the same time a sense of shame that drives them not to stumble and forfeit the prize.

The categorizing of a sense of honor as a sense of shame allows us to gain a wider perspective of how Paul uses shame to shape moral behavior.

---

29. Kaster ("Shame of the Romans," 3) writes, "Sensitivity to the emotion [*pudor*] is . . . often spoken of metaphorically as a garment, a cloak that conceals the ethically naked self and provides an acceptable social identity." See also Ferrari, *Figures of Speech*, 74–81.

30. Kaster, *Emotion, Restraint, and Community*, 29.

31. C. Barton, *Roman Honor*, 199–200. In a similar vein, Kosman ("Being Properly Affected," 89n13) writes, "The connection between shame and the desire to do what is noble is very clear in the Greek. Shame is felt for having done αἰσχρά (things disgraceful, ignoble, base), and αἰσχρά is the standard opposite of καλά (things noble, fine, honorable). Hence to do something from fear of disgrace is not incompatible with doing it for the nobility of the act itself."

32. See Cicero, *Att.* 13.31.4, for an example of how the actions of a son can shame the father. After learning of his nephew's gluttony, Cicero remarks, "I am ashamed [*pudeō*] for his father's sake."

Specifically, Paul inculcates in his readers the values of the alternative court of opinion through the development of a dispositional sense of shame. I now probe this sense of shame or prospective shame in three moves.

1. *Prospective shame: human effort and divine empowerment.* In the Greco-Roman world, the social elite who is capable of attaining great honors is at the same time capable of failing miserably. The more one exposes oneself to the reward of honor within the community, the greater the risk of slipping and falling into the abyss of disgrace and shame. Balancing the desire for honor and the concurrent aversion to shame is a high-wire act for the social elite. The higher the wire—the more exposed one is to shame—the more spectacular the achievement and performance.[33]

The Christian life may be the highest high-wire act that anyone can perform since it holds out the twin possibilities of the highest honor (glorification) and the gravest shame (destruction) before the divine judge. As a Roman citizen, Paul is clearly aware of the vertigo that one experiences while walking the wire with the requisite grace and energy. Nevertheless, he is sanguine that believers will be able to negotiate "the walk" successfully. He himself announces confidently, "It is my eager expectation and hope that I will in no way be put to shame, but that Christ will be exalted now and always in my body as I speak with all boldness" (1:20). Paul attributes this confidence to the enabling of the Holy Spirit (1:19) and the power of God that meets all their needs according to his glorious riches in Christ Jesus (4:19). Human diligence is needed (this is clearly seen in his exhortations), but human effort is complemented and supported by divine empowerment. Consequently, Paul can assure his readers that God who began a good work in them will bring it to completion until the day of Christ Jesus (1:6).

2. *Prospective shame and the social bond.* Paul seeks to cultivate in his readers a dispositional sense of shame, a consciousness that guides them to avoid what the believing community considers to be shameful and to pursue what it considers to be honorable. We gain a clearer understanding of this "guiding" force when we examine the relationship between shame and the social bond.

First, shame is the emotion of interconnectedness.[34] We have shame before those with whom we wish to be associated or identified: our parents, our relatives, our teachers, our children, our spouse, our siblings, or our fellow citizens. Since shame involves the "feeling of *a threat to the social bond*" and the fear

33. Kaster, "Shame of the Romans," 11; C. Barton, *Roman Honor*, 199–201 (introduction to part 3, "On the Wire: The Experience of Shame in Ancient Rome").

34. Scheff ("Shame and the Social Bond") considers shame to be the premier social emotion and vitally related to the formation of social bonds. Similarly, C. Barton (*Roman Honor*, 207–10) notes the importance of shame as an emotion of "relatedness."

of disconnection from the other,[35] a stronger social link invariably leads to a stronger sense of shame. In Philippians, Paul emphasizes and strengthens the social bonds of the community in three dimensions: between himself and the church, between individual members of the Christian community, and between the church and Christ. He highlights the partnership (κοινωνία) that the church has with him (1:5) and with the Holy Spirit (2:1); he exhorts them to be like-minded, being one in spirit and of one mind (2:2); and he shares his goal of knowing Christ and the κοινωνία of his sufferings (3:10). With the deepening of these social bonds, the sense of obligation that the church has to Paul, to one another, and to Christ is ratcheted up. Consequently, Paul can draw on these bonds and make bold requests. He urges the church to honor him and bring him joy by being like-minded (2:2); he exhorts individual members not to shame others by valuing themselves above others (2:3–4); he encourages them not to seek their own interests (honor) but the interests (honor) of others; and he implores the church to embrace the self-giving posture of Christ, who assumed the shameful status of a slave (2:5–11).

Second, shame is the emotion of restraint, inhibition, calibration, and social control. This inhibition arises because a dispositional sense of shame is associated with and defined by a certain kind of fear, be it the fear of disrepute or the fear of justified censure from those with whom we wish to be associated.[36] In Philippians, justified censure may come from Paul or other members within the community, but the ultimate source of this justified censure is from God. This is brought out forcefully when Paul exhorts his readers to work out their salvation with fear and trembling (2:12). This fearful or reverential attitude that Paul advocates is not directed toward individual church members or church leaders; rather, the object of this fear is God since all believers will have to give an account before him on the final day. Fear of justified censure from church leaders or other church members may influence how individual members conduct their lives. But the future orientation of Paul's exhortation with its concomitant fear of being shamed by God at the eschatological judgment functions as the ultimate basis for the dispositional sense of shame that Paul seeks to cultivate in his hearers (cf. 2 Cor. 5:9–10).

Third, shame is closely tied to a positive regard and reverence for others.[37] This understanding of shame is linked to the previous understanding of shame, the understating that shame is an emotion of restraint or inhibition. Negatively, shame restrains and inhibits us from infringing on the honor of

35. Scheff, "Shame and the Social Bond," 97.
36. See Diogenes Laertius, *Vit. phil.* 7.112; Cicero, *Rep.* 5.6; Aulus Gellius, *Noct. att.* 19.6.3; Aristotle, *Eth. nic.* 14.1–2, 1128B; Xenophon, *Mem.* 3.7.5.
37. See BDAG, s.v. "αἰδέομαι"; "αἰσχύνη," 1; "ἐντρέπω," 2.

others, guiding us to exercise appropriate humility. Positively, shame leads us to respect others, according them the honor they deserve.

The call to exercise reverential shame and humility before God is clear.[38] Believers are, nevertheless, also called to show respect to one another. In Philippians 2:3–4, Paul exhorts his readers to exercise humility, to have special regard for one another, and to care for others. Although no specific shame lexeme is employed in this context, Paul's intent is that they exercise prospective shame and respect one another. The thought is similar to the counsel that Ignatius later gives to the Magnesians: "You all should respect [ἐντρέπω] one another. No one should consider his neighbor in a fleshly manner, but you should always love one another in Jesus Christ."[39]

3. *Prospective shame, conscience, and the mindset of Christ.* The dispositional sense of shame that Paul seeks to cultivate in his readers is a Christian conscience that is centered on the mindset of Christ (2:5). I will further explore the relationship between a sense of shame, conscience, and the mindset of Christ in chapter 6. But for now I make two observations:

a. Both conscience and shame share the concept of an eyewitness. The concept of an eyewitness is inherent in our understanding of shame; it is also in our understanding of conscience (συνείδησις, σύνοιδα), for conscience's fundamental idea is "'to have knowledge of something with' another person on the basis of eye-witness."[40] In both conscience and shame, the eyewitness can be another person or oneself.

b. Paul's imperative to live worthy of the gospel, the exhortation to have the same mindset as Christ, and the call to imitate the story of Christ all suggest that one of the fundamental tasks Paul seeks to achieve is to construct a Christian conscience or sense of shame that sees the entirety of life from the perspective of Christ. In other words, Paul invites his readers to consider Christ as an eyewitness to their conduct, so that they will be able to evaluate their lives according to his mindset.

Philemon

Philemon is a letter full of pathos. Paul employs all his rhetorical skills on behalf of Onesimus. He urges Philemon to receive Onesimus back no longer as

38. For example, see the use of ἐντρέπω with reference to God in Exod. 10:3 LXX; 2 Chron. 34:27 LXX; 1 Clem. 21:6.

39. Ign. *Magn.* 6.2.

40. C. Maurer, "σύνοιδα, συνείδησις," *TDNT* 7:899.

a slave but as a beloved brother. He also tantalizingly suggests that Philemon should immediately manumit Onesimus; he should set him free.[41]

In this section, I examine how Paul uses shame to persuade Philemon to welcome Onesimus back. Even though there is no explicit occurrence of any shame lexeme in this letter, Paul's rhetoric of shame is palpable. John Chrysostom, who was trained in classical rhetoric and lived in the honor and shame culture of the fourth century, readily picks this up. In his three homilies on Philemon, Chrysostom uses "shame" or "ashamed" twenty-one times and notes repeatedly that Paul shames Philemon into compliance.

My task comprises two parts. First, I examine how Paul uses shame to persuade Philemon. Second, I explore the larger purpose of Paul's rhetoric of shame, arguing that he uses it to shape Philemon's noetic and moral apparatus.

Paul's Rhetoric of Persuasion

Philemon is a masterpiece of rhetorical persuasion. Paul skillfully adapts "every major unit of this letter—the opening, thanksgiving, body and closing—so that the persuasive force of his argument is greatly enhanced and powerful pressure is placed upon Philemon to agree to the apostle's explicit and implicit requests."[42] Given the limitations of space, I will list only the more significant moves that Paul employs.

1. In the opening address, Paul does not mention his superior status as an apostle; he does not want to appear too heavy-handed at the start. On the contrary, he calls himself a prisoner (v. 1). None of the other Pauline letters, not even the other prison epistles, begin with this designation. Moreover, Paul does not just evoke this theme once. He continues to stress his imprisonment throughout the letter, mentioning it four other times (vv. 9, 10, 13, 23). The repeated emphasis suggests that Paul specifically chose this designation for its rhetorical effect—to strike Philemon with "compunction."[43] One can imagine Paul saying to Philemon, "In light of the sacrifice that I am making, is not my request something that deserves your attention and support?"[44] But there is also another possibility. Imprisonment was shameful in the ancient world,[45]

41. Requests for manumission were not unrealistic. Manumission of slaves happened every day in the Greco-Roman world. See Treggiari, *Roman Freedmen*, 12; Harrill, *Manumission of Slaves*, 53. Moreover, there were social and economic factors that favored manumission at times. Thus, the manumission of Onesimus was a viable option to Philemon.
42. Weima, "Paul's Persuasive Prose," 30.
43. John Chrysostom, *Hom. Phlm.* 1 (NPNF[1] 13:547).
44. See the discussion in Wansink, *Chained in Christ*, 147–74.
45. Chains symbolize shame and humiliation. See Rapske, *Book of Acts*, 283–312.

and many deserted their friends who were incarcerated. In 2 Timothy, Paul himself notes that many deserted him (1:15; 4:10), and he asks Timothy not to be ashamed of his chains (1:8; cf. 1:16). Given this backdrop, Paul may therefore be saying, "If you, Philemon, are not ashamed to call me (a prisoner) your brother, you should not be ashamed to call Onesimus (a slave) your brother."

2. Another self-appellation that Paul effectively uses is "old man" (πρεσβύτης, v. 9). Since age frequently brings with it experience and wisdom, Paul's appeal to his age can be said to induce respect and obedience from Philemon. But the collocation of "old man" with "prisoner of Jesus Christ" paints a vulnerable Paul. This portrait of vulnerability is increased as Paul lays out the prospect of losing someone who is precious and useful to him (v. 11). For Onesimus is like a son to Paul, possibly a favored son, since he fathered him during his old age and imprisonment (v. 10).[46] In sending Onesimus back, Paul is giving up his own heart (v. 12). It therefore seems more likely that Paul intends to generate sympathy for his current situation by casting himself as a feeble father who needs his son's support. Philemon would thus be shameless if he did not manumit Onesimus and send him back to his aged father.[47] He would be heartless, depriving an old man of that which is essential to him.

3. The Letter to Philemon is not a private letter. Even though its message is directed to Philemon, Paul addresses not only him but also Apphia, Archippus, and the entire church that meets at his house (v. 2). This is surprising, for Paul nowhere else does this in his other letters, not even in the Pastoral Letters, which are directed toward a single individual. J. B. Lightfoot suggests that Paul includes the other addressees out of courtesy.[48] That may be so, since Apphia and Archippus are probably members of Philemon's household;[49] but it does not explain why Paul also addresses the entire church. The more probable reason is that Paul deliberately makes his request a corporate matter.

The closing of the letter also reinforces the public nature of the letter. Paul concludes the letter with a greeting that mentions five other people (Epaphras, Mark, Aristarchus, Demas, and Luke), implying that these other men know the contents of the letter. Jeffrey Weima suggests that "a modern analogy would be to request in a written letter a favor from someone and then include

---

46. See Gen. 37:3 for how Israel favored Joseph more than any other children, because he was a son born to him in his old age.

47. John Chrysostom, *Hom. Phlm.* 2 (NPNF[1] 13:551), comments, "Strange! How many things are here to shame him into compliance! Paul, from the quality of his person, from his age, because he was old, and from what was more just than all, because he was also 'a prisoner of Jesus Christ.'"

48. Lightfoot, *Saint Paul's Epistles*, 279.

49. Apphia is probably Philemon's wife, and Archippus his son.

at the bottom of the correspondence 'CC:', listing the names and perhaps even the official titles of other individuals to whom you have copied this request."[50]

The public nature of the letter increases pressure on Philemon to agree to Paul's request. Aristotle notes that "men feel shame before those whom they esteem. Now men esteem those who admire them and those whom they admire. . . . They feel more ashamed before those who are likely to be always with them or who keep watch upon them, because in both cases they are under the eyes of others."[51] Applying Aristotle's analysis to Philemon's situation, we can say that Philemon is most vulnerable to shame before Paul, his own household, and the entire church. These are the people whom he esteems, and he will accede to Paul's request so as not to be shamed before them.

4. Paul does not immediately make his request known at the beginning of the letter. He first embarrasses Philemon by heaping lavish praise on him. He calls him a beloved friend (v. 2) and brother (vv. 7, 20), he gives thanks for him because he has a reputation for generosity and love (v. 5), and he acknowledges the joy and encouragement that Philemon has given him, because the hearts of the saints have been refreshed through him (v. 7). After such laudatory comments, it will be highly embarrassing for Philemon to decline when Paul finally asks the favor.[52]

With each commendation, "Paul lays on the man a hand that is warm and heavy at the same time."[53] Its warmth is felt in the expression of joy and encouragement; its heaviness in the expectations that such impeccable behavior should continue. As one who has refreshed the hearts (σπλάγχνον) of the saints, Philemon is expected to refresh Paul's heart too. The connection to Onesimus is carefully made when Paul explicitly calls him "my heart" (σπλάγχνον, v. 12). To ensure that Philemon does not fail to pick up the innuendo, he then explicitly tells Philemon, "Refresh my heart" (σπλάγχνον, v. 20). The threefold use of the rare term σπλάγχνον is deliberate.[54] The implication is clear. "If Philemon refreshes the hearts of the saints (v. 7), and if Onesimus is Saint Paul's very heart (v. 12); then, to refresh Paul's very heart, Philemon must refresh Onesimus."[55] If he refused, Philemon would decline what he has

50. Weima, "Paul's Persuasive Prose," 57. Harrill (*Slaves in the New Testament*, 13) also notes that the address to multiple people raises "the honor-shame stakes to that of a public hearing, in the agonistic code of face-to-face rhetorical encounters."

51. Aristotle, *Rhet.* 2.6.14–18, 1384A26–1384B1.

52. John Chrysostom, *Hom. Phlm.* 2 (NPNF¹ 13:550).

53. Barth and Blanke, *Letter to Philemon*, 253.

54. The word σπλάγχνον literally means "entrails." Paul uses this term rather than the common καρδία (heart) because it is more visceral and emotive.

55. Church, "Rhetorical Structure," 24.

done for the rest of the saints. This would be highly shameful, especially since Paul is more entitled to respect by virtue of his apostolic office.[56]

5. The partnership that Paul and Philemon share in the gospel plays a significant role in Paul's rhetoric of persuasion. He first calls Philemon a co-worker (v. 1), one who shares the same ministry goals. He then emphasizes the "mutual participation" (κοινωνία) both of them share in Christ Jesus (v. 6).[57] When Paul prays for Philemon, he does not say "your faith" but "the mutual participation that you share with us in the faith" (ἡ κοινωνία τῆς πίστεώς σου, v. 6). John Chrysostom notes that with this move, Paul connects Philemon's faith with himself, "showing that it is one body, and by this particularly making him ashamed to refuse" the request that he will eventually bring forth.[58]

When Paul finally makes his appeal, he bases his request on the mutual participation (κοινωνία) both share in the faith, using the cognate word "partner" (κοινωνός). He writes, "So, if you regard me as your partner, welcome him as you would welcome me" (v. 17). The conditional particle "if" functions as a tool of persuasion, inviting Philemon to evaluate not only the nature but also the implications that stem from their relationship.

6. As Paul concludes the letter, he expresses confidence that Philemon will not only comply but will also do more than what Paul asks (v. 21). Paul is confident that Philemon will not only welcome Onesimus but also manumit him. Such expressions of confidence undergird the letter's requests, creating a sense of obligation and challenging the recipient to live up to the set expectations.[59] Plutarch notes that "when men are on the verge of giving way . . . , [challenges to honorable action] arouse in a man a desire to emulate his better self, since he is made to feel ashamed of disgraceful conduct by being reminded of his honorable actions, and is prompted to look upon himself as an example of what is better."[60]

Paul follows the expression of confidence with a note that he will visit as soon as he is released from prison (v. 22). The announcement of an apostolic *parousia* "is surely designed to make Philemon take this letter seriously: Paul will very soon be on the spot to see how Philemon has responded!"[61]

7. On several occasions Paul adopts a harsher tone in his appeal, alluding to the apostolic authority he has over Philemon. In verse 8, Paul remarks

---

56. John Chrysostom, *Hom. Phlm.* 2 (NPNF[1] 13:550), writes, "Nothing so shames us into giving, as to bring forward the kindnesses bestowed on others, and particularly when a man is more entitled to respect than they."

57. Wright, *Climax of the Covenant*, 51–52.

58. John Chrysostom, *Hom. Phlm.* 2 (NPNF[1] 13:550).

59. See Olson, "Pauline Expressions of Confidence."

60. Plutarch, *Adul. amic.* 33 (72d).

61. Barclay, "Christian Slave-Ownership," 171.

that although he has the boldness to command Philemon to do that which he ought, he prefers to appeal to him on the basis of love. In verse 14, Paul wants Philemon's favor to be voluntary rather than something forced. The softer language of "appeal" and "voluntary" balances the heavy-handedness of "command" and "forced"; nonetheless, pressure is applied on Philemon to act appropriately. The language of "obedience" in verse 21 makes this clear. In verse 19, Paul remarks that although he is very willing to pay any debt that Onesimus might have incurred, Philemon owes the apostle a much greater debt—his very self. "Thus Philemon is turned from creditor to debtor in the space of two verses, and loaded with a debt so large . . . that he is under limitless obligation to Paul."[62] He would be shameless if he declined Paul's small favor when he owes a much greater debt.

The above examples demonstrate how Paul shames Philemon into compliance. The shame that Paul employs is not retrospective but prospective. Paul does not cause Philemon to be ashamed or remorseful for things that he has already done, for the decision to welcome and manumit Onesimus is still pending. Rather, Paul instills in Philemon a fear of disrepute that would befall him if he does not fulfill his Christian obligations and principles. The shame that Paul introduces in Philemon is not reflective but inhibitory; it does not look to the past or the present but to the future. In other words, Paul seeks to inculcate in Philemon a sense of shame.

Knowledge of Every Good Thing

The immediate purpose of Paul's rhetoric of shame is to motivate Philemon to welcome Onesimus as a brother. The larger purpose, however, is to shape Philemon's moral apparatus so that he rightly understands and affirms the implications of what it means to be in a community of faith—a community in which the central relationship that defines how we truly relate to one another is spiritual rather than legal or socioeconomic. Within this community that identifies with the crucified Messiah, believers have obligations and responsibilities to one another; they are to look out not only for their own interests but also for the interests of others. This larger purpose of Paul's rhetoric is found in Paul's prayer of verses 4–7.

The crux of Paul's prayer is found in verse 6. This verse is widely recognized as the most difficult in Philemon, and it is notoriously difficult to translate.

---

62. Barclay, *Colossians and Philemon*, 104.

A literal translation gives the following: "That the partnership of your faith might become effective in the knowledge of every good thing among you for Christ." Such a translation is opaque and needs to be unpacked. Space, however, does not permit a full exegetical investigation. I summarize my understanding of this verse with a paraphrase: "Philemon, I am praying that [ὅπως] the mutual participation [ἡ κοινωνία] that arises from the faith you share with all other Christians [τῆς πίστεώς σου] might have its full impact [ἐνεργὴς γένηται] within the sphere of your understanding and affirmation [ἐν ἐπιγνώσει] of every good thing [παντὸς ἀγαθοῦ] within the community [τοῦ ἐν ἡμῖν]; may all this be done for the sake of the Messiah [εἰς Χριστόν]."

Paul's thanksgiving prayer lays the framework for Paul's subsequent request to Philemon. John Knox describes this prayer as an "overture in which each of the themes, to be later heard in a different, perhaps more specific, context, is given an anticipatory hearing."[63] Given the foundational role of this prayer, it makes sense to say that Paul's rhetoric of shame should cohere with and support this prayer. In other words, we can discern the purpose and basis of Paul's rhetoric of shame from the focus of Paul's prayer. Its purpose is to reconfigure Philemon's moral apparatus so that it is aligned with the will of God; its basis is the enabling work of God. I now expand on these observations.

Reconfiguration of Philemon's Noetic, Perspectival, and Volitional Apparatus

Paul begins his prayer with an acknowledgment about the mutual participation or communal life that Philemon shares with other believers on the basis of their common faith. But the focus of Paul's prayer quickly shifts to Philemon's noetic domain, for Paul prays that this mutual participation might have its full impact within the sphere of Philemon's "knowledge of every good thing."

In early Christian usage, "to know" is not only "to understand"; it is also "to affirm" or "to confirm." There is a theoretical element, "yet it is assumed that Christian knowledge carries with it a corresponding manner of life."[64] The outworking of Philemon's "knowledge [ἐπίγνωσις] of every good thing" (v. 6) finds its practical expression in his "consent" (γνώμη) of the "good thing" in verse 14. For not only do "knowledge" and "consent" share the same root (γνω-) in the Greek language, the term "good thing" (τὸ ἀγαθόν) is found only in these two verses in Philemon.

---

63. Knox, *Philemon among the Letters of Paul*, 22. Church ("Rhetorical Structure," 23) also notes the significance of this thanksgiving prayer for the entire letter, highlighting how key words within this prayer are recapitulated later in the letter.

64. R. Bultmann, "γινώσκω, γνῶσις, ἐπιγινώσκω, ἐπίγνωσις κτλ.," *TDNT* 1:689–719.

The word "consent" signifies an agreement to a particular course of action, but it also implies an "agreement that arises from a considered opinion about the matter."[65] There is a decision, but it is a decision that is arrived at after much deliberation and thought.[66] Paul clearly wants Philemon to agree to his request. But Paul is not *just* interested that Philemon does what he wants him to do, nor is Paul *just* interested that Philemon does the right thing. Instead, Paul wants Philemon to do the right thing *for the right reason*. If Paul's rhetoric coheres with his prayer, the emphasis on deliberation then suggests that Paul's rhetoric of shame is not meant to create an impulse decision nor subvert Philemon's noetic faculties. Rather, it is to stimulate Philemon's thinking, prompting him to discern, perceive, acknowledge, and finally comply with God's will. Although Paul's rhetoric with its rich pathos initially affects the emotional dimension of Philemon, it must nevertheless also challenge his thinking and his decision-making process. In summary, Paul's rhetoric of shame seeks to reconfigure Philemon's noetic, perspectival, and volitional apparatus—it seeks to reconfigure Philemon's moral apparatus.

Alignment with the Will of God

I noted above that the focus of Paul's prayer centers on Philemon's "knowledge of every *good* thing." Now, Paul typically uses "good" (ἀγαθός) to describe that which comes from and which pleases God (Rom. 12:9; 16:19; Gal. 6:10; 1 Thess. 5:15). The object of Philemon's knowledge thus involves, as Lightfoot puts it, "the complete appropriation of all truth and the unreserved identification with God's will."[67] Such knowledge affirms the will of God and responds in obedience and grateful submission to that which is known. When we combine this observation with the previous, we can say that Paul's rhetoric seeks to reconfigure Philemon's moral apparatus so that it ultimately aligns with the will of God.

The reconfiguration that Paul's rhetoric seeks to effect echoes what Paul wrote earlier in Romans 12:2. Paul challenges Philemon not to be conformed to worldly patterns of relationship based on the roles of master and slave. Rather, he wants Philemon's perspective to be renewed so that it affirms the will of God—that which is good for the community (Philem. 6), that which is good for Onesimus, and also that which is good for Philemon himself. Paul makes this thought explicit with the final phrase in verse 6: "for Christ" (εἰς

---

65. Moo, *Letters to the Colossians and to Philemon*, 415.

66. This emphasis on intentionality is reinforced by the subsequent phrase "of one's own free will" (κατὰ ἑκούσιον, v. 14). Barth and Blanke (*Letter to Philemon*, 389) write, "Freedom of will pertains solely to the making of a choice based on careful deliberation."

67. Lightfoot, *Saint Paul's Epistles*, 334.

Χριστόν). Philemon's "knowledge of every good thing" must ultimately have Christ as its goal; it must be actualized "for the sake of the crucified Messiah."

These findings indicate that Paul's rhetoric of shame is intended to motivate Philemon to do not so much what Paul wants as what God wants—to do not so much that which pleases Paul as that which pleases God. In essence, Paul's rhetoric of shame reconfigures Philemon's moral apparatus so that it aligns with God's will, with the divine court of opinion.

Efficacy through the Work of God

Paul prays that the mutual participation of Philemon's faith might become effective in the sphere of knowledge. But what is the agent by which this efficacy is obtained? Is it Paul's rhetoric? Is it God? Is it something else? The adjective "effective" (ἐνεργής) provides a clue. Paul often uses the ἐνεργής word group to refer to the efficacious working of God (Eph. 1:11, 20; Col. 2:12; Phil. 3:21). For example, Philippians 2:13 specifically notes that God is the one who is fundamentally at work (ἐνεργέω) in believers, enabling them both to will and work (ἐνεργέω) for his good pleasure. This theological perspective then suggests that Philemon's "knowledge of every good thing" is fundamentally made effective by God. God is the one who brings about a reconfiguration of Philemon's moral apparatus.

What then is the role of Paul's persuasive rhetoric? It is, after all, this rhetoric that challenges Philemon to consider a new reality where master and slave are brothers "both in the flesh and in the Lord" (v. 16). Paul nowhere explicitly states this in Philemon, but it seems reasonable to suggest the following: the ultimate agent by which Philemon's knowledge is made effective is God, but the means by which this is accomplished is Paul's rhetoric. In other words, Paul's rhetoric finds its efficacy in the believer through the enabling work of God.

Summary

This chapter examined Paul's use of prospective shame in Philippians and Philemon. In the first letter, Paul does not shame his readers. He nevertheless uses honor and shame discourse to inculcate in them a dispositional sense of shame that holds to a court of opinion centered on the mind of Christ rather than on the dominant culture in Roman Philippi. In the second letter, Paul evokes the occurrent experience of shame in Philemon. Paul shames Philemon so that he will receive Onesimus back as a brother as his moral thinking is aligned with God's will.

6

Constructing Paul's Use of Shame

The previous two chapters analyzed Paul's use of shame in four of his letters. This chapter builds on these exegetical findings and the earlier chapters in part 1 so as to construct a coherent understanding regarding Paul's use of shame. Paul does not provide us with a systematic treatise regarding his use of shame. Nevertheless, we may discern from his occasional letters a pattern that can function as the scaffolding for the constructive task of this chapter.

I proceed in two steps. First, I summarize Paul's construal of shame. Second, I highlight elements in his use of shame for Christic formation. This chapter concludes with a short section.

Pauline Construal of Shame

This section outlines Paul's understanding of shame from different facets. I summarize his usage of specific shame lexemes, and I list the values that Paul uses to define that which is honorable and shameful. I then clarify his understanding of shame by showing its relationship to sin, conscience, and repentance.

Lexical

Various words within the Pauline corpus fall within the concept of shame, disgrace, modesty, and respect.[1] These include αἰδώς (modesty, shame, sense

1. See *NIDNTTE* 1:72. See also L&N, 25.189–202; 88.46–50, 149–51.

of honor), ἀσχημοσύνη (shameful act), ἀτιμία (dishonor, disgrace), δειγματίζω (to make an example of, expose, disgrace), ἐντρέπω (to shame, to respect), θέατρον (public spectacle), ὀνειδισμός (disgrace, insult), ταπεινόω (to abase), and various words that share the αἰσχ- root—αἰσχρότης (shamefulness), αἰσχύνη (modesty, shame, disgrace), and καταισχύνω (to dishonor, put to shame).

Three lexemes are particularly important for my study. They are αἰδώς, αἰσχύνη, and ἐντροπή. Although there are variations, these shame lexemes and their cognates can broadly take four uses in Hellenistic Greek. Their meanings and glosses are as follows:

1. A disposition or inhibitory emotion that prevents a person from committing something dishonorable or ignominious—*modesty, reserve, sense of shame, sense of honor,* or *shamefastness.*

2. An attitude or emotional regard for the special status of others—*reverence* or *respect.*

3. The subjective feeling that is experienced after doing something objectionable or ignominious—*shame, compunction,* or *remorse.*

4. The objective state of disgrace—*humiliation, dishonor, shame, ignominy,* or *disgrace.*

Of these four uses, Paul does not explicitly employ shame lexemes to denote the second use—*reverence* or *respect.* One can, however, argue that Philippians 2:2–3 evokes this understanding without the explicit presence of the shame lexeme.

I noted in chapter 2 that αἰδώς and αἰσχύνη are generally used synonymously in classical and Hellenistic Greek. However, αἰδώς is frequently paired with σωφροσύνη (self-control), and it typically carries a loftier and nobler connotation than αἰσχύνη. The loftier connotation of αἰδώς is seen in the New Testament, despite its rare occurrence. In the textual variants of Hebrews 12:28, αἰδώς is paired with εὐλάβεια (awe) to form a hendiadys. In 1 Timothy 2:9, Paul pairs αἰδώς with σωφροσύνη, denoting the modesty and self-control that restrains women from wearing ostentatious jewelry and expensive clothes.

More significant is the distinction between αἰσχύνη (and its various cognates) and ἐντροπή. Paul distinguishes between these two lexemes when humanity is the agent that brings about retrospective shame. He uses αἰσχύνη cognates to denote a destructive and negative role for shame, such as when the Corinthians despise and humiliate those who have nothing (1 Cor. 11:22).

Paul, however, uses ἐντροπή to denote a constructive and positive role for shame, such as when he calls on the church not to associate with some so that they might be shamed and brought back to their right frame of mind (2 Thess. 3:14).

The Value That Truly Defines Honor and Shame: The Cross

The language of honor and shame enshrines and affirms values that are important to any community. Honor encourages actions, commitment, and ambitions that are essential for the preservation of communal harmony and the accumulation of social goods. Shame, on the other hand, discourages behaviors that the community considers deviant and unacceptable.

The honor and shame values of the dominant cultural rhetoric in the first century were generally predicated on human achievement, human wisdom, economic wealth, and social status. Paul, however, argues that the specific content that informs our values of honor and shame must ultimately derive from God. Thus, when Paul speaks about honor and shame, he is more concerned with the honor and shame ascribed by God than with that ascribed by society and the world.

Paul's rationale stems from his firm belief that God is the judge whose evaluation ultimately matters. He is the one before whom all humanity must appear on the final day of judgment (2 Cor. 5:10), and his approval or disapproval is of supreme importance. Paul therefore makes it his ambition and considers it an honor (φιλοτιμέομαι, 2 Cor. 5:9) to please God and not human beings (1 Thess. 2:4; Gal. 1:10). He likewise urges his readers to live worthy of the gospel of Christ (Phil. 1:27) and to seek praise from God and not from people (Rom. 2:29). Instead of marching to the drumbeat of the human court of opinion, believers are to live according to the divine mandate.

In what I have written above, Paul's understanding of honor and shame is not different from that found in the Jewish writings we examined in chapter 3. Paul, however, differs from the Jewish understanding, especially that of Ben Sira, in locating God's power and wisdom not in the Torah but in the gospel—in the "message of the cross" (1 Cor. 1:18). The gospel, with its message of a crucified Messiah, was innately shameful; it was a stumbling block to Jews and foolishness to gentiles (1 Cor. 1:20–31). Nonetheless, Paul's "claim not to be ashamed [of the gospel] signals that a social and ideological revolution has been inaugurated by the gospel" (Rom. 1:16).[2] The gospel inverts the current paradigm for honor and shame, such that the cross and

---

2. Jewett, *Romans*, 137.

its crucified Messiah are now the de facto lens through which everything and everyone must be evaluated. If people honor Christ and obey his gospel, they will be blessed and honored; if they are ashamed of the cross and disobey the gospel, they will be cursed and shamed.

The Pauline centrality of Christ thus nullifies various Jewish criteria for determining honor and shame, such as one's sexual and ethnic status. For example, Deuteronomy 23:1–8 excludes emasculated men, illegitimate children, and certain foreigners from the assembly of the Lord. The prophets do envision a time when these less than honorable statuses are overturned. If such people join themselves to the Lord and follow his commands, they will inherit an everlasting name that will endure forever (Isa. 56:3–8). Paul, however, boldly claims that all the Old Testament prophetic promises find their fulfillment in Christ (2 Cor. 1:20), such that social and ethnic markers of status are nullified in the new covenant era. In Galatians 3:28, Paul states that "there is neither Jew nor gentile, neither slave nor free, neither male nor female; for you are all one in Christ Jesus" (Gal. 3:28). Under the old covenant, only a privileged few were able to catch a glimpse of God's glory; under the new covenant, "we all, who behold the glory of the Lord with unveiled faces, are transformed into the same image from one degree of glory to another" (2 Cor. 3:18). The former markers of honor and shame are nullified and transformed in Christ.

Paul envisions the community of faith as the earthly counterpart to the divine court of opinion. Its role is to maintain the plausibility structure that undergirds the gospel worldview, instilling, perpetuating, and reinforcing in each of its members the set of values that are established by God. Thus, believers are to resist making distinctions among themselves based on external social criteria, and they are to honor and imitate those who exemplify the fundamental values of the gospel. In essence, the community must remind itself that the basis of any true honor is Christ. The ideals used in the self-evaluation component of the shame experience must be the cruciform pattern of Christ. Consequently, believers should not be ashamed if they suffer on account of Christ; they should instead boast in their sufferings, for their hope of sharing in the glory of God will not disappoint and shame them (Rom. 5:3–5).

Shame and Sin

Paul's understanding of sin is not fundamentally different from what we saw in the Jewish writings in chapter 3. At its core, sin is idolatry. It is failure to honor God (Rom. 1:21), participating in distorted systems of honor and shame that suppress the truth that God alone is the one who deserves honor

(1:18–32).[3] More broadly, sin is lawlessness. It is any failure to conform to God's moral law, and it is that which is shameful before God.[4]

As a result of their failure to fulfill the requirements of the law, sinful humanity stands under the shaming judgment of God. God shames gentiles, who refuse to glorify or give thanks to him, by handing them over to shameful lusts. They commit shameful acts with one another, receiving the penalty for their error (Rom. 1:26–27). God shames Jews, who cause his name and honor to be blasphemed among the gentiles (2:24), by giving them trouble and distress rather than glory and honor (2:9–10). Jews and gentiles each claim to possess more honor than the other. Paul, however, rejects both gentile and Jewish systems of gaining honor. He argues that *all* people sin and fall short of the glory of God (3:23), the transcendent standard of honor. All fail to conform to the glorious image of God for which they were created. As a consequence of their sin, all suffer objective shame before God.[5]

If sin results in shame, justification results in glory. Those who hope in God and rely on faith to fulfill the law will be declared righteous; they will not be put to shame (Rom. 10:11; cf. Isa. 28:16 LXX; Isa. 49:23; Ps. 25:3). On the contrary, God restores to them the glory and honor that was lost in sin (Rom. 5:1–2; 8:17, 18). This restoration comes as a gift, not by any achievement on their part, so that no one may boast (Rom. 3:27). Moreover, through the work of the Holy Spirit in sanctification, believers are progressively changed from one glory to another as they are conformed to the image of Christ (Rom. 8:29–30; 2 Cor. 3:18).[6]

Objective shame is the consequence of sin. Subjective shame *should* also be the experience of the one who sins. As John Chrysostom remarks, "Be ashamed when you sin. . . . After the sin comes the shame."[7] There are people who are shameless, whose hearts are hardened and whose consciences are seared. They do not experience subjective shame as a consequence for the wrong they have done. But if guilt is the objective fact that one has sinned (i.e., fallen short of the commands or ideals of God) *and* if one's values for honor and shame are properly calibrated according to the divine court of opinion, it then makes sense to say that subjective shame is one of the emotions that a guilty person experiences. Our analysis of Genesis 3 bears this

3. Jewett, "Honor and Shame," 266–68.

4. Heller, *Power of Shame*, 9.

5. This presentation of sin in shame categories does not deny that sin can also be understood in guilt categories. However, Chan (*Evangelism in a Skeptical World*, 77–79) notes that the shame model of sin is currently more relevant in the Western world than the guilt model. See also Pannenberg, *Apostles' Creed*, 163.

6. See Jewett, *Romans*, 280–81.

7. John Chrysostom, *Paenit.* 8.2.8 (FC 96:115).

out, for Adam and Eve experienced shame before God when they sinned. In the Pauline Letters, Paul also expects his readers to experience shame when they sin. They should be horrified if they pervert the gospel, desert the one who called them, and turn toward a gospel that is really no gospel at all (Gal. 1); they should burn with shame when there is incest within the church (1 Cor. 5); and they should grieve when brothers within the church engage in legal proceedings to destroy one another (1 Cor. 6).

Shame and Conscience

Conscience is the inner tribunal or critical self-awareness that determines whether one's actual or imagined conduct agrees with the moral norms affirmed by the mind.[8] It functions either retrospectively or prospectively, judging one's past, monitoring one's present, and guiding one's future conduct. Behavior that conforms with one's value system produces pleasure, but behavior that contravenes one's moral norm produces the feeling of pain, fear, shame, anguish, and self-condemnation.[9]

Conscience is universally present in all humanity (Jew or gentile, believer or unbeliever). It is not an external voice, nor is it the voice of God. Rather, it is an inward capacity or human cognitive faculty to critique oneself on the basis of an internalized set of values and requirements. The conscience is differentiated from the moral norms that the conscience applies to one's life. Nonetheless, as the moral norms of the individual change, so do the verdicts rendered by the conscience.

Shame and conscience are integrally related. We have already seen this in our discussion of Democritus and Epictetus. Other ancient and modern writers echo this sentiment. Clement of Alexandria relates conscience with shame rather than fear.[10] Dietrich Bonhoeffer remarks that "conscience means feeling shame before God."[11] Vladimir Solovyov similarly notes that "the ultimate foundation of conscience is the feeling of shame."[12] Shame, by definition, is a much larger category than conscience, for shame can be

---

8. For definitions of conscience, see Jewett, *Paul's Anthropological Terms*, 402–46, 458–60; J. M. Gundry-Volf, "Conscience," *DPL*, 153–56; Sorabji, *Moral Conscience through the Ages*, 216–18.

9. Thagard and Finn ("Conscience," 168) argue that "conscience is a kind of moral intuition, which is a kind of emotional consciousness."

10. Clement of Alexandria, *Strom.* 4.6 (*Ante-Nicene Fathers* 2:416).

11. Bonhoeffer, *Creation and Fall*, 128.

12. Solovyov, *Justification of the Good*, 34. He goes on to say that although conscience is a more complex development of shame, both are "no doubt essentially the same. Shame and conscience speak different languages and on different occasions, but the meaning of what they say is the same: *this is not good, this is wrong, this is unworthy.*"

elicited by moral and nonmoral lapses. When shame is, however, sufficiently circumscribed (i.e., when shame is elicited by moral failures, and the perceived standards that are determinative of the shame experience are internalized), it functions analogously to conscience. Both share the concept of an eyewitness; both are critical components of our moral apparatus; both evaluate one's conduct against some internal code; and both function prospectively and retrospectively, circumscribing future behavior that is shameful and producing the occurrent experience of pain when the person falls short of the internalized standard.

Conscience is also similar to shame in that both can register false judgments when the internalized value set is faulty. Paul is certainly aware that a person's conscience or moral yardstick may not be properly calibrated to the divine standard (cf. 1 Cor. 8:7, 10, 12; 1 Tim. 4:2; Titus 1:15).[13] The conscience may give a positive verdict, but that does not acquit a person's behavior; only the divine verdict is infallible. Judgments rendered by the conscience are normative only insofar as they cohere with God's will and the content of the Christian faith (1 Tim. 1:5, 19; 3:9). Paul writes, "My conscience is clear, but that does not make me innocent. It is the Lord who judges me" (1 Cor. 4:4 NIV). Paul therefore expends considerable energy to give his readers true knowledge so that their consciences are able to make evaluative judgments that are in line with the mind of God. In essence, Paul works to transform the consciences of his readers so that they take on the mind of Christ.[14]

Shame and Repentance

As our analysis of 1 Corinthians indicates, Paul advocates a constructive and positive role for retrospective shame. He does not rejoice in the pain that shame brings. Nonetheless, he concurs with Democritus in that those who do evil deeds must first feel shame in their own eyes. Once shame has done its work in awakening them to their error, restoration and salvation are possible.

---

13. Bosman (*Conscience in Philo and Paul*, 273) writes, "The συνείδησις [conscience] is erroneous only because it reacts on the basis of available knowledge, which may be erroneous or deficient. Deficient γνῶσις [knowledge] leads to a συνείδησις [conscience] which . . . is set into operation where it should not be operative."

14. This makes sense, for there is a close relationship between conscience (συνείδησις) and the mind (νοῦς). Both function as agents of rational discernment and moral judgment. Philo (*Post.* 59) puts both terms in parallel, equating the two. Paul makes a similar move in Titus 1:15, identifying the conscience with the mind. Thus, Eckstein (*Der Begriff Syneidesis bei Paulus*, 314) notes that the function of conscience in making concrete moral decisions is designated by Paul as the mind. See also Jewett, *Paul's Anthropological Terms*, 434, 459.

The sorrow and pain brought about by the occurrent experience of shame should lead one toward remorse, contrition, and repentance. Such a process is seen in 2 Corinthians 7.

In 2 Corinthians 7:9–10, Paul speaks about the effects of the severe letter (2:9; 7:12) he wrote to the Corinthians. The specific contents of the letter are no longer extant. It is nevertheless generally agreed that the purpose of the letter was to rebuke the church for not disciplining the man who verbally assaulted Paul and rejected his authority during his painful visit (2:1). Fundamentally, Paul wrote to shame the church into renewing their allegiance to him (7:12). His severe letter caused the church much sorrow and pain (λύπη)—a feeling that is consistent with the occurrent experience of shame, for Aristotle defines shame (αἰσχύνη) as "a kind of pain [λύπη] . . . in respect of misdeeds."[15] Paul, however, does not regret the pain that his letter evoked. For their painful sorrow resulted in their repentance (ἐλυπήθητε εἰς μετάνοιαν, 7:9)—a change of mind.[16] The painful experience of shame forced them to examine their presuppositions and evaluate them from a different frame of reference. It afforded them an opportunity to evaluate themselves no longer from a worldly mindset but from the framework of the cruciform pattern of Christ. It ultimately led them to adopt the mind of Christ.

Paul explains their repentance by outlining two kinds of pain or sorrow: godly sorrow and worldly sorrow. Godly sorrow produces repentance that leads to salvation; worldly sorrow brings death. Since the context centers on the pain that is brought about by shaming rebuke, we may make the following statements: If the pain of shaming rebuke is borne in "a manner agreeable to the mind and will of God" (κατὰ θεόν, 7:9, 10),[17] it will produce repentance that ultimately leads to salvation and will never be viewed with regret. If, however, the pain of shaming rebuke is borne with the world's attitudes and manner (ἡ τοῦ κόσμου λύπη, 7:10), it will only produce unrepentance that will ultimately lead to spiritual death and regret. What makes the pain of shaming refutation beneficial is not the experience of suffering per se but the response to it. A godly response accepts the pain of shaming rebuke as God's discipline; it submits to it, begs God for mercy, and receives forgiveness and salvation. A worldly response rejects the pain of shaming rebuke brought about by God's discipline, it considers such discipline an assault on one's autonomy, it refuses

15. Aristotle, *Rhet.* 2.6.2, 1383B12–14. See also Xenophon, *Cyr.* 6.1.35, where rebuke produces pain (λύπη) and shame (αἰσχύνη).

16. The word "repentance" (μετάνοια) etymologically means a changed (μετα-) attitude or mind (νοῦς).

17. Hodge, *Second Epistle to the Corinthians*, 182.

to submit to God, and it refuses to repent.[18] On the contrary, it provokes bitterness, anger, and resentment toward the messenger of God—Paul himself.

An arrogant and unrepentant posture toward Paul's shaming refutation is certainly possible in Corinth, for "high-status individuals in the Greco-Roman world are extremely reluctant to admit that they have made a mistake."[19] They prize consistency of character and consider any change of mind (the defining characteristic of repentance) to be a mark of fickleness and weakness. This belief is so ingrained that "even correction of mistakes was rarely acknowledged as such, and, as a result, remorse-like emotions such as *paenitentia* and *metanoia* are regularly devalued and assigned to lower-status characters."[20] Given the aversion toward repentance in the Greco-Roman world, it is no wonder that Paul had initial reservations about sending the severe letter. He was not sure how the Corinthians would receive it. Would they accept his discipline, or would they reject it? Would it lead to repentance and reconciliation, or would it cause further alienation between the Corinthians and Paul? Despite the reservations that Paul had, the goal of Paul's shaming rebuke in the severe letter was the repentance and salvation of his readers.[21]

Elements in the Pauline Role of Shame

This section examines four elements in the Pauline role of shame. Specifically, I probe his use of prospective shame, his use of retrospective shame, his rationale for shame, and the role of the Holy Spirit.

Prospective Shame in Paul's Shaming Rhetoric

Prospective shame encompasses situations where the event that causes one to feel shame is in the future. The occurrent experience of shame may or may not be present in such situations. Thus, prospective shame refers either to (1) the occurrent experience of shame concerning a prospective blow to one's honor or to (2) the prospect of shame, without necessarily experiencing the emotion of shame, that restricts one's behavior. Paul uses prospective shame in both of these senses.

---

18. Recall the response of Callicles to Socrates's shaming refutation. He becomes so uncomfortable with the occurrent experience of shame that he deflects the penetrating questions of Socrates and squirms out of the conversation. See Plato, *Gorg.* 505C–D.

19. Fulkerson, *No Regrets*, 12.

20. Fulkerson, *No Regrets*, 219.

21. Plutarch, *Adul. amic.* 12 (56a), notes that it is commonly the stinging rebuke of a philosopher's oration that brings about repentance (μετανοία).

First, Paul may engage in specific acts of shaming so as to evoke the occurrent experience of shame not for a past or present transgression but for a potential bad act in the future. He brings about the experience of prospective shame to forestall the performance of bad acts. He shames others into compliance not by pointing out their past failures but by commending their past accomplishments. He praises them for the good they have done, but also reminds them of the continued expectations that are placed on them. He emphasizes their obligations and responsibilities to one another within a community that identifies with the crucified Messiah. Thus, Paul does not harshly shame them because they are arrogantly resisting his instruction; rather, he delicately shames them so that they might heed his wise counsel and avoid making disastrous decisions. This use of prospective shame is primarily seen in Philemon.

Second, Paul may use prospective shame without necessarily evoking the occurrent experience of shame. When there is no immediate crisis, Paul does not engage in acts of shaming but uses honor and shame discourse. This includes reminding his readers that God is the ultimate judge whose opinion supremely matters, redefining that which is honorable and disgraceful, elevating worthy models, and deprecating negative examples. Through such moral education, Paul seeks to inculcate in his readers a Christian conscience that is centered on the mind of Christ and that points them toward appropriate thoughts and actions. His goal is to inculcate in his readers a sense of honor and shame that is grounded in the values of the divine court of opinion. His intent is to imprint within his readers the dispositional traits to act honorably as children of God (sense of honor) and the moral sensitivity to refrain from behaviors that dishonor their heavenly Father (sense of shame). They are to exercise appropriate humility and demonstrate proper respect toward others (Phil. 2:2–3). They must repudiate underhanded and disgraceful behavior (2 Cor. 4:2). At the same time, they must make every effort to present themselves as those approved by God, workers who have no need to be ashamed (2 Tim. 2:15; cf. Phil. 1:20). Used in this sense, shame functions more as an ethical trait than as an emotion, although the distinction cannot be too sharply held. This use of prospective shame is primarily seen in Philippians.

The cultivation of a dispositional sense of shame (shamefastness) that is centered on the mindset of Christ is not fully sufficient in itself to motivate all to adopt appropriate behaviors.[22] Failures do invariably occur, and there will

---

22. Aristotle (*Eth. nic.* 10.9.3–4, 1179B) notes that discourses on ethics only influence those who are exceptionally gifted, not the mass of humankind.

be times when believers do not live worthy of the gospel. In such situations, Paul employs retrospective shame.

Retrospective Shame in Paul's Shaming Rhetoric

Retrospective shame encompasses situations where the event that causes one to feel shame is in the past or present. This kind of shame is consequent upon having done bad acts. In retrospective shame, Paul shames others for the failures they have made or are currently making. But shaming refutation is not the first instrument of correction; restorative instruction and gentle rebuke must be first. Thus, when a believer is caught in sin, Paul exhorts the church to restore the offender to that person's former state of ethical probity. Such a rebuke is not to be conducted harshly, but "in a spirit of gentleness" (Gal. 6:1; cf. 1 Tim. 5:1–2). Paul demonstrates such an approach when he gently rebukes Euodia and Syntyche in Philippians 4:2–3.

When gentle rebuke is resisted and met with arrogance, hubris, and complacency, Paul escalates the intensity of the rebuke and engages in shaming refutation. He does not wish to be harsh. If the transgressor, however, persists in rejecting his instruction, Paul will have no choice but to dispense with "a gentle spirit." He must now use the "rod" for chastisement (1 Cor. 4:21). In shaming refutation, Paul rebukes transgressors and seeks to provoke the occurrent experience of shame in them. No one, not even the host of a house church or an apostle, is exempt from such correction if they are guilty of sin. Some of the sins that warrant shaming rebuke include factionalism (e.g., 1 Cor. 1:13–14), spiritual pride (e.g., 1 Cor. 3:1–4), and theological error that compromises key tenets of the gospel (e.g., Peter in Gal. 2).

If the person who is rebuked remains unrepentant, Paul resorts to the ultimate shaming refutation—excommunication or exclusion. The warrants for such severe disciplinary action appear to fall into three areas: persistent divisiveness and rebellion (e.g., Rom. 16:17; 2 Thess. 3:14; Titus 3:10), gross moral turpitude (e.g., the incestuous man in 1 Cor. 5), or gross theological error that subverts the gospel (e.g., blasphemy or false teaching of the gospel in 1 Tim. 1:20).[23] Failure in one of these arenas is sufficient warrant for excommunication; it is not "three strikes, you're out."

The escalating stages of Paul's disciplinary process can thus be construed as follows: restorative instruction and gentle rebuke → shaming refutation → excommunication. This sequence follows the pattern of Greco-Roman moral philosophers that we examined earlier. Paul applies the appropriate

---

23. Carson, *Love in Hard Places*, 169–70.

dose of medicine at the appropriate time, calibrating the dosage according to the severity of the sin and the response of the patient to the treatment. Light sins are treated with gentle rebukes, but grave sins require a stiffer remedy. Genuine remorse leads to the cessation of punishment and paves the way for restoration (2 Cor. 2:6–8), but unrepentance brings a severer response. Like a wise doctor, Paul ensures that the shaming refutation is not inappropriate or excessive. He also balances his harsh rhetoric with soothing words (such as praise and encouragement), so that the overall treatment regimen can be tolerated, if not embraced.

The purpose of Paul's shaming refutation is to maintain the honor of Christ, for Christ's reputation must not be tarnished through the evil done by believers. At the same time, Paul's shaming reputation is for the good of the community and the offender. The church is warned and protected against the leavening effects of sin. Moreover, the individual is disciplined with the intent of restoration. The painful occurrent experience of shame brought about by Paul and the church in acts of shaming fractures the transgressor's former mode of thinking, creating opportunities for self-reflection. If the offender feels ashamed, acknowledging that there is a breach in the shared ideals that govern the community, repentance and restoration are then possible. The sequential relationship of this process can be diagrammed as follows: act of disobedience by transgressor → shaming refutation by Paul/church → experience of shame in transgressor → repentance by transgressor → restoration by the church.

Shaming rebuke may not always be received positively. Our study of Socratic shaming noted how often Socrates failed to persuade his interlocutors. Paul himself was unsure how the Corinthian church would respond to his shaming refutation. When Paul sent the severe letter to Corinth with Titus, he held out hope for godly sorrow and genuine repentance (2 Cor. 7:9–11), yet he also feared that the church would respond with worldly sorrow and reject his call for corrective action (2 Cor. 7:5, 14). This hope and fear again gripped Paul when he announced that he would make a third visit to Corinth in response to more turmoil within the church (2 Cor. 12:14–13:10).

Although shaming rebuke may be rejected, there are pastoral insights in Paul's letters that suggest how shaming refutation can be framed in order to encourage a positive response. I summarize them as follows:

1. Paul's shaming refutation is for the sake of Christ, his gospel, and the community. Nonetheless, it must *also* be for the sake of the offender so as to bring about restoration (1 Cor. 5:5; 2 Cor. 12:19).
2. Shaming refutation is the responsibility of the entire church community rather than a single authority figure (1 Cor. 5:4; 2 Cor. 2:6; cf. Num.

15:35; Deut. 21:21). The testimony of many is more compelling, and it minimizes the likelihood that the offender perceives the shaming rebuke as a personal attack by an authoritarian individual. Moreover, participation in the disciplinary process by all the members increases conformity to the ethical standards of the community, reminding them that they are accountable to one another as members of the body of Christ.[24] When one member suffers, the entire body suffers (1 Cor. 12:26).

3. The community must demonstrate genuine love, care, and concern for the offender, even as it rebukes the offender and grieves over the sin (2 Cor. 2:4; Gal. 4:19–20; Eph. 4:15). The stronger the interconnectedness between the community and the offender, the stronger is the pressure to conform to the expectations of the community.

4. Shaming refutation cannot be excessive; it must be limited in scope (2 Cor. 2:6; cf. Deut. 25:2–3).

5. The community must be willing to forgive and embrace the offender when there is genuine repentance (2 Cor. 2:7–8). The offender must know that there is hope of rejoining the community. The shaming refutation must be restorative, not permanently stigmatic.

Rationale for Shame

The goal of Paul's shaming rhetoric is Christic formation. Paul uses shame (both retrospective and prospective) as a pedagogical tool to transform the mind of his readers into the mind of Christ so that their identity and behavior are rooted in the crucified Messiah. The goal of Paul's shaming rhetoric is clear; his rationale for doing so is more difficult to discern. Paul functions more as a practitioner than a theoretician. He uses shame, but he does not explicitly explain why he considers shame to be a vital pedagogical tool. In this section, I recall the discussions in earlier chapters (esp. the Greco-Roman backgrounds) and suggest several reasons why Paul may consider shame an important element in Christic formation.

1. *Shame, as a moral emotion, is vital to the Christian life.* Emotions are vital to the moral life.[25] For example, Aristotle noted that "moral virtue . . .

24. From a sociological perspective, Znaniecki (*Cultural Sciences*, 357) notes, "Inflicting punishment upon sinners increases the conformity and solidarity of the righteous, who are conscious that they act on the side of their god against the forces of evil. This is especially noticeable in those religious groups where the responsibility of repressing sins does not rest entirely with priests, but is shared by the whole faithful community."

25. See Williams, "Morality and the Emotions"; Prinz, *Emotional Construction of Morals*; Bagnoli, *Morality and the Emotions*; Roberts, *Emotions in the Moral Life*; Steinbock, *Moral Emotions*.

is concerned with emotions and actions."[26] Virtue is not just doing virtuous things but doing virtuous things *virtuously*. The emphasis on emotions is also true in the Christian life. Emotions play a critical role in Christian spirituality.[27] The Christian life is not just about right doing but also about right feeling. Paul remarks that sacrificial giving to the poor, self-denial, and martyrdom are meaningless if they are not accompanied with and motivated by love (1 Cor. 13:3). Given the important role that emotions play in the Christian life, it is not surprising that Paul seeks to instill in his readers a proper understanding of a key moral emotion—shame.

2. *Shame, as an emotional response, provides a window to our moral character*. Emotions are discriminating responses to values and modes of moral discernment; they are "value-laden ways of understanding the world."[28] Shame, as an emotional response of negative self-evaluation, reflects our internal moral judgments and provides some indications of the moral values we hold. The presence of the occurrent experience of shame toward a truly shameful event indicates our appropriation of the values of the divine court of opinion; the absence signals our shamelessness. Given the ability of emotional responses (particularly approbation and disapprobation) to reveal our moral character, it is no wonder that Paul reads the emotional responses of his readers for insights into their spiritual condition. Thus, when the Corinthian church did not grieve (express disapprobation) over the sin of the incestuous man in 1 Corinthians 5, but rather did boast (express approbation) in their freedom, Paul became painfully aware that their moral compass was defective.[29]

3. *Shame, as a moral emotion, has the potential to affect our belief structure*. Emotions not only reflect our belief structure but are also capable of reinforcing existing beliefs or introducing new ones.[30] Although Paul's shaming refutation seeks to transform the mind of his readers, he offers no explicit indication of how emotions affect beliefs. We may perhaps hazard a guess

26. Aristotle, *Eth. nic.* 2.6.10, 1106B16–17.

27. Theologians have generally recognized the importance of emotions in the Christian life. For Thomas Aquinas's understanding of the role of emotions in the moral life, see Cates, *Aquinas on the Emotions*. Jonathan Edwards notes that true religion must always be a matter of the affections, for "he that has doctrinal knowledge and speculation only, without affection, never is engaged in the business of religion" (*Works of Jonathan Edwards*, 2:101). For modern authors, see Elliott, *Faithful Feelings*; Roberts, *Spiritual Emotions*.

28. Nussbaum, *Upheavals of Thought*, 88.

29. Aquinas, *Summa Theologica* IIaIIae.46.1, states that a "fool is one whom shame does not incite to sorrow."

30. For essays on how emotions influence beliefs, see Frijda, Manstead, and Bem, *Emotions and Beliefs*.

using a cognitive approach to emotions, an approach that has also been applied to the study of emotions in other New Testament texts.[31] It would be anachronistic to assume that Paul has the same understanding of emotions as contemporary philosophers. Nonetheless, a cognitive approach to emotions in some form is not totally foreign to Paul's own thinking, for I have already noted the strong occurrence of cognitive or knowing lexemes in Paul's shaming rhetoric. Moreover, many Greco-Roman thinkers do adopt a cognitive understanding of emotions.[32]

I do not claim that Paul envisions his shaming rhetoric to function similarly to my following analysis. Rather, I present one way in which his shaming rhetoric can be understood. Now, recall from chapter 1 that I define an emotion as a process or script with the following five components: precipitating event, appraisal, physiological change, action tendency, and regulation. Applying this model to the case of incest in 1 Corinthians 5, the emotion process of pride that the Corinthians experience starts with a precipitating event (see fig. 6.1). In this case, it would be the situation of a socially influential man sleeping with his father's wife (5:1). The Corinthian church appraises this event positively, believing that this episode is further validation of the freedom they have in the Spirit. Sexual immorality is of no significance to the truly spiritual person. This evaluation causes them to experience pride and to boast about their current state.

When Paul shames the Corinthians, he attempts to evoke the occurrent experience of shame in his readers. If he is successful in his evocation, shame would entail an appraisal, albeit temporary, based on the current salient concerns that incest cannot be tolerated within the community. Such a new cognition (incest cannot be tolerated in any situation) in the mind of the Corinthians would clash with their prior cognition (incest can be tolerated when the violator has high social standing), resulting in cognitive dissonance and negative emotions. Cognitive dissonance theory posits that individuals, faced with this unease, will seek routes of dissonance reduction possibly through modifications of existing cognitions.[33] In essence, the Corinthians

31. See S. Barton, "Eschatology and the Emotions"; Inselmann, *Die Freude im Lukasevangelium*; Inselmann, "Zum Affekt der Freude im Philipperbrief."

32. Nussbaum (*Therapy of Desire*, 369) writes, "There is in Greek thought about the emotions, from Plato and Aristotle straight on through Epicurus, an agreement that the emotions are not simply blind surges of affect, stirrings or sensations that are identified, and distinguished from one another, by their felt quality alone. Unlike appetites such as thirst and hunger, they have an important cognitive element: they embody ways of interpreting the world. The feelings that go with the experience of emotion are hooked up with and rest upon beliefs or judgments that are their basis or ground."

33. See Harmon-Jones, "Cognitive Dissonance Theory."

may cope with the cognitive dissonance by modifying their belief structures so that they now consider incest to be truly deplorable regardless of the social standing of the offender. Through additional habituation of their affective natures to proper conduct, the temporary appraisal entailed by the emotion of shame turns into a longer-term belief, and the occurrent experience of shame becomes an emotional disposition that is constitutive of virtue.

4. *Shame, as a moral emotion, provides rhetorical amplification and deepens convictions.* Appeals to pathos complement ethos and logos arguments, for the evocation of emotions focuses attention on prior cognitions such that they are taken more seriously. Evoking the occurrent experience of shame in others thus provides more bite than merely informing someone of the wrong that they have done. It forces them to confront the issue of their sin more forcefully. It "emphasizes and makes [them] internalize the judgment that the act is wrong."[34]

Paul uses shame as a pedagogical tool to transform the minds of his readers into the mind of Christ. But the use of shame is not just to reconfigure their

Figure 6.1

Interplay of Beliefs and Affections

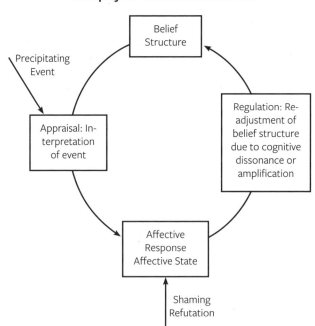

34. Curzer, *Aristotle and the Virtues*, 338.

cognitive grasp of moral principles. It is also an attempt to prod his readers to know as they ought to know—that is, to know moral truth in such a way that it affects the core of their being. It is a call to own epistemic content with emotional conditions.[35] It is a call for a deeper knowledge—a call to possess knowledge so deeply that it intuitively controls how people construe events in the world, with the result that it spontaneously leads to the appropriate feelings or affect.

5. *Shame, as the premier social emotion, supports the communal nature of Pauline ethics.* Shame is the emotion of interconnectedness; we experience shame most acutely before those who are affiliated and important to us. The stronger the social bonds, the stronger the emotional pain of shame will be. Thus, shame functions as a strong disincentive to violation of social responsibilities. Jon Elster remarks, "The emotion of shame is not only a support of social norms, but *the* support."[36] Shame plays an outsized role in regulating the social expectations of the community.

Given the significant role that shame plays in maintaining the norms of the community, it is no surprise that Paul might favor the use of shame because Pauline ethics is primarily communal.[37] Spiritual formation for Paul is not a private matter; it is a communal affair. As James Thompson notes, "Spiritual formation is corporate formation."[38] Shame has a significant role to play in the moral formation of the community. It ensures that the whole community is aware of the ethical norms of the community, and it enlists the support of the community to bring about such conformity.

6. *Shame motivates, but gratitude is the ultimate emotional motivation for doing good.* Knowledge of the noble and base informs us as to what actions are appropriate, but it cannot prompt action in itself. A strict cognitive grasp

---

35. See Roberts, "Emotions," 16, 20.

36. Elster, *Alchemies of the Mind*, 145.

37. The church is the object of God's saving activity, and God is redeeming a people (λαός) for himself. Although individuals enter into the community by faith and Paul does speak about individual character development, his focus is on the development of the individual as part of God's community. Communal edification is more important than individual edification. Thus, Paul's ire in 1 Cor. 5 is directed not so much at the incestuous man as at the community who has forgotten its moral responsibility to discipline the individual. Moreover, Paul also notes that the one who prophesies is greater than the one who speaks in tongues, for the entire church is edified through prophecy (1 Cor. 14:1–6). Finally, the communal nature of Pauline ethics is also witnessed by the heavy prevalence of ἀλλήλων (one another) in his paraenesis. Believers are to love *one another* (Rom. 12:10; 13:8; Gal. 5:13), live in harmony with *one another* (Rom. 12:16), wait for *one another* at the Lord's Supper (1 Cor. 11:33), care for *one another* (1 Cor. 12:25), do good to *one another* (1 Thess. 5:15), bear the burdens of *one another* (Gal. 6:2), and not lie to *one another* (Col. 3:9).

38. Thompson, "Spiritual Formation."

of moral principles is insufficient for moral development. A strong emotional impulse is also needed.[39] As I noted in chapter 2, Aristotle is keenly aware of this issue and considers shame to be the needed emotional impulse. It is the semi-virtue of the moral learner as it motivates the learner to have a genuine love for the noble and aversion toward the base; it propels the student to become fully virtuous rather than simply knowing what virtue demands. In essence, it bridges the moral-upbringing gap.

Paul acknowledges the role that shame plays in motivating believers to live a life worthy of their calling. When believers understand that the basis of their honor truly is Christ, their shamefastness before God and their desire to receive a crown of righteousness from him (1 Cor. 9:24–27; Phil. 3:14; 2 Tim. 4:7–8) motivate them to keep the faith and do that which pleases him. Despite the motivational impulse that shame provides, Paul would insist that the ultimate and founding motivation for Christian ethics is God's grace and love. "The starting point and basis for Paul's ethics is the saving eschatological event of Jesus' death and resurrection, in which God acted, eschatologically and finally, to save the world."[40] Theology and ethics are integrally linked. The new obedience that is required of believers is a result of the new life they have been given, such that the imperative rests on and follows the indicative. Indeed, Paul writes that Christ's self-sacrificial love controls believers so that they no longer live for themselves but for him who died on their behalf and was raised again (2 Cor. 5:14–15; cf. 1 Cor. 6:20; Gal. 2:20). Gratitude, rather than shame, then, appears to be the emotional impulse that provides the motivation for Christian living; gratitude, rather than shame, bridges the moral-upbringing gap in Pauline thought.[41] Nonetheless, gratitude cannot be completely separated from shame, for the failure to show gratitude is disgraceful and shameful.[42]

Although gratitude may be the ultimate emotional motivation for living a life that pleases God, the prior work of the Holy Spirit must not be discounted since it is the Holy Spirit who supernaturally infuses God's love into our hearts (Rom. 5:5). I now turn to the role of the Holy Spirit in Paul's use of shame.

---

39. Frijda, Manstead, and Bem ("Influence of Emotions on Beliefs," 3) write, "Although beliefs may guide our actions, they are not sufficient to initiate action. No matter how rational your thoughts about helping the needy may be, you need an emotional impulse before you actually volunteer to help. Emotions are prime candidates for turning a thinking being into an actor."

40. Schrage, *Ethics of the New Testament*, 172.

41. Question 86 of the Heidelberg Catechism affirms that believers should do good works, even though they are saved by grace through Christ, in order to show their *gratitude* to God for his blessing.

42. Seneca, *Ben.* 3.1.1. See further deSilva, *Honor, Patronage, Kinship & Purity*, 109–13.

The Role of the Holy Spirit in Paul's Use of Shame

The focus of Paul's use of shame has so far primarily centered on rhetorical, anthropological, sociological, and psychological factors. I would, however, be remiss if I ignored the role of the Holy Spirit. Paul emphasizes the necessity of both human and divine agency in moral formation, and the Holy Spirit is key to the ethical life. Gordon Fee remarks, "The Spirit is essential to Paul's ethics *because truly Christian ethics can only be by the Spirit's empowering.*"[43] If the Spirit is essential in Pauline ethics, it is just as essential in Paul's use of shame, for shaming rhetoric will never bring about genuine change without the transforming and empowering work of the Spirit. This discussion must necessarily be brief, given space constraints. I discuss three avenues in which the Spirit works according to Paul.

1. *The Holy Spirit mediates the mind of Christ.* The Holy Spirit plays a prominent role in Paul's use of shame, for he enables us to know God.[44] Specifically, the Spirit mediates the mind of Christ, enabling believers to know what pleases God. Paul's discussion of *natural* (ψυχικός) and *spiritual* (πνευματικός) people in 1 Corinthians 2:10–15 bears this out. Using the principle that "like is only known by like," Paul argues that the thoughts of God are only known by the Holy Spirit. Thus, *natural* people (those who do not have the Holy Spirit) do not accept the things of God. They consider such matters mere foolishness (2:14a). Moreover, they are not able to understand them, because such matters can only be discerned through the Spirit (2:14b). Within the context of this pericope, the things of God refer to the message of the cross and, by implication, the perspective of the crucified Messiah. Paul, in essence, therefore argues that the values of the divine court of opinion cannot be truly known and embraced by those who do not have the Spirit; it is only possible to the *spiritual*—to all believers, since they possess the Spirit.

Paul does not say that unbelievers (those who do not have the Spirit) are not able to know something about the self-giving nature of the mind of Christ. They may be able to do so, but their understanding is from the perspective of an observer or outsider (etic). Believers, however, are enabled by the Spirit so that they "truly see the cross for what it is."[45] They understand it from the perspective of an insider (emic), of one who has been empowered and transformed so as to embrace the perspective of a crucified Messiah in their cognitive, volitional, and affective spheres.

43. Fee, *God's Empowering Presence*, 878.
44. Cole, *He Who Gives Life*, 259–77.
45. Carson, *Cross and Christian Ministry*, 65.

2. *The Holy Spirit shapes our conscience and sense of shame.* I noted earlier that Democritus was one of the earlier philosophers who perceived the difficulty of external legislation to regulate moral behavior. Instead of external sanctions, he argued for an internalized standard that is bound up with one's conscience and sense of shame.[46]

The external and internal divide, embodied in the contrast between the *letter* and the *Spirit*, is also foundational in Pauline ethics.[47] In 2 Corinthians 3:1–6, Paul argues that the letter of the law inscribed on tablets of stone can only condemn. As external commands that are not enshrined in the heart, the letter pronounces death, for it can never effect true change. The Holy Spirit is needed, for he writes the law internally on human hearts (3:3; cf. Jer. 31:33; Ezek. 11:19; 36:26–27). He indwells believers and empowers them to fulfill the requirements of the law, so that the Christian life is "the natural outcome of a transformed nature rather than the laborious attempts to conform to an external code."[48]

Part of the internal transformation brought about by the Holy Spirit is the shaping of the conscience. Paul gives some evidence of this shaping when he remarks that his conscience as "guided by the Holy Spirit" (ἐν πνεύματι ἁγίῳ) testifies to his sincerity (Rom. 9:1). The Holy Spirit guides and leads (ἄγω, Gal. 5:18) a person's conscience so that it is incrementally captive to the word of God. The Holy Spirit empowers believers so that their minds are transformed, renewed, and progressively conformed to the mind of Christ (cf. Rom. 8:4–9; 12:2).[49]

Because of the transformative work of the Spirit, a well-formed conscience and sense of shame can be said to be a fruit of the Spirit. Paul, after all, remarks that self-control (ἐγκράτεια), a virtue that is closely related to a proper sense of shame, is a fruit of the Spirit (Gal. 5:23).[50]

3. *The Holy Spirit convicts believers of sin.* I noted earlier that shaming rebuke may not always elicit a favorable response, as the recipient may reject the rebuke. Shaming rebuke becomes effective only through the convicting work of the Holy Spirit, so that the transgressor is able to see the sin for what it truly is. The necessity of the Holy Spirit in shaming refutation is analogous to the necessity of the Holy Spirit in evangelism. Both require the convicting work of the Spirit. Just as the proclamation of the gospel

46. See also Cicero, *Rep.* 5.6.
47. Westerholm, "Letter and Spirit."
48. Manson, "Jesus, Paul, and the Law," 139.
49. Johnson, "Transformation of the Mind," 229–31.
50. There is a strong link between self-control (ἐγκράτεια) and shamefastness (αἰδώς). See Philo, *Sacr.* 27; *Ios.* 153; *Somn.* 1.124; *Mos.* 1.161.

does not lead to conversion unless the Holy Spirit convicts unbelievers of their sin (1 Cor. 14:24; cf. John 16:8), so also shaming rebuke does not lead to repentance unless the same Holy Spirit convicts transgressing believers of their sin. The Holy Spirit is needed not only for conversion but also for sanctification (Gal. 3:3).[51]

Shaming refutation requires the convicting work of the Holy Spirit. When Paul shames his readers, he shames them not because they do not have the Spirit but because they live as those who do not have the Spirit. Even though they should be able to assess and "discern all things" through the wisdom provided by the Holy Spirit (1 Cor. 2:15; cf. 6:3), they are instead worldly (σαρκικός) and act no differently than the rest of pagan society (1 Cor. 3:3). Moreover, they do not perceive sin as the Holy Spirit perceives sin, and they do not grieve over sin as the Holy Spirit grieves (1 Cor. 5:2; cf. Eph. 4:30).

The Holy Spirit convicts believers of sin in shaming refutation by testifying to the existential relevance of Scripture. He takes away any rationalization for sin and applies the truth of Scripture so that we perceive the sin for what it truly is. John Frame, drawing on the work of Ludwig Wittgenstein, classifies this work as a distinction between "seeing" and "seeing as."[52] Using the well-known gestalt figure of a duck/rabbit (see fig. 6.2), Frame notes that different people will see a situation differently. One person may see a duck, another a rabbit. The two people see the same lines of the picture but see different shapes. Nathan's confrontation of David in 2 Samuel 12 demonstrates the reality of this paradigm. Before the prophetic rebuke, David was not convicted of sin; he saw his relationship with Bathsheba merely as a recreational dalliance. It was only after the rebuke that David was convicted of sin; he now saw that same relationship as adultery. Frame attributes the change of perspective in David to the testifying work of the Holy Spirit. The Holy Spirit testifies to the truth of Scripture and applies it to particular experiences in our lives. As our earlier discussion on Ezekiel in chapter 3 indicated, remorse and shame for what one has done is intimately tied to knowledge of God and self-knowledge. The Holy Spirit mediates both so that we come to our senses (cf. Luke 15:17) and see sin for what it is. He guides us to the right perspective so that we construe experiences and events as Scripture rightly intends for us to construe them. The new construal that the Spirit gives invariably brings about the corresponding emotional response. Thus, the work of the Spirit

---

51. Fee (*God's Empowering Presence*, 878) states, "Both 'getting in' and 'staying in' are the work of the Spirit, and Paul sees no bifurcation between the two."

52. Frame, *Doctrine of the Knowledge of God*, 156–58.

Figure 6.2

Do You See a Duck or a Rabbit?

is not just cognitive but also emotive.[53] It is a religious experience. When the Spirit convicts us of our sin, we not only recognize that what we have done is sin but are also grieved and shamed by our sin.

Shaming Unbelievers

Paul's ethic of shame is fundamentally directed toward believers, toward those who are within the community of faith. Paul does not judge those outside the church, nor does he advocate the church to do so (1 Cor. 5:12–13). Within the context of 1 Corinthians 5, the meaning of "judge" (κρίνω) is to condemn someone formally and pursue disciplinary action against them. The church is not to judge the world in this sense, because it does not have jurisdiction over

53. Frame (*Doctrine of the Knowledge of God*, 152–53) considers the internal testimony of the Spirit or "cognitive rest" as "something very much like a *feeling*." Sometimes the feeling can be intense, as is the case when the Spirit convicted the hearts of the disciples as the risen Lord spoke to them on the road to Emmaus ("Were not our hearts burning within us?," Luke 24:32). Incidentally, Roberts (*Emotions*, 70–72) also uses the distinction between "seeing" and "seeing as" to illustrate his construal theory of emotions. Depending on how an individual perceives or construes the event, the individual will have a different emotional perception or construal. Roberts, however, uses the young woman/old woman gestalt figure rather than the duck/rabbit.

the world. That is God's prerogative. He will pass sentence on the world in the future, and the church universal will participate in that eschatological judgment (1 Cor. 6:2). But at the present time, the church's pedagogical and disciplinary focus is on its own members. The intended audience of Paul's shaming rhetoric is the community of believers. This overall comment needs two clarifications.

1. Paul's exhortation not to judge unbelievers does not mean that the church is not to speak prophetically to the world, "judging" or "shaming" it for its injustice and wickedness. One way in which believers judge and shame the world is by constantly presenting a lifestyle and advocating a worldview that is countercultural and radically different from the world. In Romans 12:17–21, Paul outlines the attitude Christians are to have toward unbelievers. He exhorts the church not to repay evil for evil, nor are they to refrain from showing kindness to their enemies (contra Sir. 12:4–5). Instead, they are to follow the advice of Proverbs 25:21–22. If their enemy is hungry, they are to feed him; if thirsty, they are to give him something to drink. In doing so, they heap burning coals on his head (Rom. 12:20). The significance of the burning coals is debated, but "most commentators agree with Augustine and Jerome that the 'coals of fire' refers to 'burning pangs of shame' which a man will feel when good is returned for evil, his shame producing remorse and contrition."[54]

This perspective of invoking shame not through harsh rhetoric but through acts of mercy recalls the inversion of shame in Ezekiel as discussed in chapter 3: Israel experiences shame not in its judgment but in its restoration. When Yahweh does his restorative work and transforms Israel's heart, Israel sees its wickedness and is stricken with remorse. In a similar way, when the Holy Spirit works in the hearts of those who oppose the church, they will see the good deeds of the church and be stricken with shame and remorse.

2. If Paul does not advocate the shaming of unbelievers through harsh rhetoric, what are we to make of the vilification of his opponents in Galatians? After all, there is reason to think that Paul does not consider the agitators to be true believers, for he warns that they will face God's eschatological judgment (Gal. 5:10).

One resolution would be to say that Paul's harsh rhetoric was directed not so much toward the agitators per se as toward the members of the church who were his brothers and sisters. The purpose of such rhetoric, then, is to persuade his readers not only to reject the agitators and their teaching but also to align themselves with him and his gospel. But a more satisfactory response would be to say that Paul has harsh words for the agitators because they are false teachers who claim to be followers of Jesus. Consequently, they fall under the jurisdiction of the church. Paul therefore exhorts the church to cast out

---

54. Waltke, *Book of Proverbs*, 331.

these false brothers (Gal. 4:30) so that the church will not be deceived by the leaven of false teaching (5:9).

Conclusion

Paul's understanding and use of shame are both similar to and different from those in the Jewish and Greco-Roman worlds. He considers shame to be an emotion that one experiences when one is guilty of sin, for shame centers on a negative self-evaluation based on a certain set of ideals that a person holds. The ideals that a person cherishes may come from different courts of opinion. For Paul, the divine court of opinion is paramount. The basis of true honor and shame is not wealth and status, but the cross. The values of the divine court of opinion cannot remain as mere external requirements or expectations of the community; they must be internally embraced so that they shape one's conscience and sense of shame. With this goal, Paul therefore seeks to shape the mind of his readers so that they evaluate all of life through the perspective of the crucified Messiah.

Paul uses shame as a pedagogical tool for Christic formation. He engages in honor and shame discourse to cultivate in his readers a dispositional sense of shame that is rooted in the mind of Christ. He also uses shaming rhetoric charged with prospective shame to discourage behavior that dishonors Christ and those for whom Christ died. When his readers persist in sinful behavior, Paul resorts to retrospective shame. He rebukes his readers with the hope that the painful experience of shame will move them to recognize the error of their ways. In extreme situations, Paul advocates excommunication to preserve the purity of the community. But even then, the door is open for the offender to rejoin the community when there is contrition. Thus, Paul shames his readers not to humiliate them but to prod them toward repentance. His shaming rhetoric is not destructive but redemptive, not disintegrative but reintegrative.

Paul's use of shaming refutation bears similarities with Greco-Roman moralists such as Plutarch, Epictetus, and Dio Chrysostom. They all believe that retrospective shame, when used circumspectly, is salutary. Nonetheless, what separates Paul from these moralists is his insistence that the Holy Spirit is vitally necessary in order for shaming refutation to be effective. Paul's shaming rhetoric is therefore not just sociological but also theological. Christic transformation through shaming refutation is not possible without the transformative and empowering work of the Holy Spirit.

PART 3

CULTURAL ENGAGEMENT

Part 3 engages Paul's ethic of shame with contemporary perspectives. Chapter 7 brings Paul into conversation with voices in our world that advocate a positive role for shame. Chapter 8 does the same with contemporary challenges to a positive use of shame.

7

Contemporary Contribution

This chapter engages Paul's ethic of shame with two voices that call for a positive role for shame: John Braithwaite's reintegrative shaming theory (RST) and the Confucian understanding of shame that undergirds Chinese families.

My reasons for putting Paul in conversation with these two voices arise from my exegetical work on Paul. Specifically, my desire is to choose one voice that advocates the use of retrospective shame and another the use of prospective shame. In looking for a contemporary voice that advocates the use of shame as a response to deviant behavior (retrospective shame), I turn to the field of criminology. This discipline raises issues that are pertinent to any community that seeks to respond to delinquent behavior. Within this discipline, Braithwaite's RST is significant as it combines insights from various criminological traditions such as labeling, subcultural, control, opportunity, and learning theories.

Reintegrative shaming is not new; aspects of it have been practiced by the Japanese, the Maoris of New Zealand, and indigenous African communities. Nonetheless, Braithwaite provides a robust theory of this practice. Since its introduction, RST has garnered wide attention such that elements of it are employed in restorative justice, a model of criminal justice that is advocated by various Christian organizations, such as Prison Fellowship. An examination of RST may afford us insights into how Pauline communities used shaming refutation to address behavior they did not approve.

In looking for a voice that advocates the use of shame as a deterrence against deviant behavior (prospective shame), I examine Confucian thought in the Chinese culture. It is generally understood that shame plays a significant role in regulating and deterring inappropriate behavior within the Chinese culture. This hypercognition or heightened sensitivity toward shame is widely attributed to the influence of Confucius. An engagement of his thought may thus prove beneficial in understanding how the Pauline community can likewise use shame as a deterrence against sinful behavior. Moreover, a better appreciation of Confucian moral psychology may further our sensitivity toward Paul's.

Although not strictly limited to a particular perspective of shame, RST focuses on retrospective and the Confucian teaching on prospective shame. Their combined foci form a complementary platform to compare Paul's ethic of shame, an ethic that comprises both retrospective and prospective shame.

The attempt to put Paul in conversation with Braithwaite's RST and Confucian thought has methodological and conceptual challenges, for there are substantial differences between them.[1] I list three:

1. The philosophical frameworks and worldviews underpinning these three voices are different. Braithwaite's RST operates within a secular, the Confucian writings within a humanistic, and Paul within a theistic framework.

2. The frame of reference for the application of shame is different for each voice. In Braithwaite's RST, it is the criminological sphere in society, encompassing everything from white-collar crime to juvenile delinquency and street crime. In the Confucian writings, it is the kingdom. In Paul's ethic of shame, it is the church, an intentional community or voluntary association that meets primarily in a household setting.

3. There are obvious lexical differences in the vocabulary of shame. The Greek word αἰσχύνη and the Chinese word 耻 (*chi*) can both be roughly translated by the English word *shame*. Nonetheless, their semantic fields do not correspond exactly.

These differences do not make comparison impossible, for it is a mistake to consider RST or Confucian thought to be utterly different with respect to the Pauline writings. My task, moreover, is not to provide a comprehensive comparison. Rather, I select certain features for comparison so that the similarities in differences and the differences in similarities between these three voices

---

1. For discussions on the complexities and fruitfulness of such comparative work, see the introductory and methodological essays in King and Schilling, *How Should One Live?*; Lloyd and Zhao, *Ancient Greece and China Compared*.

might enable a clearer perspective of Paul's vision for shame. I proceed with a discussion of Braithwaite's RST before moving to the Confucian teaching. A short conclusion will summarize the ideas of this chapter.

John Braithwaite's RST

John Braithwaite is currently a Distinguished Professor at the Australian National University. His work on RST is primarily outlined in his book *Crime, Shame, and Reintegration*. Since the publication of the book, several empirical tests were conducted to test the theory. Results were largely consistent with RST, and discrepancies led to some modification of the theory.[2] In this section, I first provide an overview of RST. I then compare and contrast it with Paul's vision of shame, noting elements that may help us further understand the latter.

Overview of the Theory

Braithwaite outlines the central thesis of his book with this claim: "The theory in this book suggests that the key to crime control is cultural commitments to shaming in ways that I call reintegrative. Societies with low crime rates are those that shame potently and judiciously; individuals who resort to crime are those insulated from shame over their wrongdoing. However, shame can be applied injudiciously and counterproductively; the theory seeks to specify the types of shaming which cause rather than prevent crime."[3] I examine Braithwaite's theory in four areas.

1. Informal Shaming and Formal Punishment

Braithwaite argues that an important factor that explains the increasing rates of crime in Western countries is the uncoupling of shame from criminal punishment (61). Since perpetrators of crime are not made to feel shame for their actions, they continue victimizing without remorse.[4] Moreover, criminal punishment administered by jurisprudential professionals that only mete out the just deserts of defendants is an "ineffective weapon of social control partly because it is a degradation ceremony with maximum prospects for

2. For modifications to RST, see Ahmed et al., *Shame Management*, 39–57.

3. Braithwaite, *Crime, Shame, and Reintegration*, 1. Subsequent page references in this section appear in the text.

4. Leibrich ("Role of Shame," 283) writes, "A study of former offenders found that shame was a significant feature in decisions to go straight." See also Murphy and Harris, "Shaming, Shame and Recidivism"; Garvey, "Can Shaming Punishments Educate?"

stigmatization" (14). The incarceration of offenders effectively breaks up meaningful relationships that can potentially help reintegrate the offender back into society after the period of punishment. As these offenders are shunted into warehouses for social deviants, they are exposed to criminal subcultures that actively support norms and rationalizations for criminal behavior.

Instead of formal criminal punishment, Braithwaite advocates informal shaming. He argues that since crime hurts, justice must heal. Justice cannot merely punish and deliver the wrongdoer's just deserts; it must restore broken communities. Shaming, especially shaming acts of injustice reintegratively, is a tool that not only prevents injustice but also fosters this needed healing and restoration.

Braithwaite argues that informal shaming within a community is more effective than purely punitive punishment meted out by an impersonal criminal system. He gives three reasons. First, "sanctions imposed by relatives, friends, or a personally relevant collectivity have more effect on criminal behavior than sanctions imposed by a remote legal authority" (69). Such disapproval poses a threat to relationships that are valued, for respect and status in the eyes of significant acquaintances are more important to most people than the opinions of justice officials.

Second, shaming within a community carries symbolic freight. It moralizes the offense and communicates reasons for the evil of a particular deviance. Shaming is "a tool to allure and inveigle the citizen to attend to the moral claims of the criminal law, to coax and caress compliance, to reason and remonstrate with him over the harmfulness of his conduct" (9). Shaming therefore views the offender as a responsible moral agent and invites him to freely comply with the norms of the community. Formal punishment, on the other hand, "is a denial of confidence in the morality of the offender by reducing norm compliance to a crude cost-benefit calculation" (72).

Third, shaming is the fundamental societal process that makes certain crimes unthinkable to most people; it "underwrites the family process of building consciences in children" (72). Conscience is a greater deterrence to deviance than punishment by the criminal justice system. The anxiety response of conscience is ever-present and immediate, but formal punishment occurs long after the crime is perpetrated and only if the offender is apprehended.

Braithwaite is not naive to think that formal punishment will be completely eliminated in any criminal justice system. He advocates that formal punishment be reserved only for offenders who are beyond conditioning by shame.

2. Disintegrative Shaming and Reintegrative Shaming

Braithwaite argues that the key to lowering crime is a cultural commitment to shaming. He defines shaming as "all societal processes of expressing social disapproval which have the intention or effect of invoking remorse in the person being shamed and/or condemnation by others who become aware of the shaming" (100). This broad definition of shaming can take multiple forms. It can be as subtle as a frown or as direct as a verbal reprimand from a judge. This definition also allows for acts of shaming that are either counterproductive or productive, acts that are injudicious or judicious. Braithwaite classifies these two types of shaming as disintegrative and reintegrative. The former is bad and harmful, the latter good and helpful.

Disintegrative shaming (DS) treats the offender disrespectfully as a fundamentally bad person. It emphasizes the labeling of deviance without much thought to de-labeling, forgiveness, and reintegration (55). The deviant label is applied primarily to the person rather than the behavior, such that the label stigmatizes as it becomes a master status that defines the person. Moreover, the shaming process is open-ended; there is no ceremony to decertify deviance. With the onset of stigmatization, the offender is progressively cast out of the community.

Reintegrative shaming (RS) is "shaming which is followed by efforts to reintegrate the offender back into the community of law-abiding or respectable citizens through words or gestures of forgiveness or ceremonies to decertify the offender as deviant" (100–101). The communal expressions of disapproval are limited in time. They are terminated before the deviance label becomes a master status that dominates all other characteristics and defines the person. They are also terminated by communal gestures of reacceptance and forgiveness. These expressions of disapproval are centered on the evil act rather than on the person, working under the assumption that the offender is fundamentally a good person that has temporarily gone astray. In short, "reintegrative shaming means treating the wrongdoer respectfully and emphatically as a good person who has done a bad act and making special efforts to show the wrongdoer how valued they are after the wrongful act has been confronted."[5]

RS is distinguished from DS not by the leniency of its gestures of disapproval; it is not weak, for it can be just as harsh as DS. Rather, RS is distinguished "by (a) a finite rather than open-ended duration which is terminated by forgiveness; and by (b) efforts to maintain bonds of love or respect through the finite period of suffering shame" (101). Moreover, RS is offense-centered (disapproval of an act) rather than person-centered (disapproval of a person).

---

5. Ahmed et al., *Shame Management*, 4.

DS is generally counterproductive. Stigmatization increases the attraction of offenders to subcultures that offer alternative routes for self-esteem that are at odds with mainstream society. In effect, DS risks pushing offenders into criminal subcultures—subcultures that provide criminal role models and techniques that make a life of crime more attractive. RS is preferable because it "minimizes risks of pushing those shamed into criminal subcultures, and because social disapproval is more effective when embedded in relationships overwhelmingly characterized by social approval" (68). Nonetheless, DS may still be superior to no shaming at all if the density of criminal subcultures in a society is low. If offenders do not encounter opportunities for participation in criminal subcultural groups, they may tire of the life of an outcast and prove themselves worthy of rehabilitation to the group that had previously labeled them as deviants. In such situations, DS and stigmatization will still reduce the crime rate of the community. It must, however, be recognized that DS increases the risk of suicide.

3. Social Conditions Conducive to RS

Braithwaite argues that "the fundamental societal conditions conducive to cultural processes of reintegrative shaming are communitarianism and interdependency" (84). Communitarianism and interdependency are related concepts. Braithwaite understands communitarianism as a characteristic of society, and interdependency as a descriptor primarily applied to individual relationships.

Social communitarianism is the sum product of individual interdependent relationships. In other words, interdependencies are the building blocks of communitarianism. A communitarian society, however, is not just the aggregation of individual interdependencies; rather, it is the aggregation of *certain* kinds of interdependencies—interdependencies that are marked by care, concern, respect, and mutual obligations. Braithwaite summarizes three elements that are necessary for a communitarian society: "(1) densely enmeshed interdependency, where the interdependencies are characterized by (2) mutual obligation and trust, and (3) are interpreted as a matter of group loyalty rather than individual convenience. Communitarianism is therefore the antithesis of individualism" (86).

All societies, whether communitarian or individualistic, can bring about shaming by the state. But communitarian societies have an advantage over individualistic societies. They "can also deliver shaming by neighbors and relatives and congregation members in a way that individualistic societies cannot. Shaming by significant others should be more potent than shaming by an impersonal state" (87). We feel shame more acutely before our friends, teachers, colleagues, and neighbors, whom we have to see every day, than from a judge (despite being a higher authority figure), whom we will perhaps see only once in our life.

Communitarian societies deliver not only more potent shaming but shaming that is also more reintegrative and less stigmatizing. Braithwaite points to research that demonstrates how social distance affects one's reaction to criminality. The less socially distant a person is to the offender, the less likely he or she will view the offender as fundamentally stigmatized. Ex-inmates affirm the different reactions close friends and socially distant people have toward them in the following manner: "Me mates know what I'm really like. They know many sides of me, whereas others just think of the criminal side first."[6] Close friends see ex-inmates as round characters with complex personalities, rather than flat characters with stereotypical master categories of criminality. Hence, their acts of shaming are least likely to be stigmatizing.

The above arguments suggest that "in communitarian societies, while pressures for shaming are greater because people are so much more involved in each others' lives, for the same reason pressures for stigmatization are less" (88). Communitarian societies are conducive to RS. Such societies foster shame and reintegration. They shame offenders without destroying the central identity that binds their interdependent relationship. They shame offenders respectfully and emphatically without permanently severing connections. They shame them reintegratively.

4. Shame Management

Subsequent research in RST focuses not so much on the act of shaming as on the reception of shame by the wrongdoer. It found that RS is "important for reducing offending not because it results in shame but because it provides a mechanism that assists offenders to manage their feeling of shame in more constructive ways."[7] There is therefore a slight focal shift in RST from *shaming* to *shame management*.

Shame management is understood as follows. In response to a shaming event, an offender can either acknowledge or dismiss the shame that should be experienced. Theorists label this as *acknowledged* or *unacknowledged* *shame*.

Acknowledged shame involves "(a) admission of feelings of shame over a wrongdoing; (b) willingness to take responsibility for the wrongdoing; and (c) a desire for making amends for what happened."[8] The offender assumes

6. Ericson, "Social Distance," 23.
7. Harris and Maruna, "Shame, Shaming and Restorative Justice," 459–60.
8. Ahmed et al., *Shame Management*, 233.

responsibility for the offense, experiences remorse, and attempts to set things right. But the shame that an offender acknowledges can be either adaptive or maladaptive; it can be either discharged and released, or it can remain persistent within the offender. Acknowledged shame that is discharged allows offenders to put the shameful event behind them and begin the process of rebuilding positive social relationships. Acknowledged shame that is not discharged leads to depression, confusion, alienation, and a loss of self-esteem.

In unacknowledged shame, the offender rejects any notion of doing anything worthy of shame. The individual feels no shame, takes no responsibility for the wrongdoing, and has no desire to make amends for what happened. If the communal disapproval persists, the fracture within the social relationships remains. The offender then blames others for the situation, directs anger toward them, and rejects those who reject them. The overall situation becomes criminogenic rather than crime inhibiting.[9]

Acknowledged shame is the likely response when acts of shaming are judiciously executed—when the shaming comes from those whom the offender highly respects. Such shame is discharged when the shaming is reintegrative, but it may remain persistent when the shaming is disintegrative. Unacknowledged shame, however, is likely when acts of shaming are injudiciously executed—when the disapproval comes from those whom the offender does not respect or only moderately respects, when the offender does not agree with the ethical standards that are applied to him, and when the shaming is disintegrative.[10]

The shift from *shaming* to *shame management* does not discount RST's primary contribution that RS reduces crime. Rather, it proposes the reason for this reduction: RS makes it more likely that wrongdoers are able not only to acknowledge their shame but also to discharge it responsibly without displacing it as anger toward others. Acts of shaming that are reintegrative rather than disintegrative bring restoration not only to the victim but also to the offender.

Interaction

RST is useful for helping us further understand Paul's ethic of shame. It provides a theoretical framework for understanding how the right kind of

9. Scheff (*Bloody Revenge*, 105–24) remarks that the appeal of Hitler during World War II was his ability to channel the shame that the people felt, from the humiliation they received at Versailles, into anger.

10. Ahmed et al., *Shame Management*, 168–70.

shame can reduce deviance. Moreover, the theory can be applied to develop procedures that encourage not only productive confrontation but also restoration of the wrongdoer. In the following, I list several dimensions that help us better understand Paul's ethic of shame and also critique some aspects of RST.

Unavoidability and Positivity

Braithwaite and his colleagues recognize that shame is an emotion that is impossible to avoid in any kind of social censure that disapproves. Some theorists advocate the importance of remorse and empathy, factors that RST also values, but they want to minimize the role of shame.[11] Research suggests, however, that it is not possible to evoke remorse, empathy, and guilt for an offense without the corresponding feeling of shame.[12]

Given the inevitability of shame, Braithwaite envisions a positive role for shame in moral formation, recognizing that shame can play a pedagogical role in deterring or reducing deviance. Braithwaite argues that RS deters crime because it develops our conscience and our "fear of shame in the eyes of intimates."[13] Moreover, it moralizes the offense, encouraging the offender to take responsibility for the wrongdoing and to make amends. Such a perspective agrees with our assessment of Paul, for he also recognizes the pedagogical value of shame. He uses shame as a pedagogical tool for Christic formation. He develops prospective shame in his readers so that their moral apparatus ultimately aligns with the will of God. He also retrospectively shames offenders so that they will examine their presuppositions and evaluate themselves from the framework of the cruciform pattern of Christ.

Disintegrative and Reintegrative Shame

Braithwaite's distinction between DS and RS is helpful. It provides needed vocabulary to distinguish between types of shaming. One benefit of this clarity is that it enables us to recognize that some criticisms of shaming are actually criticisms of DS rather than RS. For example, forcing traffic offenders to hold a placard that trumpets their offense on a busy intersection is humiliating and non-reintegrative. RST does not advocate such forms of shaming.

Paul does not explicitly distinguish between DS and RS, although I suggest that the distinction between these two concepts is connoted by his use of αἰσχύνη and ἐντροπή words.[14] Paul castigates the Corinthians for their

11. So Morris, "Shame, Guilt and Remorse."
12. Harris, Walgrave, and Braithwaite, "Emotional Dynamics."
13. Braithwaite, *Crime, Shame, and Reintegration*, 81.
14. Living in a world where honor and shame are pivotal social values, Paul is clearly aware that shame can be disintegrative and stigmatizing. One of the clearest examples of such shame in

disintegrative shaming, for their rhetoric of shame that tears down. Paul's own shaming approach can, however, be considered as reintegrative. He adopts a rhetoric of shame that builds up. Thus, shaming refutation is to be carried out by the entire community, the community must demonstrate genuine love even as it rebukes the offender, shaming refutation cannot be excessive, and the community must forgive and embrace the offender when there is genuine repentance. So far, this is not controversial. The fact that some of Paul's statements appear to be stigmatizing (e.g., "You foolish Galatians! . . . Are you so foolish?," Gal. 3:1–3) is, however, troubling. How can we claim that Paul's shaming rhetoric is reintegrative when there are stigmatizing comments embedded in his rhetoric?

Braithwaite's original theory presupposes that reintegration and stigmatization are polar opposites. Hence, any shaming encounter can be plotted along the continuum of being highly reintegrative or highly stigmatizing. Low reintegration implies high stigmatization, and vice versa. Empirical research, however, caused him to revise his view such that the oppositional polarity of reintegration and stigmatization is true at the discrete level of a single shaming comment, but not necessarily at the collective level of a mediation conference.[15] Since a mediation conference comprises multiple shaming comments, some comments may be reintegrative and others stigmatizing. Indeed, both reintegration and stigmatization may occur in the same sentence during such conferences. For example, a parent of an offending child may say something like this: "He is a naughty boy [stigmatization, since it labels the person rather than the act], but I love him [reintegration]."

If reintegration and stigmatization are not polar opposites but independent variables within a reconciliation conference, what matters, then, in evaluating such a conference is the summation and sequential order of the various shaming communications. A higher ratio of reintegrative to stigmatizing communications increases the likelihood of inducing repentance and remorse in the offender; so also will conferences that begin with stigmatizing but end with reintegrative communications.

The implication of the above research suggests that we should not be surprised to find labeling comments in Paul's shaming rhetoric, despite its *overall* reintegrative tenor. Like the Greco-Roman moral philosophers before

---

the first century CE is the tattooing (or branding) of slaves. Runaway slaves were frequently tattooed on their foreheads, thus permanently marking them with the stigma of shame (Herodotus, *Hist.* 2.113; Plato, *Leg.* 854D; Aristophanes, *Birds* 760–61; Menander, *Sam.* 323, 655; Diodorus Siculus, *Library of History* 34.2.1). Pseudo-Phocylides recognizes the harm caused by these tattoos and cautions: "Make no marks [στίγματα] on a servant, humiliating him" (Ps.-Phoc. 225).

15. Ahmed et al., *Shame Management*, 42.

him, Paul uses a mixed mode of shaming rhetoric that encompasses harsh and gentle words. Some of his statements have the potential to be stigmatizing: he castigates his readers' foolishness and intransigence. Nevertheless, the cumulative tenor of Paul's shaming rhetoric is reintegrative. He expresses genuine care and concern for them, he weeps over them, he pours out his heart for them, and he firmly believes that his readers are Abraham's seed and children of God through faith (Gal. 3:26–29). Thus, even though he might chide the Galatians for being foolish, he does not dispute their core identity as children of God. On the contrary, Paul is so harsh toward his readers *because* he affirms their identity as children of God. In essence he says, "Don't you know that you are *now* children of God? How then can you be so foolish as to turn back and be enslaved again to weak and worthless forces?" (cf. Gal. 4:8–9).

Conditions for Successful RS

Braithwaite and Paul recognize that shaming should not be the first instrument of choice to confront an offender. Braithwaite suggests beginning with "indirect methods of confrontation that seek to elicit volunteered remorse."[16] When indirect methods fail, direct verbal disapproval of the offense is then necessary. Similarly, Paul notes that gentle rebuke must be used first. When gentle rebuke is resisted and met with defiance, shaming refutation becomes necessary.

Braithwaite's discussion on the social conditions that are conducive for RS is helpful. Disapproval from respected others is preferable, as it is more likely to evoke remorse and empathy rather than anger and blame. Communitarian communities with strong interdependent relationships and social cohesiveness will also be able to conduct shaming that is more reintegrative than stigmatizing. The frame of reference for Paul's shaming rhetoric coheres with these social conditions. Paul's shaming rhetoric takes place within the church, a voluntary association that meets in a household setting. The household setting limited the numerical size of churches to about thirty people, thus promoting intimacy and accountability.[17] Moreover, Paul fosters the group identity of believers as he frequently uses the language of belonging and separation to mark the community of believers as a group that is distinct from the surrounding world.[18] Finally, Paul's metaphors for the church as a family (2 Cor. 6:18; 1 Tim. 5:1–2), a body (1 Cor. 12:12–27), a building (1 Cor. 3:9), and an olive tree (Rom. 11:17–24) echo Braithwaite's call for communitarianism and interdependency.

16. Ahmed et al., *Shame Management*, 45.
17. Gehring, *House Church and Mission*, 290.
18. See Meeks, *First Urban Christians*, 84–107.

Critique

RST cannot be uncritically accepted in its entirety, not least because the anthropology of RST and Paul are fundamentally different. RST considers people to be reasonable and good. Thus, the deviance committed by an offender is presumed to be a temporary aberration of an otherwise "mostly good" person. Paul has a darker view of humanity, for he recognizes that no one is righteous, not even one (Rom. 3:10). All people are under the power of sin (Rom. 3:9; Gal. 3:22), and all are slaves to sin (Rom. 6:20). Freedom from bondage to sin is only possible through faith in Christ (Rom. 6:18; Gal. 5:1), and the ability to live a life pleasing to God is only possible through the empowerment of the Holy Spirit (Gal. 5:13–26). Despite the above fundamental differences, both Braithwaite's and Paul's views of human nature are somewhat similar *within their respective frame of references*. The primary frame of reference for Paul's shaming rhetoric is the church, the community of believers who have the Holy Spirit. Thus, both Braithwaite and Paul view their target audience as essentially "good" people who are capable of better things.

In the attempt to hold to his view that humanity is fundamentally good, Braithwaite separates people's actions from their identities. This is seen in his differentiation between RS and DS. RS labels the act, while DS labels the person. Moreover, RS understands the person as fundamentally good, while DS treats the offender as fundamentally bad. In summary, RS "labels the act as evil while striving to preserve the identity of the offender as essentially good. It is directed at signifying evil deeds rather than evil persons in the Christian tradition of 'hate the sin and love the sinner.'"[19]

"Hate the sin and love the sinner" is good advice, but that does not mean that we should separate people from their actions. Paul makes no distinction between act and person in his shaming refutation. In fact, Paul occasionally shames his readers by highlighting not their deficient actions but their deficient character. For example, he berates the Galatians not because they act foolishly but because they are foolish (Gal. 3:1–3). Similarly, he shames the Corinthians not because they make unwise actions, but because they are unwise (1 Cor. 6:5).

Braithwaite's separation of *deed* and *identity* follows the trend of some psychologists to distinguish guilt and shame on the basis of *behavior* and *self*. I have already critiqued this bifurcation in chapter 1 and will do so further in the next chapter. But for now, note that Braithwaite's separation of deed and identity is also flawed when we observe how he applies it inconsistently. He

---

19. Braithwaite, *Crime, Shame, and Reintegration*, 101.

argues that regulating social conduct is most effective if we label the act (rather than the actor's character) as deviant when a bad act is performed. However, he argues that we should instead praise the actor's character (rather than their act) when a good act is performed. There is therefore an asymmetric labeling of deed and identity, depending on whether a good or bad act is performed.[20]

If *deed* cannot be separated from *identity*, then offenders who seek to turn a corner must accept responsibility for their past actions and acknowledge their shame. At the same time, they must also appropriately discharge this shame and begin the process of rebuilding their ethical identity—an identity that has been marred by shame. Using insights from narrative psychology, Shadd Maruna's seminal work *Making Good: How Ex-Convicts Reform and Rebuild Their Lives* shows how reform is possible when offenders re-story their life narrative, forging a "new" ethical identity for themselves that is different from their past. This autobiographical reconstruction allows ex-offenders to manage their shame, helping them overcome their stigmatization and reintegrate into mainstream society.

The narrative reconstruction advocated by Maruna, however, cannot truly create a new identity. Rather, it affords offenders "opportunities for mining their own pasts for buried themes and alternative interpretations [that foreshadow their "true self"]. . . . This narrative reconstruction is an imaginative process that blurs the distinction between fiction and nonfiction." But Maruna notes that this is not so much a denial of one's past as a way of conceptualizing it so as to enable offenders to move forward gradually.[21]

In contrast to a fictional reconstruction or reconceptualization, Pauline theology presents us with re-storying that is based on the creational power of God. When believers are united with Christ, "there is a new creation: The old has gone, the new is here!" (2 Cor. 5:17). This new life enables believers, through the power of the Spirit, to live a life pleasing to God. Paul's strategy, then, is to remind believers that their deeds must follow their core identity; the imperative must follow the indicative. When believers fall back into old patterns of behavior, Paul reminds them that they are no longer what they were: "Some of you used to be this. But you were washed, you were sanctified, you were justified in the name of the Lord Jesus Christ and in the spirit

---

20. Braithwaite modified his stance in a later book. He writes, "What we had thought we wanted offenders to feel was shame about what they had done, but not shame about themselves. Now we think this may have been a normative error" (Ahmed et al., *Shame Management*, 9). He now acknowledges that it is impossible for a person who is guilty to feel ashamed of himself or herself as a person. He only cautions that this is appropriate "so long as this does not go so far as a total rejection of self."

21. Maruna and Ramsden, "Living to Tell the Tale," 139. See also Stone, "Desistance and Identity Repair," 956–75.

of our God" (1 Cor. 6:11). As a consequence of their new status in Christ, they are to put away the old leaven of sin and be a new unleavened batch—as they really are (1 Cor. 5:7)!

Confucian Thought in Chinese Families

The prevalence and significance of shame in the Chinese culture is evident when one finds the Chinese character for shame proudly emblazoned on monuments in Chinese enclaves in America. On the ornamental arches leading to Chinatown in Chicago and Boston are inscribed four words: 礼 (*li*, ritual propriety), 义 (*yi*, righteousness), 廉 (*lian*, integrity), and 耻 (*chi*, shame or sense of shame). These four characters constitute the Four Cardinal Virtues (*siwei*, 四维) that are central in Chinese thought.[22] Thus 耻 (*chi*), "shame" or "sense of shame," is a cardinal virtue.

The importance of shame within Chinese thought is also evident when we note how shame is employed by America's top parent, the Tiger Mom. In a provocative and humorous book, Amy Chua extols the virtues of shame in grooming overachievers. She writes, "The solution to substandard performance is always to excoriate, punish, and shame the child. The Chinese parent believes that their child will be strong enough to take the shaming and to improve from it."[23]

Chua's comments cannot be easily dismissed as the overzealous comments of a fringe group of demanding parents. Research shows that Chinese parents generally consider shame to be the primary affect that is necessary not only for scholastic achievement but also for moral advancement. For example, developmental and cultural psychologist Heidi Fung affirms Martin Hoffman's theory on the importance of affect toward moral development. Her research on Taiwanese caregivers, however, leads her to argue that shame, not empathy, is the essential affect.[24]

The socialization of shame among Chinese children does not begin in the high school years, when parents fret about SAT scores and AP exams. On the contrary, it is generally well underway by the age of two and a half, as parents and caregivers use the child's rudimentary sense of shame to teach them right from wrong.[25] This hypercognition of shame in Chinese families

---

22. The Four Cardinal Virtues are recorded in "On Shepherding the People" (*mumin*, 牧民), one of the earlier chapters in *Guanzi* (管子), a compilation of politico-philosophical works attributed to Guan Zhong (管仲, d. 645 BCE).
23. Chua, *Battle Hymn of the Tiger Mother*, 52–53.
24. H. Fung, "Affect and Early Moral Socialization."
25. H. Fung, "Becoming a Moral Child."

stands in stark contrast to Euro-American families,[26] and it stems in part from the hypercognition of shame in the Chinese language. There are perhaps more shame words in the Chinese language than in any other language of the world; for there are 113 prototypical terms for shame in the Chinese language, divided into six clusters of meaning.[27] The multiplicity of lexical terms allow the concept to be elaborated and nuanced, cementing the importance of the concept within Chinese thought.

The seemingly positive valence toward shame in Chinese thought has its basis in the Confucian valorization of shame. In this section, I examine the general concept of shame in several early Confucian texts,[28] such as the *Analects* (*Lunyu*, 论语), the *Mencius* (*Mengzi*, 孟子), and the *Xunzi* (*Xunzi*, 荀子).[29] I then suggest several ways in which the Chinese approach to shame may inform our reading of Paul's vision of shame.

Overview

My overview proceeds as follows: I first summarize the Confucian construal of shame and then examine the role it plays within the Confucian project.

Confucian Construal of Shame

The concept of shame is lexically represented in early Confucian texts by terms such as *chi* (耻), *xiu* (羞), *kui* (愧), *zuo* (怍), and *can* (惭). There are different nuances of each term, many of which are debated. Nonetheless, I focus on *chi* (耻) since it occurs most often. The word *chi* (耻) is variously translated by different authors as "shame," "feeling of shame," "sense of shame," "principled shame," "self-respect," and even "conscience." Different translations reflect the different contexts in which this word occurs.

In Confucian thought, shame is an essential human trait. Mencius (ca. 372–289 BCE), the second most important sage after Confucius (ca. 551–479 BCE), remarks that "shame [*chi*, 耻] is indeed important for people" (*Mengzi* 7A7). People cannot live without shame, for "the shame [*chi*, 耻] of being shameless [*wu chi*, 无耻] is shameless [*wu chi*, 无耻] indeed!" (7A6). Xunzi

---

26. Shaver, Wu, and Schwartz ("Cross-Cultural Similarities and Differences," 199) write, "Only 10% of American mothers thought their 30- to 35-month-old children understood *ashamed*. . . . In contrast, 95% of Chinese mothers of children in the same age group said that these children could understand *shame/shyness* (羞)."

27. See Li, Wang, and Fischer, "Chinese Shame Concepts."

28. For a fuller analysis of the Confucian construal of shame, see Seok, *Moral Psychology of Confucian Shame.*

29. Unless otherwise stated, English translations and numbering of these texts come from *Confucius Analects* (trans. Slingerland), *Mengzi* (trans. Van Norden), and *Xunzi* (trans. Hutton).

(ca. 313–238 BCE), the third most important sage, considers shame to be the trait that separates people from animals. If people do not regulate themselves with shame (*lian chi*, 廉耻), they will be ignorant of right and wrong—no different from animals that desire only food and drink (*Xunzi* 4.64–68).

Shame is critical in Confucian thought because it is a moral virtue, a moral disposition, and a moral emotion. When asked what truly constitutes a scholar-official, Confucius remarks that the most important qualification is having a sense of shame (*chi*, 耻). Note that Confucius places having a sense of shame (*chi*, 耻) before other virtues such as filialness (*xiao*, 孝) and trustworthiness (*xin*, 信). Having a sense of shame is critical because it enables government officials to be deft players in the political world. Consequently, they will not disgrace (*ru*, 辱) their ruler's mandate when sent abroad as diplomats (*Lunyu* 13.20).

The Confucian texts demonstrate a concern not only to instill within people a deeper sense of shame but also to change the objects of which they are ashamed. Thus, Confucius argues that one should not be ashamed about having poor clothes or food (*Lunyu* 4.9), about seeking advice from social inferiors (5.15), or about wearing shabby clothes next to someone elegantly dressed (9.27). Rather, one should be ashamed of failing to measure up to one's words (4.22, 14.27), of toadyism and feigned friendship (5.25), and of complicity with immoral and corrupt governments (8.13). Similarly, Mencius notes that one should be ashamed of possessing an exaggerated reputation (*Mengzi* 4B18.3) and of occupying a governmental position without effecting positive ethical changes (5B5.3).

In the examples above, Confucian thought stresses the importance of ethical shame rather than social or conventional shame.[30] The criteria for shame should be measured by ethical standards that are not necessarily correlated to social standards. The basis of shame for a cultivated person should be that person's moral condition measured exclusively in terms of whether it accords with the Way.[31] The person's material well-being, external circumstances, or even reputation is not the deciding factor. Thus Xunzi remarks, "The [noble person] is ashamed of not being [morally] cultivated; he is not ashamed of being maligned. He is ashamed of not being trustworthy; he is not ashamed of not being trusted" (*Xunzi* 6.188–92). Consequently, the noble person who constantly cultivates a moral disposition will never suffer ethical disgrace (*yiru*, 义辱). Circumstances might bring conventional disgrace (*shiru*, 势辱),

30. See Van Norden, "Emotion of Shame," 67.
31. The Way (*dao*, 道) is not only the path that conforms to the intrinsic nature of the cosmos but also the path by which humanity is to walk in order to be consummately human.

but the person will never suffer disgrace in terms of that which is right and just. Conversely, the petty person who does not cultivate virtue will never attain ethical honor (*yirong*, 义荣). Circumstances might bring conventional honor (*shirong*, 势荣), but the person will never enjoy honor in terms of that which is right and just (*Xunzi* 18.528–32).[32]

Confucian shame is placed within an interconnected web of important Confucian concepts. It is related to virtue (*de*, 德), ritual propriety (*li*, 礼), humaneness (*ren*, 仁), righteousness (*yi*, 义), human nature (*xing*, 性), heart/mind (*xin*, 心), harmony (*he*, 和), and filial piety (*xiao*, 孝). A full grasp of the concept of Confucian shame requires an engagement with these conceptual clusters. Space limitations, however, do not permit me to elaborate on each of them. I will only briefly explore the relationship between shame and filial piety here.

Filial piety is the response and attempt to repay parents for the kindness that they showered on their children. It is "a cultivated disposition to attend to the needs and desires of one's parents and to work to satisfy and please them."[33] But one does not merely provide for the needs of one's parents; one must also possess a deep emotional sense of gratitude, reverence, and love for one's parents.[34] Such an attitude necessitates that children exercise their sense of shame so that they do not disgrace their family name and parents. More importantly, they must strive to bring honor to the family (*Jiyi* 2.9).[35] This posture remains valid after the children are married. It continues even after the death of their parents, as the children continue to remember and revere their spirits (*Jiyi* 1.5).[36] So important is the concept of shame to filial piety that "not to disgrace [oneself] and not to cause shame [*xiu*, 羞] to [one's] parents may be called filial duty" (*Jiyi* 2.14).[37]

Confucian Role of Shame

Nathaniel Barrett remarks that "one of the goals of the Confucian project is the cultivation of a proper sense of shame."[38] This is brought out clearly in *Lunyu* 2.3: "The Master said, 'If you try to guide the common people with coercive regulations and keep them in line with punishments, the common people will become evasive and will have no sense of shame [*chi*, 耻].

---

32. See also *Lunyu* 13.22.
33. Ivanhoe, "Filial Piety as a Virtue," 305.
34. See *Lunyu* 2.7–8.
35. ET Legge, *Li Ki*, 28:226.
36. ET Legge, *Li Ki*, 28:211.
37. ET Legge, *Li Ki*, 28:229. See also *Mengzi* 5A4.3.
38. Barrett, "Confucian Theory of Shame," 146.

If, however, you guide them with Virtue [*de*, 德], and keep them in line by means of ritual [*li*, 礼], the people will have a sense of shame [*chi*, 耻] and will rectify themselves.'" Confucius here argues that human behavior should not be governed by edicts and statutes, for the masses will only evade them as far as possible through loopholes in the legal system. Regulations and punishments can only mandate a person's external behavior; they provide no internal impetus for self-regulation. Rulers should instead regulate the people by the norms of virtue (*de*, 德) and propriety (*li*, 礼).[39] The promulgation of virtue and propriety inculcates in the people a proper sense of shame that will eventually lead them to reform themselves.

In the above passage, Confucius contrasts a sense of shame with external regulations. He thus considers shame to function like a conscience or internal regulatory apparatus. In this capacity, it guides people toward an understanding of that which is right and appropriate, compelling them to maintain an exemplary conduct even when others are unaware of their actions; it autonomously guards people against the blurring of moral boundaries, deterring them from doing that which is not acceptable;[40] and it warns against the corrupting influence of disgrace, likening disgrace to an impurity that defiles and lowers one's standing.[41]

Shame in Confucian thought acts not only negatively (inhibiting us from doing that which is wrong) but also positively (prompting us to rectify ourselves and proceed on the path of self-cultivation). In this perspective, "a sense of shame is nearly tantamount to courage" (*Zhongyong* 20.10).[42] It is the moral courage to admit one's weaknesses, to see what is right, and to act on it (*Lunyu* 2.24). It is the courage to improve oneself and to go wherever justice and righteousness lead, regardless of the circumstances (*Xunzi* 4.73–77). It is the courage to be a moral elite.

Using the framework above, Margaret Ng notes that "shame morality [in Confucian thought] . . . is an elitist morality. Here the motivating force, internal shame, seems to be as much a desire to excel the common lot as a fear of being found unworthy of membership in an idealized moral elite."[43] Confucian

---

39. *Ritual propriety* or the *rites* (*li*, 礼) are a set of religious practices, norms, and social practices that were designed to promote communal bonds not only with other people but also with one's departed ancestors and other spiritual beings. The practice of these rites allows one to cultivate oneself, to cultivate others, and to order the cosmos.

40. See Geaney, "Guarding Moral Boundaries."

41. Shun ("Early Confucian Moral Psychology," 275) understands disgrace-shame as an impurity. Thus, the idea of expunging shame is expressed by terms such as "to wash off shame" (*xi chi*, 洗耻) or "to white out shame" (*xue chi*, 雪耻).

42. ET Plaks, *Ta Hsüeh and Chung Yung*, 39.

43. Ng, "Internal Shame as a Moral Sanction," 84.

disciples cultivate moral excellence in order to be superior to the common lot. They embrace a sense of shame by applying constant effort and diligence so that they might finally attain one of three central delights that belong to the Confucian exemplary person: neither to be disgraced (*kui*, 愧) before Heaven nor to be ashamed (*zuo*, 怍) before other people (*Mengzi* 7A20.1–5).

In Mencian moral psychology, the positive role of shame receives special prominence. Mencius argues that all humans are disposed to be virtuous just as water is disposed to flow downward (*Mengzi* 6A2.2). This does not mean that all people are born with fully developed virtues. Rather, all people are similar to the sages in that all have the potential for moral development (6A7.4). This potential is due to the presence of incipient stirrings toward virtue within the heart/mind (*xin*, 心). The heart/mind (*xin*, 心) of a person "refers to the locus, or faculty, of emotions, cognition, evaluation, and judgment within the self."[44] It is the center of will, intellect, deliberation, feelings, desire, and virtue. Using a biological model for the development of moral virtue, Mencius likens the nascent tendencies of the heart/mind (*xin*, 心) to sprouts (*duan*, 端) that take root and bloom into full virtues only when they are nurtured and cultivated.[45] In Mencian thought, the sprout that has the potential to bloom into righteousness (*yi*, 义) is the "feeling of shame and aversion" (*xiuwu zhi xin*, 羞恶之心; *Mengzi* 2A6.5).

The phrase "feeling of shame and aversion" (*xiuwu zhi xin*, 羞恶之心) literally means "the heart/mind of shame and aversion," indicating that the heart/mind is the site or faculty that manifests or gives rise to shame and aversion. Given the complex understanding of the heart/mind (*xin*, 心) as the locus of emotions, cognitions, and judgment in Confucian thought, Confucian shame includes cognitive, affective, and motivational components. As an emotion, Confucian shame works in tandem with perception and judgment. It is a feeling of distress regarding one's self-image, but it is also bound up with a concern and desire for justice, self-respect, moral courage, and personal integrity.

Unlike the Four Cardinal Virtues of *Guanzi*, shame is not a cardinal virtue in Mencian thought. Nonetheless, the emotion of shame is the beginning or precursor of the cardinal virtue of righteousness (*yi*, 义). When people do something wrong, their hearts/minds induce in them a gut feeling of shame. This feeling, however, does not necessarily lead to action. It is

---

44. Virág, *Emotions in Early Chinese Philosophy*, 109–10.

45. Van Norden ("Emotion of Shame," 46) writes, "The sprouts are incipient tendencies to act, feel, desire, perceive, and think in virtuous ways." If these sprouts are not cultivated, the moral growth of the person remains stunted. The person will not realize his or her human nature and will not lead a flourishing life.

only the beginning or the sprout. People must act on these natural tendencies and do what is right. People's natures may be so corrupt that they do not do what is right, but their innate human nature is not so corrupt that they feel nothing. If they actualize the action tendencies that are embedded within the emotion of shame, they embark on the journey of cultivating righteousness (yi, 义).[46]

Mencius argues that not only must the natural tendencies of the sprouts be actualized, but they must also be extended (tui, 推; ji, 及; da, 达) or filled out (kuo, 扩; chong, 充) to encompass similar scenarios that have greater moral significance. Truly accomplishing this enables us to become fully righteous (Mengzi 7B31.1–4). When the sprouts develop, "it will be like a fire starting up, a spring breaking through! If one can merely fill them out, they will be sufficient to care for all within the Four Seas" (2A6.6). Mencius gives an example of what it means to extend the heart/mind of shame. He notes that no one, not even a beggar, will receive food that has been deliberately trampled on and given with contempt. The self-respect that is bound up with one's sense of shame inhibits one from doing so. Mencius, however, laments that people do not extend this nascent heart/mind of shame to other scenarios. Instead, people gladly accept a bribe of ten thousand bushels of grain without asking whether it is right and just to do so. According to Mencius, the sense of shame that inhibits them from receiving food given with contempt should be extended to this more significant situation, leading them to reject gifts that are done not according to propriety (li, 礼) or righteousness (yi, 义; 6A10.6–8).

Interaction

The Confucian tradition presents us with a rich understanding of shame. In the following, I note several ways it may illumine our understanding of Pauline shame, critique some of its aspects, and compare it with Braithwaite's RST.

The Importance of Moral Psychology

Our brief survey of Confucian thought demonstrates the important role that emotions play in moral formation. The link between affective and moral discourse is clear, for the opening line of the Analects suggests that "finding

---

46. Righteousness in Confucian thought is a virtue that leads one to do what is right, appropriate, fitting, or morally obligatory (Zhongyong 20.5). At the same time, it is the ability and inclination to avoid doing what is base and disgraceful. It "involves disdaining and regarding as potentially tainting to oneself what falls below ethical standards, as well as an insistence on distancing oneself from such things, even if gravely undesirable consequences may result." See Shun, Mencius and Early Chinese Thought, 62.

pleasure and joy in the important things of life are moral ends at the level of being a worthy person."[47]

The Confucian tradition emphasizes the confluence of emotion and moral action. The noble person not only does the right action but does so with the requisite attitude and emotional disposition. As Confucius said, "If I am not fully present at the sacrifice, it is as if I did not sacrifice at all" (*Lunyu* 3.12). We also saw earlier that performing filial actions out of a sense of duty cannot be considered filial unless they are accompanied with gratitude, reverence, and affection.[48] There must be integration between one's actions and interiority so that the self is brought to a coherent whole.

Mencius, too, stresses the importance of emotions in his moral psychology. Each of the four virtues central in Mencian thought is associated with a characteristic emotion: "The feeling of compassion is benevolence. The feeling of [shame and aversion] is righteousness. The feeling of respect is propriety. The feeling of approval and disapproval is wisdom" (*Mengzi* 6A6.5). By associating the beginning of each virtue with an emotion, Mencius claims that emotions function as a vehicle for moral growth. When these emotions are optimally realized and extended, human beings are able to realize their true nature.

Moral philosophers from Aristotle to Mencius recognize the important role that emotions play in moral formation. In particular, there appears to be a common assumption that there is some interplay between our belief structure and affections, between evaluations and emotions. We have already seen evidence of this in the Greco-Roman world. The same is also true for Mencius.[49] The importance of moral psychology in Greco-Roman and Confucian thought suggests that my foray into the same area in Pauline thought is not without merit. A discussion of Pauline ethics should also wrestle with his understanding of the relationship between ethical formation and emotions, not least the emotion of shame.

Shame and Moral Formation

In contrast to the common claim in present psychoanalytic and psychiatric literature, both Confucian and Pauline thought acknowledge that shame is not necessarily a dangerous and destructive affect. The specific situations in which shame is employed in each tradition differ. Nonetheless, both affirm that shame can and must play a pivotal role in moral formation. For example, both Confucian and Pauline thought affirm that the values that define true

47. Virág, "Early Confucian Perspectives on Emotion," 206.
48. See also *Lunyu* 3.26, where Confucius stresses that the correct performance of rituals requires the appropriate emotions.
49. See Van Norden, "Mencius."

honor and shame should not be determined by conventional standards such as economic wealth, social status, fame, and prestige. There is a different court of opinion to which adherents must regulate their lives. Within the Confucian tradition, the principles of humaneness, righteousness, and ritual propriety function as the yardstick to differentiate between conventional and ethical honor and shame. Within the Pauline tradition, the gospel functions as the standard by which believers are to live.

Both Confucian and Pauline thought also emphasize the importance of cultivating a proper sense of shame. The values that define honor and shame must be internalized. They must remain operative even when others are not looking. Confucius notes that the purpose of moral learning is to improve oneself, not to impress others (*Lunyu* 14.24). Mencius concurs, for he critiques the "village worthies" whose way of life is geared toward social opinion. Although "their actions seem to be blameless and pure," their conduct is disingenuous and their virtue not genuine. They are "thieves of virtue" (*Mengzi* 7B37.8–11). Paul reflects the same concern regarding the internalization of shame. He argues that the cruciform pattern of Christ must shape our mind and conscience. God sees the hearts of men. Thus, true circumcision cannot be external and physical; it must be internal and done by the Spirit (Rom. 2:28–29). Moreover, if filial piety in Confucian thought is not doing anything that would bring disgrace to one's family name and parents, then Christian filialness in Pauline thought is not doing anything that would bring disgrace to our heavenly Father.

The importance of cultivating a proper sense of shame in Confucian and Pauline thought critiques our current culture of shamelessness.[50] In response to the many cases that have come to light in the wake of the #MeToo movement, social critics lament that the epidemic of sexual violence is the result of a culture that has eviscerated shame and any notion of decency. Shame functions as a moral gyroscope for society. When it is bypassed, society loses its moral bearings with the result that injustice and anarchy prevail. In an op-ed article published shortly after allegations against Harvey Weinstein, Charlie Rose, and Al Franken surfaced, Daniel Henninger writes that "their acts reveal a collapse of self-restraint. That in turn suggests a broader evaporation of conscience, the sense that doing something is wrong. . . . So when one asks how these men could behave so boorishly and monstrously, one answer is that

---

50. The necessity for society to possess a sense of shame is not a new sentiment. In chapter 2, I noted that shame and justice (αἰδώς and δίκη) are routinely tied together in Greco-Roman thought. Thus, injustice typically follows the departure of a sense of shame. The Roman poet Ovid depicted this relationship between shame and the moral state of society in his Four Ages of the World. In the last age, the Iron Age, every evil bursts forth, as shame, truth, and loyalty have fled (*Metam.* 1.125). See also Hesiod, *Op.* 197–201.

they . . . have . . . no . . . shame."[51] Henninger further writes that these men are not outliers or exceptions. Rather, they are the product of a culture that has repealed reticence, eradicated shame, and inoculated themselves against anything that might appear morally shocking.[52] "They lived in a culture that had eliminated shame and behavioral boundaries."[53] Within such a culture, Pauline shame is sorely needed.

Critique

Despite the broad similarities in attitudes toward shame, Confucian thought differs from Pauline practice as it minimizes the use of censure or shaming rebuke. Confucian sages "do not seem to be interested in *shaming*, that is, with causing people to feel shame. The way to help people develop a proper sense of shame is *not* by shaming them, but by 'guiding them with virtue.'"[54] This does not mean that social equals did not correct one another as they pushed each other toward virtuous living, for Mencius remarks that "to demand goodness is the Way of friends" (*Mengzi* 4B30.4).[55] Moreover, Confucius even allows for subordinate persons within a hierarchical structure to remonstrate (*jian*, 谏). "If confronted by reprehensible behavior on his father's part, a son has no choice but to remonstrate with his father, and if confronted by reprehensible behavior on his ruler's part, a minister has no choice but to remonstrate with his ruler. Hence, remonstrance is the only response to immorality" (*Xiaojing* 15).[56] Nonetheless, there is hesitation in Confucian thought to rebuke others and evoke the occurrent experience of shame.[57] Confucians prefer understatement and innuendos to direct confrontation of wrong.

There are perhaps four reasons for this hesitation:

1. Demanding goodness can damage the harmonious relationship between two parties. "In order to instruct, you must correct what someone does.

51. Henninger, "Death of Self-Restraint."
52. See also Lasch, *Revolt of the Elites*, 197–212; Twitchell, *For Shame*.
53. Henninger, "Death of Self-Restraint."
54. Barrett, "Confucian Theory of Shame," 158.
55. The Neo-Confucian Wang Yang-Ming (1472–1529) develops this thought further. In a letter to his students, he writes, "To urge to virtuous action by reproof is characteristic of true friendship. However, it must be told in a loyal, devoted, virtuous way. The individual who administers reproof should approach the other man with all his loyalty and love. In a genial, obliging way he should influence him to hear and follow, thereby drawing him out to reform. If he is influenced without being angered, it may be considered well executed" (Henke, *Philosophy of Wang Yang-Ming*, 466). For further discussion, see Tu, *Neo-Confucian Thought in Action*, 142–46.
56. ET Rosemont and Ames, *Chinese Classic*, 114. See also pages 71–72 for the conditions necessary to remonstrate correctly.
57. See *Lunyu* 14.29; *Mengzi* 4A18.1–4.

If the correction does not work, one must follow it up with reprimands. If one follows it up with reprimands, then it will hurt the feelings of the [other]" (*Mengzi* 4A18.2).

2. Confucians believe in the power of virtue to exert influence over others. Just as the political leader who leads by virtue is able to govern the people without resorting to force (*Lunyu* 2.1, 3; 12.19), so also the wise sage who leads by virtue should be able to guide students without resorting to shaming refutation.

3. Confucians believe that learning is a joint effort between teacher and student. Confucius, for example, taught only those who were serious about learning. He did not instruct anyone who was not eager to learn, and he could not impart the Way to someone who did not already have a love for it (*Lunyu* 7.8, 15.16). In other words, Confucius did not waste his breath and reprimand those who were not ready to receive his words (15.8). He said, "Rotten wood cannot be carved, and a wall of dung cannot be plastered. As for Zai Wo [a lazy disciple of Confucius], what would be the use of reprimanding him?" (5.10).[58]

4. Confucius's strategy for moral cultivation is "to establish patterns of human conduct that preclude the problem in the first place."[59] The focus is on deterrence rather than correction. Thus, Confucius argues that the ruler must lead by virtue and transform the people so that they will develop a proper sense of shame. If people are constrained by prospective shame, there will be no need to employ retrospective shame in acts of shaming.

The above four reasons are valid and coherent when understood within the Confucian framework. But would Paul endorse such a laissez-faire attitude toward the spiritual growth of his readers? No. Paul uses shaming refutation that is passionate and urgent, for the eternal destiny of his readers is at stake. Some of them, such as the Galatians, are on the precipice of apostasy and damnation; they are in danger of being cursed. Paul therefore pulls out all the rhetorical stops in order to persuade his readers not to embrace a different gospel and desert the one who has called them to live in the grace of Christ Jesus (Gal. 1:6).

Paul is well aware that shaming rebuke may not always be received positively. Thus, he frames his rebuke so as to encourage a positive response. At

58. Passages that describe the difficulty that Confucius had in teaching his students include *Lunyu* 6.12; 7.34; 9.18, 24, 31; 15.13.

59. Rosemont and Ames, *Chinese Classic*, 53. See *Lunyu* 12.13.

the same time, he trusts in the power of the Holy Spirit to convict believers of their sin and bring them to repentance (cf. 1 Cor. 5:4). Pauline sanctification is dissimilar from Confucian self-cultivation in that it is not self-sanctification by self-effort; it is a cooperative endeavor. Individuals, in conjunction with the community of believers, have to work out their sanctification; nonetheless, God is the one who works in them "both to will and to work for his good pleasure" (Phil. 2:13).[60]

Braithwaite Meets Confucius

In his earlier draft of *Crime, Shame, and Reintegration*, Braithwaite included material on China's communal policing. He discarded that section, however, believing that the informal justice that was meted out involved too much stigmatization. He now considers that decision to be an intellectual mistake.[61] Further research shows that the mediation process of China's communal policing often ended with reintegrative overtures, despite beginning with stigmatizing encounters.[62] Thus, the overall encounter can be considered reintegrative. Braithwaite now argues that more attention should be paid to the Chinese restorative justice system, for he considers Confucius to be "arguably the most influential thinker about restorative justice the world has known."[63]

Reintegrative shaming is conducive in Confucian societies for two reasons, one external, the other internal.[64] Externally, Confucianism emphasizes communitarianism and interdependency. In such an environment, shaming is more likely to be reintegrative than disintegrative, and shaming episodes are taken more seriously by those who are shamed. The communitarian and interdependent ethos of Confucianism is easily seen. Let me list four examples. First, the Confucian virtue of humaneness (*ren*, 仁) is fundamentally oriented toward others; it is "care for others" (*Lunyu* 12.22). Second, Confucius considers individuals to be linked to others in "a desirable and necessary symbiosis."[65] The self is not autonomous but relational. Individualism is frowned on; harmonious interrelationships are emphasized.[66] For if one wishes to establish

---

60. There is no notion of external divine enablement in Confucian thought. Mencius notes that the two conditions necessary for moral formation within an individual are (1) the necessity of suitable environmental conditions and (2) diligence in self-cultivation. See Jiang, "Mencius on Moral Responsibility," 142.

61. Braithwaite, *Restorative Justice*, 19–20.

62. Chen, "Social Control in China," 59; Lu, "Bang Jiao," 118.

63. Braithwaite, *Restorative Justice*, 20.

64. Lu, "Bang Jiao," 122.

65. Tu, "Selfhood and Otherness," 231.

66. See Rosemont, *Against Individualism*.

oneself, one must also establish others (*Lunyu* 6.30). Third, the family is the prototype of *every* relationship.[67] For example, the kingdom is compared to a household. As the father, the ruler must use his authority for the good and welfare of the people; as the children, the people must respect and demonstrate obedience to their sovereign. This familial framework thus imbues all relationships with a deep sense of interdependent care. Such an understanding is highly significant to RST, since Braithwaite considers the family model to be the quintessential sphere in which RS best takes place.[68] Fourth, Confucian thinking stresses commonality, reciprocity, and empathy (*shu*, 恕). Those in power are especially encouraged to put themselves in the shoes of others. For example, Master Zeng counseled a new magistrate with the following words: "When you uncover the truth in a criminal case, proceed with sorrow and compassion. Do not be pleased with yourself" (*Lunyu* 19.19).

Internally, Confucianism's focus on moral learning shapes people to be amenable to correction and reform. Self-cultivation requires not only introspection, self-criticism, and inner examination but also the courage to receive criticism in good faith. Moreover, the hypercognition of shame in Confucian thought warns people of the danger of shamelessness; it sensitizes them to potential mistakes they may have committed. In such instances, those who are shamed will accept, rather than reject, valid shaming criticism. They will respond with repentance and remorse rather than anger.

The above two factors that make Confucian societies conducive to RS are also seen in Pauline communities, mutatis mutandis. Externally, the household structure of the early church and the Pauline language of belonging and separation create communities that foster communitarianism and interdependency. Internally, Pauline communities emphasize the cultivation of a dispositional sense of shame that is grounded on the mind of Christ. This inner ethos makes them more receptive to shaming rebuke. They will receive such criticism in a manner that is agreeable to the mind and will of God rather than in a manner that is consonant with the attitude of the world (2 Cor. 7:9–10).

Perception and Reception of Shame

Our brief foray into a Chinese understanding of shame shows that the perception and reception of shame diverge in different languages and cultures.

67. Rosemont and Ames (*Chinese Classic*, xi) write, "A fair argument can be made that *all* relationships within a Chinese world—social, political, and indeed cosmic relations—are conceived of in familial terms."

68. Braithwaite, *Crime, Shame, and Reintegration*, 54–68. Despite the different frames of reference between Confucian and Pauline thought (kingdom and church), both emphasize the importance of a familial or household framework in the application of shame.

Shame is highly context dependent. For example, there are significant differences in the organization, function, and socialization of shame between Chinese and Euro-American families.

First, while American parents tend to shield their children from shame, Chinese parents employ shame in the moral socialization of children. They believe that their children understand shame at an early age. "In terms of development sequence [in children], Chinese families believe that knowing shame precedes knowing right and wrong, while American parents believe the reverse."[69] Chinese parents therefore use the child's affective shame (*xiu*, 羞) to teach the cultural values of moral shame (*chi*, 耻).[70] In so doing, they evoke Mencius's understanding that the beginning of righteousness is the feeling of shame and disdain. Chinese caregivers thus nurture the child's affective shame and use this rudimentary sense of shame to teach their children right from wrong, extending it to encompass more and more complex scenarios.

Second, the effect that shaming criticism has on self-esteem depends on how that particular culture constructs its understanding of self-worth. Within individualistic cultures like the United States, one's sense of worth is typically determined by the individual; self-esteem depends on one's appraisal of oneself. Within interdependent cultures, such as those influenced by Confucianism, one's sense of worth tends to be socially constrained and is a function of how the individual is able to harmonize with others.[71] Consequently, shaming criticism by the community toward an individual in interdependent cultures is less likely to lead to anger and "may still be self-affirming . . . insofar as the experience prompts the person to restore the harmony in the relationship."[72] Among Euro-Americans, shame connotes stigmatization. Among the Chinese, however, shame "offers the promise of reintegration into the family following reestablishment of appropriate behavior. As such, shame is not primarily a threat to self-esteem: instead, it is a vehicle for social cohesion and the development of self."[73]

Given the diverse ways in which shame is construed, used, perceived, and received among different cultures, reintegrative and disintegrative shaming will mean different things in different contexts. A successful shaming program in one context may fail miserably in another. Great care must therefore be taken in the use of retrospective shame. Acts of shaming must be conducted

---

69. Fung, Lieber, and Leung, "Parental Beliefs," 102.

70. H. Fung, "Affect and Early Moral Socialization."

71. Wang and Ollendick, "Analysis of Self-Esteem."

72. Kitayama, Markus, and Matsumoto, "Culture, Self, and Emotion," 451.

73. Mascolo, Fischer, and Li, "Dynamic Development," 395.

in a manner that is cognizant of the various cultural particularities so that they will not be perceived as debilitating and destructive.

Conclusion

Braithwaite's RST and the Confucian understanding of shame are two voices that advocate a positive role for shame. Although cognizant of the challenges, both push for a careful use of shame. RST emphasizes retrospective shame, while the Confucian understanding promotes prospective shame. Together, they help us gain a more nuanced understanding of Paul's use of shame.

RST argues that the crime rate of any society is dependent on the degree to which offending is shamed and whether the shaming is reintegrative or disintegrative. Societies must communicate the shamefulness of delinquent behavior, but do so in a manner that is reintegrative rather than disintegrative. DS is counterproductive, as the offender is gradually pushed away from society. RS, on the other hand, is productive, as the offender is slowly restored to the community after confronting his or her error. Although I noted some objections and clarifications, RST's distinction between disintegrative and reintegrative shaming is helpful. It reminds us that acts of shaming are not identical. Some are truly destructive; others, however, are therapeutic, despite the bitterness of the medicine. Paul's shaming approach is therapeutic and reintegrative despite the occasional presence of harsh rhetoric and stigmatizing comments.

Confucian thought envisions a critical role for shame in moral formation, relating it to a web of other important concepts such as harmony, ritual propriety, righteousness, and filial piety. It exalts shame as a quintessential human attribute, praising it as a moral virtue or a necessary precursor to the formation of virtue. The Confucian perspective of shame contributes to our understanding of Pauline shame. It reminds us of the necessity of developing a dispositional sense of shame and cultivating a Christian conscience that is centered on the mind of Christ. It advises us that the strategy for moral formation should be preemptive rather than corrective: cultivating prospective shame as a deterrence against future sin is better than administering retrospective shame for past and present sin.

The examination of Confucian thought in Chinese families also alerts us to the social and cultural dimension of shame. The function and reception of shame is highly context sensitive; it is dependent not just on the definitional bases for honor and shame but also on the sociological structure of the community. Communitarian and interdependent communities are more receptive to the use of shame; individualistic communities less so. This presents a challenge for implementing the Pauline vision of shame in predominantly individualistic cultures. I now turn to other challenges that confront a Pauline vision of shame.

8

Contemporary Challenges

I noted in the introduction of this book that we live in a world with a fractured understanding of shame. On the one hand, we live in an anti-shame zeitgeist that wishes to avoid as much shame as possible. Psychologists declare that shame is the primary cause of emotional distress; it is the primitive emotion that must be replaced with guilt. Contemporary observers remark that shame is insidious: it shrouds itself in secrecy and deceit, and it is used to manipulate others through emotional blackmail. Celebrities and seminar speakers rail against the dangers of shame: shame is detrimental to one's self-esteem, it is the baggage that must be jettisoned in order to fulfill our destiny, and it is the shackle that must be broken so that we can stand unashamed of who we are.

On the other hand, some segments within our culture increasingly resort to shame and shaming. Historian Peter Stearns notes that there has been a resurgence of shame and shaming in the United States since the 1960s.[1] Shame is revived as a component in penology. Various judges consider public shaming to be a more effective and less expensive deterrent than incarceration. For example, Texas judge Ted Poe, an ardent supporter of shaming punishments, says, "A little shame goes a long way. Some folks say everyone should have high self-esteem, but that's not the real world. Sometimes people should feel bad."[2] The advent of new technology such as the internet, Twitter, and Facebook also took public shaming to an entirely new level. Monica Lewinsky, who

1. Stearns, *Shame*, 96–129.
2. Etzioni, "Back to the Pillory?," 46–47.

considers herself "Patient Zero" of online shaming, gave a stirring TED Talk in 2015. She lamented the culture of humiliation in which we live and made an impassioned plea that "public shaming as a blood sport has to stop."[3]

How does Paul's vision of shame speak to our fractured understanding of shame? How does it address the destructive effects of toxic shame in arenas such as online shaming? How does it answer the charge that the use of shame is manipulative or coercive? How does it compare with contemporary usage?

This chapter responds to three challenges that are problematic for a Pauline vision of shame: (1) guilt, not shame, is the preferred moral emotion; (2) the evocation of shame (or guilt) is manipulative, even coercive; and (3) shame is toxic and destructive. In my interaction with these challenges, I clarify Paul's understanding of shame with regard to the contemporary understanding of guilt and shame, maintain that Pauline shaming is neither manipulative nor coercive, and argue that Pauline shame is never toxic and destructive. Despite these challenges, I argue that Pauline shame, rightly understood, has a significant role to play in the Christic formation of the believer. A short conclusion summarizes these arguments.

Challenge 1: Guilt, Not Shame, Is the Preferred Moral Emotion

Psychologists generally consider shame to be maladaptive for moral progress. They consider shame to be heteronomous. As the subjects are dependent on the moral judgments of others, they fail to develop as responsible moral agents. Moreover, the excruciating feeling of shame causes people to deny responsibility or to blame others for their actions. In their misguided attempts to avoid or dampen this painful emotion, they may resort to destructive patterns of behavior, such as suicide and substance abuse. Guilt, on the other hand, is adaptive. It leads people to accept responsibility for their mistakes and to make reparative actions. Consequently, guilt, not shame, is the preferred moral emotion. The general assessment can be stated as follows: "Guilt is good; shame is bad. . . . Guilt about specific behaviors appears to steep people in a moral direction—fostering constructive, responsible behavior in many critical domains. Shame, in contrast, does little to inhibit immoral action."[4]

In this section, I argue that Pauline shame is important for moral formation despite contemporary aversions to shame vis-à-vis guilt. There are three reasons for my assessment: (1) Pauline shame is much more complex and nuanced than modern shame; (2) Pauline shame is not heteronomous

---

3. Lewinsky, "Price of Shame."
4. Tangney and Dearing, *Shame and Guilt*, 136–38.

but theonomous; and (3) guilt does not go far enough in reforming moral behavior. Pauline shame is needed.

The Complexity of Pauline Shame

In chapter 1, I noted that emotional lexemes in other cultures and languages may not correspond exactly to contemporary English usage. We should not assume that Pauline shame is coextensive with our modern understanding of shame. On the contrary, if we are to recover an accurate understanding of Pauline shame, we will have to analyze the concept within its own terms. As David Konstan remarks, "Rather than assume that the Greek's emotional terminology for shame was either fuzzier or more primitive than our own, we may better appreciate their idea of this emotion and its ethical significance by paying close attention to their vocabulary."[5] Having examined Pauline shame within its various contexts in chapters 4–6, we are now in a position to locate Pauline shame within contemporary understandings of shame and guilt.

I begin by recapitulating the differences between modern shame and guilt. In chapter 1, I outlined three axes commonly used to distinguish between these two moral emotions. They are (1) distinction based on the degree the person focuses either on the self or the behavior, (2) distinction based on the public and private nature of the transgression, and (3) distinction based on the nature of the eliciting event. I also argued that it is difficult to differentiate these two emotions, suggesting that the overlap between them may be explained by the argument that guilt is not an emotion in itself. Nevertheless, if the distinctions between shame and guilt as moral emotions are correct, these distinctions with their respective phenomenological experience and action tendencies can be summarized as in the following table.

	Modern shame	Modern guilt
Type of eliciting event	Moral and nonmoral	Moral
Focus of evaluation	Global self: "*I* did that horrible thing."	Specific behavior: "I *did* that horrible *thing.*"
Locus of evaluation	Public	Private
Degree of distress	Generally more painful	Generally less painful
Phenomenological experience	Shrinking; feeling small, worthless, or powerless; anger	Tension, remorse, regret

5. Konstan, *Emotions of the Ancient Greeks*, 93.

	Modern shame	Modern guilt
Concern vis-à-vis the other	Concern with others' evaluation of self (self-oriented personal distress)	Concern with one's effect on others (other-oriented empathy)
Counterfactual process[a]	Mentally undoing some aspect of the self	Mentally undoing some aspect of behavior
Motivational features	Desire to hide, escape, deny, strike back, or blame others	Desire to confess, apologize, or repair

This table slightly modifies that found in Tangney and Dearing, *Shame and Guilt*, 25.
[a] Counterfactual thinking involves imagining alternative scenarios ("If only I were . . ." or "If only I had . . .") that would lead to a different outcome.

When viewed along this grid, Paul's understanding of shame does not map exactly onto our contemporary understanding of shame or guilt. It appears to encompass elements of both. This should not be surprising. "Like many other cultures, Greece and Rome did not have distinct terms for what we call shame and guilt, and they seem to have made do with one concept where we recognize two."[6] In other words, the Greek emotional lexicon for shame appears to collapse our contemporary understanding of shame and guilt into a single concept.[7]

The Greco-Roman phenomenon of collapsing shame and guilt into a single concept is also seen in the verb ἐλέγχω. The verb can mean "to prove or convict someone to be guilty" (e.g., James 2:9: "*convicted* by the law as transgressors"), but it can also mean "to reveal or expose something to be shameful." This latter meaning is found in classical Greek, the LXX, and the New Testament.[8] Thus, the verb ἐλέγχω can denote not only the conviction of guilt but also the conviction of shame. When the verb is used in the sense of "to rebuke, reprove, correct, or discipline," it probably also carries the multivalent nuance of showing someone's shame and guilt.

Given the above cultural and linguistic backdrop, it is therefore not surprising if Paul's understanding of shame functions similarly. Let me give three examples in which Paul's understanding of shame encompasses our modern

6. Konstan, *Emotions of the Ancient Greeks*, 92. The same can be said for the Chinese. See Li, Wang, and Fischer, "Chinese Shame Concepts," 793.

7. Williams (*Shame and Necessity*, 90) writes, "If these [modern] distinctions between shame and guilt are even roughly correct, then it looks as though *aidōs* (and the other Greek terms) cannot merely mean 'shame,' but must cover something like guilt as well." Similarly, Cairns (*Aidōs*, 296–303) remarks that αἰδώς in Euripides's *Herc. fur.* comes close to the modern understanding of guilt.

8. See Xenophon, *Mem.* 1.7.2; Wis. 1;5; Eph. 5:11–13.

notion of guilt, followed by a few examples in which it encompasses our modern notion of shame.

First, Paul uses shaming refutation with the intent that it will lead to the phenomenological experience of remorse and contrition. His intent is not that his readers wallow in self-pity, lash out in anger, or languish in self-destructive thoughts. He wants the pain of retrospective Pauline shame to provide a space for deep reflection that is generative of contrition and repentance.[9] For example, Paul notes that the painful experience of shame brought about by his severe letter provoked the Corinthians to repentance (2 Cor. 7:9–10). At this level, Pauline shame encompasses the modern idea of guilt rather than shame. For the modern notion of guilt is linked with remorse and contrition, but shame is connected to feelings of worthlessness and anger.

Second, Pauline shame should be the emotion that results from the failure to hold fast to the gospel, to uphold moral standards within the community, or to love one's brother or sister. It is possible to make amends for these offenses by confessing one's wrongdoing, asking for forgiveness, and modifying one's behavior. For example, Paul expects the Galatians to repudiate the false gospel taught by the Judaizers and renew their allegiance to God; he expects the Corinthians to expel the immoral brother (1 Cor. 5:2, 7, 13) and to appoint judges that will adjudicate issues within the church (1 Cor. 6:1–6). Paul does not want his readers to hide, to deny their wrong, or to blame others. At this level, Pauline shame approximates the modern idea of guilt. For guilt is linked with a desire to make reparations, while shame is linked with a desire to hide and withdraw. Paul seeks to evoke the modern idea of guilt, despite making the bald statement "I say this to your shame" (1 Cor. 6:5).[10]

Third, Paul's shaming refutation seeks to move believers to have a genuine concern for those within the body of faith. Thus, when Paul shames Philemon, he specifically wants Philemon to empathize with Onesimus so as to receive him as a brother. Similarly, when Paul shames the Corinthians

9. In this regard, Pauline shame is not different from that presented in the Old Testament. For Old Testament writers also acknowledge that retrospective shame for sin should lead to contrition and repentance. Ezra, for example, begins his prayer of contrition and repentance to God with the statement "My God, I am too ashamed [בּושׁ] and disgraced [כלם] to lift up my face to you" (Ezra 9:6–7).

10. Another clear example where the shame of ancient Greece approximates our modern understanding of guilt is found in Sophocles's *Philoctetes*. In the play, Neoptolemus suffers remorse after stealing Philoctetes's bow through treachery. He says, "I overcame a man with shameful [αἰσχρός] trickery and deceit" (1228); "I acquired it shamefully [αἰσχρῶς] and not justly!" (1234). So struck is he by his shame that he finally remarks, "The wrong I did was disgraceful [αἰσχρός], and I shall try to undo it" (1248–49). Neoptolemus must make amends, and he does this by returning the bow to Philoctetes. In this snippet, we see that Neoptolemus's shame, with its focus on making amends, encompasses the modern idea of guilt.

in 1 Corinthians 11, he specifically wants them to empathize with those "who have nothing" (11:22). The intent of Paul's shaming refutation is to remind his readers that they have an obligation to those who are less fortunate within the body of Christ. They are to be other-oriented rather than self-oriented; they are to have empathy for others. In fact, Paul shames them precisely because they have no empathy for other believers. At this level, the aim of Paul's shaming refutation must be to evoke the modern idea of guilt. For contemporary guilt is positively related to other-oriented empathy, but shame is negatively related.[11]

In the above examples, Paul's use of shame seeks to evoke our modern understanding of guilt. Yet, when Paul tells the church not to associate with certain members who are disobeying his instructions so that they might be ashamed (2 Thess. 3:14), it is clear that he intends to elicit the modern idea of shame. Social rejection, isolation, abandonment, and severance of attachment bonds are precursors to the experience of shame. Moreover, when Paul confronts Peter in front of the entire church or when Paul castigates the church in Galatia as "foolish Galatians," it again seems clear that he intends what we understand to be shame. For the public setting of Paul's rebuke to Peter and the identification of the Galatians as those who are foolish (rather than those who have done something foolish) evoke our modern understanding of shame.

The above analysis shows that Paul's understanding of shame does not map exactly to our modern notion of shame. On the contrary, it encompasses elements of both shame and guilt. We may then reconstruct our previous table as follows:

	Modern shame	Modern guilt	Pauline shame
Type of eliciting event	Moral and nonmoral	Moral	Contrary to the gospel
Focus of evaluation	Global self: "*I* did that horrible thing."	Specific behavior: "I *did* that horrible *thing*."	Global self and specific behavior
Locus of evaluation	Public	Private	Before God
Degree of distress	Generally more painful	Generally less painful	Varied
Phenomenological experience	Shrinking; feeling small, worthless, or powerless; anger	Tension, remorse, regret	Contrition

11. Tangney and Dearing, *Shame and Guilt*, 79–89.

	Modern shame	Modern guilt	Pauline shame
Concern vis-à-vis the other	Concern with others' evaluation of self (self-oriented personal distress)	Concern with one's effect on others (other-oriented empathy)	Concern with God's evaluation of self and with one's effect on God and others
Counterfactual process	Mentally undoing some aspect of the self	Mentally undoing some aspect of behavior	Mentally undoing some aspect of the self and behavior
Motivational features	Desire to hide, escape, deny, strike back, or blame others	Desire to confess, apologize, or repair	Desire to confess, repent, and repair

Four further comments need to be made. First, the above analysis suggests that the distinction between modern shame and guilt is fuzzier than we imagine, confirming my earlier comments regarding the difficulty of distinguishing between them. Second, it is not quite adequate to say that Pauline shame is the summation of modern shame and guilt. For Pauline shame is closely tied with honor, respect, and reverence—a notion that is not present in our modern understanding of guilt and that is lost in our modern understanding of shame. Third, even though some aspects of Pauline shame can be understood by us as guilt, Pauline shame was not understood by Paul's original readers as the summation of shame and guilt; it was simply recognized as a coherent whole—as αἰσχύνη, αἰδώς, and ἐντροπή. Fourth, given the complexity of Pauline shame in encompassing elements of shame and guilt, it is a mistake simply to equate Pauline shame with our modern understanding of shame and dismiss it cavalierly.

Pauline Shame Is Not Heteronomous but Theonomous

Psychologists and ethicists disparage shame vis-à-vis guilt because they argue that shame, in contrast to guilt, is heteronomous. "An emotion is heteronomous if, in order for it to be elicited and intelligible, the judgment or attitude that triggers it (i) need not be the subject's own and (ii) the subject need not agree with the judgment or what is revealed by the attitude communicated to him."[12] Now, it is commonly assumed that shame is elicited by the evaluative judgment of an audience, a judgment with which the individual may not necessarily agree or adopt as one's own. Since shame is not necessarily dependent on

12. Teroni and Bruun, "Shame, Guilt, and Morality," 235.

the subject's autonomous moral judgment or evaluation of the circumstances, but is dependent on the moral demands impressed on the subject by others, it is argued that shame is heteronomous and cannot be morally relevant.

In response to this critique, several authors have made a defense for shame against the charge of heteronomy.[13] Most notably, Julien Deonna, Raffaele Rodogno, and Fabrice Teroni argue that the heteronomy argument against shame cannot stand.[14] They claim that shame, in fact, "is never heteronomous"; it is autonomous.[15]

In contrast to modern shame and guilt, Pauline shame is not heteronomous or autonomous but theonomous.[16] For Pauline shame is to be elicited by the subject's construal of the event according to God's criteria for honor and shame. Consequently, Pauline shame is not primarily ethical or psychological but first and foremost theological. In line with the Greco-Roman and Jewish understanding of shame, Pauline shame is also closely intertwined with one's conscience. The criterion for the elicitation of Pauline shame must be an internalized standard, for shame should not just be preoccupied with appearances or the prospects of "losing face" before others. Nonetheless, Paul is aware that a person's conscience may not be set according to the divine standard. He is therefore eager that his readers calibrate their consciences and transform their minds so that they are in sync with God's will.

If shame, as Aristotle remarks, is the fear of dishonor,[17] then Pauline shame is the fear of dishonor before God—before the one whose standard of honor and shame ultimately matters. If "the eyes are the abode of shame," as the ancient Greek proverb affirms,[18] then we learn to feel Pauline shame acutely when we see our misdeeds through God's eyes rather than through the eyes of others. We conduct ourselves "not by way of eye-service as people-pleasers, but with a sincere heart as those who fear the Lord" (Col. 3:22). Drawing on the typological correspondence between the Israelite wilderness community and the church, we may say that God (through the Holy Spirit) is the one who moves about the community. Consequently, the community must be "holy" and ready for his inspection at all times, lest he see "any shameless deed" (Deut. 23:14 LXX) and turn away from them. The community must develop

13. For example, see Williams, *Shame and Necessity*, 75–102; Kaster, "Shame of the Romans," 5–6; Calhoun, "Apology for Moral Shame."

14. Deonna, Rodogno, and Teroni, *In Defense of Shame*, 127–33.

15. Deonna, Rodogno, and Teroni, *In Defense of Shame*, 130.

16. My understanding of *theonomous* follows Gensler, *Ethics and Religion*, 25, where he remarks, "Religious moral thinking at its best is *theonomous*: based both on God's will and on a deeper part of our own will that God implanted in us. This is a responsible moral autonomy."

17. Aristotle, *Eth. nic.* 4.9.2, 1128B11–12; 3.6.3, 1115A13–14.

18. Aristotle, *Rhet.* 2.6.18, 1384A36.

a proper sense of shame that is fundamentally equivalent to an attitude of humility and reverential fear of God.

The theonomy of Pauline shame does not destroy the moral autonomy of the individual. Just as affirming God's commands to be our moral obligations does not destroy our moral autonomy,[19] so also affirming God's criteria for honor and shame as our own criteria to evaluate events does not destroy the moral autonomy of Pauline shame. On the contrary, the theonomy of Pauline shame signifies God's intention or design for our moral autonomy. The moral autonomy that Pauline shame calls for is one in which our moral thinking is based on a mind (νοῦς) that is deeply informed and constrained by God's standard.

The Inadequacy of Guilt

One of the central distinctions between modern formulations of shame and guilt is the focus of evaluation. Guilt focuses on some specific act or limited behavior ("I *did* that horrible *thing*"), shame on the global self or identity ("*I* did that horrible thing"); guilt focuses on the *deed*, shame on the *identity*; guilt focuses on the *doing*, shame on the *being*. Given this bifurcation, the counterfactual process in guilt is to envision a scenario that undoes the *act* ("If only I had not done . . ."), while that of shame is to undo the *self* ("If only I wasn't so . . ."). Consequently, the action tendency of guilt is to make reparative *actions*, but that of shame should be to reform one's *self* and modify those qualities that bring about shame.

If the above distinctions hold, then guilt is an inadequate moral emotion; it needs shame. There are three reasons for this assessment.

1. *Guilt fails to underscore the gravity of sin.* Guilt, as defined above, is a flaccid emotion that is sufficient for peccadillos but woefully inadequate for major transgressions. For example, if a person repeatedly rapes children, is it adequate for him just to experience guilt, the feeling that he has done bad acts, without acknowledging that there is something fundamentally wrong with his character and person? No! It is insufficient for that person just to know he has done wrong; he must also experience shame.[20] For shame causes us to internalize our understanding not only that the act is wrong but that the self is implicated as well; it underscores the gravity of the sin.

---

19. For arguments that divine command theory does not undermine moral autonomy, see Adams, *Finite and Infinite Goods*, 270–76; Evans, *God and Moral Obligation*, 94–98.

20. Sabini and Silver ("In Defense of Shame," 8) write, "Intense guilt, Rodion Romanavitch Raskolnokov [*sic*] guilt, *that* guilt, we suggest, has as its bite shame. . . . Acts for which we are guilty (and don't just in some weak sense feel guilty) do involve the self. And because they involve the self, they involve shame."

2. *Guilt cannot understand itself*. By focusing solely on the action apart from the subject's character or ethical consciousness, guilt lacks explanatory power. It cannot explain the factors that give rise to the action; it cannot explain why people err. If people consider guilt to be morally self-sufficient, that is because they have a distorted view of the moral life in which the moral self is devoid of character and identity.[21] Shame, with its focus on the self, provides the structure for understanding ourselves in relation to our actions. If we come to understand our shame, we come perhaps also to understand our guilt. As Bernard Williams remarks, "Shame can understand guilt, but guilt cannot understand itself."[22] Just as we cannot understand a person's actions apart from the ethical character and identity of that person, so also we cannot understand guilt without shame.

3. *Guilt treats only the symptoms*. The action tendency of guilt is ineffective in making significant moral progress. For "guilt . . . treats only the symptoms of our moral defects; it is only concerned with the defects in our actions. The self-reforming tendencies associated with shame, in contrast, treat the cause."[23] Shame gets at the root of the problem, focusing on the imperfections in our character that prompt us to go astray. Guilt is sufficient if we narrowly focus only on moral responsibility and blame. Shame, however, is needed if we extend the focus toward moral character and values.

The modern desire to favor guilt over shame and the tendency to separate *act* from *self* leave us with a neutered program for moral progress. Modern guilt in itself is inadequate for significant moral progress; shame is also necessary. The necessity of both guilt and shame makes Pauline shame an apt choice, for it contains elements of both. More significantly, Pauline shame with its grounding in Pauline ethics teaches us that it is a mistake to divide *deed* and *identity* sharply and to treat each element separately. In contrast to the modern bifurcation of deed and identity, Pauline shame addresses both. This does not mean that deed and identity, or being and doing, are identical. Rather, there is an inextricable relationship between them that is centered on the relationship between the indicative and the imperative.

Ever since Rudolf Bultmann raised the issue in his classic essay "The Problem of Ethics in Paul,"[24] the relationship between the "is" and the "ought"

21. Williams, *Shame and Necessity*, 94.
22. Williams, *Shame and Necessity*, 93.
23. Deonna, Rodogno, and Teroni, *In Defense of Shame*, 184. See also Thomason, *Naked*, 162–64.
24. Bultmann, "Das Problem der Ethik bei Paulus."

has dominated discussions on Pauline ethics. There is recognition that, for Paul, *being* precedes *doing* such that identity is the basis for ethics.[25] This picture, however, presents a relationship that may be too static. As Paul creates communities comprising Jews and gentiles from varied backgrounds, he must construct and instill within his readers a common social identity that will unify them. This constructed social identity is fragile and malleable as it is challenged by opposing worldviews within the surrounding culture. In order to reinforce the plausibility structure of the gospel in his readers, Paul must constantly remind them not only of their Christic identity but also of the ethical obligations that flow out of that identity. Depending on the exigencies of the situation, Paul emphasizes either the indicative or the imperative. Nevertheless, both are important, for they mutually reinforce each other and create a stable and coherent whole.[26]

Given the necessity to strengthen the plausibility structure of the gospel, Pauline shame looks in both directions. It looks in one direction toward who we are (modern understanding of shame) and in the other direction toward the impact of our actions on others (modern understanding of guilt). It looks toward the inner world of our dispositions and toward the outer world of harm and benefit. Pauline shame therefore fosters cruciformity in both identity and action; it cultivates a Christic identity while nurturing an ethos that is consonant with that identity. Consequently, Pauline shame presents us with a more satisfying and realistic solution to the moral problem. It accomplishes what modern guilt (or modern shame) is unable to do by itself.

Challenge 2: Evocation of Shame Is Manipulative, Even Coercive

Modern readers are generally uncomfortable with Paul's rhetoric of shame, arguing that he uses flattery, intimidation, and manipulation to achieve his ends. The use of emotions in his rhetoric is troublesome enough, but the use of an emotion such as shame (or even guilt) spells double jeopardy. His act of shaming is an illegitimate and abusive exercise of power over other moral agents.

25. Parsons, "Being Precedes Act"; Schrage, *Ethics of the New Testament*, 167–72; Thompson, *Moral Formation According to Paul*, 43–62. The anthropologist Clifford Geertz notes a similar relationship between the indicative ("the assumed structure of reality") and the imperative ("the approved way of life") in numerous religious cultures: "The powerfully coercive 'ought' is felt to grow out of a comprehensive factual 'is.'" See Geertz, *Interpretation of Cultures*, 126.

26. Geertz (*Interpretation of Cultures*, 127) writes, "The ethos [the imperative] is made intellectually reasonable by being shown to represent a way of life implied by the actual state of affairs which the world view [the indicative] describes, and the world view [the indicative] is made emotionally acceptable by being presented as an image of an actual state of affairs of which such a way of life [the imperative] is an authentic expression."

In this section, I assess whether Paul's rhetoric of shame is manipulative. I use Philemon as my test case since it is most susceptible to the charge of manipulation or coercion. For example, Alfred Suhl writes that Paul's bold request to Philemon "truly borders on extortion."[27] David Russell notes that the letter prominently displays "the subtle art of manipulation in behavioral texts."[28] More recently, Roy Jeal writes that "Paul is playing Philemon in a highly rhetoricized and manipulative fashion."[29]

I do not consider Paul's shaming rhetoric in Philemon to be manipulative or coercive; rather, it is persuasive. Before attempting to defend my stance, it is prudent to provide brief descriptions for these various terms. It is beyond the scope of this section to provide definitive accounts. I only offer conceptual distinctions along the lines of Wittgenstein's "family resemblances" that will hopefully enhance our understanding of Paul's rhetoric of shame.

Toward a Conceptual Analysis

Coercion, manipulation, and persuasion all involve influencing someone to do (or omit doing), believe, or feel something he or she would otherwise not do (or omit doing), believe, or feel. The boundaries separating manipulation, coercion, and persuasion are fuzzy. All three fall on a continuum, and it is difficult to present a simple definition of manipulation. Nevertheless, there is some consensus about which cases are clear and which are not.

Coercion and manipulation are similar in that both are often thought to be antithetical to individual autonomy. Both do not respect the choices of the individual with the result that the victim is said to be a puppet on a string. Coercion, however, differs from manipulation in four ways. First, coercion operates with a threat and diminishes a person's options.[30] Manipulation does not diminish a person's options but "perverts the way that person reaches decisions, forms preferences or adopts goals."[31] Second, coercion offers the victim the choice to comply with the coercer's demand. Third, coercion, unlike manipulation, is always transparent. In fact, coercion only works if the victim understands the nature of the threat. Fourth, since coercion involves irresistible incentives, it differs from manipulation in providing one with an excuse.[32]

27. Suhl, *Der Brief an Philemon*, 39.
28. Russell, "First-Century Appeals Letter," 21.
29. Jeal, *Exploring Philemon*, 45.
30. See Nozick, "Coercion"; Anderson, "Coercion."
31. Raz, *Morality of Freedom*, 377.
32. Rudinow, "Manipulation," 339.

Manipulation is a form of noncoercive influence. But how does it differ from persuasion? I present three popular proposals for demarcating manipulation.

1. *Manipulation as deception.* A popular proposal considers manipulation as deceptive noncoercive influence. The manipulator may lie, hide important facts, or distract the interlocutor with red herrings. Sarah Buss writes, "Manipulating/deceiving someone often prevents her from governing herself with an *accurate understanding* of her situation."[33] Persuasion, however, is always transparent. The persuader expresses a wish clearly and communicates it in ways that the other can fully understand.

2. *Manipulation as nonrational influence.* In this proposal, the manipulator bypasses or subverts the manipulee's rational capacities such that they are not sufficiently engaged or engaged in such a way that undermines their function.[34] Marcia Baron writes that "manipulativeness . . . reflects either a failure to view others as rational beings, or an impatience over the nuisance of having to treat them as rational—and as equals."[35] Unlike manipulation, persuasion offers the other person a choice and respects that person's ability to choose. Persuasion does influence how a person reaches a decision, but it does not subvert or pervert the decision-making process.

In this proposal, appeals to emotion may count as manipulation. But they need not, for emotional appeals can deepen conviction and provide rhetorical amplification. John Dryzek points to Martin Luther King Jr.'s rhetoric as a fine example of emotion working in tandem with reason. King's speeches included rational arguments. Nonetheless, "the transmission was aided, perhaps even made possible, by the accompanying rhetoric" that was largely emotional.[36]

What then separates legitimate emotional appeals from emotional manipulation in this proposal? According to Nathaniel Klemp, "Manipulation occurs when emotional rhetoric overwhelms, distracts, or bypasses listeners' rational capacities. When appeals to emotion no longer incite or aid rational reflection but, rather, interfere with the agent's capacity to reason, rhetoric turns manipulative."[37]

3. *Manipulation as intentional leading away from ideals.* Robert Noggle presents a different proposal that has gained much support.[38] He suggests that

33. Buss, "Valuing Autonomy," 226.
34. See especially Wood, "Coercion, Manipulation, Exploitation," 35; Sunstein, *Ethics of Influence*, 114.
35. Baron, "Manipulativeness," 50.
36. Dryzek, *Deliberative Democracy and Beyond*, 52.
37. Klemp, *Morality of Spin*, 54.
38. See Noggle, "Manipulative Actions."

manipulation is intentionally moving someone's belief, emotion, or desire away from that which the manipulator thinks is ideal for the manipulee. The manipulator views the victim as an object, pulling the levers of belief, emotion, or desire so that the victim strays from the norms or ideals that govern these attitudes. The ideals from which the manipulator attempts to move the victim away are "what the *influencer* thinks are ideal settings *for the person being influenced*."[39] Objective ideals or the manipulee's ideals for belief, desires, or emotions are irrelevant. What counts in manipulation is the manipulator's own ideals about what the right path should be. Noggle also considers intention to be critical. It is not possible to manipulate someone unintentionally. "An action counts as manipulation if and only if the relevant intention is present."[40]

In this proposal, manipulation intentionally seeks to move the victim away from that which the manipulator considers to be ideal beliefs, desires, or emotions. Persuasion, on the other hand, seeks to strengthen the other person's resolve to stay within the bounds of ideal beliefs, desires, or emotions.

In summary, the main features of coercion, manipulation, and persuasion are presented in a table as follows.

	Intent to lead astray from ideals	Transparent	Others given a choice	Choice of others respected	Use of sanctions or threats
Persuasion	No	Yes	Yes	Yes	No
Manipulation	Yes	Sometimes[a]	No	No	No
Coercion	Yes	Yes	Yes	No	Yes

This table has been adapted from Klemp, *Morality of Spin*, 60.
[a] Manipulation is not always deceptive, for one can manipulate by tempting, inciting, insinuating, or playing on emotions such as guilt trips. These are patently overt and transparent.

Assessing Paul's Rhetoric of Shame

I do not consider Paul's rhetoric of shame in Philemon to be manipulative or coercive. It is persuasive for the following reasons.

1. *Paul's intent is not to lead one astray from ideals.* Noggle proposes that manipulation is intentionally moving someone's belief, emotion, or desire

39. Noggle, "Manipulative Actions," 47.
40. Noggle, "Manipulative Actions," 48.

away from that which the manipulator thinks is ideal for the manipulee. With this understanding, Paul's rhetoric of shame is not manipulative because the ideals that Paul wants to instill in Philemon are what Paul considers to be true and ideal. Paul may pull the same levers of belief, emotion, and desire that a manipulator may pull, but his rhetoric is not manipulative since his intention is not to lead Philemon astray. Rather, his intention is to lead Philemon to believe rightly, to feel rightly, and to desire rightly. Philemon must believe that filial relationships *in Christ* trump social relationships *in the world*;[41] he must experience shame if he does not fulfill his obligations to a brother within the community of faith when he is capable of doing so; and Philemon must desire to do that which is good (τὸ ἀγαθόν, Philem. 14) and aligns with the will of God.[42]

A virtue of Noggle's account is that it distinguishes between nonmanipulative and manipulative appeals to emotion. This is especially significant in evaluating Paul's rhetoric of shame. According to Noggle, appeals to emotion are not manipulative if the emotion E evoked in the other is appropriate—that is, if E is based on true beliefs, and if E highlights whatever is most important in that particular situation.[43] I consider Paul's evocation of shame in Philemon to be appropriate and therefore nonmanipulative. The prospective shame that Philemon experiences is based on the true belief that members of a Christian community have obligations to one another. Moreover, the prospective shame that Paul evokes makes salient what is most crucial—that we are to evaluate matters from God's perspective. Philemon may suppose that his anger is justified, for Onesimus "wronged" him and "owes" him a debt (v. 18). But Paul's rhetoric reminds him to see the situation through the lens of the gospel—that all persons in Christ are debtors because of the grace of God and that all have equal worth. It is therefore shameful for a brother to own another brother as a slave.

2. Paul's rhetoric is transparent, not deceptive. We noted above that manipulation may be deceptive, but persuasion is not. When Paul persuades Philemon, he employs all the tools of normal rhetorical convention. He pulls out all the stops, making appeals to logos, pathos, and ethos. He praises Philemon

41. Petersen, *Rediscovering Paul*, 269.

42. Some consider Paul's rhetoric not to be manipulative because the good that Paul seeks is ultimately not for Paul's own advantage but for that of Onesimus, Philemon, and the community. Although there is some merit in this line of thought, it is not a sufficiently stringent criterion to discount all forms of manipulation. Paternalistic manipulation, for example, may move someone toward a particular ideal of desire (e.g., taking one's medicine), but does so through a process that is less than ideal for that person's emotion and belief (e.g., flattery by the nurse).

43. Noggle, "Manipulative Actions," 46.

effusively, emphasizes certain facts strategically, and plays the emotion card repeatedly. But all of this does not make Paul's rhetoric manipulative, for he does not flatter, lie, conceal relevant information, harbor ulterior motives, or exploit perceived weaknesses. As Jeffrey Weima notes, "Paul does not compromise his integrity by resorting to false praise or feigned emotions."[44] He genuinely gives thanks to God for Philemon's love in refreshing the hearts of the saints, he is sincerely confident of Philemon's obedience, he honestly wants Philemon to do the right thing, and he wholeheartedly believes that the events transpired under the providence of God. Paul's rhetoric is strong, but his intent is not to deceive, mislead, or manipulate Philemon.

3. *Paul's rhetoric gives and respects the choice of others.* Manipulation and coercion do not respect the choice of others; only persuasion does. According to this understanding, Paul's rhetoric is not coercive or manipulative, for it gives others the freedom to choose and it respects the choice of others. In verses 8–9, Paul does not exert his apostolic prerogative to command, preferring to appeal on the basis of love. In verses 13–14, Paul makes clear that he does not wish to impose his will on Philemon. Philemon's decision must be voluntary and without compulsion. Paul is so sensitive to misunderstandings that not only must Philemon's decision not be coerced, but "it must not even wear *the appearance* (ὡς) of being so."[45]

Paul will exhort and encourage, but he will not coerce or manipulate. For the good that one does cannot be commanded; it must spring "from one's own free will" (v. 14). Origen compares Paul's modus operandi with God's way of working. God could compel us to be good, but "He enjoins us to do what we do, so that what occurs is from *free will*."[46]

4. *Paul's rhetoric exerts influence, not threat or force.* Coercion involves the exercise of power over an individual; it invokes sanctions and threats to accomplish its purpose. Paul's rhetoric of shame in Philemon is clearly not coercive, for Paul writes from a posture of weakness rather than strength. As a feeble old man and powerless prisoner in Rome, he is more than a thousand miles away from the situation in Colossae and has no legal authority to compel Philemon to do anything. As a follower of the crucified Messiah, who himself rejected force when arrested by armed men, Paul himself also eschews force. Moreover, whatever authority and prestige he might have as an apostle, Paul sets it aside so that he may appeal directly to a "dear friend" (v. 1), a "fellow worker" (v. 1), a "brother" (v. 7), and a "partner" (v. 17).

44. Weima, "Paul's Persuasive Prose," 58.
45. Lightfoot, *Saint Paul's Epistles*, 340.
46. Origen, *Hom. Jer.* 20.2 (FC 97:224).

If Paul's rhetoric in Philemon is not coercive, how about his shaming rhetoric in the other letters? Should Paul's question in 1 Corinthians 4:21 ("What do you prefer? Should I come to you with a rod or with a spirit of love and gentleness?") or his language concerning the possibility of excommunication in 2 Thessalonians 3:14 ("Take note of anyone who does not obey our instruction in this letter. Do not associate with them.") be construed as threats? No. Even though Paul leverages the choices of his readers through the presentation of conditional judgments, such statements are not coercions but warnings. First, the dynamic that governs Paul and his readers is not one of power but of mutual responsibility and obligation. Second, the potential judgments embedded in the warnings are justified and in accord with the "conventions" that govern the interpersonal relationships of which Paul and his readers are a part.[47] Specifically, the measures about which Paul warns his readers are the disciplinary measures that govern the entire Christian community. Third, whatever authority Paul has as an apostle is derivative and legitimate only insofar as Paul speaks for God and the gospel. Fourth, the obedience and compliance that Paul wants from his readers is not directed to Paul per se but to the gospel. All people, even an apostle, are subject to the same gospel imperative and demands; Paul is not exempt. Thus, Paul declares that he himself would be cursed if he proclaimed a different gospel from the gospel of a crucified Messiah (Gal. 1:8).

Paul's rhetoric of shame is bold, forceful, strong, passionate, and urgent. The heavy-handedness that marks some of his rhetoric underscores his desire to infuse the conversation with the gravitas it deserves. Nonetheless, Paul's rhetoric is not coercive nor manipulative. Even John Chrysostom, who repeatedly notes that Paul shames Philemon into compliance, writes that Paul strikes a balance. Paul does not barely make a request, nor does he command. On the contrary, he makes a strong appeal "according to the rule of friendship."[48]

Since the church is a voluntary association or intentional community, persuasion must be the primary tool to effect change. Paul does not command, manipulate, or coerce, because his primary goal is not just that believers do the right thing, but that they do the right thing for the right reason. By engaging in the rhetoric of persuasion, Paul engages the minds and hearts of his readers, inviting them to embrace his vision of a cruciform community and to make that their own.

47. Carr, "Coercion and Freedom," 63–64.
48. John Chrysostom, *Hom. Phlm.* 3 (*NPNF*[1] 13:555).

Challenge 3: Shame Is Toxic and Destructive

In the introductory chapter, I noted that Brené Brown appeared on Oprah Winfrey's *Super Soul Sunday* and declared shame to be lethal and destructive. In her TED Talk "Listening to Shame," which has been viewed more than twelve million times, she notes that shame is "this web of unobtainable, conflicting, competing expectations about who we're supposed to be." It is this gremlin living inside us that repeatedly plays two thoughts in our mind: "Never good enough" or "Who do you think you are?" As a result of this feeling of inadequacy, shame drives us toward destructive patterns of behavior. Consequently, "shame is highly, highly correlated with addiction, depression, violence, aggression, bullying, suicide, eating disorders."[49]

Shame can be toxic and destructive, but it is not necessarily so. When a more expansive view of shame is adopted, shame plays a pivotal role in moral formation. We have already seen this expansive view in the Greco-Roman and Confucian traditions. Both traditions broadly consider shame to be either a virtue or a semi-virtue; both stress the importance of having a sense of shame; both stress that developing this sense of shame in children is one of the primary tasks of education.

While shame in general can be toxic and destructive, Pauline shame, rightly understood, is never toxic or destructive. It is always good. In this section, I correct two preconceptions of shame that should not be applied to Pauline shame, arguing that Pauline shame is important for the Christian moral life.

Preconception 1: Shame Destroys One's Self-Esteem

Many consider shame to be toxic and destructive because shame destroys one's self-esteem. Moreover, repeated experiences of shame cause one to have chronically diminished levels of self-esteem, and such low self-esteem in turn predisposes one to feelings of shame.[50] This creates a vicious cycle that goes from bad to worse, eventually spiraling out of control.

John Rawls is a philosopher who adopts such a view of shame. He characterizes shame as "the feeling that someone has when he experiences an injury to his self-respect or suffers a blow to his self-esteem."[51] Rawls further considers self-esteem as comprising two parts. "First . . . it includes a person's sense of his own value, his secure conviction that his conception of his good, his plan of life is worth carrying out. And second, self-respect implies a confidence

---

49. Brown, "Listening to Shame."
50. Tangney and Dearing, *Shame and Guilt*, 60.
51. Rawls, *Theory of Justice*, 442.

in one's ability, so far as it is within one's power, to fulfill one's intentions."[52] Both conditions are necessary for self-esteem. Thus, one loses self-esteem if one develops a negative opinion regarding the worthiness of one's aims and ideals or if one now comes to believe that one does not have the talent, ability, or aptitude to achieve those same ideals. If this definition of self-esteem holds, we may say that Pauline shame undercuts one's self-esteem. But it is extremely important to note that the kind of self-esteem Pauline shame clears away is a faulty self-esteem. Pauline shame removes one's faulty self-esteem in order to remind us that God's esteem is of much greater significance.

Self-esteem concerns one's overall positive opinion of oneself. However, what is critical for Paul is not so much our own positive opinion of ourselves as God's opinion of us. If our opinion of ourselves runs counter to God's opinion, Pauline shame is warranted. Pauline shame is the bitter medicine that targets our faulty conception of ourselves so as to remind us that God's perspective of us is paramount.

Pauline shame is apropos when we arrogantly hold to aims and ideals that are inimical to the gospel. For example, Paul shames the Corinthians because they hungered for power, wealth, reputation, and prestige. Their desire for wisdom and eloquence runs counter to the cruciform pattern of Christ. By critiquing their faulty aims and ideals, Paul strikes at what Rawls considers to be the first condition necessary for self-esteem. Pauline shame is also fitting when we foolishly delude ourselves into thinking that we can attain honor apart from Christ. For example, Paul shames the Galatians for wanting to be circumcised. Their desire to supplant the gospel with the teachings of the Judaizers marks their severance from Christ and their fall from grace (Gal. 5:4). This severance ultimately robs them of the ability to be justified, for it is impossible for anyone to be justified by the works of the law (Gal. 2:16; 3:10). By critiquing their ability to attain their ultimate goal of justification, Paul strikes at what Rawls considers to be the second condition necessary for self-esteem. In the above two examples, Pauline shame destroys the faulty self-esteem of the Corinthians and the Galatians. It was faulty because their aims and ideals were erroneous, based on the worldly rather than the divine court of opinion. It was also faulty because the believers, by their own human effort, lacked the means and ability to attain true honor.

Pauline shame does not just tear down; it also builds up. It constructs the proper esteem believers should have of themselves. The purpose of Pauline shame is Christic formation, reminding readers of their identity in Christ and the ethos that is consonant with that identity. Pauline shame therefore

---

52. Rawls, *Theory of Justice*, 440.

builds up the esteem of believers by reminding them of the honor they have as a result of their new identity in Christ and by outlining a set of aims and ideals that are truly significant and congruent with a cruciform ethos. Let me expand on these two points.

1. Pauline shame builds up the esteem of believers by exhorting them to embrace the honor they have in Christ. Although the Rawlsian characterization of self-esteem is helpful, it is inadequate, for it "fails to recognize aspects of our identity that contribute to our sense of worth independently of the aims and ideals around which we organize our lives."[53] Rawls only understands self-esteem that comes as a result of one's actions or doing. There is, however, a certain sense of worth that comes from one's identity, from the fact that one is a member of a certain class of noble people. For example, there is a certain dignity and honor that is afforded to Prince Louis of Cambridge despite being only an infant (he was born on April 23, 2018) and not capable of holding any magnanimous aims and ideals. He has great honor simply for the fact that he is a member of the British royal family. In the same way, Pauline shame builds up the believer's proper esteem of themselves, for it reminds them of the worth and honor they have as a result of their union with Christ—they are children of God.

When Pauline shame reminds believers of their Christic identity, it reminds them that their self-esteem, boast, pride, confidence, and identity cannot be based on the flesh (Phil. 3:3; cf. 2 Cor. 5:12, 16)—that is, on any aspect of life outside of Christ. This includes their socioeconomic status, their ethnicity, their gender, and their accomplishments or lack thereof. Regardless of whether they are rich landlords or poor slaves, regardless of whether they receive the praise or scorn of others, regardless of whether they possess all things or are exploited by others, their confidence and identity cannot be based on the opinions of the world or external standards. Rather, it is to be based on the Spirit's inner testimony that they are a new creation in Christ (2 Cor. 5:17) and are adopted children of God (Rom. 8:15; Gal. 4:5–7; Eph. 1:5). As adopted children of God, believers share in God's glory.[54] Such honor is not achieved on the basis of any human effort; it is not *attained* through the performance of some virtuous deed. On the contrary, it is a gift of God; it is an honor that is *ascribed* to believers because of their relationship to the heavenly Father.[55] As Ben Sira notes, "The glory of one's father is one's own glory" (Sir. 3:11 NRSV). Consequently, it is an honor that believers should gratefully accept and embrace.

---

53. Deigh, "Shame and Self-Esteem," 240.
54. Burke, *Adopted into God's Family*, 152–76.
55. The distinction between attained and ascribed honor is also understood as the distinction between appraisal and recognition respect. See Darwall, "Two Kinds of Respect."

2. Pauline shame builds up the esteem of believers by exhorting them to embrace aims and ideals that are truly significant, instead of chasing after shoddy ideals. Pauline shame exhorts believers to calibrate their ideals according to the divine court of opinion. Their ambition must be to press toward the goal of God's upward calling in Christ (Phil. 3:14). Such an ideal is more significant than worldly acclaim and prestige, for the prize of this goal will be given by the ultimate judge, whose opinion supremely matters. Pauline shame also builds up the esteem of believers because it reminds them that they have the means to achieve these cruciform ideals. They have this ability not because of their own intrinsic and innate competence but because God is the one who works in them, enabling them "both to will and to work for his good pleasure" (Phil. 2:13). Believers will one day attain these aims and ideals, not through their own feeble strength but through the supernatural power of the Holy Spirit.

Pauline shame, rightly understood, destroys the faulty self-esteem that believers might have. It nevertheless constructs an esteem that believers must embrace, for Pauline shame is not incompatible with Pauline honor. On the contrary, they are complementary; they are two sides of the same coin. With this understanding, Pauline shame destroys the gremlins that Brené Brown fears. In response to the thought "Never good enough," Pauline shame leads believers to affirm that they are never good enough on their own. Nevertheless, they are more than sufficient because of their union with Christ. In response to the thought "Who do you think you are?" Pauline shame leads believers to declare proudly, "I am a new creation in Christ. The old me, with its false expectations and standards, has passed away. I am now a child of God and heir according to the promise."

Preconception 2: Acts of Shaming Are Destructive

Many equate acts of shaming with humiliation. In today's age, we see the destructive power of internet-fueled shaming in the call-out and pile-on of online shaming. People are brutally shamed for public missteps and perceived antisocial behavior such as mansplaining, failing to clean up after their pets, or making obscene gestures at Arlington National Cemetery. In *So You've Been Publicly Shamed*, journalist Jon Ronson relates the horror stories of those who were at the receiving end of cyber shaming—people such as Jonah Lehrer, Justine Sacco, and Lindsey Stone. In many cases, the victims lost their jobs, showed signs of PTSD, and became stricken with insomnia, anxiety, and agoraphobia. The destructive impact of online shaming is immense. Even advocates of old-fashioned shaming, such as Texas judge Ted Poe, acknowledge that their techniques pale in comparison to the viciousness of social media.[56]

Acts of shaming can be destructive, but they need not be so. We cannot make the blanket assumption that every act of shaming is necessarily stigmatizing and humiliating. We cannot simply equate *shaming* with *mocking, despising, scorning,* or *humiliating.* Following the work of John Braithwaite, we must distinguish between reintegrative and disintegrative shaming.[57] Acts of shaming need not be destructive when expressions of disapproval are temporally limited and when efforts to maintain interdependent bonds are sustained throughout the finite period of disapproval. On the contrary, they are constructive for they enable us to envision a better self.

Paul's ethic of shame resorts to occasional acts of shaming. However, as I argued in my earlier interaction with Braithwaite's work, Paul's shaming approach is reintegrative, not disintegrative. I now briefly contrast Paul's shaming with online shaming, showing how Pauline shaming does not have the destructive elements of online shaming.

Tempo

Online shaming is toxic because it is not measured; it happens at high speed. Justine Sacco sent the unfortunate tweet "Going to Africa. Hope I don't get AIDS. Just kidding. I'm white!" an hour before she boarded her flight to South Africa. When she landed at Cape Town Airport eleven hours later, her tweet had gone viral and was the number one worldwide trend on Twitter. In fact, one Twitter user waited for her at the airport so as to take her photograph and post it online. Given the speed at which online shaming occurs, it can hardly be thoughtful, nuanced, and measured.[58] Pauline shaming, however, is graduated, calibrated, and deliberate. Just as Matthew 18 envisions an escalating response in church discipline, so also in Pauline shaming. The offender is confronted first with restorative instruction and gentle rebuke. It is only when the offender rejects this gentle instruction with arrogance and hubris that a stiffer response is necessary. The church does not have a legal rulebook to quantify specifically the amount of shaming

56. Ronson, *So You've Been Publicly Shamed*, 90.

57. Thomason (*Naked*, 172–215) makes a similar distinction using the terminology "invitations to shame" and "shaming." According to her, it is appropriate to invite people to feel shame for the moral wrong they have done. Shaming, however, is unjustified.

58. Klonick ("Re-shaming the Debate," 1032) argues that online shaming is problematic because it "(1) is an over-determined punishment with indeterminate social meaning; (2) is not a calibrated or measured form of punishment; and (3) is of little or questionable accuracy as to who and what it punishes."

discipline that should be meted out at every stage. Nonetheless, the church has the Holy Spirit as a guide. He knows what is necessary, for he is the one who is grieved by sin in the church (Eph. 4:30).

Criterion

In the past, one needed to convince an editor before a humiliating story was published. The story had to pass certain journalistic standards; it had to be newsworthy and be supported by evidence. There are, however, no official gatekeepers in today's social media. Journalist Helen Andrews remarks that "most attempts so far to devise new rules have taken ideology as their starting point: Shaming is okay as long as it's directed at men by women, the powerless against the powerful."[59] The criterion for Pauline shaming is not the ideological fad du jour nor some arbitrary human standard. It is the word of God—divinely inspired Scripture that is profitable for rebuking and correction (2 Tim. 3:16). Scripture, then, is the standard with which the people of God are to use in order to decide whether they should rebuke, censure, or exhort (2 Tim. 4:2) an erring member of the faith.

Duration and Restoration

Online shaming is toxic because it leaves a permanent stigma. Although the attention span of the internet mob is short, their scathing remarks live on forever in the cloud or until Google's servers crash without any backup. There are companies that will help you rebuild your online reputation for a fee, but your insensitive tweet and the backlash that follows are cataloged in perpetuity on the internet. Since everyone googles people they might date or hire, the first thing that prospective friends and employers will know about you is that you have been deemed a toxic liability by the internet. Online shaming thus leaves a permanent stain that continually haunts the offender, even after the person has expressed remorse and repentance. Pauline shaming, on the other hand, is limited in time and scope (2 Cor. 2:6–8). The discipline meted by the church community cannot be excessive lest the individual be overwhelmed with excessive sorrow. Moreover, the church must reaffirm their love for the individual when there is genuine repentance.

Intent

Online shaming is toxic because it does not seek the good of the offender. The intent of online shaming by the internet pitchfork mob is varied. Some seek to punish the individual. Others seek to monetize the humiliation, for any

59. Andrews, "Shame Storm," 28.

increase in clicks results in higher advertising dollars. Many others, however, pile on primarily to be part of a larger movement, to enjoy approval from fellow shamers, to demonstrate one-upmanship, and to validate one's supposed sense of righteous outrage. In the frenzy of their attack, the internet community flits between rage and Schadenfreude.

Pauline shaming of believers is never conducted with malicious intent. As with other forms of church discipline, Pauline shame is meted out with heaviness and sadness. It functions not as retributive punishment, for Christ has borne the punishment for our sins. On the contrary, Pauline shaming is ultimately redemptive and salvific. In my discussion of 1 Corinthians 11:31–32 in chapter 4, I noted that Pauline shaming is God's disciplinary judgment (κρίνω) because we have not examined (διακρίνω) ourselves sufficiently. Pauline shaming therefore becomes an invitation to confront some part of our identity and behavior that we have not confronted, so that we will not be condemned (κατακρίνω) along with the world at God's final judgment. Pauline shaming is God's firm hand of discipline on believers in the present so that we might escape his eschatological judgment.

Anonymity and Distance

Online shaming is destructive because it depersonalizes the offender. Online shamers generally have no meaningful relationship with the people they are shaming. The people whom they shame are practically strangers to them. Given this lack of relationship, the offender is often stereotyped, stigmatized, and demonized. Moreover, false narratives and imaginary rumors about the victim are hurriedly fabricated and disseminated.[60] For example, when Justine Sacco was still airborne, tweets spread the misinformation that she was a rich "heiress to a $4.8 billion fortune, as people assumed her father was the South African mining tycoon Desmond Sacco."[61] This false narrative emboldened the online community. They now saw themselves as the righteous poor who had the moral responsibility (and the power) to bring these high-status people down a peg or two.

The lack of personal proximity in social media also diminishes any unease that shamers might experience. They do not physically witness the emotional pain they inflict on the victims. Consequently, they themselves do not experience any shame for causing unnecessary harm on others. Moreover, there is a "magnitude gap . . . ; that is, there is some distance between the shamers'

---

60. Litt ("Knock, Knock. Who's There?," 331) writes, "The less an actual audience is visible or known, the more individuals become dependent on their imaginations."

61. Ronson, *So You've Been Publicly Shamed*, 76.

perceptions of their objects' great deservingness of harm and light suffering as a result of shaming, and the shamed persons' experiences with actual harm and the deep and lingering effects of online shaming."[62] While shamers are convinced that the victims will suffer no lasting effects, the reality for the shamed is much worse. They lose their jobs, their friends, and their personal security.

Pauline shaming is not conducted by people who lob shame grenades behind the veil of anonymity in a virtual community. Rather, it is conducted face-to-face within the church. Yes, Paul rebukes and shames the church through his letters, but it should be noted that these letters were delivered and read by Paul's closest associates. These associates would then relay to Paul the response of the church to his message. For example, Titus was the bearer of the severe letter to the Corinthians. When Titus failed to show up at the prearranged city of Troas, Paul was filled with dread and unease (2 Cor. 2:13). He was fearful that his shaming discipline was not well received.

Pauline shaming is never done cavalierly without thought of how it will be received, for it is conducted within a family structure in which people have significant moral and social obligations to one another. It is conducted within a communitarian and interdependent community. Those who mete out shaming discipline know the background, history, and family of the offenders; and the offenders themselves know that those who discipline them are people who walk with integrity and godly sincerity (2 Cor. 1:12). Pauline shaming is conducted by people who speak the truth in love, it is conducted by people who know and genuinely love the offenders, and it is conducted by people who know that they too will be rebuked if they fall into the same sin.

Pauline shaming is never done without exacting a heavy emotional toll on the one who metes out the discipline. Brené Brown remarks that empathy is the antidote to shame, for shame *cannot survive with* empathy.[63] Pauline shame, however, *cannot exist without* empathy. Pauline shaming cannot be conducted without deep anguish, tears, and love for the one who is shamed. In 2 Corinthians 2:4, Paul tells the Corinthians that he wrote the severe letter to them out of "much distress and anguish of heart and with many tears." The intent of the letter is not so much to cause them pain as it is to reassure them that his heart brims with love for them. Pain is not incompatible with love, and the pain of shaming rebuke is God's instrument to bring about repentance that leads to salvation. In Galatians 4:19–20, Paul pleads with the Galatians, reminding them that he is as deeply invested in their lives as a mother in labor.

---

62. Norlock, "Online Shaming," 190.
63. Brown, "Listening to Shame."

The imagery of a father will not suffice, for the imagery of a mother in labor is more visceral and apt to convey his deep love for the Galatians. After all, mothers are bound to feel deep sympathy for their children on account of the many birth pangs they suffered for them (cf. 4 Macc. 15:7). Paul wishes that he were physically present with the Galatians so that he might embrace them and adopt a gentler tone. Nevertheless, he must deliver the bitter medicine of shame, for that is the only way to ensure that Christ is formed in them.

Unlike online shaming where the shamed is promptly forgotten as the internet mob moves on to its next target, Pauline shaming maintains ties with those who have been shamed. Even in situations of excommunication, individuals within the community must continue to show basic human kindness and respect to the person.[64] This allows Pauline shaming to be truly redemptive. Consequently, when there is genuine repentance and repudiation of the sin, the community receives the offender back into the community with joy and love.

Conclusion

Given the negativity surrounding shame, many are skeptical about the moral value of shame and call for its extirpation. John Kekes argues that the good life is better lived "if instead of flagellating ourselves with the stick of shame, we concentrate on the attraction of the carrot which our conception of a good life represents."[65] Brené Brown flatly states, "There is nothing positive about shame. In any form, in any context and through any delivery system, shame is destructive. The idea that there are two types, healthy shame and toxic shame, did not bear out in any of my research."[66] Since every form of shame is bad and destructive, we must renounce its use and develop shame resilience. As Arnold Isenberg strongly notes, "There is no such thing as a right amount of shame. . . . *Every* shame, however circumscribed, must go."[67] Shame must be completely eviscerated.

It is impossible to expunge shame without crippling our humanity as moral people. Philosopher Krista Thomason, following John Rawls, argues that our moral emotions are interconnected. They do not come piecemeal; they cannot be compartmentalized. Consequently, "we cannot get rid of an emotion [such as shame] without 'disfiguring' the rest."[68] Moreover, it is not morally

---

64. So Jonathan Edwards, "The Means and Ends of Excommunication," in *Works of Jonathan Edwards*, 22:75.
65. Kekes, "Shame and Moral Progress," 294.
66. Brown, *I Thought It Was Just Me*, 62.
67. Isenberg, "Natural Pride and Natural Shame," 14.
68. Thomason, *Naked*, 147. See also pp. 164–68.

advisable to do so. The absence of shame is not, as some wrongly declare, self-esteem; it is shamelessness. Aristotle, for example, considers the opposite of shame to be shamelessness (ἀναισχυντία), a disregard concerning the things that bring dishonor.[69] Shameless people lack discipline, hold themselves to no moral ideal, and are impervious to any negative criticism that others might have concerning their character.[70] Finally, our study of Genesis 3 shows that shame is the necessary experience of sinful humanity. Just as sin entered the world through one man, so also shame. Shame cannot be extirpated as long as sin abounds.

Instead of expunging shame, a more prudent option is to rehabilitate shame. Ancient moral philosophy is helpful in this regard. Although Greco-Roman moral philosophy is acutely aware of the destructive power of shame, it acknowledges that shame, especially a sense of shame, has a pivotal and indispensable role to play in moral formation. Protagoras relates the story that shame and justice are the two gifts given by Zeus to all people so that humanity might live together peacefully under the bonds of friendship. Socrates finds shame to be a useful medicine for curing souls. Aristotle considers shame to be the semi-virtue that is necessary for one to learn to be good. Philodemus deems frank criticism and stinging rebuke to be the marks of true friendship. Seneca contends that the capacity to feel shame is necessary for moral progress.

Classical Confucian philosophy in China also undertakes a similar program. The goal of the entire Confucian project is the cultivation of a proper sense of shame. Mencius remarks that shame is important for people. A person cannot be without shame, for the shame of being without shame is shamelessness. Moreover, the emotion of shame is the sprout that blooms into the virtue of righteousness when it is properly nurtured and cultivated. Xunzi also cautions that people must regulate themselves with shame; otherwise, they will be ignorant of that which is right and wrong, no different from animals that only act instinctually.

Ancient Greco-Roman and Confucian moral philosophies present different models of how shame can be rehabilitated. Paul, however, presents believers with a better model, for he shows how shame is to function according to God's intent. Shame should be elicited according to God's criteria, not according to the individual's or society's fallen notion of what is honorable and shameful. Shame is not autonomous or heteronomous but theonomous. In this regard, the construction of Pauline shame is similar to that found in ancient Jewish literature. Nevertheless, Pauline shame differs from the Jewish understanding

69. Aristotle, *Rhet.* 2.6.2, 1383B13–17.
70. Mason, "On Shamelessness," 422.

in locating the criteria for honor and shame solely in the gospel. The cross, and the crucified Messiah, is now the lens through which everything and everyone is to be evaluated.

Given the centrality of Christ, Paul envisions shame to be a pedagogical tool for Christic formation. The goal of Pauline shame is to conform believers to Christ so that both their identity and their ethos are grounded in the crucified Messiah. The dual focus on *being* and *doing* distinguishes Pauline shame from contemporary shame or guilt. Contemporary shame focuses on being, contemporary guilt on doing. By focusing on both, Pauline shame encompasses elements of contemporary shame and guilt. Nonetheless, Pauline shame is not the summation of contemporary shame and guilt, for Pauline shame is inextricably enmeshed with honor. Pauline shame and Pauline honor are two sides of the same coin. Pauline shame therefore points believers to have the right sensitivity toward things of which they should and should not be ashamed, guiding them to live lives that are prudent, temperate, disciplined, holy, and honorable. It teaches believers to fear God and to reverence others; it teaches them to humble themselves before God and to consider others better than themselves; it teaches them to acknowledge God's honor, the honor of the church as the bride of Christ, the honor of other believers as their siblings within the family of God, and their own honor as children of God. This respect for the honor of God, the honor of others, and their own honor provides believers with the inner disposition and internal self-control that guide them to live a life pleasing to God. In essence, developing a sense of shame that is conformed to the mind of Christ is necessary "to live a life worthy of the Lord and to please him in every way" (Col. 1:10).

Believers will never perfectly calibrate their understanding of shame according to God's standard as long as they are in this world. There will be times when they are ashamed of things of which they should not be ashamed, and there will be times when they are not ashamed of things of which they should be ashamed. They will therefore need to be corrected by other believers.[71] In such situations, instruction and gentle rebuke must be employed first. If gentle rebuke is resisted and met with arrogance and hubris, stronger disciplinary measures are warranted and shaming refutation may be necessary. Nonetheless, great care and wisdom must be employed in the use of shaming refutation. It should be employed only by those who know the offender and

---

71. For practical guidelines on how shaming rebuke might be employed by a pastor, see Baxter, *Reformed Pastor*, 111–24; A. Davis, "Practical Issues of Church Discipline"; Scharf, "Pulpit Rebuke." See also Calvin, *Institutes* 4.12.1–13. For a discussion on the theory and practice of moral oversight in the consistories of Geneva during the time of Calvin, see Manetsch, *Calvin's Company of Pastors*, 182–220.

by those whom the offender knows to be trustworthy and sincere. It should be employed only by those who are painfully aware of their own weakness and frailty. It should be employed only by those who truly love and care for the offender. It should be employed only by those who are true friends of the offender so that the wounds they inflict are trustworthy and redemptive (Prov. 27:6). Used in this way, Pauline shaming refutation is never toxic and destructive; it is redemptive.

Pauline shaming may not be well received by the offenders. Some may perceive it as an attack on their autonomy and self-identity. Shaming refutation, nonetheless, is a tool that God uses to bring his people back to himself, and it is effective and redemptive through the work of the Holy Spirit. Through shaming refutation, the Holy Spirit convicts believers of their sin, shaping their consciences and sense of shame. The Holy Spirit mediates the mind of Christ, transforming believers through the renewal of their own minds so that they are progressively conformed to the image of the crucified Messiah (Rom. 12:2); he transforms them from one glory to another until they finally receive a glorious body like that of the risen Messiah (2 Cor. 3:18; Phil. 3:20).

Paul's belief in the presence and power of the Holy Spirit is the reason why Paul does not resort to manipulation and coercion. Yes, Paul's shaming rhetoric is vigorous and intense. How could it not be? For he clearly sees the destructive effects of sin. The fate of souls is in the balance.[72] Nevertheless, Paul does not cajole or inveigle his readers. He invites his readers to the table of divine forgiveness. He persuades, for he ultimately trusts in the sovereignty of God and the work of the Holy Spirit within the community. Salvation is from God; it is God's prerogative and activity, from beginning to end.

---

72. Oden (*Corrective Love*, 87–88) writes, "The church remembers the justice of the final judgment of God. . . . This eschatological view is the frame of reference for any admonition attempted within the worshipping community."

Bibliography

Ancient Texts

Chinese Texts

Henke, Frederick Goodrich, trans. *The Philosophy of Wang Yang-Ming*. London: Open Court, 1916.

Hutton, Eric L., trans. *Xunzi: The Complete Text*. Princeton: Princeton University Press, 2014.

Johnston, Ian, and Ping Wang, trans. *Daxue and Zhongyong*. Hong Kong: Chinese University of Hong Kong, 2012.

Lau, D. C., trans. *The Analects*. Harmondsworth: Penguin Books, 1979.

———. *Mencius*. London: Penguin Books, 1970.

Legge, James, trans. *Li Ki*. The Sacred Books of the East 27–28. Oxford: Clarendon, 1885.

Plaks, Andrew H., trans. *Ta Hsüeh and Chung Yung*. London: Penguin Books, 2003.

Rickett, W. Allyn, trans. *Guanzi: Political, Economic, and Philosophical Essays from Early China*. Rev. ed. 2 vols. Boston: Cheng & Tsui, 2001.

Rosemont, Henry, Jr., and Roger T. Ames, trans. *The Chinese Classic of Family Reverence: A Philosophical Translation of the "Xiaojing."* Honolulu: University of Hawai'i Press, 2009.

Slingerland, Edward G., trans. *Confucius Analects: With Selection from Traditional Commentaries*. Indianapolis: Hackett, 2003.

Van Norden, Bryan W., trans. *Mengzi: With Selections from Traditional Commentaries*. Indianapolis: Hackett, 2008.

Greco-Roman, Jewish, and Christian Texts

Achilles Tatius. *Leucippe and Clitophon*. Translated by S. Gaselee. LCL. Cambridge, MA: Harvard University Press, 1969.

Aquinas, Thomas. *The "Summa Theologica" of St. Thomas Aquinas*. Translated by Fathers of the English Dominican Province. 22 vols. London: Burns, Oates & Washbourne, 1912–42.

Aristophanes. *Birds; Lysistrata; Women at the Thesmophoria*. Edited and translated by Jeffrey Henderson. LCL. Cambridge, MA: Harvard University Press, 2000.

Aristotle. *The "Art" of Rhetoric*. Translated by John Henry Freese. LCL. Cambridge, MA: Harvard University Press, 1926.

———. *The Nicomachean Ethics*. Translated by H. Rackham. LCL. Cambridge, MA: Harvard University Press, 1926.

Arnim, Hans Friedrich August von. *Stoicorum Veterum Fragmenta*. 4 vols. Leipzig: Teubner, 1903–24.

Augustine. *Augustine's Commentary on Galatians*. Translated by Eric Plumer. Oxford: Oxford University Press, 2003.

Aulus Gellius. *Attic Nights*. 3 vols. LCL. Cambridge, MA: Harvard University Press, 1927.

Calvin, John. *Institutes of the Christian Religion*. Edited by John T. McNeill. Translated by Ford Lewis Battles. Library of Christian Classics 20–21. Louisville: Westminster John Knox, 2006.

Charlesworth, James H., ed. *The Old Testament Pseudepigrapha*. 2 vols. Peabody, MA: Hendrickson, 2009.

Cicero. *Brutus; Orator*. Translated by G. L. Hendrickson and H. M. Hubbell. LCL. Cambridge, MA: Harvard University Press, 1939.

———. *Letters to Atticus*. Edited and translated by D. R. Shackleton Bailey. 4 vols. LCL. Cambridge, MA: Harvard University Press, 1999.

———. *On Old Age; On Friendship; On Divination*. Translated by W. A. Falconer. LCL. Cambridge, MA: Harvard University Press, 1923.

———. *On the Republic; On the Laws*. Translated by Clinton W. Keyes. LCL. Cambridge, MA: Harvard University Press, 1928.

———. *Pro Archia; Post Reditum in Senatu; Post Reditum ad Quirites; De Domo Sua; De Haruspicum Responsis; Pro Plancio*. Translated by N. H. Watts. LCL. Cambridge, MA: Harvard University Press, 1923.

———. *Pro Lege Manilia; Pro Caecina; Pro Cluentio; Pro Rabirio Perduellionis Reo*. Translated by H. Grose Hodge. LCL. Cambridge, MA: Harvard University Press, 1927.

———. *Rhetorica ad Herennium*. Translated by Harry Caplan. LCL. Cambridge, MA: Harvard University Press, 1954.

Demosthenes. *Orations*. Translated by J. H. Vince, C. A. Vince, A. T. Murray, N. J. De Witt, and N. W. De Witt. 7 vols. LCL. Cambridge, MA: Harvard University Press, 1926–49.

Dio Chrysostom. *Discourses*. Translated by J. W. Cohoon and H. Lamar Crosby. 5 vols. LCL. Cambridge, MA: Harvard University Press, 1932–51.

Diodorus Siculus. *Library of History*. Translated by C. H. Oldfather, Charles L. Sherman, C. Bradford Welles, Russel M. Geer, and Francis R. Walton. 12 vols. LCL. Cambridge, MA: Harvard University Press, 1933.

Diogenes Laertius. *Lives of Eminent Philosophers*. Translated by R. D. Hicks. LCL. Cambridge, MA: Harvard University Press, 1917–25.

Epictetus. *Discourses*. Translated by W. A. Oldfather. 2 vols. LCL. Cambridge, MA: Harvard University Press, 1925–28.

Euripides. *Suppliant Women; Electra; Heracles*. Edited and translated by David Kovacs. LCL. Cambridge, MA: Harvard University Press, 1998.

Freeman, Kathleen, trans. *Ancilla to the Pre-Socratic Philosophers: A Complete Translation of the Fragments in Diels, Fragmente Der Vorsokratiker*.

Cambridge, MA: Harvard University Press, 1962.

Gaius. *The Institutes of Gaius and Rules of Ulpian*. Translated by James Muirhead. Edinburgh: T&T Clark, 1880.

García Martínez, Florentino, and Eibert J. C. Tigchelaar, eds. *The Dead Sea Scrolls: Study Edition*. 2 vols. Leiden: Brill, 1997–98.

Herodotus. *The Persian Wars*. Translated by A. D. Godley. 4 vols. LCL. Cambridge, MA: Harvard University Press, 1920–25.

Hesiod. *Theogony; Works and Days; Testimonia*. Edited and translated by Glenn W. Most. LCL. Cambridge, MA: Harvard University Press, 2018.

Iamblichus. *On the Pythagorean Way of Life*. Translated by John M. Dillon and Jackson P. Hershbell. Society of Biblical Literature Texts and Translations 29. Atlanta: Scholars Press, 1991.

Jerome. *Commentary on Galatians*. Translated by Andrew Cain. FC. Washington, DC: Catholic University of America Press, 2010.

John Chrysostom. *On Repentance and Almsgiving*. Translated by Gus George Christo. FC. Washington, DC: Catholic University of America Press, 1998.

Josephus. *Jewish Antiquities*. Translated by H. St. J. Thackeray, Ralph Marcus, Allen Wikgren, and Louis H. Feldman. 9 vols. LCL. Cambridge, MA: Harvard University Press, 1930–65.

———. *The Jewish War*. Translated by H. St. J. Thackeray. 3 vols. LCL. Cambridge, MA: Harvard University Press, 1927–28.

———. *The Life; Against Apion*. Translated by H. St. J. Thackeray. LCL. Cambridge, MA: Harvard University Press, 1926.

Luther, Martin. *Luther's Works*. Edited by Jaroslav Pelikan. 55 vols. St. Louis: Concordia, 1955.

Martial. *Epigrams*. Edited and translated by D. R. Shackleton Bailey. 3 vols. LCL. Cambridge, MA: Harvard University Press, 1993.

Menander. *Samia; Sikyonioi; Synaristosai; Phasma; Unidentified Fragments*. Edited and translated by W. G. Arnott. LCL. Cambridge, MA: Harvard University Press, 2000.

Musonius Rufus. *Musonius Rufus: "The Roman Socrates."* Translated by Cora E. Lutz. Yale Classical Studies 10. New Haven: Yale University Press, 1947.

Origen. *Homilies on Jeremiah; Homily on 1 Kings 28*. Translated by John Clark Smith. FC. Washington, DC: Catholic University of America Press, 1998.

Ovid. *Metamorphoses*. Edited by G. P. Goold. Translated by Frank Justus Miller. 2 vols. LCL. Cambridge, MA: Harvard University Press, 1916.

Philo. *On Abraham; On Joseph; On Moses*. Translated by F. H. Colson. LCL. Cambridge, MA: Harvard University Press, 1935.

———. *On Flight and Finding; On the Change of Names; On Dreams*. Translated by F. H. Colson and G. H. Whitaker. LCL. Cambridge, MA: Harvard University Press, 1934.

———. *On the Cherubim; The Sacrifices of Abel and Cain; The Worse Attacks the Better; On the Posterity and Exile of Cain; On the Giants*. Translated by F. H. Colson and G. H. Whitaker. LCL. Cambridge, MA: Harvard University Press, 1929.

———. *On the Confusion of Tongues; On the Migration of Abraham; Who Is the Heir of Divine Things?; On*

Mating with the Preliminary Studies. Translated by F. H. Colson and G. H. Whitaker. LCL. Cambridge, MA: Harvard University Press, 1932.

Philodemus. *On Frank Criticism.* Translated by David Konstan, Diskin Clay, Clarence E. Glad, Johan C. Thom, and James Ware. Society of Biblical Literature Texts and Translations 43. Atlanta: Scholars Press, 1998.

Plato. *Charmides; Alcibiades I and II; Hipparchus; the Lovers; Theages; Minos; Epinomis.* Translated by W. R. M. Lamb. LCL. Cambridge, MA: Harvard University Press, 1927.

———. *Euthyphro; Apology; Crito; Phaedo; Phaedrus.* Translated by Harold North Fowler. LCL. Cambridge, MA: Harvard University Press, 1914.

———. *Laches; Protagoras; Meno; Euthydemus.* Translated by W. R. M. Lamb. LCL. Cambridge, MA: Harvard University Press, 1924.

———. *Laws.* Translated by R. G. Bury. 2 vols. LCL. Cambridge, MA: Harvard University Press, 1926.

———. *Lysis; Symposium; Gorgias.* Translated by W. R. M. Lamb. LCL. Cambridge, MA: Harvard University Press, 1925.

———. *The Republic.* Translated by Paul Shorey. 2 vols. LCL. Cambridge, MA: Harvard University Press, 1930–35.

———. *Theaetetus; Sophist.* Translated by Harold North Fowler. LCL. Cambridge, MA: Harvard University Press, 1921.

———. *Timaeus; Critias; Cleitophon; Menexenus; Epistles.* Translated by R. G. Bury. LCL. Cambridge, MA: Harvard University Press, 1929.

Plutarch. *Lives.* Translated by Bernadotte Perrin. 11 vols. LCL. Cambridge, MA: Harvard University Press, 1914–26.

———. *Moralia.* Translated by Frank Cole Babbitt, G. Cyril Armstrong, Hugh Tredennick, Harold North Fowler, W. C. Helmbold, Harold Cherniss, Benedict Einarson et al. 16 vols. LCL. Cambridge, MA: Harvard University Press, 1927–2004.

Quintilian. *The Orator's Education.* Edited and translated by Donald A. Russell. 4 vols. LCL. Cambridge, MA: Harvard University Press, 2002.

Roberts, Alexander, and James Donaldson, eds. *The Ante-Nicene Fathers.* 10 vols. 1885–87. Repr., Peabody, MA: Hendrickson, 1994.

Schaff, Philip, and Henry Wace, eds. *Nicene and Post-Nicene Fathers.* 28 vols. in 2 series. 1886–89. Repr., Peabody, MA: Hendrickson, 1994.

Schuller, Eileen M., and Carol Newsom. *The Hodayot (Thanksgiving Psalms): A Study Edition of 1QH^a.* Early Judaism and Its Literature 36. Atlanta: Society of Biblical Literature, 2012.

Seneca. *Epistles.* Translated by Richard M. Gummere. 3 vols. LCL. Cambridge, MA: Harvard University Press, 1917–25.

Stobaeus. *Ioannis Stobaei Anthologium.* Edited by Curt Wachsmuth and Otto Hense. 5 vols. Berlin: Weidmann, 1884–1912.

Tacitus. *Histories.* Translated by John Jackson and Clifford H. Moore. 2 vols. LCL. Cambridge, MA: Harvard University Press, 1925.

Wachsmuth, Curt. *Studien zu den griechischen Florilegien.* Berlin: Weidmann, 1882.

Xenophon. *Cyropaedia.* Translated by Walter Miller. 2 vols. LCL. Cambridge, MA: Harvard University Press, 1914.

———. *Memorabilia; Oeconomicus; Symposium; Apology.* Edited by

Jeffrey Henderson. Translated by E. C. Marchant and O. J. Todd. LCL. Cambridge, MA: Harvard University Press, 2013.

Reference Works

Bauer, Walter. *A Greek-English Lexicon of the New Testament and Other Early Christian Literature*. Edited by Frederick W. Danker. Translated by William F. Arndt, and F. Wilbur Gingrich. 3rd ed. Chicago: University of Chicago Press, 2000.

Botterweck, G. Johannes, Helmer Ringgren, Heinz-Josef Fabry, and Holger Gzella, eds. *Theological Dictionary of the Old Testament*. Translated by John T. Willis, Douglas W. Stott, David E. Green, and Mark E. Biddle. 16 vols. Grand Rapids: Eerdmans, 1974–2018.

Hawthorne, Gerald F., and Ralph P. Martin, eds. *Dictionary of Paul and His Letters*. Downers Grove, IL: InterVarsity, 1993.

Kittel, Gerhard, and Gerhard Friedrich, eds. *Theological Dictionary of the New Testament*. Translated by Geoffrey William Bromiley. 10 vols. Grand Rapids: Eerdmans, 1964–76.

Köhler, Ludwig, Walter Baumgartner, and Johann Jakob Stamm. *The Hebrew and Aramaic Lexicon of the Old Testament*. Edited and translated by M. E. J. Richardson. 2 vols. Leiden: Brill, 1994–2000.

Liddell, Henry George, Robert Scott, and Henry Stuart Jones. *A Greek-English Lexicon*. 9th ed. with revised supplement. Oxford: Clarendon, 1996.

Louw, J. P., and Eugene A. Nida, eds. *Greek-English Lexicon of the New Testament: Based on Semantic Domains*. 2nd ed. 2 vols. New York: United Bible Societies, 1989.

Silva, Moisés, ed. *New International Dictionary of New Testament Theology and Exegesis*. 2nd ed. 5 vols. Grand Rapids: Zondervan, 2014.

VanGemeren, Willem, ed. *New International Dictionary of Old Testament Theology and Exegesis*. 5 vols. Grand Rapids: Zondervan, 1997.

Secondary Literature

Adams, Robert M. *Finite and Infinite Goods: A Framework for Ethics*. New York: Oxford University Press, 1999.

Ahmed, Eliza, Nathan Harris, John Braithwaite, and Valerie Braithwaite. *Shame Management through Reintegration*. Cambridge: Cambridge University Press, 2001.

Anderson, Scott. "Coercion." *The Stanford Encyclopedia of Philosophy*. Edited by Edward N. Zalta. Winter 2017 ed. https://plato.stanford.edu/archives/win2017/entries/coercion/.

Andrews, Helen. "Shame Storm." *First Things*, January 2019.

Armstrong, David. "'Be Angry and Sin Not': Philodemus versus the Stoics on Natural Bites and Natural Emotions." Pages 79–121 in *Passions and Moral Progress in Greco-Roman Thought*. Edited by John Fitzgerald. London: Routledge, 2008.

Arzt-Grabner, Peter. "Paul's Letter Thanksgiving." Pages 129–58 in *Paul and the Ancient Letter Form*. Edited by Stanley E. Porter and Sean A. Adams. Pauline Studies 6. Leiden: Brill, 2010.

Aubry, Timothy Richard, and Trysh Travis, eds. *Rethinking Therapeutic Culture*. Chicago: University of Chicago Press, 2015.

Ausubel, David P. "Relationships between Shame and Guilt in the Socializing

Process." *Psychological Review* 62 (1955): 378–90.

Avrahami, Yael. "בוש in the Psalms—Shame or Disappointment?" *JSOT* 34 (2010): 295–313.

Bagnoli, Carla, ed. *Morality and the Emotions*. New York: Oxford University Press, 2011.

Barclay, John M. G. *Colossians and Philemon*. New Testament Guides. Sheffield: Sheffield Academic, 1997.

———. "Paul, Philemon and the Dilemma of Christian Slave-Ownership." *NTS* 37 (1991): 161–86.

Baron, Marcia. "Manipulativeness." *Proceedings and Addresses of the American Philosophical Association* 77 (2003): 37–54.

Barrett, Nathaniel F. "A Confucian Theory of Shame." *Sophia* 54 (2015): 143–63.

Barth, Markus, and Helmut Blanke. *The Letter to Philemon*. Eerdmans Critical Commentary. Grand Rapids: Eerdmans, 2000.

Barton, Carlin A. *Roman Honor: The Fire in the Bones*. Berkeley: University of California Press, 2001.

Barton, Stephen C. "Eschatology and the Emotions in Early Christianity." *JBL* 130 (2011): 571–91.

Baxter, Richard. *The Reformed Pastor*. Edited by William Brown. Edinburgh: Banner of Truth Trust, 1974.

Bechtel, Lyn M. "Shame as a Sanction of Social Control in Biblical Israel: Judicial, Political, and Social Shaming." *JSOT* 49 (1991): 47–76.

Benedict, Ruth. *The Chrysanthemum and the Sword: Patterns of Japanese Culture*. Boston: Houghton Mifflin, 1946.

Ben-Ze'ev, Aaron. "The Thing Called Emotion." Pages 41–62 in *The Oxford Handbook of Philosophy of Emotion*. Edited by Peter Goldie. Oxford: Oxford University Press, 2010.

Berger, Peter L. *The Sacred Canopy: Elements of a Sociological Theory of Religion*. Garden City, NY: Doubleday, 1969.

Blocher, Henri. *In the Beginning: The Opening Chapters of Genesis*. Translated by David G. Preston. Leicester: Inter-Varsity, 1984.

Blum, Alon. "Shame and Guilt, Misconceptions and Controversies: A Critical Review of the Literature." *Traumatology* 14 (2008): 91–102.

Bonhoeffer, Dietrich. *Creation and Fall: A Theological Exposition of Genesis 1–3*. Edited by John W. De Gruchy. Translated by Douglas S. Bax. Dietrich Bonhoeffer Works. Minneapolis: Fortress, 1997.

Bosman, Philip. *Conscience in Philo and Paul*. WUNT 2/166. Tübingen: Mohr Siebeck, 2003.

Braithwaite, John. *Crime, Shame, and Reintegration*. Cambridge: Cambridge University Press, 1989.

———. *Restorative Justice and Responsive Regulation*. Oxford: Oxford University Press, 2002.

Brand, Miryam T. *Evil Within and Without: The Source of Sin and Its Nature as Portrayed in Second Temple Literature*. Journal of Ancient Judaism Supplements 9. Göttingen: Vandenhoeck & Ruprecht, 2013.

Brickhouse, Thomas C., and Nicholas D. Smith. "The Socratic *Elenchos*?" Pages 145–57 in Scott, *Does Socrates Have a Method?*

———. *Socratic Moral Psychology*. Cambridge: Cambridge University Press, 2010.

Brinton, Alan. "Pathos and the 'Appeal to Emotion': An Aristotelian Analysis."

History of Philosophy Quarterly 5 (1988): 207–19.

Broadie, Sarah. *Ethics with Aristotle.* New York: Oxford University Press, 1991.

Brown, Brené. *I Thought It Was Just Me: Women Reclaiming Power and Courage in a Culture of Shame.* New York: Gotham, 2007.

———. "Listening to Shame." TED2012, March 2012. Video, 20:24. https://www.ted.com/talks/brene_brown_listening_to_shame.

Brown, Colin. "Ernst Lohmeyer's *Kyrios Jesus.*" Pages 6–42 in *Where Christology Began: Essays on Philippians 2.* Edited by Ralph P. Martin and Brian J. Dodd. Louisville: Westminster John Knox, 1998.

Bruce, F. F. *Philippians.* New International Biblical Commentary on the New Testament. Peabody, MA: Hendrickson, 1989.

Brucker, Ralph. *"Christushymnen" oder "epideiktische Passagen"? Studien zum Stilwechsel im Neuen Testament und seiner Umwelt.* Forschungen zur Religion und Literatur des Alten und Neuen Testaments 176. Göttingen: Vandenhoeck & Ruprecht, 1997.

Brueggemann, Walter. *Genesis.* Interpretation: A Bible Commentary for Teaching and Preaching. Atlanta: John Knox, 1982.

Bullmore, Michael A. *St. Paul's Theology of Rhetorical Style: An Examination of I Corinthians 2.1–5 in Light of First Century Graeco-Roman Rhetorical Culture.* San Francisco: International Scholars Publications, 1995.

Bultmann, Rudolf. "Das Problem der Ethik bei Paulus." *Zeitschrift für die neutestamentliche Wissenschaft und die Kunde der älteren Kirche* 23 (1924): 123–40.

———. "The Significance of the Historical Jesus for the Theology of Paul." Pages 220–46 in *Faith and Understanding I.* Translated by Louise Pettibone Smith. London: SCM, 1969.

Burgo, Joseph. "Challenging the Antishame Zeitgeist." *Atlantic,* June 17, 2013. http://www.theatlantic.com/health/archive/2013/06/challenging-the-anti-shame-zeitgeist/276833/.

Burke, Trevor J. *Adopted into God's Family: Exploring a Pauline Metaphor.* New Studies in Biblical Theology 22. Downers Grove, IL: InterVarsity, 2006.

Burnyeat, M. F. "Aristotle on Learning to Be Good." Pages 69–92 in *Essays on Aristotle's Ethics.* Edited by Amélie Oksenberg Rorty. Berkeley: University of California Press, 1980.

Burton, Ernest DeWitt. *A Critical and Exegetical Commentary on the Epistle to the Galatians.* International Critical Commentary. Edinburgh: T&T Clark, 1921.

Buss, Sarah. "Valuing Autonomy and Respecting Persons: Manipulation, Seduction, and the Basis of Moral Constraints." *Ethics* 115.2 (2005): 195–235.

Cairns, Douglas L. *Aidōs: The Psychology and Ethics of Honour and Shame in Ancient Greek Literature.* Oxford: Clarendon, 1993.

———. "Ethics, Ethology, Terminology: Iliadic Anger and the Cross-Cultural Study of Emotion." Pages 11–49 in *Ancient Anger: Perspectives from Homer to Galen.* Edited by Susanna B. Braund and Glenn W. Most. Yale Classical Studies 32. Cambridge: Cambridge University Press, 2003.

Calhoun, Cheshire. "An Apology for Moral Shame." *Journal of Political Philosophy* 12 (2004): 127–46.

Carmichael, Calum M. *The Laws of Deuteronomy*. Ithaca, NY: Cornell University Press, 1974.

Carpenter, Michelle, and Ronald M. Polansky. "Variety of Socratic Elenchi." Pages 89–100 in Scott, *Does Socrates Have a Method?*

Carr, Craig L. "Coercion and Freedom." *American Philosophical Quarterly* 25 (1988): 59–67.

Carson, D. A. *The Cross and Christian Ministry: An Exposition of Passages from 1 Corinthians*. Grand Rapids: Baker, 1993.

———. *Love in Hard Places*. Wheaton: Crossway, 2002.

———. "Mirror-Reading with Paul and against Paul: Galatians 2:11–14 as a Test Case." Pages 99–112 in *Studies in the Pauline Epistles: Essays in Honor of Douglas J. Moo*. Edited by Matthew S. Harmon and Jay E. Smith. Grand Rapids: Zondervan, 2014.

Cassuto, Umberto. *A Commentary on the Book of Genesis*. Translated by Israel Abrahams. 2 vols. Jerusalem: Magnes, 1961.

Cates, Diana Fritz. *Aquinas on the Emotions: A Religious-Ethical Inquiry*. Washington, DC: Georgetown University Press, 2009.

Chan, Sam. *Evangelism in a Skeptical World: How to Make the Unbelievable News about Jesus More Believable*. Grand Rapids: Zondervan, 2018.

Chapman, David W. *Ancient Jewish and Christian Perceptions of Crucifixion*. WUNT 2/244. Tübingen: Mohr Siebeck, 2008.

Chen, Xiaoming. "Social Control in China: Applications of the Labeling Theory and the Reintegrative Shaming Theory." *International Journal of Offender Therapy & Comparative Criminology* 46 (2002): 45–63.

Chow, John K. *Patronage and Power: A Study of Social Networks in Corinth*. JSNTSup 75. Sheffield: JSOT Press, 1992.

Chua, Amy. *Battle Hymn of the Tiger Mother*. New York: Penguin, 2011.

Church, F. Forrester. "Rhetorical Structure and Design in Paul's Letter to Philemon." *Harvard Theological Review* 71 (1978): 17–33.

Cole, Graham A. *He Who Gives Life: The Doctrine of the Holy Spirit*. Wheaton: Crossway, 2007.

Collins, John J. *Jewish Wisdom in the Hellenistic Age*. Old Testament Library. Louisville: Westminster John Knox, 1997.

Cook, John Granger. *Crucifixion in the Mediterranean World*. WUNT 327. Tübingen: Mohr Siebeck, 2014.

Cooper, John M. *Reason and Emotion: Essays on Ancient Moral Psychology and Ethical Theory*. Princeton: Princeton University Press, 1999.

Creighton, Millie R. "Revisiting Shame and Guilt Cultures: A Forty-Year Pilgrimage." *Ethos* 18 (1990): 279–307.

Curzer, Howard J. *Aristotle and the Virtues*. Oxford: Oxford University Press, 2012.

Darwall, Stephen L. "Two Kinds of Respect." *Ethics* 88 (1977): 36–49.

Daube, David. "The Culture of Deuteronomy." *Orita* 3 (1969): 27–52.

Davis, Andrew M. "The Practical Issues of Church Discipline." Pages 157–85 in *Those Who Must Give an Account: A Study of Church Membership and Church Discipline*. Edited by John S. Hammett and Benjamin L. Merkle. Nashville: B&H Academic, 2012.

Davis, Ellen F. *Swallowing the Scroll: Textuality and the Dynamics of Discourse in Ezekiel's Prophecy.* Bible and Literature Series 21. Sheffield: Almond Press, 1989.

Debanné, Marc J. *Enthymemes in the Letters of Paul.* The Library of New Testament Studies 303. London: T&T Clark, 2006.

Deigh, John. "Shame and Self-Esteem: A Critique." *Ethics* 93 (1983): 225–45.

Demos, John. "Shame and Guilt in Early New England." Pages 69–85 in *Emotion and Social Change.* Edited by Carol Z. Stearns and Peter N. Stearns. New York: Holmes & Meier, 1988.

Deonna, Julien A., Raffaele Rodogno, and Fabrice Teroni. *In Defense of Shame: The Faces of an Emotion.* Oxford: Oxford University Press, 2011.

deSilva, David A. *Despising Shame: Honor Discourse and Community Maintenance in the Epistle to the Hebrews.* SBLDS 152. Atlanta: Scholars Press, 1995.

———. *Honor, Patronage, Kinship & Purity: Unlocking New Testament Culture.* Downers Grove, IL: InterVarsity, 2000.

———. *Introducing the Apocrypha: Message, Context, and Significance.* 2nd ed. Grand Rapids: Baker Academic, 2018.

Dodds, E. R. *The Greeks and the Irrational.* Sather Classical Lectures 25. Berkeley: University of California Press, 1951.

Douglas, Mary. *Purity and Danger: An Analysis of the Concepts of Pollution and Taboo.* London: Routledge & Kegan Paul, 1966.

Dow, Jamie. *Passions and Persuasion in Aristotle's "Rhetoric."* Oxford: Oxford University Press, 2015.

"Dr. Brené Brown: 'Shame Is Lethal.'" Oprah.com, March 24, 2013. http://www.oprah.com/own-super-soul-sunday/Dr-Brene-Brown-Shame-Is-Lethal-Video.

Dryzek, John S. *Deliberative Democracy and Beyond: Liberals, Critics, Contestations.* Oxford: Oxford University Press, 2000.

Du Toit, Andreas B. "Alienation and Re-identification as Pragmatic Strategies in Galatians." *Neotestamentica* 26 (1992): 279–95.

———. "Vilification as a Pragmatic Device in Early Christian Epistolography." *Biblica* 75 (1994): 403–12.

Eckstein, Hans-Joachim. *Der Begriff Syneidesis bei Paulus.* WUNT 2/10. Tübingen: Mohr Siebeck, 1983.

Edwards, Jonathan. *Works of Jonathan Edwards.* 26 vols. New Haven: Yale University Press, 1957–2008.

Ekman, Paul. *Emotion in the Human Face.* 2nd ed. Cambridge: Cambridge University Press, 1982.

Elison, Jeff. "Shame and Guilt: A Hundred Years of Apples and Oranges." *New Ideas in Psychology* 23 (2005): 5–32.

Elliott, Matthew. *Faithful Feelings: Rethinking Emotion in the New Testament.* Grand Rapids: Kregel, 2006.

Elster, Jon. *Alchemies of the Mind: Rationality and the Emotions.* Cambridge: Cambridge University Press, 1999.

Engberg-Pedersen, Troels. "Is There an Ethical Dimension to Aristotelian Rhetoric?" Pages 116–41 in *Essays on Aristotle's "Rhetoric."* Edited by Amélie Oksenberg Rorty. Berkeley: University of California Press, 1996.

Ericson, Richard V. "Social Distance and Reaction to Criminality." *British Journal of Criminology* 17 (1977): 16–29.

Etzioni, Amitai. "Back to the Pillory?" *American Scholar* 68.3 (1999): 43–50.

Evans, C. Stephen. *God and Moral Obligation*. Oxford: Oxford University Press, 2013.

Fee, Gordon D. *God's Empowering Presence: The Holy Spirit in the Letters of Paul*. Peabody, MA: Hendrickson, 1994.

Ferguson, Tamara J., Hedy Stegge, and Ilse Damhuis. "Children's Understanding of Guilt and Shame." *Child Development* 62 (1991): 827–39.

Ferrari, Gloria. *Figures of Speech: Men and Maidens in Ancient Greece*. Chicago: University of Chicago Press, 2002.

Fischer, Kurt W., and June Price Tangney. "Self-Conscious Emotions and the Affect Revolution: Framework and Overview." Pages 3–22 in *Self-Conscious Emotions: The Psychology of Shame, Guilt, Embarrassment, and Pride*. Edited by June Price Tangney and Kurt W. Fischer. New York: Guilford, 1995.

Fisher, N. R. E. *Hybris: A Study in the Values of Honour and Shame in Ancient Greece*. Warminster: Aris & Phillips, 1992.

Fortenbaugh, William W. *Aristotle on Emotion*. London: Duckworth, 1975.

Fowl, Stephen E. *The Story of Christ in the Ethics of Paul: An Analysis of the Function of the Hymnic Material in the Pauline Corpus*. JSNTSup 36. Sheffield: JSOT Press, 1990.

Frame, John M. *The Doctrine of the Knowledge of God*. Phillipsburg, NJ: Presbyterian and Reformed, 1987.

Fredriksen, Paula. *From Jesus to Christ: The Origins of the New Testament Images of Christ*. 2nd ed. New Haven: Yale University Press, 2000.

Frijda, Nico H., A. S. R. Manstead, and Sacha Bem, eds. *Emotions and Beliefs: How Feelings Influence Thoughts*. Cambridge: Cambridge University Press, 2000.

———. "The Influence of Emotions on Beliefs." Pages 1–9 in Frijda, Manstead, and Bem, *Emotions and Beliefs*.

Fulkerson, Laurel. *No Regrets: Remorse in Classical Antiquity*. Oxford: Oxford University Press, 2013.

Fung, Heidi. "Affect and Early Moral Socialization: Some Insights and Contributions from Indigenous Psychological Studies in Taiwan." Pages 175–96 in *Indigenous and Cultural Psychology: Understanding People in Context*. Edited by Uichol Kim, Kuo-Shu Yang, and Kwang-Kuo Hwang. New York: Springer, 2006.

———. "Becoming a Moral Child: The Socialization of Shame among Young Chinese Children." *Ethos* 27 (1999): 180–209.

Fung, Heidi, Eli Lieber, and Patrick W. L. Leung. "Parental Beliefs about Shame and Moral Socialization in Taiwan, Hong Kong, and the United States." Pages 83–109 in *Progress in Asian Social Psychology: Conceptual and Empirical Contributions*. Edited by Kuo-Shu Yang, Kwang-Kuo Hwang, Paul B. Pedersen, and Ikuo Daibo. Westport, CT: Praeger, 2003.

Fung, Ronald Y. K. *The Epistle to the Galatians*. New International Commentary on the New Testament. Grand Rapids: Eerdmans, 1988.

Furnish, Victor Paul. *Theology and Ethics in Paul*. Nashville: Abingdon, 1968.

Futter, D. B. "Shame as a Tool for Persuasion in Plato's *Gorgias*." *Journal of the History of Philosophy* 47 (2009): 451–61.

Garvey, Stephen P. "Can Shaming Punishments Educate?" *University of Chicago Law Review* 65 (1998): 733–94.

Geaney, Jane. "Guarding Moral Boundaries: Shame in Early Confucianism." *Philosophy East and West* 54 (2004): 113–42.

Geertz, Clifford. *The Interpretation of Cultures: Selected Essays.* New York: Basic Books, 1973.

Gehm, Theodor L., and Klaus R. Scherer. "Relating Situation Evaluation to Emotion Differentiation: Nonmetric Analysis of Cross-Cultural Questionnaire Data." Pages 61–77 in *Facets of Emotion: Recent Research.* Edited by Klaus R. Scherer. Hillsdale, NJ: Erlbaum, 1988.

Gehring, Roger W. *House Church and Mission: The Importance of Household Structures in Early Christianity.* Peabody, MA: Hendrickson, 2004.

Gensler, Harry J. *Ethics and Religion.* New York: Cambridge University Press, 2016.

Gibson, Jack J. *Peter between Jerusalem and Antioch: Peter, James and the Gentiles.* WUNT 2/345. Tübingen: Mohr Siebeck, 2013.

Gilbert, Paul. "Evolution, Social Roles, and the Difference in Shame and Guilt." *Social Research* 70 (2003): 1205–30.

———. "What Is Shame?" Pages 3–38 in *Shame: Interpersonal Behavior, Psychopathology, and Culture.* Edited by Paul Gilbert and Bernice Andrews. New York: Oxford University Press, 1998.

Gill, Christopher. *Greek Thought.* New Surveys in the Classics 25. Oxford: Oxford University Press, 1995.

Gish, Dustin A. "Rivals in Persuasion: Gorgianic Sophistic versus Socratic Rhetoric." *Polis* 23 (2006): 46–73.

Glad, Clarence E. *Paul and Philodemus: Adaptability in Epicurean and Early Christian Psychagogy.* NovTSup 81. Leiden: Brill, 1995.

Graver, Margaret. *Stoicism and Emotion.* Chicago: University of Chicago Press, 2007.

Hadjiev, T. S. "Honor and Shame." Pages 333–38 in *Dictionary of the Old Testament: Prophets.* Edited by Mark J. Boda and J. Gordon McConville. Downers Grove, IL: IVP Academic, 2012.

Hafemann, Scott J. *Suffering and the Spirit: An Exegetical Study of II Cor. 2:14–3:3 within the Context of the Corinthian Correspondence.* WUNT 2/19. Tübingen: Mohr Siebeck, 1986.

Hansen, G. Walter. *Abraham in Galatians: Epistolary and Rhetorical Contexts.* JSNTSup 29. Sheffield: JSOT Press, 1989.

Harmon-Jones, Eddie. "A Cognitive Dissonance Theory Perspective on the Role of Emotion in the Maintenance and Change of Beliefs and Attitudes." Pages 185–211 in Frijda, Manstead, and Bem, *Emotions and Beliefs.*

Harrill, J. A. *The Manumission of Slaves in Early Christianity.* Hermeneutische Untersuchungen zur Theologie 32. Tübingen: Mohr Siebeck, 1995.

———. *Slaves in the New Testament: Literary, Social, and Moral Dimensions.* Minneapolis: Fortress, 2006.

Harrington, Daniel J., and James F. Keenan. *Paul and Virtue Ethics: Building Bridges between New Testament Studies and Moral Theology.* Lanham, MD: Rowman & Littlefield, 2010.

Harris, Nathan. "Reassessing the Dimensionality of the Moral Emotions." *British Journal of Psychology* 94 (2003): 457–73.

Harris, Nathan, and Shadd Maruna. "Shame, Shaming and Restorative Justice: A Critical Appraisal." Pages 452–62 in *Handbook of Restorative Justice: A Global Perspective*. Edited by Dennis Sullivan and Larry Tifft. London: Routledge, 2006.

Harris, Nathan, Lode Walgrave, and John Braithwaite. "Emotional Dynamics in Restorative Conferences." *Theoretical Criminology* 8 (2004): 191–210.

Harris, William V. *Restraining Rage: The Ideology of Anger Control in Classical Antiquity*. Cambridge, MA: Harvard University Press, 2001.

Hays, Richard B. *First Corinthians*. Interpretation: A Bible Commentary for Teaching and Preaching. Louisville: Westminster John Knox, 1997.

Heller, Agnes. *The Power of Shame: A Rational Perspective*. London: Routledge & Kegan Paul, 1985.

Hellerman, Joseph H. *Reconstructing Honor in Roman Philippi: Carmen Christi as Cursus Pudorum*. Society for New Testament Studies Monograph Series 132. Cambridge: Cambridge University Press, 2005.

Hengel, Martin. *Crucifixion in the Ancient World and the Folly of the Message of the Cross*. Philadelphia: Fortress, 1977.

———. *Judaism and Hellenism: Studies in Their Encounter in Palestine during the Early Hellenistic Period*. Translated by John Bowden. 2 vols. Philadelphia: Fortress, 1981.

———. *Saint Peter: The Underestimated Apostle*. Translated by Thomas H. Trapp. Grand Rapids: Eerdmans, 2010.

Henninger, Daniel. "The Death of Self-Restraint." *Wall Street Journal*, December 7, 2017, sec. A.

Hodge, Charles. *An Exposition of the Second Epistle to the Corinthians*. New York: Robert Carter & Brothers, 1872.

Horrell, David G. *Solidarity and Difference: A Contemporary Reading of Paul's Ethics*. 2nd ed. London: Bloomsbury T&T Clark, 2016.

Inselmann, Anke. *Die Freude im Lukasevangelium: Ein Beitrag zur psychologischen Exegese*. WUNT 2/322. Tübingen: Mohr Siebeck, 2012.

———. "Zum Affekt der Freude im Philipperbrief: Unter Berücksichtigung pragmatischer und psychologischer Zugänge." Pages 255–88 in *Der Philipperbrief des Paulus in der hellenistisch-römischen Welt*. Edited by Jörg Frey and Benjamin Schliesser. WUNT 353. Tübingen: Mohr Siebeck, 2015.

Irwin, Terence. *Aristotle: Nicomachean Ethics*. 2nd ed. Indianapolis: Hackett, 1999.

Isenberg, Arnold. "Natural Pride and Natural Shame." *Philosophy and Phenomenological Research* 10 (1949): 1–24.

Ivanhoe, P. J. "Filial Piety as a Virtue." Pages 297–312 in *Working Virtue: Virtue Ethics and Contemporary Moral Problems*. Edited by Rebecca L. Walker and P. J. Ivanhoe. Oxford: Clarendon, 2007.

James, William. "What Is an Emotion?" *Mind* 9 (1884): 188–205.

Jeal, Roy R. *Exploring Philemon: Freedom, Brotherhood, and Partnership in the New Society*. Atlanta: SBL Press, 2015.

Jewett, Robert. "The Agitators and the Galatian Congregation." *NTS* 17 (1971): 198–212.

———. "Honor and Shame in the Argument of Romans." Pages 258–73 in

Putting Body and Soul Together: Essays in Honor of Robin Scroggs. Edited by Virginia Wiles, Alexandra R. Brown, and Graydon F. Snyder. Valley Forge, PA: Trinity Press International, 1997.

———. *Paul's Anthropological Terms: A Study of Their Use in Conflict Settings.* Arbeiten zur Geschichte des antiken Judentums und des Urchristentums 10. Leiden: Brill, 1971.

———. *Romans.* Hermeneia. Minneapolis: Fortress, 2007.

Jiang, Xinyan. "Mencius on Moral Responsibility." Pages 141–59 in *The Examined Life—Chinese Perspectives: Essays on Chinese Ethical Traditions.* Edited by Xinyan Jiang. Binghampton, NY: Global Publications, 2002.

Jimenez, Marta. "The Virtue of Shame: Aristotle on the Positive Role of Shame in Moral Development." PhD diss., University of Toronto, 2011.

Johnson, Luke Timothy. "The New Testament's Anti-Jewish Slander and the Conventions of Ancient Polemic." *JBL* 108 (1989): 419–41.

———. "Transformation of the Mind and Moral Discernment in Paul." Pages 215–36 in *Early Christianity and Classical Culture: Comparative Studies in Honor of Abraham J. Malherbe.* Edited by John T. Fitzgerald, Thomas H. Olbricht, and L. Michael White. NovTSup 110. Leiden: Brill, 2003.

———. *The Writings of the New Testament: An Interpretation.* 3rd ed. Minneapolis: Fortress, 2010.

Joyce, Paul M. *Divine Initiative and Human Response in Ezekiel.* Journal for the Study of the Old Testament Supplement Series 51. Sheffield: JSOT Press, 1989.

Jumper, James N. "Honor and Shame in the Deuteronomic Covenant and the Deuteronomistic Presentation of the Davidic Covenant." PhD diss., Harvard University, 2013.

Kahn, Charles H. "Drama and Dialectic in Plato's *Gorgias.*" *Oxford Studies in Ancient Philosophy* 1 (1983): 75–121.

———. *Plato and the Socratic Dialogue: The Philosophical Use of a Literary Form.* Cambridge: Cambridge University Press, 1996.

Kamtekar, Rachana. "ΑΙΔΩΣ in Epictetus." *Classical Philology* 93 (1998): 136–60.

Kaster, Robert A. *Emotion, Restraint, and Community in Ancient Rome.* Oxford: Oxford University Press, 2005.

———. "The Shame of the Romans." *Transactions of the American Philological Association* 127 (1997): 1–19.

Kaufman, Gershen. *The Psychology of Shame: Theory and Treatment of Shame-Based Syndromes.* 2nd ed. New York: Springer, 2004.

Kekes, John. "Shame and Moral Progress." *Midwest Studies in Philosophy* 13 (1988): 282–96.

Kelly, J. M. *Studies in the Civil Judicature of the Roman Republic.* Oxford: Clarendon, 1976.

Keltner, Dacher, and LeeAnne Harker. "The Forms and Functions of the Nonverbal Signal of Shame." Pages 78–98 in *Shame: Interpersonal Behavior, Psychopathology, and Culture.* Edited by Paul Gilbert and Bernice Andrews. New York: Oxford University Press, 1998.

King, R. A. H., and D. Schilling, eds. *How Should One Live? Comparing Ethics in Ancient China and Greco-Roman Antiquity.* Berlin: de Gruyter, 2011.

Kinman, Brent. "'Appoint the Despised as Judges!' (1 Corinthians 6:4)." *Tyndale Bulletin* 48 (1997): 345–54.

Kirk, Marshall, and Hunter Madsen. *After the Ball: How America Will Conquer Its Fear and Hatred of Gays in the '90s.* New York: Doubleday, 1989.

Kitayama, Shinobu, Hazel Rose Markus, and Hisaya Matsumoto. "Culture, Self, and Emotion: A Cultural Perspective on 'Self-Conscious' Emotions." Pages 439–64 in *Self-Conscious Emotions: The Psychology of Shame, Guilt, Embarrassment, and Pride.* Edited by June Price Tangney and Kurt W. Fischer. New York: Guilford, 1995.

Kleinginna, Paul R., Jr., and Anne M. Kleinginna. "A Categorized List of Emotion Definitions, with Suggestions for a Consensual Definition." *Motivation and Emotion* 5 (1981): 345–79.

Klemp, Nathaniel J. *The Morality of Spin: Virtue and Vice in Political Rhetoric and the Christian Right.* Lanham, MD: Rowman & Littlefield, 2012.

Klonick, Kate. "Re-shaming the Debate: Social Norms, Shame, and Regulation in an Internet Age." *Maryland Law Review* 75.4 (2016): 1029–65.

Klopfenstein, Martin A. *Scham und Schande nach dem Alten Testament: Eine begriffsgeschichtliche Untersuchung zu den hebräischen Wurzeln bôš, klm und ḥpr.* Abhandlungen zur Theologie des Alten und Neuen Testaments 62. Zürich: TVZ, 1972.

Knox, John. *Philemon among the Letters of Paul.* Rev. ed. New York: Abingdon, 1959.

Konstan, David. *The Emotions of the Ancient Greeks: Studies in Aristotle and Classical Literature.* Toronto: University of Toronto Press, 2006.

Kosman, L. A. "Being Properly Affected: Virtues and Feelings in Aristotle's Ethics." Pages 103–16 in *Essays on Aristotle's Ethics.* Edited by Amélie Oksenberg Rorty. Berkeley: University of California Press, 1980.

Kugler, Karen, and Warren H. Jones. "On Conceptualizing and Assessing Guilt." *Journal of Personality and Social Psychology* 62 (1992): 318–27.

Lambrecht, Jan. "Paul and Epistolary Thanksgiving." *Ephemerides Theologicae Lovanienses* 88 (2012): 167–71.

Lapsley, Jacqueline E. *Can These Bones Live? The Problem of the Moral Self in the Book of Ezekiel.* Beihefte zur Zeitschrift für die alttestamentliche Wissenschaft 301. Berlin: de Gruyter, 2000.

Lasch, Christopher. *The Revolt of the Elites and the Betrayal of Democracy.* New York: Norton, 1996.

Lebra, Takie Sugiyama. "Shame and Guilt: A Psychocultural View of the Japanese Self." *Ethos* 11 (1983): 192–210.

Leibrich, Julie. "The Role of Shame in Going Straight: A Study of Former Offenders." Pages 283–302 in *Restorative Justice: International Perspectives.* Edited by Burt Galaway and Joe Hudson. Monsey, NY: Criminal Justice Press, 1996.

Leighton, Stephen R. "Aristotle and the Emotions." Pages 206–37 in *Essays on Aristotle's "Rhetoric."* Edited by Amélie Oksenberg Rorty. Berkeley: University of California Press, 1996.

Lemos, T. M. "Shame and Mutilation of Enemies in the Hebrew Bible." *JBL* 125 (2006): 225–41.

Lendon, J. E. *Empire of Honour: The Art of Government in the Roman World.* Oxford: Clarendon, 1997.

Lewinsky, Monica. "The Price of Shame." TED2015. Video, 22:19. https://www

.ted.com/talks/monica_lewinsky_the _price_of_shame/.

Lewis, Helen Block. *Shame and Guilt in Neurosis*. New York: International Universities, 1971.

Lewis, Michael. "Self-Conscious Emotions: Embarrassment, Pride, Shame, and Guilt." Pages 742–56 in *Handbook of Emotions*. Edited by Michael Lewis, Jeannette M. Haviland-Jones, and Lisa Feldman Barrett. 3rd ed. New York: Guilford, 2008.

Li, Jin, Lianqin Wang, and Kurt W. Fischer. "The Organization of Chinese Shame Concepts." *Cognition and Emotion* 18 (2004): 767–97.

Lightfoot, J. B. *Saint Paul's Epistles to the Colossians and to Philemon*. London: Macmillan, 1890.

Litt, Eden. "Knock, Knock. Who's There? The Imagined Audience." *Journal of Broadcasting & Electronic Media* 56 (2012): 330–45.

Lloyd, G. E. R, and Jenny Jingyi Zhao, eds. *Ancient Greece and China Compared*. Cambridge: Cambridge University Press, 2018.

Lu, Hong. "Bang Jiao and Reintegrative Shaming in China's Urban Neighborhoods." *International Journal of Comparative and Applied Criminal Justice* 23 (1999): 115–25.

Lutz, Catherine. *Unnatural Emotions: Everyday Sentiments on a Micronesian Atoll and Their Challenge to Western Theory*. Chicago: University of Chicago Press, 1988.

Lyons, George. *Pauline Autobiography: Toward a New Understanding*. SBLDS 73. Atlanta: Scholars Press, 1985.

Machen, J. Gresham. *The Origin of Paul's Religion*. New York: Macmillan, 1921.

Malina, Bruce J. *The New Testament World: Insights from Cultural Anthropology*. 3rd ed. Louisville: Westminster John Knox, 2001.

Malina, Bruce J., and John J. Pilch. *Social-Science Commentary on the Letters of Paul*. Minneapolis: Fortress, 2006.

Mallon, Ron, and Stephen P. Stich. "The Odd Couple: The Compatibility of Social Construction and Evolutionary Psychology." *Philosophy of Science* 67 (2000): 133–54.

Manetsch, Scott M. *Calvin's Company of Pastors: Pastoral Care and the Emerging Reformed Church, 1536–1609*. Oxford Studies in Historical Theology. New York: Oxford University Press, 2013.

Manson, T. W. "Jesus, Paul, and the Law." Pages 125–41 in *Law and Religion*. Edited by Erwin I. J. Rosenthal. Vol. 3 of *Judaism and Christianity*. London: Sheldon, 1938.

Marshall, Peter. *Enmity in Corinth: Social Conventions in Paul's Relations with the Corinthians*. WUNT 2/23. Tübingen: Mohr Siebeck, 1987.

Martin, Troy W. "The Voice of Emotion: Paul's Pathetic Persuasion (Gal 4:12–20)." Pages 181–202 in *Paul and Pathos*. Edited by Thomas H. Olbricht and Jerry L. Sumney. Symposium Series 16. Atlanta: Society of Biblical Literature, 2001.

Martínez de Pisón, Ramón. *Death by Despair: Shame and Suicide*. New York: Peter Lang, 2006.

Maruna, Shadd. *Making Good: How Ex-Convicts Reform and Rebuild Their Lives*. Washington, DC: American Psychological Association, 2001.

Maruna, Shadd, and Derek Ramsden. "Living to Tell the Tale: Redemption Narratives, Shame Management, and Offender Rehabilitation." Pages 129–49 in *Healing Plots: The Narrative*

Basis of Psychotherapy. Edited by Amia Lieblich, Dan P. McAdams, and Ruthellen Josselson. Washington, DC: American Psychological Association, 2004.

Mascolo, Michael F., Kurt W. Fischer, and Jin Li. "Dynamic Development of Component Systems of Emotions: Pride, Shame and Guilt in China and the United States." Pages 375–408 in *Handbook of Affective Sciences*. Edited by Richard J. Davidson, Klaus R. Scherer, and H. Hill Goldsmith. New York: Oxford University Press, 2003.

Mason, Michelle. "On Shamelessness." *Philosophical Papers* 39.3 (2010): 401–25.

McKim, Richard. "Shame and Truth in Plato's *Gorgias*." Pages 34–48 in *Platonic Writings, Platonic Readings*. Edited by Charles L. Griswold Jr. London: Routledge, 1988.

Meeks, Wayne A. *The First Urban Christians: The Social World of the Apostle Paul*. 2nd ed. New Haven: Yale University Press, 2003.

———. "The Man from Heaven in Paul's Letter to the Philippians." Pages 329–36 in *The Future of Early Christianity: Essays in Honor of Helmut Koester*. Edited by Birger A. Pearson. Minneapolis: Fortress, 1991.

Mesquita, Batja, and Nico H. Frijda. "Cultural Variations in Emotions: A Review." *Psychological Bulletin* 112 (1992): 179–204.

Milgrom, Jacob. *Cult and Conscience: The Asham and the Priestly Doctrine of Repentance*. Studies in Judaism in Late Antiquity 18. Leiden: Brill, 1976.

———. "Rationale for Cultic Law: The Case of Impurity." *Semeia* 45 (1989): 103–9.

Miller, William Ian. *The Anatomy of Disgust*. Cambridge, MA: Harvard University Press, 1997.

Moo, Douglas J. *The Letters to the Colossians and to Philemon*. Pillar New Testament Commentary. Grand Rapids: Eerdmans, 2008.

Morris, Allison. "Shame, Guilt and Remorse: Experiences from Family Group Conferences in New Zealand." Pages 157–78 in *Punishing Juveniles: Principle and Critique*. Edited by Ido Weijers and Antony Duff. Oxford: Hart, 2002.

Morrison, Andrew P. *The Culture of Shame*. New York: Ballantine, 1996.

Moskowitz, Eva S. *In Therapy We Trust: America's Obsession with Self-Fulfillment*. Baltimore: Johns Hopkins University Press, 2001.

Moss, Jessica. "The Doctor and the Pastry Chef: Pleasure and Persuasion in Plato's *Gorgias*." *Ancient Philosophy* 27 (2007): 229–49.

———. "Shame, Pleasure, and the Divided Soul." *Oxford Studies in Ancient Philosophy* 29 (2005): 137–70.

Muravchik, Stephanie. *American Protestantism in the Age of Psychology*. Cambridge: Cambridge University Press, 2011.

Murphy, Kristina, and Nathan Harris. "Shaming, Shame and Recidivism: A Test of Reintegrative Shaming Theory in the White-Collar Crime Context." *British Journal of Criminology* 47.6 (2007): 900–917.

Nathanson, Donald L. *Shame and Pride: Affect, Sex, and the Birth of the Self*. New York: Norton, 1992.

Neyrey, Jerome H. "Despising the Shame of the Cross: Honor and Shame in the Johannine Passion Narrative." *Semeia* 68 (1994): 113–37.

Ng, Margaret N. "Internal Shame as a Moral Sanction." *Journal of Chinese Philosophy* 8 (1981): 75–86.

Nieuwenburg, Paul. "Learning to Deliberate: Aristotle on Truthfulness and Public Deliberation." *Political Theory* 32 (2004): 449–67.

Noggle, Robert. "Manipulative Actions: A Conceptual and Moral Analysis." *American Philosophical Quarterly* 33 (1996): 43–55.

Nolan, James L. *The Therapeutic State: Justifying Government at Century's End.* New York: New York University Press, 1998.

Norlock, Kathryn J. "Online Shaming." *Social Philosophy Today* 33 (2017): 187–97.

Nozick, Robert. "Coercion." Pages 440–72 in *Philosophy, Science, and Method: Essays in Honor of Ernest Nagel.* Edited by Sidney Morgenbesser, Patrick Suppes, and Morton White. New York: St. Martin's Press, 1969.

Nussbaum, Martha C. *The Therapy of Desire: Theory and Practice in Hellenistic Ethics.* Princeton: Princeton University Press, 1994.

———. *Upheavals of Thought: The Intelligence of Emotions.* Cambridge: Cambridge University Press, 2001.

O'Brien, Peter T. *Introductory Thanksgivings in the Letters of Paul.* NovTSup 49. Leiden: Brill, 1977.

Odell, Margaret S. "The Inversion of Shame and Forgiveness in Ezekiel 16.59–63." *JSOT* 56 (1992): 101–12.

Oden, Thomas C. *Corrective Love: The Power of Communion Discipline.* St. Louis: Concordia, 1995.

Olson, Stanley N. "Pauline Expressions of Confidence in His Addressees." *Catholic Biblical Quarterly* 47 (1985): 282–95.

Olthof, Tjeert, Anneke Schouten, Hilde Kuiper, Hedy Stegge, and Aagje Jennekens-Schinkel. "Shame and Guilt in Children: Differential Situational Antecedents and Experiential Correlates." *British Journal of Developmental Psychology* 18 (2000): 51–64.

Olyan, Saul M. "Honor, Shame, and Covenant Relations in Ancient Israel and Its Environment." *JBL* 115 (1996): 201–18.

Ortlund, Eric. "Shame in Restoration in Ezekiel." *Scandinavian Evangelical e-Journal* 2 (2011): 1–17.

Ortony, Andrew. "Is Guilt an Emotion?" *Cognition and Emotion* 1 (1987): 283–98.

Pannenberg, Wolfhart. *The Apostles' Creed in the Light of Today's Questions.* London: SCM, 1972.

Parsons, Michael. "Being Precedes Act: Indicative and Imperative in Paul's Writing." *Evangelical Quarterly* 60 (1988): 99–127.

Parussini, Gabriele. "If You Don't Pay These Taxes, Expect a Troupe of Drummers at Your Door." *Wall Street Journal*, April 17, 2016.

Pattison, Stephen. *Shame: Theory, Therapy, Theology.* Cambridge: Cambridge University Press, 2000.

Penner, Terry. "Socrates." Pages 164–89 in *The Cambridge History of Greek and Roman Political Thought.* Edited by C. J. Rowe and Malcolm Schofield. New York: Cambridge University Press, 2000.

Petersen, Norman R. *Rediscovering Paul: Philemon and the Sociology of Paul's Narrative World.* Philadelphia: Fortress, 1985.

Pitt-Rivers, Julian. "Honour and Social Status." Pages 19–77 in *Honour and Shame: The Values of Mediterranean*

Society. Edited by John G. Peristiany. Chicago: University of Chicago Press, 1966.

Planalp, Sally. *Communicating Emotion: Social, Moral, and Cultural Processes.* Cambridge: Cambridge University Press, 1999.

Pogoloff, Stephen M. *Logos and Sophia: The Rhetorical Situation of 1 Corinthians.* SBLDS 134. Atlanta: Scholars Press, 1992.

Polsky, Andrew J. *The Rise of the Therapeutic State.* Princeton: Princeton University Press, 1991.

Price, A. W. "Emotions in Plato and Aristotle." Pages 121–42 in *The Oxford Handbook of Philosophy of Emotion.* Edited by Peter Goldie. Oxford: Oxford University Press, 2010.

Prinz, Jesse J. *The Emotional Construction of Morals.* Oxford: Oxford University Press, 2007.

Rad, Gerhard von. *Deuteronomy: A Commentary.* Old Testament Library. Philadelphia: Westminster, 1966.

Rapp, Christof. "Aristotle on the Moral Psychology of Persuasion." Pages 589–611 in *The Oxford Handbook of Aristotle.* Edited by Christopher John Shields. Oxford: Oxford University Press, 2012.

Rapske, Brian. *The Book of Acts and Paul in Roman Custody.* Vol. 3 of *The Book of Acts in Its First Century Setting.* Grand Rapids: Eerdmans, 1994.

Rawls, John. *A Theory of Justice.* Cambridge, MA: Belknap, 1971.

Raz, Joseph. *The Morality of Freedom.* Oxford: Oxford University Press, 1986.

Renz, Thomas. *The Rhetorical Function of the Book of Ezekiel.* Supplements to *Vetus Testamentum* 76. Leiden: Brill, 1999.

Rieff, Philip. *The Triumph of the Therapeutic: Uses of Faith after Freud.* New York: Harper & Row, 1966.

Roberts, Robert C. *Emotions: An Essay in Aid of Moral Psychology.* Cambridge: Cambridge University Press, 2003.

———. "Emotions in the Epistemology of Paul the Apostle." Pages 11–29 in *Passion and Passivity.* Edited by Ingolf U. Dalferth and Michael Rodgers. Religion in Philosophy and Theology 61. Tübingen: Mohr Siebeck, 2011.

———. *Emotions in the Moral Life.* New York: Cambridge University Press, 2013.

———. *Spiritual Emotions: A Psychology of Christian Virtues.* Grand Rapids: Eerdmans, 2007.

Ronson, Jon. "How One Stupid Tweet Blew Up Justine Sacco's Life." *New York Times Magazine*, February 15, 2015.

———. *So You've Been Publicly Shamed.* New York: Riverhead Books, 2015.

Roon, A. van. *The Authenticity of Ephesians.* NovTSup 39. Leiden: Brill, 1974.

Rosemont, Henry, Jr. *Against Individualism: A Confucian Rethinking of the Foundation of Morality, Politics, Family, and Religion.* Lanham, MD: Lexington Books, 2015.

Rosner, Brian S. *Paul, Scripture, and Ethics: A Study of 1 Corinthians 5–7.* Arbeiten zur Geschichte des antiken Judentums und des Urchristentums 22. Leiden: Brill, 1994.

———, ed. *Understanding Paul's Ethics: Twentieth Century Approaches.* Grand Rapids: Eerdmans, 1995.

Rowe, Christopher. "Socrates in Plato's Dialogues." Pages 159–70 in *A Companion to Socrates.* Edited by Sara Ahbel-Rappe and Rachana Kamtekar. Oxford: Blackwell, 2006.

Rubin, Julius H. *Religious Melancholy and Protestant Experience in America.* New York: Oxford University Press, 1994.

Rudinow, Joel. "Manipulation." *Ethics* 88 (1978): 338–47.

Russell, David M. "The Strategy of a First-Century Appeals Letter: A Discourse Reading of Paul's Epistle to Philemon." *Journal of Translation and Textlinguistics* 11 (1998): 1–25.

Sabini, John, Brian Garvey, and Amanda L. Hall. "Shame and Embarrassment Revisited." *Personality and Social Psychology Bulletin* 27 (2001): 104–17.

Sabini, John, and Maury Silver. "In Defense of Shame: Shame in the Context of Guilt and Embarrassment." *Journal for the Theory of Social Behaviour* 27 (1997): 1–15.

———. "Why Emotion Names and Experiences Don't Neatly Pair." *Psychological Inquiry* 16 (2005): 1–10.

Sampley, J. Paul. "Paul's Frank Speech with the Galatians and the Corinthians." Pages 295–323 in *Philodemus and the New Testament World.* Edited by John T. Fitzgerald, Dirk Obbink, and Glenn S. Holland. NovTSup 111. Leiden: Brill, 2004.

Sanderman, Daniel. "Why Socrates Mocks His Interlocutors." *Skepsis* 15 (2004): 431–41.

Sanders, Jack T. "Ben Sira's Ethics of Caution." *Hebrew Union College Annual* 50 (1979): 73–106.

Scharf, Greg R. "The Pulpit Rebuke: What Is It? When Is It Appropriate? What Makes It Effective?" *Journal of the Evangelical Homiletics Society* 15 (2015): 60–78.

Scheff, Thomas J. *Bloody Revenge: Emotions, Nationalism, and War.* Boulder, CO: Westview, 1994.

———. *Microsociology: Discourse, Emotion, and Social Structure.* Chicago: University of Chicago Press, 1990.

———. "Shame and Conformity: The Deference-Emotion Systems." *American Sociological Review* 53 (1988): 395–406.

———. "Shame and the Social Bond: A Sociological Theory." *Sociological Theory* 18 (2000): 84–99.

Scherer, Klaus R. "What Are Emotions? And How Can They Be Measured?" *Social Science Information* 44 (2005): 695–729.

Schmitz, Thomas A. "The Second Sophistic." Pages 304–16 in *The Oxford Handbook of Social Relations in the Roman World.* Edited by Michael Peachin. Oxford: Oxford University Press, 2011.

Schneider, Carl D. *Shame, Exposure, and Privacy.* Boston: Beacon, 1977.

Schrage, Wolfgang. *The Ethics of the New Testament.* Translated by David Green. Philadelphia: Fortress, 1988.

Scott, Gary Alan, ed. *Does Socrates Have a Method? Rethinking the Elenchus in Plato's Dialogues and Beyond.* University Park: Pennsylvania State University Press, 2002.

Seok, Bongrae. *Moral Psychology of Confucian Shame: Shame of Shamelessness.* Lanham, MD: Rowman & Littlefield, 2016.

Shaver, Phillip R., Shelley Wu, and Judith C. Schwartz. "Cross-Cultural Similarities and Differences in Emotion and Its Representation." Pages 175–212 in *Emotion.* Edited by Margaret S. Clark. Thousand Oaks, CA: Sage, 1992.

Sherman, Nancy. *The Fabric of Character: Aristotle's Theory of Virtue.* Oxford: Clarendon, 1989.

———. *Making a Necessity of Virtue: Aristotle and Kant on Virtue.* Cambridge: Cambridge University Press, 1997.

Shun, Kwong-loi. "Early Confucian Moral Psychology." Pages 263–89 in *Dao Companion to Classical Confucian Philosophy.* Edited by Vincent Shen. New York: Springer, 2013.

———. *Mencius and Early Chinese Thought.* Stanford: Stanford University Press, 1997.

Shweder, Richard A. "Toward a Deep Cultural Psychology of Shame." *Social Research* 70 (2003): 1109–30.

———. "'You're Not Sick, You're Just in Love': Emotion as an Interpretive System." Pages 32–44 in *The Nature of Emotion: Fundamental Questions.* Edited by Paul Ekman and Richard J. Davidson. New York: Oxford University Press, 1994.

Shweder, Richard A., Jonathan Haidt, Randall Horton, and Craig Joseph. "The Cultural Psychology of the Emotions: Ancient and Renewed." Pages 409–27 in *Handbook of Emotions.* Edited by Michael Lewis, Jeannette M. Haviland-Jones, and Lisa Feldman Barrett. 3rd ed. New York: Guilford, 2008.

Silva, Moisés. *Interpreting Galatians: Explorations in Exegetical Method.* 2nd ed. Grand Rapids: Baker Academic, 2001.

Simkins, Ronald A. "'Return to Yahweh': Honor and Shame in Joel." *Semeia* 68 (1994): 41–54.

Skehan, Patrick W., and Alexander A. Di Lella. *The Wisdom of Ben Sira.* Anchor Bible. Garden City, NY: Doubleday, 1987.

Smith, Christian. *Soul Searching: The Religious and Spiritual Lives of American Teenagers.* Oxford: Oxford University Press, 2005.

Smith, Craig A., and Heather S. Scott. "A Componential Approach to the Meaning of Facial Expressions." Pages 229–54 in *The Psychology of Facial Expression.* Edited by James A. Russell and José Miguel Fernández-Dols. Cambridge: Cambridge University Press, 1997.

Smith, Richard H., J. Matthew Webster, W. Gerrod Parrott, and Heidi L. Eyre. "The Role of Public Exposure in Moral and Nonmoral Shame and Guilt." *Journal of Personality and Social Psychology* 83 (2002): 138–59.

Solomon, Robert C. *The Passions.* Notre Dame, IN: University of Notre Dame Press, 1983.

———. "The Philosophy of Emotions." Pages 3–16 in *Handbook of Emotions.* Edited by Michael Lewis, Jeannette M. Haviland-Jones, and Lisa Feldman Barrett. 3rd ed. New York: Guilford, 2008.

Solovyov, Vladimir. *The Justification of the Good: An Essay on Moral Philosophy.* Translated by Nathalie A. Duddington. 2nd ed. Grand Rapids: Eerdmans, 2005.

Sommers, Christina Hoff, and Sally L. Satel. *One Nation under Therapy: How the Helping Culture Is Eroding Self-Reliance.* New York: St. Martin's, 2005.

Sorabji, Richard. "Aristotle on the Role of Intellect in Virtue." Pages 201–19 in *Essays on Aristotle's Ethics.* Edited by Amélie Oksenberg Rorty. Berkeley: University of California Press, 1980.

———. *Moral Conscience through the Ages: Fifth Century BCE to the Present.* Chicago: University of Chicago Press, 2014.

South, James T. *Disciplinary Practices in Pauline Texts*. Lewiston, NY: Mellen, 1992.

Stearns, Peter N. *Shame: A Brief History*. Urbana: University of Illinois Press, 2017.

Steinbock, Anthony J. *Moral Emotions: Reclaiming the Evidence of the Heart*. Evanston, IL: Northwestern University Press, 2014.

Stiebert, Johanna. *The Construction of Shame in the Hebrew Bible: The Prophetic Contribution*. Journal for the Study of the Old Testament Supplement Series 346. London: Sheffield Academic, 2002.

Stocker, Michael. "Emotional Thoughts." *American Philosophical Quarterly* 24 (1987): 59–69.

Stone, Rebecca. "Desistance and Identity Repair: Redemption Narratives as Resistance to Stigma." *British Journal of Criminology* 56 (2016): 956–75.

Striker, Gisela. "Emotions in Context: Aristotle's Treatment of the Passions in the *Rhetoric* and His Moral Psychology." Pages 286–302 in *Essays on Aristotle's "Rhetoric."* Edited by Amélie Oksenberg Rorty. Berkeley: University of California Press, 1996.

Suhl, Alfred. *Der Brief an Philemon*. Zürcher Bibelkommentare. Zürich: TVZ, 1981.

Sunstein, Cass R. *The Ethics of Influence: Government in the Age of Behavioral Science*. New York: Cambridge University Press, 2016.

Tangney, June Price, and Ronda L. Dearing. *Shame and Guilt*. New York: Guilford, 2002.

Tangney, June Price, Jeff Stuewig, and Debra J. Mashek. "Moral Emotions and Moral Behavior." *Annual Review of Psychology* 58 (2007): 345–72.

Tarnopolsky, Christina H. *Prudes, Perverts, and Tyrants: Plato's Gorgias and the Politics of Shame*. Princeton: Princeton University Press, 2010.

Taylor, Gabriele. *Pride, Shame, and Guilt: Emotions of Self-Assessment*. Oxford: Clarendon, 1985.

Teroni, Fabrice, and Otto Bruun. "Shame, Guilt, and Morality." *Journal of Moral Philosophy* 8 (2011): 223–45.

Thagard, Paul, and Tracy Finn. "Conscience: What Is Moral Intuition?" Pages 150–69 in *Morality and the Emotions*. Edited by Carla Bagnoli. New York: Oxford University Press, 2011.

Thiselton, Anthony C. *The First Epistle to the Corinthians: A Commentary on the Greek Text*. New International Greek Testament Commentary. Grand Rapids: Eerdmans, 2000.

Thom, Johan C. *The Pythagorean Golden Verses: With Introduction and Commentary*. Religions in the Graeco-Roman World 123. Leiden: Brill, 1995.

Thomason, Krista K. *Naked: The Dark Side of Shame and Moral Life*. New York: Oxford University Press, 2018.

Thompson, James. *Moral Formation according to Paul: The Context and Coherence of Pauline Ethics*. Grand Rapids: Baker Academic, 2011.

———. "Spiritual Formation Is Corporate Formation: The Transformative Church in Romans and 2 Corinthians." Pages 103–26 in *The Church according to Paul: Rediscovering the Community Conformed to Christ*. Grand Rapids: Baker Academic, 2014.

Tolmie, D. F. *Persuading the Galatians: A Text-Centred Rhetorical Analysis of a Pauline Letter*. WUNT 2/190. Tübingen: Mohr Siebeck, 2005.

Treggiari, Susan. *Roman Freedmen during the Late Republic*. Oxford: Clarendon, 1969.

Trench, Richard Chenevix. *Synonyms of the New Testament*. 9th ed. London: Macmillan, 1880.

Tu, Wei-Ming. *Neo-Confucian Thought in Action: Wang Yang-Ming's Youth (1472–1509)*. Berkeley: University of California Press, 1976.

———. "Selfhood and Otherness in Confucian Thought." Pages 231–51 in *Culture and Self: Asian and Western Perspectives*. Edited by Anthony J. Marsella, George A. DeVos, and Francis L. K. Hsu. New York: Tavistock, 1985.

Twitchell, James B. *For Shame: The Loss of Common Decency in American Culture*. New York: St. Martin's, 1997.

Van Nes, Jermo. *Pauline Language and the Pastoral Epistles: A Study of Linguistic Variation in the* Corpus Paulinum. Linguistic Biblical Studies 16. Leiden: Brill, 2018.

Van Norden, Bryan W. "The Emotion of Shame and the Virtue of Righteousness in Mencius." *Dao* 2 (2002): 45–77.

———. "Mencius." *The Stanford Encyclopedia of Philosophy*. Edited by Edward N. Zalta. Spring 2017 ed., 2017. https://plato.stanford.edu/archives/spr2017/entries/mencius/.

Vasiliou, Iakovos. "Virtue and Argument in Aristotle's Ethics." Pages 37–78 in *Moral Psychology*. Edited by Sergio Tenenbaum. Amsterdam: Rodopi, 2007.

Vegge, Ivar. *2 Corinthians—a Letter about Reconciliation: A Psychagogical, Epistolographical, and Rhetorical Analysis*. WUNT 2/239. Tübingen: Mohr Siebeck, 2008.

Virág, Curie. "Early Confucian Perspectives on Emotion." Pages 203–25 in *Dao Companion to Classical Confucian Philosophy*. Edited by Vincent Shen. New York: Springer, 2013.

———. *The Emotions in Early Chinese Philosophy*. New York: Oxford University Press, 2017.

Waltke, Bruce K. *The Book of Proverbs: Chapters 15–31*. New International Commentary on the Old Testament. Grand Rapids: Eerdmans, 2005.

Wang, Yanping, and Thomas H. Ollendick. "A Cross-Cultural and Developmental Analysis of Self-Esteem in Chinese and Western Children." *Clinical Child and Family Psychology Review* 4 (2001): 253–71.

Wansink, Craig S. *Chained in Christ: The Experience and Rhetoric of Paul's Imprisonments*. JSNTSup 130. Sheffield: Sheffield Academic, 1996.

Watson, Duane F. "A Rhetorical Analysis of Philippians and Its Implications for the Unity Question." *Novum Testamentum* 30 (1988): 57–88.

Watson, Francis. *Paul, Judaism, and the Gentiles: A Sociological Approach*. Society for New Testament Studies Monograph Series 56. Cambridge: Cambridge University Press, 1986.

Wechsler, Andreas. *Geschichtsbild und Apostelstreit: Eine forschungsgeschichtliche und exegetische Studie über den antiochenischen Zwischenfall (Gal 2, 11–14)*. Beihefte zur Zeitschrift für die neutestamentliche Wissenschaft 62. Berlin: de Gruyter, 1991.

Weima, Jeffrey A. D. *Paul the Ancient Letter Writer: An Introduction to Epistolary Analysis*. Grand Rapids: Baker Academic, 2016.

———. "Paul's Persuasive Prose: An Epistolary Analysis of the Letter to Philemon." Pages 29–60 in *Philemon in Perspective: Interpreting a Pauline*

Letter. Edited by D. Francois Tolmie. Beihefte zur Zeitschrift für die neutestamentliche Wissenschaft 169. Berlin: de Gruyter, 2010.

———. "Sincerely, Paul: The Significance of the Pauline Letter Closings." Pages 307–45 in *Paul and the Ancient Letter Form*. Edited by Stanley E. Porter and Sean A. Adams. Pauline Studies 6. Leiden: Brill, 2010.

Weinfeld, Moshe. *Deuteronomy and the Deuteronomic School*. Oxford: Clarendon, 1972.

Wenham, David. *Paul: Follower of Jesus or Founder of Christianity?* Grand Rapids: Eerdmans, 1995.

Westerholm, Stephen. "Letter and Spirit: The Foundation of Pauline Ethics." *NTS* 30 (1984): 229–48.

Wierzbicka, Anna. *Emotions across Languages and Cultures: Diversity and Universals*. Cambridge: Cambridge University Press, 1999.

Williams, Bernard. "Morality and the Emotions." Pages 207–29 in *Problems of the Self*. Cambridge: Cambridge University Press, 1973.

———. *Shame and Necessity*. Berkeley: University of California Press, 1993.

Wilson, P. Eddy. "Deuteronomy XXV 11–12—One for the Books." *Vetus Testamentum* 47 (1997): 220–35.

Witherington, Ben, III. *Paul's Letter to the Philippians: A Socio-rhetorical Commentary*. Grand Rapids: Eerdmans, 2011.

Wood, Allen W. "Coercion, Manipulation, Exploitation." Pages 17–50 in *Manipulation: Theory and Practice*. Edited by Christian Coons and Michael Weber. Oxford: Oxford University Press, 2014.

Woodruff, Paul B. "Socrates and the Irrational." Pages 130–50 in *Reason and Religion in Socratic Philosophy*. Edited by Nicholas D. Smith and Paul B. Woodruff. Oxford: Oxford University Press, 2000.

Wright, N. T. *The Climax of the Covenant*. Minneapolis: Fortress, 1992.

Wu, Daniel. *Honor, Shame, and Guilt: Social-Scientific Approaches to the Book of Ezekiel*. Bulletin for Biblical Research Supplements 14. Winona Lake, IN: Eisenbrauns, 2016.

Zimmerli, Walther. "Knowledge of God according to the Book of Ezekiel." Pages 29–98 in *I Am Yahweh*. Atlanta: John Knox, 1982.

Znaniecki, Florian. *Cultural Sciences: Their Origin and Development*. Urbana: University of Illinois Press, 1952.

Name Index

The letter *t* following a page number denotes a table. The letter *f* following a page number denotes a figure.

Scripture Index

Ancient Writings Index